The Birth of the Past

The Birth

The Johns Hopkins University Press
Baltimore

of the Past

ZACHARY SAYRE SCHIFFMAN

Foreword by
ANTHONY GRAFTON

8/21/12
ww
65 —

The Johns Hopkins University Press
2715 North Charles Street
Baltimore, Maryland 21218-4363
www.press.jhu.edu

Library of Congress Cataloging-in-Publication Data

Schiffman, Zachary Sayre.
The birth of the past / Zachary Sayre Schiffman.
p. cm.
Includes bibliographical references and index.
ISBN-13: 978-1-4214-0278-9 (hardcover : alk. paper)
ISBN-10: 1-4214-0278-5 (hardcover : alk. paper)
1. History—Philosophy. 2. Historiography—Philosophy. 3. Historiography—
Western countries. 4. Western countries—Intellectual life. 5. Civilization, Western.
I. Title.
D16.8.S268 2011
901—dc22 2011008229

A catalog record for this book is available from the British Library.

*Special discounts are available for bulk purchases of this book. For more information please
contact Special Sales at 410-516-6936 or specialsales@press.jhu.edu.*

The Johns Hopkins University Press uses environmentally friendly book materials,
including recycled text paper that is composed of at least 30 percent post-consumer
waste, whenever possible.

For *Hanna Holborn Gray*
and
Karl Joachim Weintraub (1924-2004)

"And I too am a painter," have I said with Correggio.
—Montesquieu, *The Spirit of the Laws,*
quoting Correggio's reputed words
upon first viewing Raphael's *St. Cecilia*

Contents

Foreword

Americans know that history matters. Jurists and politicians, pundits and bloggers invoke history to support their visions of the form of government we should live under and the sort of wars we should wage, the schools and universities we should build and support and the ways in which we should exploit our natural resources. But as Jill Lepore and others have pointed out, most of the history that is retold in such contexts is actually unhistorical.[1] Ordinary citizens and politicians alike assume that past thinkers can guide us in a present they could not have envisioned: that the founders of the United States can tell us everything we need to know about women's rights, nuclear weapons, and the exploration of space. We ask what Jesus would have driven, without reflecting that he rode a donkey rather than a car.

Historians look at the past in a very different way. Like L. P. Hartley, they assume that "the past is a foreign country: they do things differently there." Past societies and leaders certainly offer examples that we can still study with profit. But we can learn from them only if we bear in mind that they are part of a past—a continuum of social and cultural, economic and political development, their place in which was different from ours. We judge our colleagues and graduate students by their ability to put this principle into practice, and we train our undergraduates, or try to train them, to do so as well.

When did Western intellectuals first begin to think about the past in these distinctive terms? In this book, Zachary Schiffman offers a powerful and engaging answer. For a quarter of a century, he has explored, in articles that are now classics, in a remarkable study of French historical thought, and in a prescient collaborative book, the history of Western ways of preserving and imagining the past.[2] His work has shaped that of his colleagues and of younger scholars—for example, the distinguished Harvard historian Ann Blair, whose own brilliant inquiries into the history of information management began from a read-

ix

ing of one of Schiffman's articles.[3] But for all the clarity of his thought and the elegance of his prose, he has found his readers among his fellow specialists.

In his new book Schiffman develops a sweeping argument about the origins of what he describes as "our"—that is, the modern Western—vision of the past, as a country different from the one we inhabit. The argument is carried on with great gusto and stylistic virtuosity, growing into a book-length essay that challenges comparison with some of the great past essays on the vision and meaning of history. Classic works by Isaiah Berlin, R. G. Collingwood, and H. Stuart Hughes come immediately to mind. But Schiffman's work also rests on close reading of texts and friendly debate with many interpreters, both old and new. The combination of broad-gauged argument and tightly focused interpretation of particular witnesses gives Schiffman's book a special distinction.

Beginning with the Greeks, Schiffman argues—using Thucydides as his chief witness—that it is in fact an anachronism, a sin against Western historical consciousness, to ascribe that sort of consciousness to the ancients. Augustine dismissed secular history as one long noisy nightmare. Yet he and other Christian thinkers did more to create a sense of the past, as a continuum, than the secular historians of Greece. For they forged the concept of a single, continuous *sæculum*—a vision that was novel, sophisticated, and powerful even if, as Schiffman argues from the works of the Venerable Bede, it rested on a causal understanding of the past that differs radically from that of most moderns.

More than half a century ago, Erwin Panofsky argued that Renaissance scholars and artists arrived at a new vision of the past—a new historical perspective. As their new system of visual perspective enabled them to see the world around them from a fixed distance and in three dimensions, so their historical perspective enabled them to do the same for the ancient past. Where medieval scholars and artists had pulled antiquity apart, separating form from content, their Renaissance successors reassembled antiquity as a single coherent mosaic.[4]

Schiffman agrees that Renaissance humanists came to see the ancient past as distant from the world of fragments they were forced to inhabit. But he also shows that they deliberately read the past anachronistically in order to make it live, using allegory and other traditional tools. Their historical consciousness lived in this tension, and in many cases—Schiffman explores that of Petrarch with special care—the dialectical power of their sense of the past crackled with energy. In some instances—in their confrontations with the individual writers whose works they combed for lessons and in their confrontations with alien cultures—the humanists moved towards a sense of the multiplicity of perspectives. Yet they never abandoned the search for examples that could serve as direct models for action in the present.

In the end, even the most capacious and original scholars of the Renaissance—such as those pioneering writers on the art of history, Francesco Patrizi and Jean Bodin—remained caught in a web of contradictions as they contemplated and used the past. Schiffman offers a wonderful treatment of Bodin's effort, and that of other late humanists, to use notebooks to master, organize, and impose a coherent interpretation on the vast heaps of information that confronted them in the burgeoning world of print. For all the richness and variety of the material they assembled, they did not arrive, he argues, at a coherent, rigorous vision of a single past, ordered on a single timeline.

Intellectual historians have often tried to identify particular early modern thinkers as the creators of the modern sense of history.[5] In an especially rich and complex series of arguments, Schiffman examines his beloved Montaigne, imagining the conquest of the New World from the standpoint of its native inhabitants, and moves from them to the brilliant jurists Lorenzo Valla and Hermann Conring, those cocky critics of medieval Roman lawyers, whom they dismissed as unable to understand the very texts that were the basis of their practice. In each case, Schiffman argues, the "contextualizing move" of the early modern intellectual, for all its brilliance, is motivated by a particular situation and individual prejudices, which general accounts have tended to obscure.

It took the Enlightenment, and Montesquieu—so Schiffman concludes, in a very original chapter—to lay the foundation for a truly comprehensive vision of the past. Here, as in many other passages, Schiffman is a polite but determined revisionist. From the nineteenth century to the recent work of Reinhart Koselleck and Peter Fritzsche, scholars have normally argued that Europeans developed a full sense of the past only after the destruction of the Ancien Regime by the French Revolution and Napoleon and the rise of the romantic sense of national identities and their evolution.[6] Schiffman, by contrast, argues that Montesquieu—using a new epistemology deriving from Malebranche, but applying it to the realm of the human sciences—first managed to see in the past both the individuality of particular places and times and the general social rules that made them comparable to one another.

In an epilogue, Schiffman examines other vital ways of approaching the past: Herder's philosophy of history, with its insistence on the individuality of peoples and ages, and antiquarianism, with its new tools for setting artifacts into their contexts and reconstructing rituals, beliefs, and institutions. For all their richness, he argues, it was the fusion of these traditions with the "relationalism" of the Enlightenment that created the modern sense of the past. This is a bold thesis, and it will certainly provoke discussion.

The Birth of the Past is not a comprehensive history but an essay, highly selective and dramatic in its organization. But it is also a guide to a vast and fascinating intellectual territory. A special virtue of Schiffman's approach lies in his emphasis on the concrete ways in which historians and historical thinkers read and interpreted their sources. Drawing on recent work by Daniel Woolf and others, Schiffman connects historians' visions of the past with the practices of reading and interpretation—private and public, silent and oral—that flourished around them.[7] By drawing the history of material texts into connection with the history of ideas, Schiffman gives his work a compelling vividness and intimacy that most intellectual histories lack.

Schiffman's book is a uniquely eloquent and engaging guide to a profound and valuable tradition, one that many Americans—and most students—find increasingly foreign. Schiffman not only tells the story of how this intellectual tradition took shape, but also makes clear its richness and its vitality. With the ropes and pitons he offers, many more readers will be able to climb Mt. Thucydides and Mt. Montesquieu— and see a vital prospect, brilliantly displayed.

Anthony Grafton
Princeton University

Gestation

The intuition that inspired this book occurred to me more than thirty years ago, while I was crossing a quadrangle at the University of Chicago, trudging along in my customary state of graduate-student befuddlement. Somewhere around Botany Pond I experienced a brief moment of intellectual clarity, the memory of which has stayed with me ever since. I had been musing about the Renaissance "attitude toward the past"—the ever-elusive subject of my dissertation—when I suddenly found myself questioning the very appropriateness of that formulation, which assumed the existence of "the past" as an object of thought. This assumption now began to trouble me deeply, and at the farthest reach of my mind there flitted the barest hint of an idea: that the conceptual entity we call "the past" didn't exist in the Renaissance. At the time, though, I was hardly capable of expressing this idea, let alone substantiating it; and as I struggled to make sense of it, a sea of confusion closed over me, diffusing the light.

My subsequent academic career has been like one long in-held breath, as I have fought my way back toward the surface and the light of that intuition. In my first book, on the problem of relativism in the French Renaissance, I finally succeeded in describing a fundamental difference between Renaissance and modern attitudes toward the past, but in a way that still took the idea of the past for granted, despite my already having begun to question this assumption openly in my teaching. While completing that book, I had the good fortune to meet Leonard Barkan, who was studying similar issues from an interdisciplinary perspective that combined literary criticism and art history, an approach that would eventually bear fruit in his magisterial work on Renaissance archaeology and aesthetics, *Unearthing the Past*. In the course of our many discussions about how to conceptualize the past, some during a highly illuminating NEH summer seminar he directed, I began to acquire the means of making sense of my insight back at Botany Pond. These means have been augmented by my long association, nurtured over many a luncheon, with Constantin Fasolt, an early modern historian who trained as a medievalist with a distinctly philosophical bent. Constantin and I talked our way through several drafts of his *Limits of History,* an exploration of the nature of modern historical consciousness that has profoundly influenced my own thinking on the topic and on which I have relied heavily in the present volume. At the same time Constantin was working on his book, I was coauthoring a history of information with another friend and early modern historian, Michael E. Hobart, who studies the "analytical temper" that accompanied the rise of modern science and mathematics. Michael and I had long debates over the role of this temper in the formation of modern historical thought—in which I defended nineteenth-century historicism against the claims of eighteenth-century rationalism—and these debates subtly shaped my thinking on this subject, without my even having realized it. Finally, I owe to another friend and colleague, Susan E. Rosa, a more nuanced appreciation of the role of Enlightenment in the emergence of a new conception of history. Indeed, she encouraged me toward the study of Montesquieu, which revealed to me the full extent of the early modern analytical temper, whose influence Michael Hobart had championed against my own initial resistance.

These friends and scholars offered me critical lifelines as I struggled to regain the surface and the light first glimpsed at Botany Pond, and I confess a deep and abiding debt to them. But my greatest debt is to my teachers at the University of Chicago, who (though I didn't realize it at the time) were very much with me as I trudged my befuddled way across the university quadrangle. Hanna Holborn Gray had first introduced me to the study of Renaissance historiography and directed me toward the topic that would become my dissertation. Her wealth of insights into Renaissance historical thought was almost too rich for me to digest, and the present volume stands as paltry testimony to some comments she tossed off in passing decades ago. If she embarked me on my dissertation, Karl Joachim Weintraub saw me safely to port, and in the process showed me how to navigate my way as a self-avowed historicist. He also tried to inculcate the highest standards of intellectual responsibility by which scholars should test their ideas, especially the flashy ones that most appeal at first glance, only to fade upon closer scrutiny. That my insight at Botany Pond would survive not only my initial confusion but also my subsequent skepticism—that it would become the basis for my questioning of historicism itself—is an irony he surely would have savored, had he only lived to see it.

IN THE PERVERSE EXPRESSION OF ANOTHER dearly departed friend, "I am but the nexus of those around me." The history of my insight at Botany Pond would seem to support this claim, despite its provocative phrasing. Thus, with a mind suitably molded by my mentors, I experienced a moment of intuition that, sparking a quest that resonated in relation to the thought of my colleagues, has shaped the course of my academic life . . . or so it would seem. But then again, in tracing the gestation of this idea, perhaps I have merely privileged a modern tendency to contextualize thought and action, to explain them in relation to spatial and temporal reference points, rather than by other means. Did the insight really occur at Botany Pond, or is that locale merely a mnemonic placeholder, an evocative talisman for something that actually happened elsewhere—on the main quadrangle, or during my walk to campus, or the night before, as I lay pensively in bed? Did my advisers wittingly or unwittingly nurture this idea, or did it result from too much coffee—or not enough—or from something seen or smelled that triggered a random connection in the brain? Did each of the above-mentioned friends and colleagues come along at just the right moment to play a decisive role in the emergence of this idea? Though my debts to them are genuine, I should be so fortunate as to have such prescient and versatile friends! And surely the lame imagery of my prolonged ascent toward the light is, at best, a clumsy instance of poetic (or, better yet, "historic") license.

Such are the stories we make for (and of) ourselves. My point is not that I have actively interpreted my academic life—and that all such interpretations are open to question—but that I have contextualized it with reference to a spatial and temporal matrix, epitomized by the faux concreteness of Botany Pond. This kind of storytelling has a special appeal for us; it has the ring of truth. (Despite acknowledging the perversity of his self-conception, my friend nonetheless maintained it in complete seriousness.) We use spatial and temporal reference points to make sense of all things tangible and intangible—our ideas, our selves, our polity, our culture, and its products. (On the wall to my left, as I write these words, hangs one of my departed friend's prized possessions, a photo of a 1930s airship floating above Central Park, the perfect image of early twentieth-century modernism.) "The past" is enmeshed in this contextualizing habit of mind, the origins of which I seek.

ALTHOUGH THE PRODUCT OF OVER THIRTY YEARS of reading, this book is more a work of synthesis than of scholarship. In keeping with this distinction, I have tried to minimize the use of notes and, whenever possible, to give credit where credit is due in the text, acknowledging in narrative form the scholarly works that have most influenced me. In the case of primary sources, I have generally provided references in parentheses in the text. References to classical sources are by book and chapter number, a practice I have tried to uphold with more recent primary sources as well. In general, I have referred to well-known primary sources by their most common English titles; lesser-known sources, such as Renaissance educational treatises, I have referred to by their original-language titles, which I have translated in parentheses (the titles of works with published English translations are either italicized or in quotes; those of works that haven't been translated are not italicized or in quotes). For each of the four parts of this book I have provided a separate section in the selected bibliography, which lists the chief works I consulted while writing the part in question, along with the primary and secondary sources referenced in the part. In general, I have avoided notes when citations in the narrative, combined with listings in the appropriate section of the bibliography, provide readers with unambiguous reference information. Although the bibliography comprises the works that have contributed most immediately to my synthesis, it in no way represents the sum total of my research.

IN CLOSING THESE PRELIMINARY REMARKS, I would like to acknowledge a generous grant from Northeastern Illinois University to help offset the cost of publishing this volume. In particular, I am grateful to the Office of the President, the Office of the Provost, and the Office of the Dean of the College of Arts and Sciences, all of which contributed liberally to this grant, despite severe budgetary constraints. I would also like to acknowledge the sage guidance of the late Henry Y. K. Tom, former executive editor at the Johns Hopkins University Press, on whose professional advice I relied heavily in writing this book. I have also greatly benefited from the advice of Suzanne Flinchbaugh, associate editor at the Press.

Finally, I would like to acknowledge the forbearance of my family during the long composition of this book. Such testimonials often come off rote-sounding, but mine is most genuine and heartfelt. My wife, Amy Truelove, sacrificed much of her weekend schedule to my writing habits without ever once complaining, despite the fact that her own demanding career rendered her weekends precious to her. And my children, Aaron and Leah, endured my long absences in my study—and my absentmindedness outside of it—with good humor and grace. My son is old enough to have lived through the composition of an earlier book, but my daughter was at first unaccustomed to Daddy emerging from his study on the weekends at 2 p.m., still dressed in his bathrobe. Authors always seem to acknowledge their families, and now I know why they can never do so enough.

The Birth of the Past

The Past Defined

We need to put aside all of the usual ideas about what history is or ought to be and take a good close look instead at the one thing that underlies all forms of history. That one thing is the distinction between past and present. This is so elementary, so necessary for the very possibility of thinking about the past at all, that it may be considered the founding principle of history.

—Constantin Fasolt, *The Limits of History*

The title of this book invites reflection, for it posits the birth of something forever and always dead. To explain away this paradox, one might presume I am referring to the birth of what will become the past; but if I were, I would have entitled the book "The Birth of the Present"—a questionable project for a historian. One might also presume that I mean "the birth of our idea of the past," a notion expressed more gracefully by omitting the first prepositional phrase. But "the birth of our idea of the past" is not quite the same thing as "the birth of the past," for the former expression assumes the existence of a past about which we have a particular idea, whereas the latter expression refers to the birth of that assumption itself. We take the existence of "the past" for granted as a commonsense notion, yet I will argue that this notion has a history that began only fairly recently, during the Renaissance, and did not culminate until the eighteenth century, after which it acquired its commonsense status.

Because this argument is almost entirely counterintuitive, flying in the face of a host of unquestioned assumptions, let me lay it out logically (if a bit laboriously) in order to clarify exactly what I am claiming and why I am claiming it.

First, in our daily lives we take the past for granted as being, quite simply, the time before the present. As such, it is less an object of thought than a mundane reality reinforced by the tenses of everyday language and by the passage of time, as one moment of awareness gives way to the next, forming memories.

Second, when we do bother to focus on the past as an object of thought—a task we have for the most part relegated to historians—we tend to conflate this mundane notion with another: that the past is not simply *prior* to the present but *different* from it. The perception of difference reflects an awareness that each historical entity exists in its own distinctive context, that (for example) Shakespeare's world—as reflected in its language, customs, dress, and whatnot—differs from our own. Following Constantin Fasolt's lead, I will declare this awareness of the difference between past and present "the founding principle of history" (4). (Those familiar with the language of postmodern literary criticism should note that the "perception of difference" about which I am writing has nothing in common with the Derridean notion of *différance,* a neologism that denotes the indeterminate status of the meaning conveyed by words and signs.)

Third, despite our tendency to conflate the past as a time prior to the present with the past as a time different from the present, the two ideas are distinct. In and of itself, priority in time does not entail difference. Because this principle grounds my entire argument, let me pause here to illustrate it briefly. Above I described the passage of time as "one moment of awareness giv[ing] way to the next." Viewed from this basic existential perspective, the time prior to the present constitutes an undifferentiated expanse, all of which is equally "not present." Even if we were to divide it into years arranged chronologically, it would still remain essentially undifferentiated. An excerpt from the *Anglo-Saxon Chronicle* epitomizes this homogeneous quality:

803   In this year Hygebald, bishop of Lindisfarne, passed away on 24 June; and Egbert was consecrated in his place on 11 June [following]. And archbishop Æthelheard passed away in Kent, and Wulfred was consecrated archbishop.

804   In this year archbishop Wulfred received the pallium.

805   In this year king Cuthred passed away in Kent, and abbess Ceolburh and Heardberht.

806   In this year there was an eclipse of the moon on 1 September. And Eardwulf, king of Northumbria, was driven from his kingdom, and Eanberht, bishop Hexham, passed away. . . .

812   In this year king Charlemagne passed away. He reigned forty-five
years. And archbishop Wulfred and Wigberht, bishop of Wessex,
went to Rome. . . .[1]

This medieval chronicle, written in at least thirteen different monkish hands,
covers the expanse of time from the birth of Christ to 1154, virtually year-by-
year. Granted, most of the later entries are more elaborate than these earlier
ones, but the annalistic mode—which slots an eclipse of the moon alongside the
defeat of a Northumbrian king, and the death of Charlemagne alongside the travels of English bishops and archbishops—renders all entries qualitatively equal.
In and of itself priority in time does not entail difference. The distinction between past and present that constitutes "the founding principle of history" rests
on something other than mere priority in time; it reflects an abiding awareness
that different historical entities exist in different historical contexts.

Fourth, the flip side of this awareness is a sense of anachronism, triggered
when we encounter things that appear out of context. (Imagine Shakespeare
dressed in jeans and a tee shirt.) For the sake of convenience I will refer to the
awareness of the difference between past and present as an *idea of anachronism*,
for this idea enables us to distinguish between historical contexts.

Fifth, the idea of anachronism has a history. To illustrate this point, we need
only consider the decontextualized entries in the above-quoted chronicle, which
commingles disparate events without regard for their widely different contexts.
One might object that the mere presence of a decontextualized form of record
keeping does not preclude the existence of an idea of anachronism; after all, we
moderns have ready reference to almanacs, encyclopedias, and the Internet, and
these decontextualized forms of information storage coexist with an abiding
awareness of historical context. The difference, however, between our lists and
those of the medieval chroniclers is that ours are subtended by a vast body of
contextualized historical knowledge, whereas theirs constitute, for all practical
purposes, *the* historical record. Hence it would be reasonable to conclude either
that the chroniclers didn't have an idea of anachronism or that it so differs from
ours as to have played no role in their historical account.

Sixth, if the idea of anachronism has a history, we can assume it originated
at some point, before which—for lack of a distinction between past and present—
there would have been no conception of the past. This bald statement highlights the objection that mine is a purely semantic argument, devoid of real
substance: I have narrowly defined the idea of the past so that it rests upon

a sense of anachronism, and then I have whisked that sense away, making "the past" inconceivable on logical grounds. Mere academic flapdoodle! Logic notwithstanding—so the objection runs—memory remains a universal human faculty, providing practical proof of the existence of the past, along with myriad references to it in everyday language. Confronted with this objection, I must insist that the past is constituted by something more than the mere memory of what we had for lunch yesterday or who we voted for in the last election; the past is not simply *prior* to the present but *different* from it. We conflate this sense of difference with priority in time—assuming that any memory of a prior event constitutes proof of the existence of the past—in part because of the imprecision of everyday language and in part because the idea of anachronism has become second nature for us. So deeply rooted is this idea that we literally find the recollection of prior times inconceivable without it. Once we distinguish between priority and difference, however, we confront the possibility that "the past" has a history extending back to a point of origin, before which it did not exist as a conceptual entity.

I MAINTAIN THAT THE IDEA OF ANACHRONISM originated in the Renaissance. This claim breaks little new ground; in one form or another it underlies most modern interpretations of the period. Rather, the novelty of my argument lies in the consequences of this claim for ancient and medieval as well as Renaissance and modern thought. As regards antiquity, I stake out two counterintuitive positions: (1) that ancient historians did not write about "the past" and (2) that the ancients in general did not have an idea of anachronism. Since these positions lie at the foundation for all that follows in the book, I will briefly outline them here.

At first glance the claim that the great historians of classical antiquity had no idea of the past seems absurd. After all, they pioneered the literary genre of history, and they were capable of making subtle linguistic distinctions about actions in the past. In fact, the Greek and Latin languages distinguish between three kinds of past tense, denoting action begun in the past (aorist or perfect indefinite), action continued in the past (imperfect), and action completed in the past (perfect definite); in addition, these languages have other ways of expressing the past by means of what linguists call "aspect" and "mood," such as the pluperfect, the future perfect, the imperfect subjunctive, and so on. By contrast, the English language has only the simple past tense and relies on aspect and mood to express other forms of the past. The ancients were thus at least as capable as we are of describing past actions and relating them to each other in sophisticated ways.

Recall, though, that the past is constituted as such not simply by priority in time but by *difference* from the present. A sense of the difference between past and present implies a unitary conception of "the" past—an entity containing the people and events under consideration—which differs from all other such entities (Periclean Athens differs from Elizabethan England differs from modern America). These differences reflect not some Hegelian "spirit of an age" but the sensibilities influencing the innumerable choices made by individuals living at a particular time, sensibilities and choices contributing to shared mental and physical properties that define the people and events under consideration as distinct from other peoples and events.

Classical historians, however, did not perceive these differences. Instead of "the" past—whatever kind of entity it might encompass—they conceived of multiple "pasts" characterized by different time frames, each disassociated from the next, without privileging any particular one. As we will see, for example, Thucydides begins his history in a time frame that describes the progress toward sea power in the ancient world, switches to another time frame to describe the rise of the Athenian empire, and then to yet another to describe the sequence of events leading up to the Peloponnesian War. All these time frames and more coexist in the first book of his history, which leads to the introduction of an entirely new time frame in book 2, the "time of the war" as measured by summers and winters.

Ancient Greeks and Romans could not subsume these pasts under a single entity—"the" past—because they could not integrate these time frames. They faced an intellectual obstacle greater, and altogether different, from that of finding a uniform measure of time—itself no mean obstacle. As we will see, classical historians employed not only diverse quantitative, linear time schemes but qualitative, episodic ones. The linear time frames—which varied with the events under consideration—described them with reference to temporal chains of cause and effect, while the episodic ones analyzed events without regard to any quantitative measure of time. The coexistence of frameworks differing in kind as well as degree militated against a unitary conception of the past.

Without this unitary conception, the ancients could not distinguish systematically between past and present. In other words, they could not have an idea of anachronism. Again, this claim sounds absurd. How could they fail to recognize the differences between their world and that of their parents and grandparents? The question, though obvious to us, obscures the fundamental problem described above. The world of their forefathers did not constitute a "world" at all—a coherent intellectual entity—but rather comprised "worlds" defined by different conceptions of time. For lack of a coherent intellectual entity, the ancients had no fulcrum with which to lever past from present in a systematic, consistent manner. They perceived "local" distinctions between past and present—individual instances of anachronism, each defined by its own time frame—but they did not integrate these instances into a larger, "global" view of the differences between past and present. Instead, they noted such instances only in passing, for specific rhetorical purposes, after which the ancient authors set them aside, effectively relegating them to oblivion.

So—one might object at this point—they had an idea of anachronism after all, but not our modern one! This objection embroils us in a tricky question: is my view of anachronism itself anachronistic? In other words, am I assuming that our modern view is the defining one? Might not the ancients' "local" awareness of the differences between past and present count as a legitimate idea of anachronism? Here I must confess to a degree of uncertainty, for as a historian I am always on the alert for anachronisms in my own thinking. As I reread my opening line in the preceding paragraph—"Without a unitary conception of the past, the ancients could not distinguish systematically between past and present"—my eye fixes on the adverb *systematically*. Is this qualifier a fudge? Might it be possible to have an unsystematic idea of anachronism? On purely semantic grounds I would have to say "yes." But on logical grounds I'm inclined to say "no," if only (to reiterate Fasolt's point) because the distinction between past and present is so elementary, so clearly necessary for the very possibility of thinking about the past at all, that it counts as the founding principle of history. This fundamental distinction is by definition systematic, implying a unitary conception of the past, without which the distinction itself would have been unsustainable.

Of course, logic is no defense against anachronism, and even a distinction that seems so elementary may yet be contextualized. In fact, that's precisely what I hope to do. I am using Fasolt's distinction between past and present as a heuristic device for breaking out of the hermeneutical circle of anachronism, within which all views of anachronism remain potentially anachronistic. I am employing this distinction as if it were universally true in order to explore the extent to which it is, in fact, historically grown. (I might add here that this effort constitutes the merest footnote to Fasolt's *Limits of History,* a work I deeply admire.) So, even though my view of anachronism may itself be anachronistic, my conscience is clear.

I hope by these convoluted ways to show that what historians call "the past" is an intellectual construct. This claim goes beyond acknowledging that we interpret the past according to our circumstances; rather, it calls into question the objective existence of the thing called "the past" that we interpret. The past it-self, as an object of thought distinct from the present, is less a universal given than the intellectual creation of a particular historical moment.

Let me try to describe what I am saying by analogy to Michael Faraday's dis-covery of "energy."[2] Faraday's studies of magnetism and electricity reflect his conviction that all the various forces of nature, which natural philosophers had always studied in isolation, are in fact interconnected. Before Faraday, people per-ceived diverse forces—the lightning that flashes across the sky, the prickle of static generated by the rustle of clothes, the insistent movement of the compass's nee-dle—as discrete and separate. After Faraday's linkage of magnetism and electric-ity, however, people became aware that all these forces and more shared some-thing in common—"energy"—which eventually became the basis for Einstein's most famous equation. Similarly (although there's no Faraday in my story), before a certain point in our intellectual development, there were "pasts"—analogous to the "forces" that natural philosophers studied in isolation—each construed as distinct from the next; but after a crucial turning point there was "the past"—analogous to the idea of "energy"—an intellectual entity that did not previously exist but whose appearance made possible a whole new way of thinking about the world.

We should not mistake this new way of thinking for late eighteenth-century "historicism," despite the fact that my study culminates in the eighteenth cen-tury. In his classic history of historicism, *Die Entstehung des Historismus* (1936)—translated as *Historism: The Rise of a New Historical Outlook*—Friedrich Meinecke described it as the coming together of the ideas of individuality and development, such that one can explain the ineffable uniqueness of an entity by showing how it came to be that way through time. According to this line of rea-soning, I am unique because I was born at a particular and unrepeatable point in time and space, from which I have evolved in relation to ever-changing circum-stances that, in turn, bear the distinctive imprint of my ever-changing self. Enti-ties thus conceived are thoroughly and absolutely historical in the sense that they are so constituted by their context as to be, for all practical purposes, inseparable from it.

Historicism embodies a version of the idea of anachronism, but the idea it-self did not originate with historicism, as Meinecke effectively acknowledged. Although he counted British and French enlighteners—Voltaire, Montesquieu, Hume, Gibbon, Robertson—among the forerunners of historicism, he did not regard them as full-fledged historicists because they viewed their own enlight-ened age as the pinnacle from which to judge all others. This bias ran counter to the truly historicist tendency—manifested by early German romantics like Möser, Herder, and Goethe—to regard each historical entity from *within* its own context. When they judged the present better than the past, enlighteners manifested a nonhistoricist idea of anachronism.

The roots of their idea extend back to the Renaissance. Unlike enlighteners, who would compare past to present and find the former wanting, Renaissance humanists compared the two and found the latter wanting. Their desire to resurrect ancient culture in all its glory reflects an acute awareness of the differences between past and present. This sense of anachronism manifested itself in the search for lost classical manuscripts, in the desire to restore the texts of classical literature to their original purity, and in the program of *imitatio* that used classical models as the basis for modern literary efforts.

Strictly speaking, though, the Renaissance desire to resurrect classical culture—to make it live again—was not historical. True, it proceeded by means of what Meinecke would have called the *Hilfswissenschaften,* sciences auxiliary to history, such as philology, which brought new exactitude to the Renaissance study of classical antiquity; and these auxiliary sciences would eventually contribute to the rise of early modern historical scholarship and to the subsequent emergence of Enlightenment historiography and romantic historicism. But in the Renaissance, philology had yet to become a *Hilfswissenschaft,* for the historical viewpoint it would aid had not yet come into being. Instead, philology served—recalling Meinecke's terms—to articulate a notion of individuality unaccompanied by that of development. In other words, the Renaissance witnessed the emergence of the idea of anachronism pure and simple, unsullied by what we have come to know as historical thought.

The birth of anachronism thus differs from and precedes the birth of the past, which is in the broadest sense a historical notion. For all its intellectual power and utility, historical understanding holds the past at arm's length, defining it as irretrievably "other," as dead and buried. In the Renaissance, however, the idea of anachronism served to define the past without cutting off access to it. Machiavelli's famous letter of 10 December 1513, about the tedium of his life in exile from politics, captures the immediacy of the past in the Renaissance:

> In the evening, I return to my house and go into my study. At the door I take off the clothes I have worn all day, mud spotted and dirty, and put on regal and courtly garments. Thus appropriately clothed, I enter into the ancient courts of ancient men, where, being lovingly received, I feed on that food which is mine alone and which I was born for; I am not ashamed to speak with them and to ask

the reasons for their actions, and they courteously answer me. For hours I feel no boredom and forget every worry; I do not fear poverty, and death does not terrify me. I give myself completely over to the ancients.[3]

"Death does not terrify me"—what better evocation of the living power of the past in the Renaissance, before it became historicized! Appropriately attired for noble discourse, Machiavelli finds himself transported, not back through time but beyond it.

ANY STUDY OF THE BIRTH OF THE PAST must necessarily confront a basic methodological problem: where to begin? Constantin Fasolt has unwittingly provided me with a starting point by arguing simply, powerfully, and eloquently for the centrality of the idea of anachronism to historical understanding. Fasolt cannot be blamed for my stubborn persistence in maintaining that the Greeks did not have an idea of anachronism, a position stemming from my long struggle to understand one of the most difficult and rewarding of ancient authors, Thucydides. My conviction about the Greeks provides my inquiry with a logical foundation, which I excavate down to the bedrock of Greek culture, namely Homer.

We are accustomed to thinking of Homer as a historian before the fact, whose myths constitute the distilled and distorted memory of actual events. Instead of the past, though, I will argue that Homer's epics evoke a "past-made-present" that collapses the distinction between the two. As oral storytelling gave way to written narrative—especially in Herodotus's great compendium—a vision emerged of multiple pasts differing in kind as well as degree. The profusion of pasts—especially apparent in Thucydides—served narrative purposes far more ambitious than those of a modern historian, accounting for the enduring value of ancient historical writing. This profusion persisted even in Polybius's attempt to create a unified view of events centering on the rise of the Roman Empire, and it effectively prevented the nostalgia of a Livy or a Tacitus from engendering an idea of "the" past.

My survey of ancient historiography raises an obvious question: if ancient thought could not accommodate an idea of "the" past, how did that idea originate? The ancients lacked a unified conception of human activity that could gather all the various "pasts" into a single entity. The first step toward the creation of such an entity came not in the field of historiography but in theology, as classical culture became Christianized. In his *Confessions* Augustine of Hippo marks a great transition in Western thought, away from the classical ideal of philosophical transcendence of the world and toward a more existential stance, one that sees our consciousness as embedded in our earthly circumstances. This stance undergirds Augustine's idea of the *sæculum,* as expressed in *The City of God.* The *sæculum* constitutes an entity encompassing all human activity, both sacred and secular, though at first this unity existed not in time but in a kind of space, for the *sæculum* lay distended between God and the Devil.

The "figural" mode of scriptural analysis transformed the *sæculum* from a spatial to a temporal entity. This form of interpreting scripture unified the Old and New Testaments by viewing them from the perspective of the Incarnation— whereby events in the Old prefigured those in the New—but Augustine extended it beyond the Incarnation to encompass the Parousia, or Second Coming. With Augustine's innovation the figural mode of analysis came to circumscribe all of human history. Men like Gregory of Tours and the Venerable Bede subsequently used it to sacralize the *sæculum,* which for them comprised the workings of divine will in human affairs rather than simply circumscribing the world of human action. It thus acquired a more linear, temporal quality. Divine will, however, ultimately transcends time—past, present, and future are one in the mind of God. The Christian notion of the simultaneity of time in the omnipresence of God's mind ultimately precluded the emergence of an idea of the past in the Middle Ages.

The figural view of reality began to break down in the Renaissance with the emergence of an idea of anachronism. During the fourteenth century, Italian humanists awakened to the expressive power of classical Latin, a language more subtle and sophisticated than its cruder medieval offspring. Along with the resurrection of classical Latin came the revival of classical authors and the culture they conveyed, chiefly as excerpted in collections of commonplaces. These collections, and the classical rhetoric that underlay them, fostered the shift from a figural to an "exemplary" view of the world, characterized by the emulation of classical literary models. The emulative urge created a paradox—a "living past" that was, at one and the same time, different from the present and of vital importance to it as a cultural norm. Francesco Petrarca, the greatest of the early humanists, best exemplifies the appeal of the living past. He despaired of his own "dark age" that had lost the light of classical eloquence, and he yearned to plug directly into the cultural powerhouse of antiquity, jumping over the "middle" age that separated him from it. The past thus defined existed not "back there" in time but in a realm beyond time, in a symbolic space accessible by means of imitation.

The paradoxical nature of the living past became ever more apparent as growing awareness of the differences between past and present increasingly undermined the relevance of classical models. Humanist legal education illustrates how attempts to revive the text of Roman law, in order better to apply it to the modern world, gradually revealed it as the law of a past society. In response sixteenth-century French legal theorists like Jean Bodin sought to create a new body of universal law abstracted from the best laws of the most noteworthy peoples. But attempts to resuscitate the living past only served to suffocate it further under an avalanche of customs, laws, and institutions revealed by humanistic scholarship. Ironically, then, the emergence of an idea of anachronism in the Renaissance served to circumscribe—and ultimately undermine—the exemplarity it fostered.

A tendency to historicize entities while contextualizing them—to distinguish systematically between past and present—began to emerge in the sixteenth and seventeenth centuries. In part this tendency evolved as a natural consequence of humanist reading habits, which encouraged the kind of empathic engagement with the great heroes of antiquity evidenced by Michel de Montaigne. But instances of local empathy did not necessarily entail the sort of historical imagination that regards the past from a consistent perspective, rendering it remote from the present. Although the development of humanistic scholarship in the seventeenth century lent greater stability and consistency to the understanding of the past, it still did not privilege a sustained distinction between past and present. The furor excited in the late seventeenth and early eighteenth centuries by the French *Querelle des anciens et des modernes* and by the English "Battle of the Books" testifies to the fact that the historicizing viewpoint had by no means carried the day. It required support from outside itself to gain in assurance, and this it acquired from a Cartesian, relational view of truth.

Underlying Descartes's epochal invention of analytical geometry—by which he correlated lines and numbers—was his realization that every point on a line is the ratio of two numbers and that each ratio implies an ordered series of numbers in the same relation. Descartes expanded on this relational insight when he detailed a method of thinking that extended outward from "clear and distinct" ideas via chains of reasoning that measured the intervals between objects of thought. He regarded this activity as the chief task of reason, which used such comparisons to derive new knowledge from existing relations. Descartes's greatest disciple and popularizer, Nicholas Malebranche, expanded on this relational vision of knowledge, distilling from it the essence of the cardinal and ordinal principles of number that underlie modern mathematics. By means of the nascent principles of number thinking, Malebranche sought to assess all sorts of ideas—embracing moral as well as natural philosophy—by measuring the relations between them.

In his seminal *Spirit of the Laws* Montesquieu fashioned from Malebranche's relational vision of truth the prototype of a modern social science. Here he defined laws as relations, and he took as his proper subject not the laws themselves but the relations they represented, and the relations of these relations. All this he revealed through cross-cultural and cross-historical comparisons that (in effect) measured the distance between entities, thereby determining the order of relations to which they belonged. Customs, laws, institutions, states, religions, peoples—all these and more partook of general types of relations, which were themselves modified by a host of variables. Montesquieu thus conceived of any given entity as enmeshed in a web of relations that define it as unique and, at the same time, typify it. A sustained conception of the past emerged from this relational viewpoint, which consistently and systematically separated past from present in a logical way.

Montesquieu represents the tip of an analytical iceberg, wherein the principles, patterns, and metaphors of number thinking reshaped Western thought. Eighteenth-century rationalism is often contrasted with nineteenth-century historicism, which cherished the unique instead of the typical. But we can already see in the complexity of Montesquieu's relational view of the world a tremendous tension between the unique and the typical that reinforced the tension between past and present. The past born of this tension was defined as such from *without*, through a comparative method that differentiated any given entity in relation to other such entities. Historicists would subsequently view the past from *within*, seeing each entity as the product of its own unique process of development. Before they could do so, however, the past had to emerge in all its contextual distinctiveness from the network of relations that defined it. The past had to be born before it could be historicized.

AS THE ABOVE SYNOPSIS SHOULD MAKE abundantly clear, I have written a historiographical *essay* rather than a comprehensive *survey* of historical thought. I aim to reveal a hidden aspect of historical knowing that traditional surveys have obscured; consequently, my approach is highly selective, despite (or perhaps on account of) the broad chronological scope of the argument. My focus is explicitly Western, for I am not qualified to judge the sense of the past in other cultures. Within this Eurocentric emphasis I have further limited the range of my inquiry in order to bring its object more clearly into view. Thus I have dealt with the Hebrew sense of God's temporal agency only to the extent that it enters into the mainstream of Western culture via Christianity; and even Christian biblical versions of the past appear only as part of a later, figural reading of history. I have addressed early modern philology and antiquarianism—the subjects of much recent scholarship—only to the extent that they contribute to the information overload that French enlighteners sought to resolve. I have limited discussion of travel and travel literature—also subjects of recent scholarly interest—to the eighteenth century, when they started to exert widespread influence on European thinking, despite their importance for the intellectual development of earlier figures covered in the essay, such as Herodotus and Montaigne. Finally, and perhaps most glaringly, I have treated the towering figure of Giambattista Vico only as an outlier in the history of historiography, an exception proving a rule, notwithstanding his prominence in the overall story of Western historical consciousness. Were I more learned, I might have found the means to address these and other lacunae without sacrificing the thread of my argument, but my own limitations confront me at every turn.

Although I can claim to have read widely and deeply in some aspects of the history of historiography, one will not find here a comprehensive analysis of the modern authorities who treat the subjects I cover. As I stated earlier, this is more a work of synthesis than scholarship, and I have reserved the right to employ and discuss only those authorities who have most immediately shaped my thinking. Some of them are old—perhaps even old-fashioned—but I have not hesitated to use them if their scholarship, sound though unfashionable, serves in some way to advance my argument. I have honed the edge of that argument precisely through the selection of topics and authorities. And it is to the argument itself, about the strangeness of our modern perception of the past, that I ask the reader to direct his or her attention: if it proves worthy, perhaps others will expand upon it.

PART ONE

Antiquity

In flat appearance we should be and be,
Except for delicate clinkings not explained.

—Wallace Stevens, "Description without Place"

Flatland

A rguably the greatest of all historians, Thucydides remains at best intensely difficult for modern readers and at worst utterly boring. In part the reason for his inaccessibility lies in his deadpan description of even the most horrific events, embroiling a complex cast of characters—aloof statesmen, pandering demagogues, egocentric rogues, decent fools—depicted with the severest economy of expression. The pulse of the narrative barely quickens as Spartans slaughter the courageous Plataeans after a heroic siege, as Athenians eradicate the luckless Melians for choosing to resist imperialist aggression, as Corcyraeans massacre one another in an unstoppable internecine bloodbath. Even the outcome of the famous "Mitylenian debate"—when the Athenian Assembly recoils from its previous resolve to execute all the adult males of the rebellious city of Mitylene and enslave all the women and children—still entails the deaths of the rebel leaders, "the number being rather more than a thousand." Thus, with these dispassionate words, they exit the scene of a narrative that flows on and on, from horror to horror, almost in a monotone. And the perpetrator of the Mitylenian bloodletting, the Athenian demagogue Cleon—who insisted on at least a thousand heads if he could not have more—merely garners the title "most violent man in Athens," opprobrium of such concision that it might pass unnoticed had not some scholars fastened upon it as a rare instance of Thucydidean ire.

Of course, all this reticence serves the interests of what we now call "historical objectivity," which Thucydides would regard less grandiosely as "accuracy," a scholarly virtue he is widely regarded as personifying. Indeed, he does not entitle his work a "history," perhaps because of that term's association with Herodotean storytelling. And, lest anyone confuse his efforts with the tales of his predecessor, Thucydides expressly disavows entertainment in favor of instruction. To this end he stretches every nerve to appear impartial. The whole narrative takes its structure from this drive for accuracy, being organized by the chronological scheme of successive summers and winters that marks the campaign seasons of the war. Thucydides justifies this novel scheme as more precise than the traditional form of dating by the names of a city's annual magistrates, for it better enables him to locate events within any given year. This aspect of the drive for accuracy, though, has the effect of further flattening the narrative, confining it to a recurrent pattern, a monotony of seasons that (ironically) strikes our sensibilities as unnatural.

But for the modern reader, the real source of the narrative's impenetrability lies beneath its unruffled surface. The work begins with a striking statement: "Thucydides, an Athenian, wrote the history of the war between the Peloponnesians and the Athenians, beginning at the moment that it broke out, and believing that it would be a great war, and more worthy of relation than any that had preceded it." From this point he launches into a nineteen-chapter digression (about a dozen pages in English translation) ostensibly proving that the Peloponnesian War was the greatest yet fought. This digression begins innocuously with the words "For instance" and—after a highly imaginative and detailed reconstruction of the material circumstances of the Greeks from the remote past to the present—ends abruptly with the phrase, "Having now given the result of my inquiries into early times . . ." The digression is so famous and insightful that tradition accords it a title: the Archaeology. Yet, regardless of its ultimate significance, its immediate effect is to bewilder the modern reader, who quickly loses sight of the Peloponnesian War as Thucydides details patterns of ancient migration, the subsequent establishment of walled communities, the gradual accumulation of material resources, and the eventual rise of navies and sea power. Instead of presenting a linear argument about the present, he takes a giant looping detour into the distant past. And this is only the first of many such loops, which classicists term "ring compositions." These loops begin so imperceptibly that readers unaccustomed to Thucydides's style only gradually become aware that they are lost in the thicket of a digression and, to recapture the general line of argument, must backtrack to the mere word or two that initiated the loop many pages earlier.

In addition to ring compositions, Thucydides exhibits a tendency to digress on a smaller scale. The concluding chapter of the Archaeology, where he emerges from his long digression into the remote past, is itself a minidigression. This chapter (roughly a paragraph in translation) concerns widespread ignorance about the recent, as well as remote, past, with the bulk of the chapter devoted to misconceptions about the overthrow of the Pisistratid tyranny in Athens, only some eighty years before the Peloponnesian War. The reader easily becomes lost amid the details of the plot against the Pisistratids, which constitutes a freestanding story whose relation to the main argument threatens to become tenuous. Woe to the inattentive reader when such minidigressions occur—as they inevitably do—within ring compositions!

A venerable and judicious classicist, John H. Finley Jr. likens these digressions (both large and small) to footnotes and appendices. He speculates that, in the absence of any conventional scholarly apparatus, Thucydides brought the full force of his learning to bear wherever he deemed proof necessary to the credibility of his argument. Ring compositions and their lesser kin thus appear as by-products of Thucydides's concern for accuracy. But Finley also allows that the practice is to some extent unconscious on the part of the author, who becomes so absorbed by the details and ramifications of his story at any given point that he all too readily gets carried away with them. Thus secondary elements in the story receive the same thorough treatment as primary ones. Another equally venerable and judicious scholar, the philologist Erich Auerbach, traces this same tendency to get caught up in details back to the Homeric epics, where the poet obviously had no scholarly pretenses. In fact, Auerbach sees this tendency at work in ancient Roman narratives, as well as Greek ones. It is so pervasive that we can—reversing Finley's emphasis—regard it first and foremost as an unconscious habit of mind, one that has the incidental effect of lending scholarly support to Thucydides's account of events.[1] His mental landscape was thus structured in such a way that he could not subordinate what we regard as the secondary (and tertiary) to the primary levels of his argument.

This quality of mind creates a flat, almost featureless, historical terrain, which modern readers have difficulty navigating. We expect a historian to view events, such as those constituting a war, from a perspective that relates parts to whole, just as an artist orients the elements of a landscape in relation to a vanishing point. Historical perspective would subordinate the immediate causes of a war (say, the German invasion of Poland on 1 September 1939) to its underlying causes (Germany's late development as a nation-state in the nineteenth century, its humiliation at Versailles after the First World War, a worldwide economic depression that undermined the Weimar Republic, the rise of the Nazi Party and a reinvigorated nationalism). The war would thus emerge not merely as a clash of combatants but as an upheaval from below, from events (the Versailles Treaty) decades prior to the war, from forces (the Great Depression) unrelated to diplomacy, from ideologies (racial and nationalist) deep-seated in the culture of nineteenth-century Europe. Depending on the historian's perspective, all these features would take their appropriate place—in the foreground, middle ground, or background—providing the reader with an orientation amid events.

Of course, one might object that Thucydides actually does view the Peloponnesian War in this way, when he distinguishes between what he calls the "real" and the "immediate" causes of the war. Coming hard on the heels of the Archaeology, this distinction constitutes one of the organizing principles of the entire work. Indeed, one might even argue—along with Finley—that the Archaeology itself demonstrates the extent to which Thucydides has "grasped the significance of the economic advances of his time."[2] Naval power had given rise to a new kind of state—Athens with its commercial, seaborne empire—which inevitably came into conflict with the traditional agrarian, continental power of Sparta. After all (one might argue), how else could Thucydides have known that the coming war was bound to be a great one, if not by perceiving that deep-seated historical forces had come to a head?

Yet no sooner does he make the distinction between real and immediate causes than he launches into such a detailed discussion of the latter—stemming from a clash between Corinth and Corcyra—that the reader quickly loses sight of the former, ostensibly more important topic. Furthermore, the clash between Corinth and Corcyra appears to us moderns as clearly driven by economic considerations. The merest glance at a map indicates that the two states are natural competitors in the east-west trade between the Greek cities of Asia Minor and those of Italy; and the proximity of Athens and Corinth heightens their own commercial competition, explaining for us why Athens will side with the more distant Corcyra in this quarrel. Nowhere, though, does Thucydides subsume the immediate causes of the war under this economic rubric. Instead, he simply recounts the minute steps by which Corinth and Corcyra (and eventually Athens) came to blows over internal affairs in the remote city of Epidamnus, affairs themselves detailed with equal, mind-numbing thoroughness.

And when he moves on to consider the real cause of the war—the fear of growing Athenian power that induced the Spartans to side with Corinth—he nowhere analyzes the source of that power. Instead, he launches into another famous ring composition (now known as the Pentecontaetia, from the Greek for "fifty years"), detailing the period between the Persian and Peloponnesian wars when Athens emerged to rival Sparta. Modern historians like Finley have distilled from this account the essence of Athenian growth: how it became a sea power after the Persian wars, how sea power encouraged the expansion of democracy (the poorest citizens rowed the ships), how democracy fostered imperialism (more ships entailed more rowers, strengthening the political hold of the democracy). Thucydides himself understood this pattern perfectly well; indeed, it was common knowledge at his time, as we can infer from the acerbic observations of the so-called Old Oligarch, an Athenian curmudgeon who recognized these developments, didn't particularly like them, but saw no alternative to being ruled by the riffraff. Despite having these connections clearly in mind, however, Thucydides did not use them to explain the remarkable rise of Athens in the Pentecontaetia. Rather, he details that rise event by event: how, after their victories over the Persians, the Greeks sought to liberate their kinsmen in Asia Minor; how the Spartans bungled their leadership of this crusade; how the Athenians took over from them, forming the Delian League; how, as the Persian threat diminished and individual states sought to leave the League, Athens conquered them one by one, creating the Athenian Empire; how success bred success, as Athens's imperialistic reach expanded toward ever richer prizes; how, all the while, Sparta saw its power steadily eclipsed and grew ever more fearful. All this Thucydides recounts in a narrative of surface events, without recourse to the underlying forces that figure so prominently in modern historical accounts of this period, forces that Thucydides himself surely recognized.

Or did he? We divine the motive force behind Athenian expansion because of what Thucydides has written about navies in the Archaeology, about democracy in the "Funeral Oration," and about empire in the Periclean policy speeches. Yet even though he perceived the connection between these elements, he did not grant that connection explanatory power; thus, we may reasonably question whether he recognized it as constituting a historical force, a vector abstracted from events. His account has exactly the opposite thrust, toward the concrete rather than the abstract, toward the visible rather than the invisible, toward the surface of events rather than whatever may underlie them. For Thucydides, historical explanation resides in the account of the events themselves, whose meaning is manifestly clear (given all that detail how could it not be?) and requires no interpretation. There are no ineffable forces at work here shaping events, at least not of the kind we would recognize.

Thus, what we have been calling the primary, secondary, and tertiary levels of his account are for him all one and the same. Instead of consciously taking a perspective on events—instead of interpreting them in a way that makes one more important than another—he simply relates them in sequence (including illustrative digressions) such that no one event stands above another in explanatory value. Of course, noteworthy events—the plague at Athens, the Corcyraean revolution, the capture of Pylos, the Melian dialogue, the Sicilian expedition—occur throughout the history, but they simply happen within the frame of the account rather than structuring that frame. Indeed, given the uniformity of his historical landscape, we may justifiably question whether Thucydides shares our notion of "event." For us an event is something that stands out—something "salient"—yet this is precisely what is missing from his account. To borrow a distinction from mathematics, we may say that he recounts not a closed "series" of events (delimited by a historical perspective) but an open "sequence" of occurrences ("This occurred, then this, then this . . ."). Occurrences as such are linked by their proximity to each other, not by the chains of cause and effect that bind events together.

We have come thus far at our (relative) ease, thanks to the labor of many scholars. Erich Auerbach, for one, has brilliantly depicted the "foregrounded" nature of classical narrative, which leaves nothing in the "background," nothing in the shadows where it might be subject to interpretation. He attributes this habit of revealing all with equal clarity to an aristocratic "separation of styles," which utilizes a "high style" for serious matters (the stuff of history, epic poetry, and tragedy) and a "low style" for mundane matters (as in comedy and romance). The separation of styles precludes the serious consideration of daily life, the arena where historical forces—vectors abstracted from events—most readily manifest themselves. (From the mundane reality of my writing these words on a computer while dressed in cheap clothing made in some third world country, we can infer the digital revolution and the globalization of the economy, vectors that would pass unnoticed were my historical vision focused solely on "serious" matters, such as diplomacy and war.) And another fine classicist, Virginia Hunter, has shown convincingly that neither Herodotus nor Thucydides shares our notion of "event"; rather, they see history as constituted by universal and ineluctable "processes," recurrent patterns that unfold inexorably when catalyzed by occurrences. Thus the Archaeology discloses a "process" of growth via sea power to empire—obviously a mid-fifth-century pattern—which Thucydides reads back in time to encompass the rise of the Minoans, Achaeans, and, ultimately, the Athenians. This emphasis on historical patterns tends to rob "events" of their distinctiveness, transforming them into "occurrences."[3]

In the wake of this scholarship we can assert with confidence that the Thucydidean conception of history differs radically from our own. "Forces," "events," "interpretations"—this is the stuff of modern historical understanding, which (as Auerbach amply demonstrates) is itself historically grown. Thoroughly imbued with this sense of relativism, we would scarcely assume that Thucydides viewed the world as we do—or, at least, we would reject that assumption once we became aware of having made it. But, even in full consciousness of our relativism, we would still freely assume that he had a conception of "the past." After all, what do historians—even chroniclers of recent events—write about? Of course, we would grant that Thucydides's conception of the past might not be the same as ours—that his concerned different subject matter (war rather than, say, economics) and had different content (occurrences rather than events). But this caveat still assumes the notion that he had an idea of the past as an objective space existing "back there" in time. And underlying this assumption is another—equally tenacious and even more fundamental—that "the past" is different from "the present." Not simply prior, but different. Indeed, this difference constitutes the past as a separate realm. Ultimately, however, the flattened nature of the Thucydidean narrative calls into question the very existence of the past as an objective space in time distinct from the present.

At this point a skeptic might object that we are committing the sin of anachronism by denying Thucydides any conception of the past just because he fails to share ours. I've already explored this objection in my introduction, but let us now consider how the charge itself highlights the importance of the idea of anachronism for our conception of the past. We are so conditioned by this idea that things taken out of their historical context strike us as being either odd or humorous. (In the now classic British comedy *Monty Python and the Holy Grail*, for example, medieval knights dispatch the beast guarding the Grail by means of "The Holy Hand Grenade of Antioch.") Historians strive to avoid anachronism as the worst of scholarly sins. We have even coined our own special pejorative—"Whig history"—to disparage judgments about the past that privilege contemporary practices and ideals.

By contrast, Thucydides demonstrates an awareness of differences between past and present without elevating that awareness to a principle of historical knowledge. In the Archaeology he refers to past practices no longer in use—such as the custom of always carrying arms for self-defense or of wearing belts during athletic contests rather than contending naked—from which he adduces changes in the material and cultural circumstances of the Hellenes, changes that chart the course of Hellenic progress. And this awareness of historical differences is not new with Thucydides, for even Homer manifests it. Although he lived in an Iron Age culture, Homer sings of past heroes hefting bronze weapons, as they would have done in the "olden days." Yet for Homer and Thucydides this awareness did not constitute a sustained and systematic perception of the difference between past and present. Rather, it remained a local phenomenon, a literary device or a logical point that, once employed, was quickly forgotten. After illustrating his argument about Hellenic progress, Thucydides makes hardly any mention of archaic practices or historical differences; and aside from the weight of the bronze in their hands, Homer's heroes fight as Iron Age warriors. We may justifiably question whether the Greeks (or the Romans, for that matter) had an idea of anachronism if they did not consistently distinguish past from present.

Their use of the past remained fundamentally instrumentalist for a number of reasons. The above-mentioned classical separation of styles detailed by Auerbach precludes an idea of anachronism, for the differences between past and present manifest themselves first and foremost in the circumstances of daily life. (The computer on which I write these words is already "outdated"; and, though I may think my off-the-rack clothing stylish, it too is probably "old-fashioned.") When Thucydides scorns mundane subject matter as unbefitting the seriousness of history, he cuts himself off from the economic, social, and cultural realms that best establish what we have come to know as "historical context." Recently Aldo Schiavone, a noted historian of classical antiquity, has developed a related argument, that the slave economy of imperial Rome (and by extension that of classical Athens) obscured the daily reality of labor, relegating it to something contemptible and beneath notice in a fundamentally aristocratic culture. The consequent lack of a labor theory of value impeded conceptions of economic and social progress, encouraging instead a static view of the world that focused on recurrent patterns in history rather than singular events, on the universal and immutable over the contingent and variable.

I would like to supplement these explanations with an entirely different and even more basic reason for the absence of a systematic idea of anachronism: the ancients conceived not of "the" past but of "pasts," which intertwined with different conceptions of time. The flattening of Thucydides's historical perspective occurs as he shifts temporal vantage point, allowing one kind of past to intrude on another without privileging either, without "taking a perspective." The absence of an idea of "the" past militates against a systematic distinction between past and present. It permits the operation of a localized sense of anachronism without transmuting that awareness into a principle of historical knowledge.

This explanation may appear more abstract and seemingly more detached from the reality of ancient lives than those offered by Auerbach and Schiavone, yet it takes precedence because it stands prior in time to their explanations and closer in proximity to the immediate concerns of the ancients. As we will see, the perception of multiple pasts ultimately constitutes the very genre of history, in which Thucydides traditionally stands as but the second innovator, behind his older contemporary Herodotus. True, this genre issued from an aristocratic culture, but its germination antedates that culture's implementation of a separation of styles. Although we can detect some aspects of this separation as far back as Homer, the literary doctrine and its strict implementation did not arise until much later, after Hellenic culture had given way to the Hellenistic one adopted by the Romans. Slavery, of course, is as old as humankind, and Athenian slavery, in particular, has a long history; but, as best we can tell, a full-blown slave economy did not develop in Athens until well after the Persian wars. By contrast, the genre of history emerges from these very wars, which constitute a transformative event occurring as the society evolved from orality into literacy. Our seemingly more abstract factor actually connects with surprising immediacy to the reality of ancient lives lived in the shadow of a heroic struggle that (in the minds of contemporaries) rivaled or even eclipsed the deeds of the Homeric heroes. It thus called forth innovative attempts at preserving the memory of that heroism, attempts that enshrined multiple pasts.

BEFORE TURNING TO AN EXAMINATION of the oral culture from which history would emerge, I must insert a caveat. In the argument that follows, I will increasingly emphasize the distinction between a conception of "the" past and that of multiple "pasts." At some point one may begin to wonder whether I have overdrawn this distinction. Specifically, one may question whether moderns actually have a conception of "the" past. Each modern historian obviously takes a perspective on the events he or she recounts. But the sum of these differing accounts does not add up to "the" past; rather, it constitutes a collection of "pasts." Some might claim that each account exists primarily as an intellectual construct that cannot be correlated to an objective reality in time. Indeed, in the wake of modern literary criticism some might even seek to do away with any notion of "the" past altogether, substituting in its place an idea of "texts," broadly construed as artifacts existing in the present, from which any inference to a past "back there" in time is entirely gratuitous.

The tendency to deny the objective reality of the past originates from a reaction to nineteenth-century historicism. This modern (as opposed to postmodern) form of historical consciousness explains the uniqueness of historical entities as developing over time in relation to their circumstances. It has become a habit of mind so deeply engrained that people naturally tend to understand themselves and their world as historically grown, assuming that all others have always done likewise. They hardly realize that this stratum of our consciousness settled out from the convergence of several intellectual currents in the eighteenth century—that it is itself a historical deposit. In effect, the historicist habit of mind has fostered a conception of the past as an objective entity, a cultural given that transcends our diverse accounts of it. This conception is reinforced by our everyday linguistic usage, where "the past" presumes a referent whose reality we scarcely question. As this chapter proceeds, I will gradually distinguish this usage, and the habit of mind it reflects, from other conceptions by emphasizing the definite article; hence, I shall contrast "the" past with multiple "pasts." This distinction merely serves to help illuminate the assumptions underlying the intellectual inheritance of modern historicism, which we can no longer take for granted.

Pasts Present

P rimo Levi's account of concentration camp life shows us that the figure of the storyteller is ubiquitous and irrepressible, even in Auschwitz:

> From the outside door, secretly and looking around cautiously, the storyteller comes in. He is seated on Wachsmann's bunk and at once gathers around him a small, attentive, silent crowd. He chants an interminable Yiddish rhapsody, always the same one, in rhymed quatrains, of a resigned and penetrating melancholy (but perhaps I only remember it so because of the time and the place that I heard it?); from the few words that I understand, it must be a song that he composed himself, in which he has enclosed all the life of the Lager in minute detail. Some are generous and give the storyteller a pinch of tobacco or a needleful of thread; others listen intently but give nothing.

Levi characterized the labor camp as a "gigantic biological and social experiment" conducted under the most rigorous circumstances. This very rigor enables us to isolate some of the features of oral storytelling, in part by contrast with the above scene. From these features, we can begin to infer the idea of a "past-made-present" fostered by oral traditions.[4]

Although Levi did manage to keep some notes about his experiences, such record keeping was punishable by death, a stricture that naturally encouraged storytelling instead. This activity took place at night, after the evening ration and before "lights out." The storyteller was obviously skilled in his craft and benefited materially (albeit unreliably) from his skill. He "chants" his story in "rhymed quatrains" as an *aide-mémoire*, for it is "always the same one"—though how could Levi be sure if he didn't understand the words? Clearly, the chant *sounded* the same to him, though its details may have varied with each retelling.

But most striking for our purposes are two features: the silence of the audience and the nature of the tale. The severity of the biological experiment on the prisoners—they were being starved and worked to death—reduced them to silence. Otherwise, they would have engaged in give-and-take with the storyteller, and his story would thus have evolved more perceptibly from one telling to the next. Finally, the story "enclosed all the life of the Lager"—it concerned the present—for these people surely had no future, and, as Levi details everywhere in his study, they had through the harshest conditioning been stripped of their past, leaving them immersed in a pitiless here-and-now.

By contrast, storytelling in ancient Greece was at least ostensibly about the past—"ostensibly" because the real subject of oral traditions in pre- and early literate societies concerns the present, namely the continuity of the community. But let us leave this social function aside for the moment and concentrate instead on the subjective side of oral tradition, its pretense of providing an account of the past. This pretense is inherent in the very nature of oral tradition, which originates "as messages are transmitted beyond the generation that gave rise to them."[5] By this definition, storytelling in Auschwitz was, so to speak, a dead end; but in those cases where storytelling did entail an oral tradition, we can distinguish between stories told in formal language (such as epic poetry) and in everyday language (such as narrative tales). Both genres evoke what we might term a "past-made-present," which conflates the two temporal realms, creating a symbolic space apart from time. By collapsing the differences between past and present, this space affords an immediate connection to the past. The ancient Greeks accessed the symbolic space of the past first and foremost through the Homeric epics. The very success of these epics eventually fixed their form and content. As they ceased to evolve along with the society that told them, they became supplemented in their historical role by narrative tales. We will consider both of these storytelling genres in order to gain some understanding of oral and early literate notions of the past from Homer to Herodotus.

THE ANCIENT GREEKS IDENTIFIED THEIR remote past with the Trojan War as memorialized by "Homer," the semilegendary, blind poet from Ionia credited with composing the *Iliad* and the *Odyssey*. Although some scholars claim these epics have distant, Indo-European roots, most regard them as originating from warrior songs performed during the early Mycenaean period on mainland Greece, maybe as far back as 1500 BC. During its heyday (c. 1400-1200 BC) this civilization profited not only from trade but also from piracy, as raiders fanned out across the eastern Mediterranean. One of Odysseus's many sobriquets is "sacker of cities," and one of the many cities sacked around this time was a commercial center near the Hellespont, now widely regarded as the "real" Troy. The site actually comprises nine Troys, one atop the other, and who destroyed Troy VIIa around 1250 BC—whether Mycenaean pirates or other marauders—remains unclear. Suffice it to say that the ever-evolving warrior songs came to encompass these piratical adventures, too, which intertwined with earlier tales. The whole amalgam continued to evolve during the Greek "Dark Age" that followed the twelfth-century collapse of Mycenaean civilization and persisted until the eighth century.

The Mycenaeans had an unwieldy form of syllabic writing too cumbersome for everyday use, and the Greeks of the Dark Age lost even this art, so the heroic songs enjoyed a long period of oral gestation. One imagines they were originally sung in the evening by warriors, whether around a campfire, in a Mycenaean lord's palace, or in a village chieftain's house during the Dark Age. These performances probably involved some degree of give-and-take between singer and audience that served progressively to shape each song. Successful warriors may have eventually begun sponsoring singers of special ability, remunerating them formally or informally. Whatever the case, singing inevitably became a craft, the preserve of bards who began to distill the myriad songs into basic metrical patterns, archetypal figures, and narrative themes. When Greece stood at the cusp of alphabetic literacy (around the eighth century), these bardic compositions coalesced into the epics we now know as the *Iliad* and the *Odyssey*—whether at the hands of one, two, or several singers, and whether they were literate or nonliterate, will forever remain a mystery.

Although the epics purport to be about the past, they really serve to sanction the current ideals, aspirations, and practices of the community, especially as embodied by the warrior elite that subsidized their performance. The social function of the epics is part and parcel of their production. In this regard the oral model of spontaneous "composition in performance" seems to fit the Homeric bards best, with the caveat that they may also have utilized some rehearsal and memorization. A bard would chant his song in the prescribed meter, reinforced by (say) the pounding of his staff, fabricating his verse from stock "formulas" and "themes"—metrical and narrative elements—that fit an ever-evolving story cast in what we now know as "dactylic hexameter." As the fundamental building blocks of this mode of composition, formulas and themes would remain relatively stable, while the details of the story would evolve along with the tastes and experience of the audience. The success of the performance depends on the audience already knowing the basic story, so listeners could follow it without effort, immersing themselves in its flow. And this requirement circumscribes the past with the present, necessitating that the details and context of the story remain either current or well within the memory of the audience. Memory in preliterate cultures extended from as much as 125 years or so—measured from the youngest of one generation to the youngest three generations on—to as little as a generation. (This range depends not only on the average life span in a society but also on the society's time frame, as reflected by its system of time measurement—whether by generations, reigns, priestly officeholders, or whatnot). In any case the bardic past remained in fairly close orbit around the present.

Regardless of the depth of the society's time frame, the audience experienced the bardic past as essentially timeless. One obvious indication of this has largely escaped notice. The bards lived amid the ruins of the Mycenaean civilization of which they sang, yet neither they nor their auditors connected the songs to the ruins, even though (for example) the "Catalogue of Ships" in book 2 of the *Iliad* makes specific reference to the mighty walls of Tiryns and Mycenae. Granted, names like *Tiryns* and *Mycenae* may not have had geographical meaning for the Homeric Greeks; nonetheless, they attributed the massive constructions we now associate with these names to a mythical race of Cyclopes. And this attribution continued long after the Greeks had emerged from their Dark Age, long after they had attained the technological means and intellectual sophistication to connect the ruins to the culture they valorized. Of course, we cannot expect them to have undertaken modern archaeological excavations; but, just the same, we cannot help being struck by their relative lack of curiosity about the ruins, despite their having been steeped in epics about Mycenaean kings and heroes.

Commenting on the similar indifference of Renaissance Romans to the possibility that the classical world they cherished might lie buried beneath their feet, Leonard Barkan has remarked, "You cannot travel through symbolic space with a shovel" (25). Like Barkan's Renaissance Romans, the ancient Greeks felt no inclination to dig for their past because they did not identify it with ruins existing on a spatial/temporal plane. Rather, it resided in a symbolic space apart from time. The timelessness of this symbolic space is reflected in two features of the Homeric epics: the "foregrounded" nature of their narrative action and the agelessness of their heroes. These features fostered an immediate connection between a Greek audience and its past as embodied in the epics, a connection unmediated by time.

The oral performance of the epics had the effect of riveting the audience in a perpetual here-and-now of vivid stories flowing imperceptibly from one to the next. In the famous first chapter of his masterwork, *Mimesis,* Erich Auerbach aptly illustrates the foregrounded quality of the narrative in his analysis of the passage in the *Odyssey* where Odysseus returns home after a twenty-year absence, disguised as a road-weary traveler. Even though his wife, Penelope, fails to recognize him, she dutifully instructs their faithful housekeeper, Euryclea, to wash his feet in a traditional gesture of hospitality. As the servant does so, her fingers graze a telltale scar on Odysseus's leg, which had been gored during a boar hunt in his youth, and she suddenly realizes that her master has returned. At this point the narrative abruptly loops far back in time to the boar hunt with Odysseus's grandfather, Autolycus, that occasioned the scar. This digression details the genealogy and character of Autolycus, his long-standing love for his grandson, the youth's visit, the welcoming banquet held in Odysseus's honor, the next day's early reveille, the stages of the hunt, the fateful wound, Odysseus's convalescence and return home, his parents' anxiety and relief at having their son back in one piece—and then, just as abruptly, the narrative resumes where it left off, as an astonished Euryclea lets her master's foot fall back into the water basin.

Here we have a succession of stories, each told for its own sake. Auerbach describes how the narrative places the action at hand entirely in the foreground, revealing all through its attention to detail and leaving nothing in the shadows, in the background. Homer (to utilize the authorial convention) moves from scene to scene, elaborating each exhaustively, regardless of what we might deem its relative importance to the story. He thus composes as if in a ubiquitous present, shedding equal light on all scenes. Even what we would term a "flashback"—a regressive plot movement subordinate to the main action—receives the same full treatment as the scenes preceding and following it, such that it hardly seems like a flashback at all. Yet we automatically process it as such—so accustomed are we to modern assumptions about the plotting of a narrative—all the while remaining oblivious to the distinct possibility that a Greek audience, immersed in the narrative flow, might not have done so. The temporal sequencing of the plot might have been less important to the audience than the immediacy of each scene.

This possibility appears all the more likely when we ask ourselves certain logical questions arising from the narrative as it moves forward toward its denouement—Odysseus's slaughter of the fifty suitors who had taken to besieging his wife and consuming his livelihood during his absence. How could an aging Penelope attract so many suitors in their prime? Economic motives, we moderns assume cynically, though the poet lingers on her beauty. And how could an aging, footsore Odysseus dispatch them all with such alacrity? The image of a grizzled, battle-hardened veteran arises before us, though unbidden by the poet. Rather, in his mind's eye, and in that of his audience, neither Penelope nor Odysseus has aged a day, their twenty-year separation notwithstanding. Time's passage is not an element in a story that remains firmly fixed in the present.

Auerbach notes this timeless quality when he remarks that Odysseus's innermost self remains unchanged despite his travails, that the experience of ceaseless war and wandering leaves no mark on his personality. But Auerbach neglects to point out that Odysseus remains essentially unchanged in body as well as soul, that the wanderer's years are washed away like grime from a traveler's feet, that the hero who springs into action against the suitors is indistinguishable from the king who left home twenty years before. Twenty years! What we think of in some specificity as an eventful passage of time the ancient audience processed as duration—an indeterminate continuum—through which the characters remain completely unchanged in all their aspects. "They are," to quote M. I. Finley, "as timeless as the story itself."[6]

Perhaps Aristotle epitomized this timeless past best in his famous distinction between poetry (by which he means chiefly epic) and history: "Poetry is something more philosophic and of graver import than history, since its statements are of the nature rather of universals, whereas those of history are singulars. By a universal statement I mean one as to what such or such a kind of man will probably or necessarily say or do—which is the aim of poetry, though it affixes proper names to the characters; by a singular statement, one as to what, say, Alcibiades did or had done to him."[7]

We tend to approach this oft-cited passage from the wrong side of the divide between history and poetry, from a perspective that claims to have supplanted myth with fact. The passage retains its interest for us chiefly as the philosopher's only substantial comment on history, as if he should have said more. Yet Aristotle's virtual silence on this matter reveals him as a true son of Homer. From the Greek point of view, time-bound historical facts are mired in contingency and offer no fit subject for knowledge. Who cares whether Alcibiades did this or that particular thing at this or that particular moment? Obviously, we moderns care because we have a conception of the world that cherishes contingency, that sees it as constitutive of events, and sees events as links in causal chains. But even Thucydides, the great chronicler of Alcibiades's actions, can only make sense of events by balancing historical contingency against timeless universality. Thus, long before history existed as a literary genre, the Homeric epics embodied the eternal, living truth of the past, which retained a vitality and immediacy unmatched by our time-bound, contingent view. For a Greek audience the past lives in the medium of the epics, through which it speaks directly to the present.

And not only to the present, but the future. The true subject of the epics concerns the continuity of the community, an amalgam of past, present, *and* future. Past practices, consented to by the community in the present, become cultural archetypes projected into the future. Thus Aristotle's universals concern "what such or such a kind of man will probably or necessarily say or do." The constructs that we regard as "timeless" are in reality "timeful," intermixing the temporal states we so carefully distinguish; indeed, universals cannot exist unless the community consents to project its past into its future. The latter constitutes something more than what we would today regard as a mere collection of hopes and dreams. It has fully as much reality as the past, precisely because it is constructed out of the past. Further, these projections—authorized and participated in by the community as a whole—have extraordinary power. Whereas our hopes and dreams are private, theirs were public, embodied in the performance of the epics; and whereas our public aspirations are a matter of constant debate and dispute, theirs were held with much greater unanimity because they constituted virtually the entire cultural inheritance. Our sustained sense of anachronism precludes the Homeric amalgam of past, present, and future. Useful though it may be, the analytical distinction between past and present comes at the cost of their more fully integrated vision of life.

ALTHOUGH HOMER WOULD ALWAYS RETAIN his magic for the ancient Greeks—some pale reflection of which we can still sense today—the immediacy of the temporal amalgam began to weaken as the bardic tradition gave way to a rhapsodic one dedicated to the preservation of Homeric genius. By the seventh and sixth centuries BC, if not earlier, the influence of writing helped stabilize the epics. (The earliest instances of alphabetic writing date from the late eighth century and record snatches of verse, leading some scholars to speculate that the alphabet originated when Greek traders adapted Phoenician characters to the task of remembering Homeric verse during their long absences from home.) Despite the stabilizing effect of early literacy, which probably didn't extend much beyond an *aide-mémoire*, the poems surely continued to evolve in the process of rhapsodic performance, although at a much slower rate. We can thus hypothesize that a gap gradually opened between the world of the poems and that of the audience— between a heroic age of gods and an age of men—leading the Greeks to begin memorializing their more recent past through prose narratives, which now served as an additional means of reinforcing social consensus. This emphasis on storytelling in ordinary language would generate much of the raw material from which, more than two centuries later, Herodotus would fabricate a new conception of the past.

A tradition of oral storytelling in everyday prose had presumably coexisted with epic poetry and probably even predated it, as we can assume from the omnipresence of this activity. Actual evidence of this oral tradition in Greece, however, is largely limited to inferences from etymology. Herodotus referred to himself as a *logios,* a "man versed in *logoi,*" which he apparently performed orally for decades before finally assembling them in the written form of the *Histories.* The term *logoi* meant for Herodotus something more akin to "narratives," "accounts," or "arguments" than simply "stories," though Thucydides later took a dimmer view, deriding the *logographoi* ("chroniclers") as mere storytellers seeking public praise at truth's expense (1.21). The term *logographoi* incorporates the activity of writing, from which we can infer that, by the late fifth century BC, "men versed in *logoi*" had taken to recording traditional narratives rather than performing them orally. Etymology thus suggests that a centuries-old tradition of oral storytelling coexisted with literacy at least until the late fifth century BC.

Modern anthropological and historical research, especially Jan Vansina's pioneering fieldwork in Africa, confirms the role of storytellers in societies touched by literacy. Vansina distinguishes in general between memorized and nonmemorized stories. Memorized stories achieve a remarkable degree of fidelity to an original across many generations, whereas nonmemorized ones are of indeterminate origin: "There is no question of reconstructing any original or even of assuming that there was but one original."[8] Vansina found that well-established African kingships could support the existence of storytellers specializing in memorized messages, such as official chronicles and royal genealogies. The more decentralized *polis* world of ancient Greece, however, probably did not support the same degree of mnemonic specialization found in Africa. On this account the vast bulk of Greek prose narratives probably consisted of non-memorized stories that evolved with each retelling. Vansina terms these compositions "tales," and they approximate what Herodotus meant by *logoi.*

Contemporary anthropology sheds some light on the raw material from which Herodotus would fabricate his *Histories.* Vansina distinguishes among four kinds of tales: (1) historical tales of a general, local, or family nature; (2) didactic tales, especially concerning etiological myths; (3) "artistic" tales designed as pure entertainment; and (4) personal recollections passed on to subsequent generations. These varieties share one feature in common, for "all record history to some extent."[9] The "prosaic" past is structured in much the same way as the poetic past of the Homeric epics. Regardless of whether the tales are "historical," "didactic," or "artistic," they all depict a past that orbits the present, as Vansina himself discovered to his embarrassment. While a youthful researcher, he touted the apparent exactitude of an oral chronicle of the Kuba of Zaire; but some twenty years later, on hearing the "same" chronicle again, he realized that it simply constituted a mutable record of what the Kuba believe in the present rather than what had actually happened in the past. This mutability is part and parcel of the oral composition and transmission of such nonmemorized stories, which evolve along with the society that retells them.

Contemporary anthropological evidence about oral traditions enables us to imagine a scenario for the evolution of the *logoi* that eventually found their way into Herodotus's *Histories*. Here we will focus on what Vansina termed "historical tales," which he subdivided into family, local, and general or regional stories. (Note that Herodotus drew inspiration from the whole gamut of oral storytelling, "fictional" as well as "factual," and that his vast work reflects a wide range of other influences as well.) Prominent families had their own oral histories, incorporating accounts of great deeds intermixed with genealogies tracing a family's lineage back to divine or heroic origins. These accounts might be passed on from father to son or performed by an entertainer for a lord. Through continual retelling, the individual stories would gradually mutate in an incremental way unnoticeable to an ancient audience. Furthermore, the audience would regard the whole ensemble of stories as constituting a family history that stretched uniformly from the remote past to the present, leaving no gaps in the account. To a modern observer, however, this ensemble would assume a kind of "hourglass" pattern, with a narrow, sketchy middle ground separating broadly detailed accounts of recent events and distant origins. Vansina terms this narrow waist the "floating gap" because it tends to advance steadily toward the present as (typically) the oldest material at the base of the hourglass gets forgotten or amalgamated with material filtering down from the top.[10]

Not only would family narratives follow this pattern, but so, too, would local and regional narratives. Competition or cooperation among prominent families might lead, after a degree of negotiated storytelling, to the emergence of an informal account acceptable to an entire community ("informal" because most *poleis* lacked the kind of centralized rule that might have fostered the memorization of an "official" account). Likewise, regional narratives would arise, reconciling divergent local accounts and permitting the attainment of a broader (though still informal) consensus. The emergence of the *logios,* the man versed in *logoi,* would parallel these developments, as not just families but communities began hosting and rewarding skilled narrative recitations. We can further imagine the evolution of a class of itinerant *logioi,* men who circulated from *polis* to *polis,* cementing a regional heritage, itself further reinforced by performances at Panhellenic festivals.

These narratives, especially the larger-scale productions, must have had much the same effect on a Greek audience as the Homeric epics did. Time would have assumed the aspect of duration; any sustained narrative would have consisted of *logoi* flowing imperceptibly from one to the next, so as to foreground the action of each scene; and the narrative would have transcended the contingent and aspired to the universal. As Vansina notes, the historical nature of tales was always subordinated to another aim, "being either to instruct, give pleasure, or vindicate rights."[11] We are here in the realm of the past-made-present, which retains its immediacy in public performance, by which it is projected into the future. This oral tradition of prose narrative coexisted with alphabetic literacy, which initially served merely as an *aide-mémoire.* Indeed, not only did oral storytelling in public performance flourish well into the fifth century BC, but throughout Greco-Roman antiquity oral recitation remained the primary mode of "publishing" compositions.

BEFORE A HERODOTUS COULD EVEN CONCEIVE of distilling the vast body of oral tales into a written history, there had to exist a prior tradition of prose writing. Although oral prose narrative existed from time immemorial, written prose narrative did not appear until relatively late, around the mid-sixth century BC. The etymology of the Greek term for prose—*psilos logos* ("naked language") or *pedzos logos* ("language that walks on foot")—reveals its perceived inferiority to poetry, a status that retarded its literary development. But the expansion of Greek intellectual horizons, stimulated in part by a wave of colonization spreading through the Mediterranean and Black Seas in the seventh and sixth centuries BC, led some thinkers to challenge the intellectual primacy of the poetic heritage. These challengers hailed chiefly from the Greek cities of Ionia, or Asia Minor, most prominently from the city of Miletus. Ionia's status as a cultural and commercial crossroad helped stimulate new, critical thinking about the natural world intended to supplement, if not supplant, the mythological views derived from Homer and Hesiod. Thales of Miletus launched this philosophical revolution in the early sixth century BC; and his student, Anaximander (also from Miletus), "penned" European literature's first extant line of prose, an obscure statement about the nature of the *cosmos,* or natural order, that scholars still puzzle over.

The trickle of prose grew in the late sixth and early fifth centuries BC, as Ionian authors expanded beyond natural philosophy to launch new inquiries into geography, ethnology, chronology, and genealogy. We know the names of some figures associated with this movement, though we know little about when they lived, and we can only glean what they wrote from fragments preserved in the works of later authors. Chief among them is Hecataeus of Miletus, a student of Anaximander, who lived around 500 BC and composed two prose works, the *Genealogies* and the *Circuit of the Earth.* As best we can tell, the former work attempts to order a vast body of genealogical lore extending back to Homer, and the latter follows the circuit of the known world, describing each region, its peoples, and its marvels. Another important figure, and a likely contemporary of Herodotus, is Hellanicus of Lesbos, best remembered for Thucydides's criticism of his chronological efforts. Other figures—like Xanthus the Lydian and Charon of Lampsacus—wrote chiefly about Persian matters.

Taken together, this group of prose authors testifies to a further expansion of intellectual horizons, as Greeks now began actively to critique the heritage of epic poetry. Hecataeus heralds this new critical spirit in his *Genealogies,* which starts by taking the Greeks to task for telling "a great many foolish stories."[12] Herodotus stands as heir to these Ionians. In addition to rejecting the gullibility of the epic poets, he also chronicled Persian expansion, as did Xanthus and Charon, and indulged in lengthy geographical and ethnographical excursions, in the manner of Hecataeus. These debts notwithstanding, the sprinkling of Ionian writings hardly portends the great inundation of prose literature that began with the thunderclap of the *Histories.*

The Herodotean Achievement

A t almost twice the length of the only previous large-scale account of a Hellenic war, the *Histories* dwarf the *Iliad.* Whereas Homer dealt with the last year of one war, and chiefly with the actions of one hero, Herodotus chronicled two mighty wars between Greece and Persia spanning more than a decade, as well as the phenomenal sixty-year expansion of Persian power that had led to these wars. His cast of characters—including such larger-than-life figures as Cyrus, Darius, and Xerxes, to say nothing of the Greeks—far exceeds Homer's. Indeed, his subject transcends war to deal with a theme altogether greater and more important—the source of the enmity between East and West, an enmity rooted in a clash of cultures and, even more fundamentally, in the very dynamic of empire.

The enormity and complexity of this undertaking called forth an entirely new conception of the past. In place of the timeless past of the epic poets and *logioi,* Herodotus substituted a past characterized by a linear, directional flow of time, which provided the organizing principle for his vast work. Yet this conception did not lead to our notion of a past "back there" in time, linked to the present by chains of cause and effect. Everything in such a past would necessarily hinge on what came before it, opening the door to a world of contingencies ultimately meaningless to a Greek, the kind of world that Aristotle dismissed in his distinction between poetry and history. Instead, linear time served Herodotus as a giant container for innumerable *logoi,* which constituted episodes illustrating universal truths. The order of occurrences within an episode had no significance for the truth it illustrated, which remained unaffected by such causal relations. In other words, linear time transformed freestanding *logoi—* disparate narratives, accounts, and arguments—into instances of episodic time. In place of the timeless past, Herodotus thus substituted multiple pasts formed by two distinct notions of time, linear and episodic.[13]

Although his Ionian predecessors had criticized epic traditions, they only questioned specific stories and genealogical relations; nothing in their extant writings suggests that they reconceived the timeless past enshrined by the epics. In doing so, Herodotus broke entirely new ground. This achievement was part of a larger process of critical "inquiry"—his famous use of the term *historia* in the opening line of his work—that subjected earthly and especially human matters to new kinds of scrutiny, reflecting fifth-century "Greek Enlightenment" developments in medicine, ethnography, geography, natural philosophy, and rhetoric. In this wide-ranging inquiry Herodotus balanced the contingent against the universal. To label his undertaking a "history"—at least in our narrow, modern sense of the term—would be anachronistic. Nonetheless, his work evidences a deep concern for the contingencies of this world, from which he sought to distill universals rendered all the more meaningful by their temporality. Neither the poets nor the *logioi,* nor the Ionians, nor even his contemporaries had anticipated this accomplishment. In the inimitable words of Arnaldo Momigliano, "There was no Herodotus before Herodotus."[14]

About his life we know hardly more than we do about those of his predecessors. Herodotus was born in the Ionian city of Halicarnassus around 490 BC, and he probably died between 425 and 420. One tradition has him fleeing his native *polis* after an unsuccessful coup against the local tyrant, though later admirers may have fabricated this story to suit the life of a man who memorialized the Greek struggle against Persian tyranny. Another questionable tradition places him at the founding of the colony of Thurii, in southern Italy, around 443 BC, an Athenian-led Panhellenic enterprise that (suspiciously) recalls the Panhellenic league against Persia. Tradition also has him sojourning in Athens and Sparta at various points—a likely possibility given the preeminence of these *poleis*—and by his own testimony he traveled widely throughout the eastern Mediterranean and Near East. But even these probabilities have been questioned recently by some hypercritics, who dismiss most of his travel claims as mere literary flour-ishes because of geographical inaccuracies in his account. Fortunately, all this uncertainty gives us a free hand to speculate about the likely genesis of the *Histories,* exploring the emergence of his new conception of the past.

Let us imagine a man by avocation well versed in *logoi,* living in the afterglow of incredible events—the remarkable victory at Marathon in 490, the unprece-dented league of Greek states against Xerxes (a league unparalleled in Hellenic memory since Homeric times), the heroic battles of 480 and 479 (Thermopylae, Salamis, Plataea, Mycale). In short, let us imagine a man living in the shadow of what we might today call (with reference to those who fought in the Second World War) a "greatest generation," one that was already beginning to pass from the scene. And along with it was perishing the memory of its accomplish-ments, a memory chiefly preserved in oral tales that were steadily being swal-lowed by the oblivion of Vansina's "floating gap." Of course, Herodotus would not have seen it this way, but he would have felt the impending loss, the perish-ability of the past, far more acutely than we (with our vast and growing accumu-lation of records in every conceivable form) could possibly imagine. Let us as-sume that his life's work was born of an anxiety for and obligation to the memory of these deeds, which had eclipsed even those of the Homeric heroes.

Opinions vary as to when Herodotus discovered his mission in life, but let us assume (purely for the sake of argument) that he found it early on, that he pur-sued it by means of travel throughout the Persian Empire as well as Greece, and that—after collecting numerous accounts and stories—he subsequently began composing what would become the *Histories.* (A popular alternative scenario—that he originally worked in the ethnographic mode of Hecataeus and only later discovered his true calling—would suit our purposes equally well.) Despite oc-casional errors in his description of localities, we need not go to the hypercriti-cal extreme of dismissing all his travel claims. Indeed, we have every reason to assume, at the very least, that he visited Egypt (to which he would devote an entire book of his *Histories*), for this region had recently been absorbed by the Persian Empire, whose rise he was chronicling. Even if he drew his original inspiration from Hecataeus's ethnographic efforts, he would have likely traveled to Egypt in the footsteps of his predecessor.

Egypt made a profound impression on Herodotus, confronting him with the prospect of a vastly older and more sophisticated civilization, whose written records and remains dated back thousands of years. (The Roman peasant-soldiers who conquered Greece some three hundred years later would experience a similar kind of awe in the presence of Hellenistic civilization.) Herodotus's concept of linear, directional time derives from his exposure to and confrontation with Egyptian culture. This experience, later recorded in book 2 of the *Histories,* led him to attribute the Hellenic pantheon of gods to the influence of Egyptian religion, thus subsuming Greek myth under an Egyptian chronology.

In a reference to Hecataeus in book 2, Herodotus describes meeting a sect of Egyptian priests in Thebes that had been visited a generation or two earlier by his predecessor (2.142–44). The priests recounted how Hecataeus had traced his family back to a god in the sixteenth generation, in response to which they had humbled him with their lineage of 341 generations, embodied in the physical record of 341 statues, one for each hereditary holder of the office of high priest. Leading Herodotus into the great hall where they kept these statues, the priests asserted that during the entire time represented by this collection—11,340 years by Herodotus's calculation—no god had ever assumed mortal form. So much for Hecataeus's genealogical fancies!

This priestly anecdote only served to underscore for Herodotus the immense discrepancy between Egyptian and Greek time frames, for the Greek "age of the gods" seemed to fall squarely within the Egyptian "age of men." Herodotus devoted considerable effort and ingenuity to resolving this discrepancy, ultimately creating a framework of linear, directional time to contain his accumulation of *logoi*. He started by granting priority to Egyptian religious traditions because their great antiquity was bolstered by physical remains and written as well as oral priestly records. In modern parlance he adopted a "diffusionist" view of religion, tracing the Greek pantheon back to the Egyptians. As he would later declare in the *Histories*, "The names of nearly all the gods came to the Greeks from Egypt" (2.50). In reality Herodotus's Egyptian interpreters may have unintentionally fostered this view by drawing analogies between Egyptian gods and Greek ones; and no doubt the priests intentionally reinforced this assumption because it flattered their own vanity. Regardless of its origins, though, this viewpoint created an interesting problem for Herodotus concerning the relation between the Egyptian god known to him as "Heracles" (scholars still puzzle over the identity of this deity) and the Greek hero-god of the same name. In the process of resolving this problem Herodotus discovered the linear time frame that subsumed Greek events under an Egyptian chronology.[15]

According to Herodotus's priestly informants, Heracles appeared when the original eight gods of Egypt transmuted into the twelve of the classical pantheon, some seventeen thousand years before the reign of Amasis (the last pharaoh before the Persian conquest of Egypt in 525 BC). In order to test this information—which indicated that the Egyptian god far predated the Greek hero—Herodotus traveled to the Phoenician city of Tyre, site of an ancient temple of Heracles that (according to the priests there) dated back at least twenty-three hundred years. While at Tyre, Herodotus saw another temple, dedicated to the Thasian Heracles. This discovery prompted him to journey to the Ionian island of Thasos, where he located a temple of Heracles built by the Phoenicians "five generations before Heracles the son of Amphitryon made his appearance in Greece" (2.44). Of this last Heracles the Egyptians have no knowledge, so (Herodotus concluded) he must be a much later figure—a hero, not a god. The worship of Heracles thus radiated outward from Egypt to Tyre, from Tyre to Thasos, from Thasos to Greece, in a gradual, multimillennial diffusion.

Herodotus took considerable time, effort, and expense to resolve this problem—journeying from Egypt to Tyre to Thasos, all ostensibly to check some dates—but the payoff came with the creation of a time frame with fixed reference points that exposed and clarified the confusion of Greek traditions. The enormity of this achievement becomes apparent when we consider that the Greeks had no uniform chronology of their own but only a set of local schemes that varied from one *polis* to the next, that remained largely oral, and that attained little time depth. By contrast, Herodotus used written as well as oral priestly records to devise a chronology spanning seventeen thousand years between two fixed points, the appearance of Heracles and the reign of Amasis, the latter ending little more than two generations before Herodotus's own day. From his standpoint in the present, then, Herodotus could cast back, interpolating Egyptian and Greek developments (the latter dated from their own genealogical traditions). Thus, twenty-three hundred years had elapsed since the founding of the temple of Heracles at Tyre, which preceded the founding of the temple on Thasos, which preceded the appearance of the Greek Heracles by five generations, which occurred a mere nine hundred years before Herodotus's own day. Dionysus (a younger god than Heracles) made his appearance fifteen thousand years before Amasis, even though Greek tradition renders him only one thousand years old; and Pan, a god even more ancient than Heracles, is said by the Greeks to have originated barely eight hundred years ago, "a shorter time than has elapsed since the Trojan War" (2.145). On this ironic note in the *Histories* Herodotus would invite his readers to draw their own conclusions about the reliability of Greek traditions.

During his travels Herodotus found confirmation for the precedence of the Egyptian religion and time frame in another linear sequence of great antiquity, the formation of the very land of Egypt itself. Ionian natural philosophers and geographers had held that Egypt came into being with the silting action of the Nile. Although Herodotus quibbled with this view—maintaining that the land and people of Egypt preexisted the formation of the delta—he nonetheless accepted their theory about alluvial deposits, arguing that sedimentation from the Nile caused the original land of Egypt (which he claimed had centered on Thebes) to extend gradually toward the Mediterranean. More important for our purposes are Herodotus's efforts to create a time frame for this process. Employing some very rough comparisons, he estimated that it occurred over a period of about ten thousand years. Further, he noted that the region between Memphis and the sea had risen steadily, as indicated by the river's flood crest, which (to judge by Egyptian records) had increased twelve feet in nine hundred years. Admittedly, the calculations here are very imprecise; nonetheless, they serve to describe a directional sequence of events, much as did the diffusion of Egyptian religion to the Phoenicians and ultimately to the Greeks. Indeed, the creation of Egyptian and Greek religion occurs against the backdrop of the creation of the land of Egypt, connecting past to present in a process that literally "grounds" time (2.10–16).

The existence of a documented time frame of great antiquity made such a profound impression on Herodotus precisely because he was a *logios,* heir to and proprietor of a large corpus of undifferentiated stories. *Logioi* before Herodotus had told their stories either as individual tales or as discrete aggregates of tales gathered around (say) genealogical or geographical themes. In principle the Egyptian chronology provided a means of ordering these stories temporally in much larger collections; it thus offered the prospect of storytelling on a grander scale than had been previously conceivable. In so doing, it also transposed the essentially timeless stories of the past-made-present to a chronological realm where (to recall Aristotle's distinction between history and poetry) their contingency threatened to obscure their universality. This threat forced Herodotus to reconceive the past, an undertaking that necessarily placed him in direct confrontation with its chief architect, Homer.

THE FIRST LINE OF THE *HISTORIES* EXPRESSLY ECHOES the Homeric goal of preserving renown. Indeed, reverberations of Homer sound throughout a text that similarly recounts a heroic struggle between East and West, combining an *Odyssey*-like first half (about the marvelous East) with an *Iliad*-like second half (about the fascination and horror of war). But right from the start Herodotus intentionally distinguishes his enterprise from Homer's. The very first line concludes by asking whence the quarrel between East and West arose, in response to which Herodotus lists a series of rape and abduction myths—about Io, Europa, and Helen—which he then promptly dismisses as irrelevant. Herodotus makes this slap against Homeric mythologizing all the more backhanded by pointedly choosing to recount the Persian rather than the Greek version of these myths.

Hecataeus, too, had questioned the gullibility of the epic poets, but Herodotus goes far beyond his predecessor's critique of individual stories. Using the immensity of the Egyptian time frame as his critical lever, Herodotus challenged the antiquity, and hence the reliability, of whole traditions about the remote past in Greece. This achievement stands revealed in book 2—about the geography, customs, and history of Egypt—which strikes most modern readers as an overlong digression, sandwiched between more "historical" accounts of the rise of Cyrus in book 1 and the Egyptian campaign of his successor Cambyses in book 3. We miss the significance of the religious and geological time frames introduced in book 2 because Herodotus did not expressly combine them to create an overarching chronology for the *Histories*. Although he clearly saw the relation between them, he treated the formation of the land of Egypt and the formation of Egyptian religion as separate episodes. He submerged them in a sequence of accounts that flows imperceptibly from one story to the next and, ultimately, from one book to the next. Indeed, his storytelling has such a breathless quality that he often interrupts himself, as one interesting episode calls to mind another, and sometimes another, carrying him far afield before he returns to the original inquiry that generated all the intervening stories. For the modern reader, at least, these "ring compositions" obscure—and even seem to belie—the presence of a linear time frame in the *Histories*.

The technique of ring composition extends back to Homer, as exemplified in the above-described story of the boar hunt that interrupts the foot-washing scene in the *Odyssey*. Yet Herodotus employs this technique on a much grander scale than Homer, using it as the chief compositional device for stitching to-gether a long, complex prose narrative comprising innumerable *logoi*. These he joins by means of what Henry Immerwahr, a noted student of Herodotus's style, has termed "framing sentences"—introductory comments at the beginning of each story and summary ones at the end. Commenting on this form of composi-tion, Immerwahr states, "In outlining the units of the work we must free our-selves from the notion of subordination, for Herodotus' *logoi* are of every con-ceivable length; they are in turn composed of other *logoi*, and there is no specific hierarchy of major and minor units" (15). At this point a logical question arises: if ring compositions obscure and even belie the existence of a linear time frame for a modern audience, would they have had the same effect on Herodotus's Greek audience? Or to put the question differently, would an audience accustomed by the Homeric poems to immersing itself in the flow of stories and devoting itself wholly to each one in sequence have noted and retained the importance of Herodotus's chronological innovations?

We can only speculate about audience reactions twenty-five hundred years ago, but it seems highly likely that Greeks—who took their religion very seriously—could not but register the importance of Herodotus's claims about the Egyptian origin of their gods, claims reflecting an expressed criticism of Homer and Hesiod, who together served as the foundation and touchstone of their cul-ture. And even if some members of his audience had managed to snooze through the chronological portions of Herodotus's composition—as do many modern readers—they certainly would have awakened with a start when he began using Egyptian records to rework Homer's version of the siege of Troy.

After laying out his diffusionist model of Greek religion, Herodotus pro-ceeded to chronicle the noteworthy pharaohs, starting with the first (Min), end-ing with the last (Amasis), and dwelling at considerable length on the reign of the pharaoh known in Greek as Proteus. According to Herodotus's priestly in-formants, Proteus gave Helen sanctuary after her abductor, Paris, was forced by bad weather to land in Egypt while returning to Troy. Proteus sent the cad pack-ing, while allowing Helen to remain a guest until Menelaus eventually came to fetch her, after ten years of mistakenly besieging Troy in the belief that his wife was held captive there! Herodotus claims that Homer himself had hinted at the accuracy of this priestly account through various allusions to visits by Paris and Menelaus to Egypt. And if this were not enough proof, Herodotus further claims (in a distinctly unheroic exercise of political calculation) that the Trojans would have been mad to imperil their city for ten minutes—let alone ten years—just so that Paris could keep his prize. Obviously, Helen wasn't there, as the Trojans had protested all along, and only divine intervention kept the Greeks from realizing this. In the final analysis Homer knowingly embroidered the truth in an instance of poetic license (2.112–20).

Even in a sequence of stories stitched together one after another, this one would stand out. And it would resonate deeply with previous stories about the antiquity of Egyptian records and the origin and diffusion of the Egyptian gods, in a multimillennial process that paralleled and overlapped the formation of the land of Egypt. Book 2 thus expressly serves as an antidote to Greek parochialism by asserting the priority of Egyptian records, Egyptian religion, and (most important) an Egyptian time frame that subsumes and explains significant aspects of Hellenic culture. Despite the foregrounded nature of the narrative, which immerses the audience in the particular story at hand, Herodotus clearly intended book 2 to teach his fellow Greeks a lesson in perspective that would illuminate the whole of his *Histories*.

BUT WHY TEACH THIS LESSON? And how did it illuminate the rest of the work? The benefits of historical perspective appear so obvious to us that they obscure Herodotus's real purpose in writing book 2. Recall that, as the Homeric epics became increasingly fixed by rhapsodes and by writing, the *logoi* circulating among families, cities, and regions assumed a larger role in the presentation of the past-made-present. But these stories remained disparate and uncoordinated. Each family, each city, each region had its own "past," combining recent with remote accounts. To a modern observer each of these amalgams would typically assume an hourglass pattern, with a narrow waist (the "floating gap") separating broad extremes. An ancient Greek, however, would not have perceived this pattern but only a unified account flowing uniformly from one generation to the next. Thus Hecataeus could without any incongruity claim descent from a god over sixteen generations, even though his genealogy was doubtless rather spare in the middle. Herodotus vastly expanded this middle ground by locating the Homeric age of gods and heroes on a temporal continuum characterized by an unrepeatable sequence of events—the formation of the land of Egypt and the diffusion of Egyptian religion. In so doing, he transformed the shape of the past; from our modern perspective he eliminated the floating gap by anchoring the mythological base in time and by filling out the narrow "hourglass" waist. For all practical purposes he created something approaching our conception of "historical time."

Yet his creation is not quite identical to our conception. To paraphrase Immerwahr, we must free ourselves from modern notions of subordination when thinking about the structure of the Herodotean past. We subordinate the story of events to a directional time frame that explains them; Herodotus essentially did the reverse, subordinating directional time to the flow of stories. Even in book 2 he didn't impose a single, linear time frame but, rather, treated the geological and religious schemes as distinct (though clearly related) stories. And after telling one story, he moved on in serial fashion to the next, and the next, and the next. So wherein lies, for Herodotus, the utility and importance of linear time?

By expanding the middle ground between recent and remote events, linear time creates a space where Herodotus can bring together and coordinate different historical traditions represented by innumerable *logoi*. If we were to array them on a time line, the key stories of the *Histories* extend back well over two hundred years from Herodotus's day. They thus reach far into the region of Vansina's "floating gap," giving substance to a period that had previously been obscure. No one had sought to collect and coordinate these stories—at least not on the Herodotean scale—for this activity would have been inconceivable without the theoretical posit of an expanded middle ground. The posit remained "theoretical" because it did not actually serve to structure the middle ground— time lines reflect our mentality, not Herodotus's. He simply asserted the existence of a large temporal space—a framework, if you will—which he then proceeded to fill with stories. That space takes its internal structure not from the directional flow of time but from the episodic flow of stories. In other words, linear time transformed undifferentiated *logoi* into a sequence of episodes in a larger story, and in so doing, it imparted to them a kind of nonlinear temporality. The real importance of linear time for Herodotus lies in its creation of "episodic time."

LET US TRY TO GRASP THIS STRANGE NOTION of episodic time by illustrating it. After having dismissed the rape and abduction myths at the beginning of book 1 as irrelevant to the story of the struggle between East and West, Herodotus traces the real source of this struggle to the Lydian king Croesus's subjugation of the Ionians, from whom he extracted tribute—the first official and tangible sign of foreign domination over a Greek people. Because the imperialistic ambitions of East against West initiate from this point, Herodotus explicitly locates it in time: Croesus was the fifth generation of the Mermnadae to rule the kingdom of Lydia; and the Mermnadae took power from the Heraclids, who had reigned for twenty-two generations, or 505 years. The appearance of precision here is merely an illusion. In book 2, where Herodotus translates 341 generations of priests into 11,340 years, he specifies that a generation equals thirty-three years; here a generation apparently equals twenty-three years, if one bothers to do the math. What Herodotus really signified by twenty-two generations, or 505 years, is akin to what Homer signified by Odysseus's twenty-year absence from home—namely duration, a very long time.[16]

The antiquity of their dynasty lends drama to the fall of the Heraclids, the last of whom, Candaules, is led by his good fortune to an act of injustice. Inordinately proud of his wife's beauty, he forces his reluctant bodyguard, Gyges, to hide in her bedroom and watch her undress. When she discovers this affront, she induces Gyges to avenge her honor by killing the king in the very same room. After wedding the queen and inaugurating the new dynasty of the Mermnadae, Gyges seeks to have his reign confirmed by the oracle at Delphi, which prophesies that the Heraclids will have their revenge on the Mermnadae in the fifth generation, thus anticipating the fall of Croesus. Herodotus then follows this dire prediction with a generation-by-generation account of the Mermnadae, culminating with the reign of Croesus, whose defeat by Cyrus led to the incorporation of the kingdom of Lydia into the Persian Empire, thus bringing Persia into contact with the Ionian Greeks and, eventually, with their kin on the mainland.

These stories appear loosely situated in time, to the extent that they consist of a sequence of actions beginning in the more remote past and ending in the more recent past. Candaules's act of injustice sets in motion a process of injustice and retribution that works itself out inexorably over the generations. His wife's retribution through her instrument, Gyges, itself entails an act of injustice, for the bodyguard betrayed the king he had sworn to protect, hence setting the stage for other instances of retribution and injustice that ripple outward from this epicenter. It seems to us moderns as if Herodotus has established an (albeit quaint) chain of cause and effect here, for Gyges's actions determine the fate of Croesus, which in turn brings the Ionian Greeks under Persian domination. But we should note that our bare outline obscures innumerable intervening *logoi* whose vividness disrupts the causal sequence. In the short narrative span between the rise of Gyges and the fall of Croesus we encounter memorable tales of Arion rescued by the dolphin, of Solon's wisdom at the court of Croesus, of the Pisistratid tyranny in Athens, of Lycurgian reform in Sparta, to name only the most noteworthy. Herodotus thinks not in terms of the flow of causation but the flow of stories, which carries him (willy-nilly) forward and backward in time, and from one locale to another. Amid these far-flung digressions only the framing sentences manage to recall the audience to the general line of argument. By virtue of its inclusion in the narrative, each story constitutes an episode in the overarching theme about the struggle between East and West, but the meaning of the episode does not hinge on what happens before and after it.

Meaning resides primarily in the universal principle embodied in the episode and only secondarily (at best) in the episode's position in the narrative. The assassination of Candaules exemplifies the universal principle of "just retribution." Not coincidentally, it occurs at the very site of the insult—the queen's bedroom—and it initiates a recurring pattern of injury and revenge. For a Greek audience schooled in the multigenerational workings of "fate," the fall of Croesus constitutes just retribution for Gyges's betrayal of his king. Attuned to genealogical nuances, the audience would have also noted that Croesus married his sister to Astyages, king of the Medes, who had unjustly attempted to kill the infant Cyrus. On reaching manhood, Cyrus seeks retribution by capturing Astyages, usurping his throne, and liberating Persia from the Medes. In response to this injury to his brother-in-law, Croesus invades Persia and (in turn) falls prey to a counterinvasion. This cycle of injury and revenge is paralleled and echoed by another. Cyrus's usurpation of power had been spurred on by Harpagus the Mede's quest for vengeance against his king, Astyages, who had had Harpagus's son killed, cooked, and served to the unsuspecting father at a banquet—in an act of revenge for an earlier injury. Harpagus's betrayal of Astyages recalls Gyges's betrayal of Candaules; and, again not coincidentally, it is Harpagus who, as one of Cyrus's henchmen, conquers the Ionians for Persia, thus drawing a thematic connection between that event and the initial affront in the bedroom generations earlier. The above summary makes these stories appear causally connected; however, they are told not in chronological order but in widely dispersed episodes that serve to resonate with a universal theme rather than reveal a causal chain. These episodes constitute instances of nonlinear temporality; they occur in time, but their meaning is timeless.

The unity of the *Histories* lies in the dimension of episodic time. The work ends with a group of stories that bring it full circle, back to where it began. The first of these echoes the Gyges affair. After his defeat and return to Persia, Xerxes developed an unrequited passion for his brother's wife, leading him to make an injurious promise that brought down horrible vengeance on both the brother and the wife. This story of royal willfulness helps bring closure to a work structured by (among other things) an ever-expanding cycle of injury and revenge: the Gyges affair entails the Persian conquest of Ionia, which leads to the revolt of that region, which spurs Darius's attempt to punish the Athenians for aiding the rebels, which prompts Xerxes's invasion of Hellas. This theme intertwines with another, equally familiar to a Greek audience. Xerxes's lust for his brother's wife is but the final instance of his hubris, in a history full of such acts, the most notorious of which concern his bridging the Hellespont and his whipping the waters when a storm destroyed his bridges. In the Greek moral economy the gods reward such arrogant acts with *atê*, the willful blindness that eventually entails *nemesis,* one's downfall.

References to the Greek moral economy, however, do not exhaust the underlying unity of the *Histories.* The cycles of injury and revenge, and of hubris and nemesis, cluster about a larger theme: the dictates of empire and their contribution to *metabolê,* the reversals of fortune whereby (to paraphrase the opening of the *Histories*) small states have become great and once-great ones have become small (1.5). Imperial power must seek retribution for every injury, lest it appear weak; and it must ceaselessly expand at the expense of lesser neighbors, lest it stagnate. Poor states—toughened by need—have become great by conquering rich ones, and great states—proud but softened by wealth—eventually fall prey to the poor ones they encounter in the course of imperial expansion. In the very last episode of his work Herodotus again casts back to the beginning—to the conquest of Croesus's rich Lydian Empire by Cyrus's rude Persians—when he recounts in closing how Cyrus had refused to shift the seat of his empire from Persia to Lydia, for fear that the Persians might become soft. Perhaps Herodotus, who brought his massive work to completion during the opening phase of the Peloponnesian War, intended a message here for his host city of Athens, a poor state transformed into an aggressive imperial power by the Persian wars.

TO SUMMARIZE, THE EXISTENCE OF A LINEAR TIME FRAME enabled Herodotus to differentiate a vast body of *logoi* into episodes of a larger story that occupies temporal space extending backward, beyond the recent past into a previously uncharted middle ground. Linear time thus engendered episodic time. But the meaning of each episode remains timeless, and the temporal space takes its structure from the flow of stories. The two kinds of time correspond to two kinds of past: the contingent past of linear, directional time, and the episodic past, embodying universals that speak directly to the present. Before Herodotus, there was only one kind of past depicted in prose and verse: the undifferentiated "olden days" of the epics and the *logoi.* This too was a past that spoke directly to the present; yet, unlike Herodotus's episodic past, the olden days were not anchored to any time frame but floated in an ether, in a symbolic or mythical space apart from time. Herodotus's critique of Homer announces to his audience the transformation of these olden days into something entirely new, an episodic past anchored in time.

To our modern eye, this invention creates a remarkably flat historical land-scape, accentuating the phenomenon of foregrounding—the tendency to im-merse the audience in the particular story at hand—far more than Homer ever did. The story of the boar hunt that interrupts the foot-washing scene in the *Odyssey* is one of the more pronounced examples of ring composition in the Homeric epics. Of course, this style of composition abounds throughout Homer, but it is generally limited to short digressions and only rarely imperils the plot. In contrast, Herodotean storytelling is by its very nature digressive to an extreme. For example, in his account of the five generations of Mermnadae from Gyges to Croesus, Herodotus happens to mention an event in the reign of Croesus's father that peripherally involved Periander, the future ruler of Corinth. From this in-cident Herodotus segued forward in time to a tale about Arion, a musician in Periander's court, who was robbed and tossed overboard by Corinthian sailors while traveling home from Italy. His miraculous rescue by a dolphin enabled him eventually to return to Corinth and expose his would-be murderers. This story digresses far from the matter at hand—the fate of the ruling dynasty of Lydia—and it is only one of hundreds of such digressions, which sometimes contain stories within stories. What we would regard as the important events of the his-tory lie buried beneath this avalanche of tales.

Only as Herodotus approaches the more recent past—the Persian expeditions to mainland Greece—does the temporal thrust of the narrative strengthen, pro-viding more conspicuous instances of linear, causal explanation. At the end of book 6, for example, he recounts the downfall of Miltiades, who had led the Athenians to victory at Marathon. Flushed with his recent success, Miltiades convinces the Athenian assembly to provide him with a fleet for the conquest of the Persian-occupied island of Paros, where he quickly becomes bogged down in a fruitless siege, which he has to abandon after falling and injuring his leg. Upon his return to Athens, political enemies put him on trial, and he is lucky to escape with a mere fine before dying of gangrene. All this is presented in linear fashion as a sequence of events that build one upon the other. Indeed, we would expect Herodotus to end the story of Miltiades here and thus conclude book 6 with the account of his downfall, disgrace, and death. Instead, Herodotus chooses to break the linear narrative and cast back to a much earlier episode in Miltiades's career, his capture of Lemnos, which in turn draws Herodotus further back, to a consid-eration of the ancient quarrel between the Athenians and the Pelasgians who would eventually settle Lemnos. The book thus concludes with a digression within a digression. Despite the growing linearity of the narrative as it approaches more recent events, the *Histories* still remain fundamentally episodic.

The invention of the episodic past militates against the kind of historical perspective that we regard as constitutive of "the" past, an overarching temporal framework that organizes events in the foreground, middle ground, and background, according to their significance for the account in question. Rather, Herodotus moves almost indiscriminately from story to story to story. Amid this flow, there are no events in the modern sense—nothing stands out as "salient," as definitively shaping subsequent developments. Instead of events, one finds occurrences, catalysts that set in motion inexorable processes, which themselves stand as instances of universal phenomena. Although one instance of "just retribution" may draw in its train specific consequences for certain peoples at particular times, it is qualitatively no different from any other instance of that phenomenon. To the extent that it always entails the same kind of consequence, it serves not to shape events in distinctive ways but to catalyze a sequence of predictable actions and reactions. Indeed, for Herodotus the value of history lies in this very element of predictability, which offers the possibility of attaining prudence in human affairs.

In the previous paragraph I described the flow of episodes as "almost indiscriminate," for it seems to follow the tenuous logic of storytelling (". . . and this reminds me of the one about Arion and the dolphin . . ."). But undue emphasis on Herodotus as *logios* obscures the operation of his highly critical intelligence, already apparent in his challenge to Homeric traditions. Although he inherited the critical spirit of the Ionians, recent research has also revealed that the form and substance of his arguments owe much to the so-called Greek Enlightenment of the fifth century BC. The seemingly indiscriminate flow of stories mirrors in large part the logic of contemporary critical inquiry, as shaped especially by the debates of medical writers, natural philosophers, and sophistic rhetoricians. By its very nature this inquiry ranges widely, from assessing the true geography of Egypt to determining the reason why Persian skulls are thinner than Egyptian ones, to describing the strange customs of the Scythians, to explaining why this version of a story is more convincing than that one. In other words, the shape of Herodotus's account owes as much to the intellectual debates of his day as to the imperatives of storytelling. Nonetheless, these diverse instances of critical inquiry themselves constitute episodes contained within a chronological framework, just like the more traditional *logoi*. In effect, they reduce to instances of episodic time that militate against the attainment of a temporal perspective constitutive of "the" past.

Thucydides and the Refashionings
of Linear Time

S tung by emulation, Thucydides supposedly wept on hearing Herodotus recite his *Histories* in Athens . . . or so reports Marcellinus in his late antique biography. A fanciful image, perhaps—much like the story of the young Herodotus attempting to overthrow a tyranny—but nonetheless evocative of the many resonances between Thucydides's work and that of his elder contemporary. Although he chose to muffle these echoes, intentionally distancing himself from the *logographoi* and their questionable tales about uncertain events, Thucydides betrays a considerable debt to Herodotus right from the start, in the Archaeology, the very place where he had sought most assiduously to distinguish himself from his predecessor. At base a thought experiment about the remote past, the Archaeology would have been literally inconceivable had not Herodotus posited a linear time frame subsuming Greek myth under an Egyptian chronology—had he not (at least in theory) connected the remote past to the present. This connection freed Thucydides to cast his mind back in time, to imagine what life must have been like *before* the Trojan War. The Archaeology thus stands as an unwitting monument to the Herodotean achievement.

Thucydides, however, expressly denigrates that achievement. Although he criticizes only Hellanicus by name, his real target is undoubtedly Herodotus, two of whose errors he pointedly corrects toward the end of the Archaeology, where he disavows "romance" in favor of "an exact knowledge of the past as an aid to the interpretation of the future." "In fine," he concludes, "I have written my work, not as an essay which is to win the applause of the moment, but as a possession for all time" (1.22). Scholars debate the meaning of this claim (to which we will return later), but for now we can say that it rests largely on an appreciation of the analytical uses of linear time. Whereas Herodotus had treated it as a container for innumerable *logoi,* linear time became for Thucydides a medium for something resembling what we would today call "historical analysis."

The chief feature distinguishing our form of analysis from Thucydides's is that ours claims to hold a single object in view, "the" past, whereas his embraces multiple pasts. These reflect differences between episodic and linear time, as well as differences within linear time itself, which Thucydides frequently refashions to suit the changing needs of his argument. The refashionings of linear time, when combined with subtle shifts between the linear and episodic frames, make Thucydides's work hard for modern readers to follow. Our familiarity with the genre of history leads us to expect an account written from an overarching perspective that links one event to the next. Instead, we encounter a work that links not events but temporal frames, which serve to illustrate the universal patterns of history.

IN A FAMOUS JUDGMENT OF THUCYDIDES's writing style, R. G. Collingwood decries it as "harsh, artificial, repellent"—in comparison to Herodotus's more genial self-presentation—and concludes that Thucydides wrote with a "bad conscience," trying to turn history into something more scientific (29). What Collingwood sees as a sign of bad conscience, however, is for us the hallmark of an analytical mind working within the framework of linear time. This framework required that Thucydides advance his argument in a systematic fashion, without digressions. He could not afford the Herodotean luxury of recounting different versions of the same story; instead, he distilled them into a single account of any given event in order to accentuate the logical flow of his narrative. He only rarely digresses. Even the ring compositions that so disorient the modern reader serve clearly announced analytical purposes. Instances of gratuitous storytelling are so rare in Thucydides that they stand out as aberrations. The chief among them—a lengthy digression in book 6 about the overthrow of the Pisistratid tyranny in Athens—is the exception that proves the analytical rule. A close reading of this passage reveals how it resonates with the account of the Sicilian expedition it interrupts, establishing a parallel between the tyranny of the last of the Pisistratids and the tyrannical behavior of the Athenian Assembly some eighty years later.[17]

The Archaeology stands as the manifesto of this new analytical approach to recounting events. While ostensibly showing that the Peloponnesian War was the greatest yet fought, the Archaeology also serves to introduce the dimension of linear time as a medium of historical analysis. Thucydides details a story of progress from the remote past to the present, marked by the steady rise of sea power. Tradition has it that King Minos of Crete first established a navy, from which Thucydides infers the existence of a seaborne Minoan empire. This achievement was eventually eclipsed by that of Agamemnon, who mounted the ten-year naval expedition against Troy. A consideration of Homeric ship capacities makes clear the extent of this expedition and its relative weakness in comparison to modern efforts. Thucydides states that some three hundred years ago (dating from the end of the Peloponnesian War) the Corinthians pioneered the development of modern naval architecture; and some 260 years ago they engaged in the first genuine sea battle, heralding the kind of naval warfare by which the Athenians would eventually win their empire and preeminence. The forward thrust of the argument is unmistakable, advancing a story of material progress in tandem with the march of time.

The familiar feel of the Archaeology lulls us into thinking it "recounts the past," whereas in reality it "creates a past" through a set piece of historical analysis all the more impressive for its innovative use of scant information. Thucydides has barely four chronological reference points for the early history of sea power—the reputed naval empires of kings Minos and Agamemnon and the naval innovations of Corinthian shipwrights and admirals—only the last two of which were even remotely dateable. Our modern knowledge that Minoan civilization precedes Mycenaean obscures the fact that the chronological relation between Minos and Agamemnon was not so readily apparent in Thucydides's day. Granted, his use of these figures as temporal reference points was not exactly bold, but neither was it commonplace, especially given that the Greeks had no uniform chronology of their own remote past, let alone one coordinating it with that of non-Greek Minoans.[18] Indeed, Thucydides was probably the first to formulate this particular chronological relation in writing. The bolder assertion that Agamemnon ruled a naval empire rests on a single line of Homer ("Of many an isle, and of all Argos king"). And the most substantial "fact" cited—that Ameinocles, a Corinthian shipwright, made four galleys for the Samians three hundred years before the Peloponnesian War—seems, on reflection, rather odd proof of a revolution in naval architecture. (It probably derives from oral stories perpetuated by a leading family on the island of Samos; and in keeping with Greek oral traditions, the dating of this event, and of the first sea battle, is at best impressionistic.) Thucydides obviously had little information to work with, but his analysis appears so rigorous that we hardly think to question it, though undoubtedly his contemporaries would have recognized its novelty.

He intended this analysis of the remote past to stand as earnest for what he could accomplish with the more abundant evidence of recent events. It showcases a form of retrospective reasoning that reads the present back into the past. (Indeed, with scant historical material, how else could he have proceeded?) Starting from the reality of the Athenian naval empire, he sought its previous iterations in a pattern that builds throughout the Archaeology, which in turn forecasts the pattern for the entire history. He showed how the most successful states culminate as naval powers, how naval power entails empire, how an empire seeks to expand by overseas expeditions, how it eventually succumbs to an opposing confederation and/or to internal dissention, both of which are products of its very success. In this manner history spirals forward in time, as one empire supplants another—from the Minoans, to the Mycenaeans, to the Athenians, and (by implication) to the Syracuseans, who in Thucydides's estimation seemed poised to supplant the Athenians. Of course, he conspicuously omits the example of Persia, lest he appear too Herodotean, but the recurrent pattern clearly derives from his predecessor.[19] Whereas Herodotus developed this pattern episodically, Thucydides sought to reveal its operations in linear time, thereby gaining for it greater credence as a product of historical reason rather than literary imagination.

In contrast to our modern expectations, however, Thucydides did not subordinate historical reason to linear time. Rather, he did the reverse, subordinating linear time to the requirements of historical analysis. He thus consistently refashioned linear time to suit his changing needs, structuring it differently to bolster different forms of retrospective analysis. And, in keeping with this principle of temporal relativity, he occasionally discarded the linear approach entirely, in favor of episodic time, if he felt the latter better suited the requirements of his analysis.

Nowhere are these temporal shifts more apparent than in book 1, where they present an enormous stumbling block to the modern reader. The broadly sketched rise of sea power in the Archaeology gives way to a minute account of the immediate causes of the war, an account that begins without a starting date, though it proceeds in an intensely linear fashion to detail a long chain of events that leads up to Sparta's decision to declare war on Athens. This minute account bears no relation to the big picture sketched in the Archaeology; the two inhabit different linear time frames. The analysis of the immediate causes of the war leads Thucydides to a consideration of the real, underlying cause, namely Sparta's fear of the growing power of Athens, which he illustrates in a digression, the Pentecontaetia. This section breaks the previous linear flow by casting the reader back fifty years, to the origins of the Athenian Empire that would eventually arouse Spartan fears. Thucydides presents these origins in linear fashion, though he abandons linear for episodic time at the point in his account where the empire becomes an established fact. From this point on in the Pentecontaetia, one has difficulty discerning the chronological interrelation of events, though one has no difficulty at all discerning each event as an episode illustrating the contrast of national characters, of Athenian daring versus Spartan caution.[20] Episodic then gives way to linear time, as Thucydides details Sparta's actual declaration of war and the diplomatic sparring that followed. The linear account, in turn, yields to a series of episodes—about Cylon's attempted coup in Athens (c. 620 BC), about the death of the Spartan general Pausanius (c. 470 BC), about the last years of Themistocles (468-462 BC)—which ostensibly explain the diplomatic sparring but ultimately segue into issues of political leadership. From this theme Thucydides returns to a linear frame, recounting Pericles's first policy speech on the eve of the war, which reveals him as the ultimate proponent of the naval strategy first prophesied by Themistocles.

Lest all this chronological confusion make Thucydides appear artless, we should note that he concludes book 1 where he started, with a consideration of sea power. Clearly, a historical pattern underlies the book, though the modern reader may be hard pressed to find it amid all the temporal shifts. And matters are not helped when, at the beginning of book 2, Thucydides introduces yet another linear time frame, the "time of the war" as measured by the novel scheme of successive summers and winters. This he anchors to a starting date confirmed by no less than five different chronological means: the war began in the fifteenth year of the Thirty-Years' Truce, in the forty-eighth year of the priesthood of Chrysis at Argos, in the ephorate of Aenesias at Sparta, in the archonship of Pythodorus at Athens, and six months after the battle of Potidaea. Obviously, he could have provided an overarching chronology for much of book 1 had he had an overarching conception of "the" past.

ONCE WE ENTER THE "TIME OF THE WAR," the account appears to stabilize, moving forward at a steady (some might say monotonous) pace as Thucydides details events in the chronological order of summers and winters. In his mind this sequence begins in 431 BC and ends in 404 BC. It delimits a war that he insists lasted twenty-seven years, despite the intervening Peace of Nicias (421-413 BC), which he dismisses as little more than an armed truce characterized by proxy warfare. This claim—maintained at length in the so-called Second Preface of book 5, where Thucydides reintroduces himself to the reader—evidences the importance he attached to the "time of the war" as a linear, directional sequence encompassing the downfall of Athens (5.25–26).

Despite its importance, the sequence does not suffice, in and of itself, to explain the outcome of a war that led to the defeat of the stronger power. Rather, it simply demarcates the analytical field for retrospective reasoning. In this regard it functions in a manner analogous to Herodotus's Egyptian chronology, as a container for the "stuff" of history. Thucydides refashions this chronological stuff in both linear and episodic ways to explain the paradoxical outcome of the war. That outcome appears not as a single chronological development but as the unfolding of tendencies revealed in discrete temporal frames.

A linear frame dominates the first part of book 2, which moves in sequence from the "Funeral Oration" to the plague in Athens to Pericles's second policy speech. The plague establishes the directional axis of this sequence, for its ravages changed Athens irrevocably. The Periclean strategy of withdrawing everyone within the walls of the city intensified the effects of the plague, thus necessitating his speech in defense of this strategy when people began to criticize his leadership. The directional sequence unfolds a theme: the erosion of public spirit by private interest. The "Funeral Oration" lays out the dimensions of Athenian civic-mindedness; the account of the plague shows how civic pride of purpose gives way to a carpe diem attitude characterized by self-centered hedonism; Pericles's policy speech resolutely defends civic resolve against the encroachments of private self-interest. Thucydides concludes this part of book 2 with his famous estimation of Pericles as the embodiment of a transcendent civic-mindedness, which will after his untimely death from the plague give way to the partisan politics of private interest, thereby sapping the strength of the community. The entire linear sequence reflects the operation of retrospective reasoning, which takes the outcome of the war as its standpoint.

With the assessment of Pericles that concludes the first half of book 2, Thucydides offers us a critical perspective on the war as a whole. Indeed, most readers pay little attention to the second half of the book, which constitutes a dull sequence of occurrences, punctuated by detailed accounts of the Spartan investment of Plataea, a long-standing Athenian ally, and of the Athenian admiral Phormio's naval victories over the Peloponnesians. If we give these accounts the attention Thucydides obviously thought they merit, we lose our perspective on the war, as the linear frame gives way to an episodic one. Among other things, the Plataean episode models the typical stages of a siege narrative—the opening negotiations, the commencement of hostilities, the progress of operations— which will recur throughout the work, albeit more briefly now that Thucydides has established the general pattern. Similarly, the account of Phormio's victories lays out the pattern of naval warfare, characterized by an Athenian monopoly of seamanship and tactics, which Thucydides details here so as to reference it more briefly later.

Book 2 thus consists of multiple temporal frames—both linear and episodic— abstracted from the "time of the war" and linked by the flow of occurrences. The latter take the form of open-end sequences ("this happened, then this, then this"), characterized by chronological rather than causal connections. Unlike these

interstitial occurrences, the temporal frames they link establish themes that resonate throughout the work, providing it with its coherence. The theme of public
versus private interest resounds again and again, most notably in the debate
between Nicias and Alcibiades over the fateful Sicilian expedition. Even the apparently innocuous episodes about Plataea and Phormio have deeper resonances. Later, in a work that increasingly showcases the principle of expediency,
the Athenians will callously abandon the loyal Plataeans after having encouraged them to resist the Spartans; and, as the Athenians overreach themselves
militarily, especially in Sicily, the Peloponnesians will break the Athenian naval
monopoly as they too "become nautical" during the long school of the war.
Writing from the perspective of the defeat of Athens, Thucydides fully intends
the reader to make these connections early on in the work. Its unity lies not in
the "time of the war" itself but in the refashioning of this time into new temporal
frames perceived in the light of retrospective analysis.

WHY DOESN'T THE TENDENCY TOWARD RETROSPECTIVE analysis
itself exemplify an idea of "the" past? Surely (skeptics may argue) when Thucydides looks back on the war, he sees it as a whole. He's even gone out of his
way to define it as such by insisting on its twenty-seven-year length. Similarly,
in the Archaeology he looks back upon a much longer past. Indeed, don't all
people—ancients as well as moderns—conceive of a unitary past when they look
back in time? They use the past tense in speech and writing; they conceive of
"now" and "then," of "before" and "after." Armed with these kinds of objections,
a skeptic might conclude that Thucydides's use of multiple time frames simply
constitutes a narrative strategy and says nothing about his conception of the past.

Ideas of the past, however, transcend the temporal distinctions of everyday
language, which (in the above instances) merely denote priority in time. The
past is defined as such by its *difference* from the present, which is more than a
matter of priority. Rather, it results from a sustained sense of anachronism. Although Thucydides's temporal frames in effect separate past from present, their
multiplicity militates against a systematic idea of anachronism. That idea might
appear in one particular frame, as it does in the Archaeology (where he mentions customs no longer practiced), without carrying over to the next frame
(where he details the immediate causes of the war). Thucydides is intently focused on defining individual "pasts" rather than "the" past.

This intensity of purpose derives from the fact that, until his own day, past
remained essentially indistinguishable from present. Thucydides comments at
the very beginning of the Archaeology that his own recent past—the time im-

mediately preceding the Peloponnesian War, the time of his youth and early manhood—was already sunk in obscurity. He reiterates this claim in the Pentecontaetia, where he criticizes Hellanicus's chronological inaccuracies; and he elsewhere repeatedly highlights the Athenians' ignorance of their own past, especially the overthrow of the Pisistratid tyranny. Looking back in time, Thucydides could surely recall the details of his youthful upbringing, but the connections between his personal history and any larger historical framework remained at best incidental and at worst nonexistent, for even recent political events were already murky. Or, to phrase the matter less negatively—for the judgment in the previous sentence already betrays too much modern bias—when Thucydides looked back in time, he perceived (in both personal and political terms) a past inextricably bound up with the present—a past-made-present—the product of traditional commemorative practices.

In a recent reassessment of the origins of Greek historiography, Mark Munn has described some of the ways in which Athenians commemorated the events of Thucydides's youth, the period that set the seal on Athenian democracy at home and empire abroad. According to Munn, these civic achievements were celebrated in choral songs, tragedies, funeral orations, and other public rituals, all of which blended past with present. Such performances utilized mythological and historical materials to define the current aspirations of the community. Thus, in the wake of the Persian wars, the mythological Athenian king Theseus became reinterpreted as the defender of Athens against the barbarians, and his personal heroism became identified with the civic heroism of the Athenians, who had not only defeated the Persians but were by great effort extending their rule to Thrace and Asia Minor. Even more ostensibly historical productions, like Aeschylus's *Persians,* ultimately served to authorize the newly-formed Athenian Empire, which originated with the downfall of the prideful Xerxes. Commenting on these and other public performances, Munn concludes, "The past is thus, in a sense, timeless, and the eternal present is everything, always carrying with it the significance of the past" (33).

Keeping the effect of these commemorative practices in mind, we must re-evaluate what it meant for an Athenian like Thucydides to "look back in time." He surely did not regard himself as a child of the emerging Athenian Empire or of the newly expanded democracy—as (say) our parents or grandparents might regard themselves as children of the Great Depression or the New Deal—for such a view requires a distinction between past and present that he could not sustain. In the absence of this he would have processed the temporal relations of everyday language—"now" and "then," "before" and "after"—differently than we do; at the very least these terms would lack the directional, linear quality we attribute to them. Of course, he could readily understand how a current event might have been caused by an immediately prior one, but he could not sustain this kind of analytical stance against the inexorable encroachment of commemorative practices that steadily blended past with present. Indeed, according to Munn, this very problem led Thucydides to write history, to distinguish the reality of past events from current aspirations, so that he and his contemporaries might make sound political judgments. To Munn's conclusion we need only add that sound political judgment was grounded in a new appreciation of linear time as directional sequence.

The notion of a twenty-seven-year war obviously did not spring fully formed from Thucydides's brow, even though he began writing at the outbreak of hostilities. He had to construct his vision of the Peloponnesian War out of pieces—a speech, a siege, a battle, a massacre. Or, better yet, he first had to construct the pieces—to fix them apart from the commemorative flow—before he could eventually abstract from them the "time of the war." The coherence of this linear frame, therefore, resides in the thematic interrelation of the pieces from which it is abstracted. Of course, modern historians do something similar when they seek in retrospect to identify the enduring forces or tendencies underlying events. But the modern historian's starting point—the assumption of a linear, directional sequence—is Thucydides's end point. This crucial difference means that the overarching connections between the pieces of his account are thematic rather than causal, for the latter would necessarily presume the existence of a linear frame. Thucydides thus fashions the "time of the war" from themes whose significance exists apart from time.

This conceptual barrier to any notion of "the" past—even one limited to the Peloponnesian War—is reinforced by a characteristically Greek philosophical disposition. Recall Aristotle's horror of contingency in his distinction between poetry and history. Temporal chains of cause and effect are inherently contingent and, as such, meaningless to a Greek. "Facts"—that Alcibiades did this or that particular thing—are important not in themselves but only when they reveal some underlying universal truth. The significance of Alcibiades's actions lies in (among other things) their illustration of the growing tension between public and private interests. This tension "grows" with the impact of the plague and the death of Pericles—it has temporal boundaries and a linear thrust—but it is not defined by them. It can be expected to play itself out again and again, in polities other than Athens. Even if he could have conceived of a past characterized by a chain of cause-and-effect relations, he would not have valued that perception for its own sake. Instead, he still would have sought the timeless themes bounded by those temporal relations.

THE GENIUS OF THUCYDIDES SURELY LIES IN (among other things) the subtlety, multiplicity, and density of his thematic interrelations, which enabled him to unify the disparate temporal frames of his work. We can illustrate these resonances by briefly exploring some of the relations between books 3 and 5 on the one hand, and the Archaeology on the other. Taken as a whole, book 3 strikes many readers as the most substantial of the eight Thucydides completed. It offers a meditation on the transformation of *logos*—taken as both "reason" and "speech"—during the course of the war.[21] This theme interlinks three famous accounts in the book: the Mitylenian debate, the trial of the Plataeans, and the Corcyraean revolution.

The Mitylenian debate of 427 BC concerns the fate of a rebellious city on the island of Lesbos, whose leadership broke its alliance with Athens and attempted to bring the entire island over to the Spartans. By the time of this debate Pericles had been dead for two years, and Cleon ("the most violent man in Athens") held sway in the Athenian Assembly. Here he argues that justice requires the severest punishment of all Mitylenians, the people as well as their leaders, for everyone was complicit in the betrayal of Athenian trust. At the same time, he questions the integrity of those orators who want to prolong debate on this matter, and he blasts the Assembly for indulging itself in oratorical contests that showcase clever speechifying. In response, Diodotus (an otherwise unknown orator) delivers a very clever speech indeed, defending the role of debate in public policy decisions and arguing that considerations of expediency, not justice, should govern the deliberative process. On this account, he concludes, only the ringleaders of the revolt should suffer punishment, lest Athens alienate the popular element in its subject cities and transform each revolt into a fight to the death. In the end Diodotus's arguments appear to carry the day, for the populace of Mitylene was spared, though the triumph of *logos* is subtly undercut when Thucydides mentions in passing the execution of a thousand "ringleaders" and the enserfment of the rest of the population. Apparently, Cleon's notion of justice still carried some weight.

The ideal of expediency receives unexpectedly brutal application in the next major account of book 3, when the Spartans trick the Plataeans into surrendering after a heroic siege by offering them the prospect of a fair hearing before a commission of Spartan judges. Since the siege resulted from a failed Theban attempt to seize their city, the Plataeans surrender, expecting to make the reasonable plea that they were only resisting unprovoked aggression; they never suspect that the commission is nothing but a kangaroo court. After asking their captives a single, loaded question—essentially, "What have you done for us lately?"—the judges choose expediency over justice and, siding with their Theban allies, sentence the Plataeans to death for having courageously resisted a Theban sneak attack.

In the famous account of the Corcyraean revolution, near the end of book 3, arguments from expediency serve as a cloak for horrific acts perpetrated not against foreign powers but against one's very own family and neighbors. Strife had erupted in Corcyra in 427 when an oligarchical coup against the pro-Athenian democracy sparked civil war, during which the hard-pressed oligarchs burned their own warehouses, destroying the economic heart of this rich and powerful city. The Athenians, aghast at the self-immolation of their ally, attempted to reconcile the contending parties, but their intervention only lent encouragement to a democratic assault on the oligarchs. The ensuing generalized massacre transgressed all limits: "Sons were killed by their fathers, and suppliants dragged from the altar or slain upon it" (3.81). Thucydides sums up the breakdown of social consensus in his chilling coda: "Words had to change their ordinary meanings and to take those which were now given them" (3.82). The transformation of *logos*—of reason and speech—first glimpsed in the Mitylenian debate is now complete. Read in isolation, the latter appears as the triumph of reason over passion, of Diodotus over Cleon. But by the time one finishes book 3, Diodotus's espousal of expediency portends the breakdown of reason and speech in the Corcyraean revolution, as expedient actions born of excessive partisanship transmute virtues into vices and vices into virtues. Once words lose their meanings, consensus disintegrates and factionalism spirals out of control, in a free fall that can end only when one party has exterminated the other. This stark realization casts a long shadow across the rest of the work, darkening book 5 in particular.

This book is best known for the "Melian dialogue" of 416 BC, when the Athenians sent a powerful expedition to conquer the tiny island of Melos. Before resorting to force, they attempted to win over their opponents with words. Ultimately, however, they failed to convince the Melians of the hopelessness of resistance. The ensuing siege ended, inevitably, with the complete eradication of the Melians and the resettlement of the island by Athenian colonists.

Readers often approach this famous dialogue with the kind of reverence that tends to single it out, even when one tries to understand it in its context. Indeed, book 5 seems a rather shabby setting for the dialogue, which is preceded by a series of drab verbatim treaties that most scholars assume Thucydides would have edited out or paraphrased had he completed the work. Yet the language of these treaties—redolent with the most solemn oaths—stands in utter contrast to the expectations and actions of the signatories, who regard the treaties purely as cynical ploys. Clearly, words have changed their meanings, not only in Corcyra but throughout Greece. Against this backdrop, the Melian dialogue appears not only as a ruthless exercise in *Machtpolitik* but also as a heroic attempt to restore the meaning of words through straight talk. Despite all the unpalatable truths they will later voice about the will to power of gods and men alike, the Athenians take a noble stance at the outset, when they propose to dispense with clever speechifying before the multitude and, instead, engage in a frank exchange of views with the Melian leadership. The confidence that truth will out, that reason will prevail, marks them indelibly as Athenians, for whom every problem has a solution, if only one tries hard enough to find it. The ultimate failure of the dialogue highlights not only the sappy moralism of the Melians but the misguided rationalism of their opponents.

That the dialogue will fail is apparent from the very outset. The Athenians begin by proposing that both sides consider only what is expedient, not what is right. The Melians respond with a clever counterargument: that appeals to justice and honor, to what's fair and right, might be more expedient than the Athenians realize: "And you are as much interested in this as any, as your fall would be a signal for the heaviest vengeance and an example for the world to meditate upon" (5.90). This notion the Athenians dismiss out of hand, arguing that rival empires treat each other differently than they do their subject cities. Writing from the perspective of the war's end—and Sparta's harsh treatment of Athens—Thucydides could not have intended this portion of the dialogue as anything other than ironic. Athenian shortsightedness leads them to focus solely on the present, on the actual resources states have at hand, without any concern for the future. By contrast, Melian shortsightedness leads them to focus solely on hope for the future, without any consideration of their actual resources. With their different perspectives and different imperatives, the two sides are doomed to talk past each other, and any expectation otherwise can only have been naive.

The Melian dialogue culminates the decay of *logos* that had begun in book 3. Once words have lost their meanings—once expediency and self-interest become the rulers of action—one can find no firm ground for reasoning, not even in the logic of expediency itself. The hopelessness of this conclusion contrasts sharply with the more optimistic tone of the earlier books. The Archaeology presents (at least ostensibly) a story of progress toward sea power. The subsequent narrative of book 1 bears out this story, charting the emergence and growth of the Athenian Empire, especially under the wise guidance of Pericles. Indeed, Periclean naval policy reflects the same kind of rational calculation and analysis of resources that one finds displayed in the Archaeology. Yet, the Archaeology ends on a surprisingly dark note, calling into question the sunny faith in the power of reason and the progress it has revealed: "The Median war, the greatest achievement of past times, yet found a speedy decision in two actions by sea and two by land. The Peloponnesian [War] was prolonged to an immense length, and long as it was it was short without parallel for the misfortunes that it brought upon Hellas" (1.23). There follows a catalog of concentrated man-made misery—of numerous battles and revolutions, of bloodshed and banishment on an enormous scale. Even nature gets into the act, redoubling the best efforts of men with earthquakes, famine, and plague.

This brief glimpse into the abyss immediately follows Thucydides's claim to have written a possession for all time. Perhaps we ought to understand this claim in its narrative context, one in which material progress can entail widespread misery, in which reason can lead to miscalculation. Seen from this perspective, Thucydides counsels prudence, lest the quick-witted discover they've been too clever by half. This moral is indeed a possession for all time. It emerges not from a linear narrative that piles effect upon cause but from the accumulation of discrete temporal frames, both episodic and linear, that resonate powerfully with each other. And the metacritical message they convey is fully ironic, for Thucydides cautions against the overly enthusiastic use of his own methodology, against a reckless faith in the power of rational analysis.

This message is timeless not only in its wise insistence on human fallibility but also in its ultimate distrust of the kind of analysis that showcases linear time. For Thucydides, as for Herodotus, the richness of historical inquiry lies in the manifold interactions between different kinds of linear past and between the linear and episodic pasts. Any attempt to reduce this multiplicity to a single, overarching interpretation of events—"the" past—would have impoverished their undertaking. It would have cut off past from present, leaving the past dead and buried, accessible only through the evocation of its context. Instead, Herodotus and Thucydides succeeded in transplanting the past-made-present preserved by Homer and the *logioi* to a temporal realm without killing it off, rendering its lessons all the more vivid and meaningful by bringing them down to earth.

Hellenistic Innovations

The ruinous Peloponnesian War symbolizes the demise of Hellenic civilization. Although the great age of Greek philosophy had just begun to dawn, the final years of the war also brought with them a shift in the Hellenic world's political center of gravity, away from the endlessly contentious Greek city-states and toward larger political entities, first Persia (the makeweight in the final stages of the war) and ultimately Macedonia. The emergence of Thebes and of a revitalized Athenian Empire in the early to mid-fourth century did little to alter the political instability of Greece, which Philip of Macedon adroitly exploited in his conquest of the mainland. When his son Alexander extended Macedon's reach into Egypt, Persia, and India, he also expanded the scope of Hellenic culture beyond its narrow, parochial boundaries to encompass a wider world, thus giving rise to Hellenistic, or "Greeklike," culture.

The expansion of Greek culture spurred the diffusion of historical writing and the enlargement of historical horizons. The fourth and third centuries BC mark the spread of an interest in historical writing outward from mainland Greece to the wider Greek-speaking world. Sicily, for example, developed an especially rich historiographical tradition, culminating in the work of Timaeus of Tauromenium (c. 345–c. 250 BC), who wrote a comprehensive history of the western Greeks in thirty-eight books (only fragments of which have survived). Timaeus may also exemplify the enlargement of historical horizons, for he was probably the first to employ the system of dating events by Olympiads, though whether he did so consistently remains unclear. This system had the potential of coordinating far-flung events that had formerly been dated by a multitude of local means, such as archonship, priesthood, and kingship.

The development of this dating system culminated in the great universal history of Polybius (c. 205–c. 125 BC). Although he regarded himself as Thucydides's intellectual heir, Polybius drew his inspiration for universal history from Ephorus of Cyme (c. 400–c. 330 BC). As best we can tell from the surviving bits of text—and from the comments of other ancient authors—Ephorus wrote a history universal in time and space, measured by the standards of his day. In contrast, Polybius wrote a history universal only in space. By this means he aimed to highlight a singular achievement that had occurred chiefly during his own lifetime: the unification of the known world under Roman power. Polybius symbolized this achievement with the system of dating by Olympiads, which enabled him to explain how far-flung events all contributed to the same end, the creation of a unified Mediterranean world—the Oecumene.

One might anticipate the emergence of an idea of "the" past from Polybius's unified view of events, even though it did not extend far back in time. He begins his history proper with the outbreak of the Second Punic War during the 140th Olympiad, a date suggesting to modern readers the potential for temporal depth; and his account has an unmistakably linear thrust, with strong chains of cause and effect only rarely broken by forays into episodic time. Despite the temporal possibilities apparent in his universal history, however, Polybius demonstrates the impossibility of conceiving of a unified past in antiquity. Not only did he share Thucydides's tendency to refashion linear time schemes to suit his various needs, but he also ended up showcasing a form of episodic time entirely at odds with the predominantly linear thrust of the work. In the final analysis these different frameworks did not partake of the same kind of temporality, thus militating against the possibility of a past "back there" in time.

FOR SIXTEEN YEARS POLYBIUS LIVED IN A GILDED CAGE in Rome as one of a thousand prominent hostages to the good behavior of the Achaean League, a powerful confederation of Greek states whose cavalry he commanded prior to his detention. Although the Achaeans had scrupulously honored their alliance with Rome during its Third Macedonian War (171-167 BC), their attempts to retain some shred of political independence after Rome's conquest of Greece incited Rome's jealousy and subsequent hostage-taking. Unlike his compatriots, who remained for years scattered throughout Italy in virtual imprisonment, Polybius sojourned in Rome as "guest" of consul Aemilius Paullus, victorious general in the recent war, with whom Polybius had become acquainted during the Macedonian campaign. He tutored and befriended Aemilius's sons, one of whom—Publius Scipio Aemilianus—would complete the destruction of Carthage in the Third Punic War, becoming the greatest Roman of his day. From this vantage point at the pinnacle of Roman power, Polybius conceived of the project of chronicling and explaining for a largely Greek audience the startling fifty-year rise of Rome, from its crushing defeat by Hannibal at Cannae in 216 BC to its decisive victory in the Third Macedonian War by 167 BC, which eliminated the last challenge to its hegemony. Eventually, after completing the analysis of Rome's rise to hegemony in thirty-two books, Polybius added eight more books on Rome's exercise of hegemony from 167 to 146 BC, when his friend Scipio Aemilianus laid waste to Carthage. Of the forty books of this history, only the first five have survived in their entirety, along with numerous scattered fragments (some lengthy) of the remaining books.

Although the history proper begins in the 140th Olympiad—the quadrennial span starting with the prelude to the Second Punic War and culminating with the Roman disaster at Cannae—Polybius prefaced his account with two introductory books on the previous fifty years. These recount the completion of Rome's conquest of Italy, the beginning of its quarrel with Carthage, its hard-fought victory in the First Punic War, its subsequent seizure of Sardinia and Corsica, and the Carthaginian attempt to recoup its empire by expanding into Spain—an expansion that ultimately set the stage for the Second Punic War. In addition to these events in Italy, Sicily, North Africa, and Spain, Polybius detailed affairs on the other side of the Adriatic, as the emerging power of Rome also made itself felt in Illyria and Macedonia, instigating a scramble for precedence in Greece between Macedonia on the one hand and the Aetolian and Achaean leagues on the other.

Polybius recounts these events in an intensely linear narrative that quickly develops a momentum of its own, running so breathlessly from one occurrence to the next that he must occasionally pause to remind us of why he's writing, lest we lose our bearings in the seemingly endless sequence of happenings. This narrative is especially noteworthy for its variety of dating systems. After announcing that the history proper will begin in the 140th Olympiad (1.3), he declares the necessity of prefacing this account with events beginning in the 129th Olympiad (1.4)—that is, with the quadrennial span of 264-261 BC, encompassing the outbreak of the First Punic War. This, in turn, he prefaces with an account of Rome's conquest of Italy in the previous century, an account that abandons Olympiads entirely, beginning in "the nineteenth year after the battle of Aegospotami and the sixteenth before that of Leuctra, the year in which the Spartans ratified the peace known as that of Antalcidas with the King of Persia, that in which also Dionysius the Elder, after defeating the Italiot Greeks in the battle at the river Elleporos, was besieging Rhegium, and that in which the Gauls, after taking Rome itself by assault, occupied the whole of that city except the Capitol" (1.6). Polybius established this foundational date (387/386 BC) not with an Olympiad but rather by reference to events affecting the major powers of that distant era—Athens, Sparta, Thebes, Persia, and Syracuse—in comparison to which Rome was but a weak and insignificant state with an uncertain future. Rome's insignificance rendered Olympiads inappropriate, for the state that would unify the Mediterranean did not yet exist, though its lineaments would become apparent by the beginning of the First Punic War, which could thus be dated by that universal means. The use of different dating systems undercuts the linearity of the account by highlighting discontinuities between past and present, with different time frames reflecting different kinds of past.[22]

The reader, however, does not notice this discontinuity, for no sooner does Polybius establish his foundational year than he submerges the reader in a deluge of occurrences that rushes toward the outbreak of the First Punic War in the 129th Olympiad. Although Polybius had previously referred to this date at the beginning of book 1, it does not appear in the body of his account, which flows almost seamlessly from Rome's conquest of Italy through the First Punic War and beyond, with the passage of time denoted by the annual election of consuls. This standard of measurement changes in book 2, which treats affairs across the Adriatic in Illyria, Macedonia, and Greece, where the rise and fall of regional rulers provide the chief chronological reference points. Polybius blends this variety of times into one long narrative of occurrences, punctuated by occasional digressions explaining where he's been, where he's going, and why he's writing. Not until the outbreak of the Second Punic War in book 3 do we arrive officially at the system of dating by Olympiads, at which point the work assumes a predictable chronological rhythm, with two books allotted to each Olympiad. The onrush of occurrences obscures the variety of temporal schemes. As Donald J. Wilcox observes, "Before the Roman conquest there were times, each measured in its own way and each possessing its own order and significance. After the conquest there was a single time, needing a new standard of measurement" (89). In essence, each measure of time constitutes a past, with the Oecumene—the unification of time—signifying a new kind of past.

The linearity of the account makes the new kind of past appear as the product of singular events, but it isn't. Rather, it lies at the end of a long chain of occurrences—itself subdivided into different kinds of links—which terminate in the present without actually explaining how the present came to be. From the very start of the work, Polybius intended to offer that particular explanation in an instance of episodic time entirely distinct from the predominant linearity of the narrative: "For who is so worthless or indolent as not to wish to know by what means and under what system of polity the Romans in less than fifty-three years have succeeded in subjecting nearly the whole inhabited world to their sole form of government—a thing unique in history?" (1.1). Book 6—Polybius's famous digression on the nature of the Roman constitution—actually explains the singular developments of his day in an entirely nonlinear way, with reference to a "mixed constitution," which managed to forestall (albeit temporarily) the eternal cycle of constitutional change.

This cycle begins with one-man rule, in which primitive monarchy (based on the dictates of a strongman or chieftain) gives way to kingship (grounded in notions of justice and moral suasion), which eventually degenerates into tyranny. The latter form of one-man rule then gives way to aristocracy, which gradually degenerates into oligarchy, which then leads to democracy and its degenerate form, mob-rule . . . which prompts the reemergence of a strongman. In Polybius's view the Romans managed to forestall this cycle of change through a mixed constitution in which monarchical, aristocratic, and democratic elements coexisted, counterbalancing each other. The Roman version of the mixed constitution was especially noteworthy because it had emerged naturally, during the early days of the republic, rather than being imposed by a lawgiver (as Lycurgus had done for Sparta). The natural strength of the Roman constitution was, in turn, reinforced by the indigenous habits and customs of the Romans, which encouraged a spirit of obedience, self-sacrifice, and community-mindedness. These supports, however, could not entirely offset the effect of another natural process—the biological pattern of birth, maturity, and decay—which would eventually overtake even the mixed constitution of the Romans, thus renewing the inevitable cycle of constitutional change. Polybius did not fully reconcile these two natural patterns, perhaps because Rome's continued growth allowed him to sidestep the issue of decay and focus on the stability afforded by the mixed constitution.[23]

Book 6 interrupts the narrative at a crucial juncture—the nadir of Roman fortunes—when Rome's disastrous defeat at Cannae incited the rebellion of its Italian allies and encouraged Philip V of Macedon to ally with Hannibal. Rome seemed doomed. That it not only absorbed these tremendous body blows—coming on top of a string of previous defeats—but soon rebounded to achieve world dominance required for Polybius a special kind of explanation, disrupting the newly established sequence of Olympiads and entirely transcending the confines of linear time. Book 6 constitutes a very lengthy excursion into episodic time, but one in which the eternal, recurrent processes that drive events are subjected to much closer scrutiny than ever before. In place of vague Herodotean appeals to *metabolê*—the reversals of fortune whereby insignificant states become great and great ones insignificant—Polybius identifies the motive force of political change and subjects it to detailed analysis. The cycle he describes has some linear features—monarchy is always followed by aristocracy, which is always followed by democracy—but the cycle, being eternal, essentially stands apart from the flow of time.

Polybius's account ultimately highlights the discontinuity between linear and episodic time frames. More so than any other ancient author, he could have reconciled the two—he could have superimposed the cycle of constitutional development onto the linear narrative, using a state's position in the cycle to help explain the outcome of events. The narrative was especially ripe for this approach after book 6 because Polybius had reduced the varieties of linear time to one—Olympiads—and he had introduced a form of episodic time so compelling that it overshadowed his subsequent episodic excursions, which remained brief and infrequent. Yet the fragmentary remainder of the history contains no evidence that he ever reconciled the two temporal schemes. In his mind they remained incommensurable. Like a true Greek, he could only understand the welter of occurrences occasioning the rise of Rome by ascending to a more general level of explanation, detached from all specificity.

ALTHOUGH POLYBIUS'S MEANS OF DATING by Olympiads ultimately did not catch on, his annalistic form of writing influenced subsequent authors, most notably Livy and Tacitus. These historians organized their accounts by consular year, named after the two annually elected chief executives of the Roman republic. In a thoroughly Roman-dominated world this traditional Roman means of dating probably made more sense than Greek Olympiads, and it proved no less useful for the coordination of far-flung events. Livy and Tacitus combined the narrative unity afforded by the annalistic form with a distinctive sense of nostalgia, a yearning for "the good old days," before Rome's acquisition of empire undermined the simple virtues of the yeoman farmer. One might think to find in this pervasive nostalgia at least some intimation of a systematic distinction between past and present, which could serve as the foundation for an idea of "the" past. Ironically, though, the annalistic form giving narrative unity to these accounts militated against the distinction between past and present.

"Men ever praise the olden time, and find fault with the present."[24] Machiavelli's observation in the *Discourses on the First Ten Books of Titus Livius* holds just as true for antiquity as it does today. In the *Iliad* the wise old Nestor attempts to reconcile the wrathful Achilles and the haughty Agamemnon by saying that in olden days—when men were *really* men—they nonetheless heeded his advice. In the *Works and Days* Hesiod gives this kind of idealization enduring expression in the myth of humanity's descent from a golden age. But the note of nostalgia sounded by Livy and Tacitus—and Sallust before them—expresses something more than the natural human tendency to idealize the olden days. Rather, it issues from actual events, specifically from the decline of the yeoman farmer in Italy after the First Punic War. This process, which accelerated with Rome's acquisition of empire, led to the agrarian reforms of the brothers Gracchi and eventually to the civil wars—between Marius and Sulla and, ultimately, Pompey and Caesar—that destroyed the republic. In his pathbreaking monograph on the conspiracy of Catiline, however, Sallust did not attribute this civil strife to complex historical processes—economic, social, or political—but rather to a decrease of virtue corresponding to an increase of wealth. He portrayed Catiline as a traditional Roman gone bad, who employed characteristic Roman energy, resourcefulness, and courage in an attempt to seize the republic rather than serve it. Sallust's nostalgia—if we may term it that—was not for a sepia-hued bygone world but for native virtues actively twisted into vices by a misbegotten desire for wealth.

Although Livy developed this theme within a much larger time frame—a history of the city of Rome from its founding to his own day—he did not gain any greater temporal perspective on the differences between past and present. He introduces his account with a lamentation on the loss of ancient simplicity, but the annalistic form he adopted does not portray the olden days as far removed from the present. His history begins with the founding of Rome, an event that convention enabled him to date with some precision (for example, one section of Livy's account concludes, "Thus 310 years after the foundation of Rome military tribunes with consular power first entered upon office" [4.7]). He could have used the founding of Rome as the touchstone for all subsequent events, establishing a linear sequence of years extending all the way to the present. Instead, he dates events by a variety of means—the reigns of the kings, the years of wars, and (most important) the annual consulships. The Romans maintained an official list of consuls, along with their accomplishments, but Livy's audience did not have ready access to this list and could not have translated the names of the consuls into a meaningful sequence of years. Without an overarching linear sequence to give it structure and direction, the annalistic form privileged instances of episodic time. As it moves from one consulship to the next, Livy's account details (for example) the ongoing struggle between patricians and plebeians that would eventually lead to *concordia,* the virtue underlying Rome's imperial rise. But this theme is crosscut by a multitude of stories—episodes illustrating instances of virtue and vice—that bear little linear relation to each other or to the larger theme; rather, they exist as freestanding episodes offset from each other by the annalistic form. These forays into episodic time best enabled Livy to explore the moral issues that motivated his writing, issues rooted in the present rather than the past; and Livy's episodic treatment of these issues foregrounds them, presenting them to his audience as alive and vital.[25]

In his magisterial survey of Latin literature the Italian classicist Gian Biagio Conte epitomizes Livy's attitude toward the past: "The mythology of the past, in short, not only *has* meaning for contemporary men but also *gives* meaning to their actions, in that it can illustrate through examples their own ideological needs" (371). When Livy prescribed history as "the best medicine for a sick mind" (1.1), he gave voice to an "ideological need," to a loosely connected set of associations constituting "Romanness," associations that dwelled in the breast of each Roman and that required (and, indeed, awaited) reactivation. The cure Livy prescribed resided in the episodic content of the history, and the nostalgia he expressed was not for something lost in the past but for something buried in the present.

With Tacitus this pattern remains fundamentally unchanged, though "Romanness" becomes redefined for the autocratic age of the principate. In the *Agricola* Tacitus commemorates the life of his father-in-law, which showed the kind of renown one could achieve without exciting the jealousy of the *princeps*. In the *Germania* he not only highlights the martial vigor of the northern barbarians, by implicit contrast with the moral corruption of the Romans, but he also implies the need to revive Roman virtue to fend off this threat. In the *Histories* he describes the decay of the old republican values and further elaborates the new imperial ones necessary for life in the principate, values he had first explored in the *Agricola*. Only in the *Annals* does he seem to give way to a pervasive darkness and despair. But even here there are prominent rays of light, as soldiers like Germanicus and Corbulo advance the glory of Rome in wars against the Germans and Persians. Indeed, as his vision of the present grew ever darker, Tacitus voiced an ideological need that grew ever stronger. And the medicine of history—along with the episodic means of its administration—remained as efficacious for him as it had been for Livy. If in his darkest moments he feared that the present could no longer benefit from it, he still hoped that the future might.

IN MY ANALYSIS OF ANCIENT HISTORIOGRAPHY, and of ancient historical consciousness, I have exploited the crucial distinction between a modern unitary notion of "the" past on the one hand and an ancient conception of multiple "pasts" on the other. Before concluding my analysis, I want to reflect briefly on the meaning of this notion of multiple pasts, lest we relapse into our accustomed mode of thinking—which takes the existence of "the" past for granted as a universal given—all the while paying lip service to the notion of multiple pasts. Our accustomed habit of mind might resurface in a tendency to conceive of the multiple pasts of antiquity as if each afforded its own perspective on "the" past, as if each viewpoint sustained a sense of perspective distance between past and present. This possibility is all the more probable because (as I suggested earlier) I may have overdrawn the antithesis between antiquity and modernity. Specifically, I may have overstated the unity of the modern conception of the past, in response to which one might reasonably claim that there are as many pasts as there are historical viewpoints. What separates these multiple pasts from those of antiquity?

The crucial yet counterintuitive answer is that all modern forms of historical understanding and the pasts they evoke—including even those sociological visions of *la longue durée* that emphasize continuity over change—are marked by a sense of anachronism, by an awareness that the past is fundamentally different from the present. Precisely this feature is missing from ancient historical accounts. Ancient authors demonstrate a sense of anachronism at a local level—when, for example, Homer has Achilles wield a bronze sword—but this awareness does not extend beyond the local level to color the whole account; it is instrumentalist rather than systematic. It appears in one time frame without carrying over into the next, if only because the time frames are incommensurable; they address different problems and issues. For lack of a systematic sense of anachronism, the ancients could not sustain a distinction between past and present and, consequently, had no idea of the past. Here I have intentionally omitted quotation marks from the definite article to underscore a larger point, namely, that a whole dimension of consciousness that we take for granted is entirely absent from ancient thought. Instead of "the past," they conceived of things that had passed; the distinction is crucial, for (as I have stressed repeatedly) priority in time does not necessarily entail a sense of difference between past and present—it does not constitute the past as an intellectual construct.

Perhaps the counterintuitive nature of my contention still intrudes, for the very expression "multiple pasts" appeals to a concept whose existence I am denying. So let us try a different approach. Instead of arguing a negative—that the ancients did *not* have a systematic idea of anachronism separating past from present—let us try to establish a positive. Specifically, let us try to establish what multiple pasts "felt" like—that is, how they were experienced. In his evocative essay "History, Histories, and the Formal Structures of Time," Reinhart Koselleck offers us a window onto this form of consciousness when he describes three modes of premodern temporal experience:

1. The irreversibility of events, before and after, in their various processual contexts.

2. The repeatability of events, whether in the form of an imputed identity of events, the return of constellations, or a figurative or typological ordering of events.

3. The contemporaneity of the noncontemporaneous *(Gleichzeitigkeit der Ungleichzeitigen)*.[26]

The first two are familiar to us, but the third is distinctly foreign to our sensibilities, and not simply on account of its Germanic ungainliness.

Koselleck applies this strange notion specifically to "the prognostic structure of historical time"—such as the Polybian cycle of constitutional change—"for each prognosis anticipates events which are certainly rooted in the present and in this respect are already existent, although they have not actually occurred." Thucydides's Archaeology epitomizes the contemporaneity of the noncontemporaneous, for it lays out in a linear temporal framework the recurrent pattern of material progress through sea power, beginning in the remote past, culminating in Periclean Athens, and pointing beyond in an ever-widening gyre. Recall how Virginia Hunter described this pattern as an ineluctable "process" that unfolds inexorably when catalyzed by occurrences, and how such processes obscure for the Greeks the significance of what we call "events." The process is always present—"contemporaneous"—though not all at once in all its features. We should note that such processes are entirely distinct from the modern notion of "historical forces"—vectors of historical change distilled from events—because they are not about events at all but occurrences. Whereas events generate novelty, occurrences catalyze predictable processes, even though they may happen within an ongoing linear time frame. In their predictability all the stages of a process are contemporaneous, in the sense of *immanent*. But this English term, though more elegant than the literal translation of Koselleck's German expression, fails to capture the synchronicity implicit in the original. *Die Gleichzeitigkeit der Ungleichzeitigen* denotes the simultaneous coexistence of all the stages of a historical process, stages that can be rendered diachronically only because they have been grasped synchronically. The underlying synchronicity of this historical viewpoint militates against the possibility of a systematic distinction between past and present.

As a mode of temporal experience the contemporaneity of the noncontemporaneous encompasses instances of both episodic and linear time, for recurrent historical processes can operate within either temporal frame. Thus, the future stages of progress toward sea power are immanent at any given point in Thucydides's *linear* account of the distant past, and the future stages of the constitutional cycle are immanent at any given point in Polybius's *episodic* account of political change. In fact—and here we can effectively move beyond Koselleck's more narrow use of the formulation—the principle of the contemporaneity of the noncontemporaneous operates not only within these temporal frames but between them, as the narrative flow of an ancient historical account switches from one linear or episodic frame to another. These "multiple pasts," as I have been calling them, are all contemporaneous because each one denotes a different kind of synchronic process or pattern. These patterns—be they of progress toward sea power, of constitutional change, of reversals of fortune, of injury and revenge—are all predictable. Each one lies immanent, just below the flat surface of a sea of occurrences stretching to every horizon, in a monotony of campaign seasons, Olympiads, consular reigns, or whatnot. The nondescript uniformity of this sea—devoid of those salient outcroppings we call "events"—enhances the synchronicity of these multiple pasts, which is experienced as their contemporaneity, regardless of which particular process has risen (momentarily) to the surface. The synchronicity of recurrent themes thus serves to bind the history together, emphasizing universals while repressing contingencies.

Let me try to describe the ancient experience of contemporaneity—albeit grossly and imperfectly—in Livy's historical enterprise. If he did not write about the past as we know it, what did he write about? Granted, Livy's historical vision encompasses seven centuries and is packed full to bursting with the individuals and events that transformed a small, insignificant community into the greatest power in the world. Granted, too, he felt the weight of these centuries—experienced as the enormity of the Roman achievement—and he revered the heroes whose wisdom, courage, and self-sacrifice had made it possible. Despite adopting an annalistic approach, however, Livy did not recount the Roman achievement diachronically but episodically, as a series of stories celebrating the virtues that made Rome great and condemning the vices that might have destroyed it. A moment's reflection reveals that these stories are patterned: the lust of Tarquin's son for Lucretia during Rome's kingship parallels the lust of the decemvir Appius Claudius for Verginia during the early days of the republic, as do the fates of the two women, and the actions of their avengers; similarly, neither Lucius Junius Brutus nor Publius Horatius nor Titus Manlius hesitate to execute family members for disloyalty to the state or disobedience to its magistrates—one can multiply such exemplary patterns at one's leisure. Livy is enough of a moralist that one hesitates to call these patterns processes, in the analytical sense disclosed by Thucydides and Polybius; nonetheless, they arise repeatedly amid the flow of occurrences and follow predictable courses. The moral truths illustrated by these episodes thus share a fundamental contemporaneity, regardless of which one is actually in play.

This contemporaneity forms the base and foundation of Livy's history, which is not about the past at all. Rather, he wrote history by way of communing with the ancients who personified the greatness of Rome, in much the same way as a Roman paterfamilias dwelled with his ancestors, whose death masks kept watchful eye over him from the household atrium—death masks (we might add) that he paraded in the family name at various public ceremonies. Livy sought to remind his contemporaries of the necessity—the expectation—of keeping faith with their ancestors, lest his generation undermine the immense achievement that its forefathers had made possible. If the dead had resided in a past different from the present, they would not have exerted such power over the present or embodied such ability to address its ideological needs. This power is altogether different from the modern one of a revered past, embodied in (say) the Constitution of the United States—yellowed with age and poured over by legal scholars with the aim of determining the "original" intent of the Founding Fathers. Livy felt the weight imposed by his *patres*—and the obligation it entailed—all the more heavily because they were still very much with him. Though they were dead, they had not departed; they had passed . . . but not into the past.

PART TWO

Christianity

Time present and time past
Are both perhaps present in time future,
And time future contained in time past.
If all time is eternally present
All time is unredeemable.

—T. S. Eliot, "Burnt Norton"

Can't Get Here from There

Between antiquity's profusion of pasts and modernity's single, unitary past lies an unbridgeable divide, though we fail to see it as such. Looking back from our side of the divide, we naturally assume that earlier notions contribute to later ones, that some feature or features of classical thought evolved, perhaps in combination with other elements, to produce what we regard as "the" past. We thus have convenient recourse to the commonplace about Western civilization as the coming together of two traditions—the Greco-Roman and the Judeo-Christian—whose mixture combined the Hellenic spirit of empirical inquiry into events with the Hebraic sense of God's purposive action in the world, yielding the basis for our distinctively Western historical sensibility. This commonplace is of great utility for conceptualizing an entity so unwieldy as a civilization, but it is nonetheless an artifact of our modern conception of the past, which is indelibly marked by an idea of anachronism. Perceiving the past as fundamentally different from the present, we naturally seek to explain how one could have evolved into the other, in a process that assumes continuity rather than discontinuity. Yet—at the risk of sounding clever—this urge to connect past to present discloses an anachronism at the very heart of our sense of anachronism!

Despite its utility, the above commonplace about Western civilization obscures the processes at work in the formation of our idea of the past. The more closely one scrutinizes these processes, the more improbable the commonplace explanation becomes, if only for lack of common ground among the multiple pasts of classical antiquity, let alone between them and the Hebrew sense of God's action in the world. In our recitation of the commonplace, we created that ground by sleight of hand, positing an empirical urge to understand events that evolves, under Hebraic influence, into a directional conception of history—as if one thing combines with another to yield a third. But there was no single conception of past time in classical antiquity, despite the Hellenic invention of history as a literary genre. At base there were two different kinds of past—linear and episodic—and the linear one was as varied as the phenomena it described. Thus classical historical accounts flip repeatedly between the linear and the episodic— and within the linear from one measure of time to another—bewildering and exasperating modern readers. The irreducible multiplicity of these pasts argues against their direct combination with the Hebrew sense of God's action in the world.

So how did we get here from there? The short answer is, We didn't. An intellectual leap from these myriad pasts to a unitary past would have been impossible. We fail to see this from our side of the divide because we readily assume that myriad pasts are simply multiple takes on the same object—"the" past— whose existence as a category of thought we take for granted. But this category didn't exist on the other side of the divide, so the ancient mind could conceive neither the leap nor the need for it—which brings us back to the question of how this category of thought originated in the first place. If it did not spring forth fully formed, it must have begun as something else, something unrelated to those concerns we regard as "historical." Indeed, the first signs of a new way of thinking lie in the conscious rejection of classical sensibilities, which had to be cleared away before the past as a category of thought could even begin to emerge.

AURELIUS AUGUSTINUS, BISHOP OF HIPPO—more commonly known as St. Augustine—played the decisive role in this process, though we would look in vain throughout his writings for any sign of the modern attitude toward the past. One of the foremost products of the classical culture of his day, Augustine turned away from that tradition, toward a new conception of human existence that enabled him to perceive it as an integrated whole, as transpiring in a space specifically designated for human action. This space was more existential than historical; time factored into it as an abiding sense of the here-and-now, obliterating the traditional notion of time's passage. Augustine's existential space stands as the logical precursor to our idea of the past, if only because it circumscribed all human actions, subjecting them uniformly to the same kind of analysis.

Before one could conceive of the past, one had to be able to think of the variety of human actions as constituting a single conceptual entity. Episodic time could not create this unity because it excluded linear time—a facet of the human condition—and linear time itself could not provide an adequate frame because it remained mired in a contingency that obscured universal truths. Indeed, a conception of the unity of human action in space had to precede that of its unity in time, if only because time is ineffable—"unredeemable," in T. S. Eliot's fluid expression, denoting (on one level) the fleeting nature of consciousness, which always comes into play after the fact. As Reinhart Koselleck notes, "Time is not manifest and cannot be intuited"; thus the categories of modern historical thought rely on spatial metaphors.[1] We think of an "age" as constituting a "space of time," of events as forming a "chain," of time as "progressing" sequentially—these expressions all reflect the fact that time manifests itself first and foremost as motion in space. Before one could conceive of the past as remote from the present, one had to regard the human world, in all its diversity and variety, as constituting a distinctive spatial entity. Augustine termed this new entity the *sæculum,* though it was not specifically "secular" in the modern sense. Rather, it constituted the realm in which sacred and secular intertwine, where past, present, and future converge in the here-and-now.

The issue of redemption rendered this new entity distinct from its natural surroundings. Only humanity participates in salvation, for only humanity fell in need of a redeemer. The perceived necessity of redemption shaped the world of human action, imparting to it a theological unity revealed by a method of biblical interpretation that sought parallels between the Old and New Testaments, whereby actors or events in the Old "prefigured" their "fulfillment" in the New. Augustine extended this "figural" mode of interpretation beyond the events in scripture to encompass the end of time, where all Christ's promises are fulfilled. He thus used a theological instrument to circumscribe the space of human action. Within this space he sharply distinguished between biblical and postbiblical events. Whereas God revealed the meaning of biblical events in scripture, he left the meaning of postbiblical events obscure until Judgment Day.

Augustine's disciples and successors can be forgiven for abusing his chosen theological instrument. By extending the scope of the figural interpretation to the end of time, Augustine blurred his own dividing line between biblical and postbiblical events, encouraging the figural analysis of contemporary events. Born more than a century after Augustine's death, Gregory of Tours offers the perfect evocation of the *sæculum* in his *Ten Books of History,* where tales of innumerable "miracles and slaughters" reveal the intertwining of sacred and secular.[2] Yet Gregory makes no distinction between biblical and postbiblical events, for he draws figural parallels between events in the Old Testament and those in his own day. During the next two centuries the figural mode of analysis would loose its anchor in scripture and break entirely free. In his *Ecclesiastical History of the English People,* the Venerable Bede draws figural parallels between pairs of contemporary events, without any reference to scripture whatsoever.

These figural parallels enabled Bede to fabricate chains of events that create (for the modern reader) the illusion of historical cause and effect. When one examines the chains closely, though, one discovers that effect sometimes precedes cause, thus disclosing the underlying simultaneity of time in the *sæculum,* where past, present, and future converge in the here-and-now. The chain nonetheless seems historical to us, and herein lies an irony. By detaching the figural view of the world from its anchor in scripture, Bede has lent providential direction and organization to events that otherwise would have remained, in the manner of Gregory of Tours, a confused collection of miracles and slaughters. He thus imparted a narrative order to the *sæculum,* which is the first step in its transformation from a spatial to a temporal entity. The emergence of this temporal dimension constitutes the leading edge of the modern idea of the past, in which the distinction between past and present would eventually subvert the simultaneity of time in the *sæculum.*

We must now begin our descent into theology in order to divine the origins of the past. I use the term *descent* advisedly, for this is a harrowing world, full of traps and snares for the unwary. Augustine will be our guide, and we will cleave initially to a biographical approach—a well-trodden path, thanks to the work of Peter Brown and those who have followed him. I hope not simply to retrace their steps but to show how their path leads in an unexpected direction, toward the birth of the past, albeit via a circuitous route. Along the way I will demonstrate through Augustine's own account of his life that he did not share our modern idea of the past. Only by ridding ourselves of this tenacious assumption can we open ourselves to the (strange) theological notion of the simultaneity of time. Augustine translated this notion from his *Confessions* to *The City of God,* where it constitutes the nucleus of the *sæculum* that Gregory of Tours and Bede would later begin to transmute into a historical space.

The Power of Prayer

The opening lines of Augustine's *Confessions* set the tone for the entire work:

Great art thou, O Lord, and greatly to be praised: great is thy power, and thy wisdom is infinite. And man, who being a part of what thou hast created, is desirous to praise thee; this man, bearing about his own mortality with him, carrying about him a testimony of his own sin (even this testimony, that God resisteth the proud); yet this man, this part of what thou hast created, is desirous to praise thee; thou so provokest him, that he even delighteth to praise thee. For thou hast created us for thyself, and our heart cannot be quieted till it may find repose in thee. Grant me, Lord, to know and understand what I ought first to do, whether to call upon thee, or praise thee, and which ought to be first, to know thee, or to call upon thee? But who can rightly call upon thee, that is yet ignorant of thee (for such a one may instead of thee call upon another)? Or art thou rather first called upon, that thou mayest so come to be known? But how then shall they call upon him, in whom they have not believed, and how shall they believe, without a preacher? And again, they shall praise the Lord that seek after him: for, they that seek shall find; and finding they shall praise him. Thee will I seek, O Lord, calling upon thee; and I will call upon thee, believing in thee: for thou has been declared to us. My faith, O Lord, calls upon thee, which thou hast given me, which thou hast inspired into me; even by the humanity of thy Son, and by the ministry of thy preacher.[3]

Thus, in its entirety, reads the first chapter of a work that may well rank as the longest sustained prayer in Western literature. Its fervent tone grows ever more intense as Augustine moves from the more "personal" books to the more "philosophical" ones that conclude the *Confessions*. Ask any religious devotee: prayer is endlessly—indeed devilishly—difficult ("When we call upon thee, how can we be assured that we calleth not upon another?"). Cast from consideration any vulgar notion of "petitioning the Lord with prayer," as if one could without sacrilege appeal to some sort of anthropomorphized deity: genuine prayer is foremost an intensely focused meditation on the inconceivable mystery of God, in which the never-ending problem of "staying on task" represents only the first—and least—of many obstacles.

Magnus es, domine, et laudabilis valde. . . . Augustine launches the work with a line from Psalms that, in and of itself, constitutes a complete, self-contained prayer of a specific type, a *confessio* or "confession," from the Latin verb *confiteri*. Unfortunately, modern English usage encourages multiple misunderstandings of the term. It summons images of interrogation-room disclosures, of steamy "tell-all" books, or of dark confessionals and whispered secrets, all far from Augustine's intent (the sacrament of penance—along with the cloistered space reserved for its practice—didn't even exist yet). Further, all these English meanings take nominative form, evoking a "deed" rather than a "doing." By contrast, the meaning of the original Latin term lies closer to the verb from which it derives, implying the ongoing act of "confessing." This act has manifold meanings extending beyond our modern associations: Augustine praises God in the *confessio laudis* and declares his faith in the *confessio fidei,* as well as admitting to sin in the *confessio peccati.* Taken together, all these acts bear witness, in the sense of actively testifying, to the glory of God.

Each form of confession makes extraordinary demands on the worshiper. The initial confession of praise, for example, harbors unexpected depths. This ostensibly straightforward declaration of God's infinite greatness evokes, at one and the same time, a sense of our own feebleness, our unimaginable distance from him, our yearning for him. These feelings give rise to a host of apprehensions: How span this unbridgeable divide? By praising God or calling upon him? How call upon him without knowing him? How know him without believing in him? How believe in him without a preacher? All this anxious questing—and more—from a simple *confessio laudis!*

If Augustine aimed merely to embroil us in hermeneutics, though, his book would never have found a large audience. He intends to ensnare us with not only the substance of what he says but the way he says it—indeed, by the very saying of it. His restless, labyrinthine confessings have a disturbing effect, not only for their anxious piling of question on question but also for the strange intimacy they evoke. While publicly baring his soul, Augustine resolutely refuses to address us, his readers, directly. In his indispensable commentary on the text, James O'Donnell likens the effect of the opening lines to that of "coming into a room and chancing upon a man speaking to someone who isn't there," a man so intent on what he's saying that he scarcely acknowledges our presence.[4] Augustine's very act of speaking so intently to God becomes self-validating, and we find ourselves swept into a novel inner reality that leaves our mundane external one behind. Nothing in classical literature prepares us for such an opening.

It roots us firmly in the present, in the here-and-now of ongoing prayer. This "presentness" differs qualitatively from the "eternal present" depicted in the foregrounded literature of antiquity. As the latter moves from scene to scene, it plants each one firmly before us in such overwhelming detail as to push from consideration the previous, richly detailed scene. The unity of a foregrounded narrative lies in the dense interrelation of its episodic themes, the meaning of each episode emerging from the universal truths it illustrates rather than from its position in a causal chain of events. In the foregrounded literature of antiquity episodic time trumps linear time.

Scion of classical culture, Augustine retains both these conceptions of time, along with their relative weighting. He conceives the story of his life as a linear sequence in the *Confessions,* and he synchronizes the events of sacred and secular history in *The City of God.* Indeed, according to Donald J. Wilcox, he even integrates personal and historical time, seeing them as parts of a single temporal series created by God (122). Despite this linear viewpoint, however, he nonetheless privileges instances of episodic time. The famous pear-stealing incident in book 2 of the *Confessions* springs immediately to mind, along with the remarkable story in book 6 of Alypius seduced by a gladiatorial spectacle. The two episodes interlink thematically, for in both, friends lead friends astray. And the pear-tree episode recalls the Fall in Genesis, while Alypius's bloodlust manifests the effects of that primal event. These and myriad other episodes serve to illustrate a divine pattern whose workings transcend linear time.

Yet in recounting these episodes, Augustine evokes not an eternal but a very temporal present, the one he is in *now,* as we witness him confessing to God. This literary effect is a deliberate attempt to confront us with the reality of our existential situation, so as to encourage our spiritual ascent. Augustine regards all humanity as condemned to live in the time—and world—of God's creation, which separates us from him. The constant press of temporal cares, desires, and ambitions obscures from us the ever-present workings of the divine hand. Yet something within our fragmented and distracted souls longs for God, yearns to be gathered in wholeness with him, in a mystical unity that transcends not only our mundane mind and body but also our temporal identity as individual human beings. The way to God lies within—through the soul—by means of prayer, in a confessing that rediscovers and bears witness to the presence of God, even when our hearts have seemingly strayed farthest from him.

In marked contrast to the foregrounded literature of antiquity, Augustine creates his "here-and-now" by stripping away the world rather than embellishing it, by revealing the divine presence amid life's desiderata. This realization emerges during the actual process of remembering, a plowing of the soul that unearths hidden truth. Augustine emphasizes the act of recollection more than the things remembered—the past itself hardly interests him. In his penetrating analysis of the *Confessions,* Karl Joachim Weintraub notes Augustine's "impatience to be done with this personal past," the recollection of which only serves the interests of self-clarification in the present (36). Thus, notes Weintraub, Augustine's "autobiographical" books constitute a mere prelude to his "philosophical" ones—on time, memory, and the meaning of scripture—where he engages the logos more directly and intimately.

This engagement remains rooted in the *now* of Augustine's ongoing consciousness—what he calls *attentio*—the portal through which he seeks God.

The past has no existence apart from the mind that conceives it; it merely constitutes an instance of recollecting in the present. So, too, the future is an instance of anticipating. Augustine thus speaks in the *Confessions* of "a present time of past things; a present time of present things; and a present time of future things" (11.20). Our consciousness is an attending in, and to, the moment, an ineffable point "distended" between memory of what has gone before and expectation of what is to come, between a past and a future that have no intrinsic reality outside the attentive mind. By reducing all time to the *now*, Augustine seeks to overturn our mundane sense of time's passage, which obscures the presence of time's Creator. Indeed, Augustine sees intimations of divinity in the mind's trinity of memory, perception, and expectation. Delving into the soul, he finds God in the *now* of ongoing prayer.

Surprisingly, though, Augustine denies us the possibility of transcending time through prayer. The way to God is blocked. Despite our intense yearning for wholeness in God, we remain fragmented beings stranded in time. Ours is a *distentio animi* (which Garry Wills freely translates as a "tugged-about-soul") pulled between past and future—a flitting awareness that shuttles ceaselessly from memory to expectation—knowing no rest and finding no purchase for ascent toward God. Augustine likens us to "pilgrims"—*peregrini*—literally "aliens" cut off from God and mired in time. Once we recognize our earthly alienation, our unfulfilled longing cannot but manifest itself in the process of confessing, as we lovingly bear witness to our Creator. This act naturally becomes an ongoing exercise of the soul *(exercitatio animi)* that progressively strips away the illusions of the mundane world, sharpens our awareness of our existential condition, and readies us for the final reward beyond time, when yearning will yield to fulfillment.

By denying the possibility of spiritual transcendence in this life, Augustine, in his chosen form of prayer, privileges the present in an entirely new way. Whereas the Socrates of the *Apology* or the *Crito* encourages his fellow Athenians to attend to their souls rather than (say) their possessions, his kind of self-attention is not "radically reflexive" (to borrow an expression from Charles Taylor's masterful analysis of Augustine). Socrates trains the minds of his interlocutors to think logically about the world and the ideas that inform it, reaching outward to grasp the universal truths that validate mental operations. By contrast, Augustine turns his mind inward and rivets its attention on its own operations. When he "attends" to himself, he becomes aware of his own awareness; he literally becomes "present" to himself as an inescapably temporal entity, as a being caught in time.

His insistent orientation in the present establishes a fixed point of view—a sustained perspective—from which to interpret the course of his own life and that of all humanity, a viewpoint that overrides the multiple pasts of linear and episodic time. We are here at a critical juncture, for Augustine's insistent orientation in the present might have enabled him to distinguish past from present in a systematic and sustained fashion, engendering the idea of anachronism characteristic of "the" past as an autonomous intellectual entity. Yet precisely the opposite happens: past, present, and future all coalesce for him in the *now;* qualitative distinctions between them vanish, precluding any possibility of the past as we know it.

Of course, Augustine does not deny that he has a past, that in his boyhood he once stole some pears. But he nonetheless insists that the time of his boyhood has ceased to exist: "My own childhood, which no longer exists, is in past time, which also no longer exists" (11.18). This assertion would remain fairly innocuous were it not for the conclusion Augustine draws from it—that the "past" is merely an instance of recollecting in the present. Only through the ambiguities of everyday language does the past acquire a referent outside the moment. In her challenging study of ancient and medieval memory, Janet Coleman observes, "There is a sense, then, in which Augustine the Roman orator has destroyed the past as meaningfully distinct from the now, and made all Christians paradoxically memoryless" (100). Although their religion is characterized by belief in a seminal event—the Incarnation—they worship not a "historical" but a "living" Christ whose eternal Truth is ever-present. Augustine evokes this Christian "presentness" in the act of confessing, through which he artfully draws us into the *now,* intending to make it as alive for us as it is for him. In effect, this existential stance leaves no room for an autonomous past.

This assertion may still seem counterintuitive. How could the author of *The City of God,* commonly touted as the "first Christian philosophy of history," not conceive of the past as an autonomous entity? Here we must introduce a crucial distinction between "real" and "historical" events. Augustine is aware of real events—the Incarnation, the pear-stealing incident, and (as we will see) the sack of Rome—but their meaning is not historical in any classical or modern sense. Although they exist for him in a linear time frame, he does not understand them in terms of their sequencing; and although they may partake of episodic qualities, the human truths they illuminate have little explanatory value for him. Rather, whatever meaning they have is revealed by God, as known through scripture. Since God's Word is limited to biblical events, his ultimate plan for humanity remains unknown, though some of its outlines can be inferred from what we do know about the divine will. The light of scripture thus reveals events as temporal parts of an eternal whole.

Christ is both the capstone and linchpin of scripture, the point toward which the entire account tends, from Genesis onward, and the key to understanding the events it contains. The fact of the Incarnation—of God made flesh—informs this account from start to finish, imparting extraordinary significance to the human experience of time. The mind that seeks truth does not have to ascend from the temporal to the eternal—as if that were even possible—rather it need only descend into the moment, into the very essence of God's creation. By reducing time to the *now,* Augustine has not narrowed his horizons but vastly expanded them, enabling him to find linkages between events that transcend the materialistic constraints of cause and effect or the superficial resonance of episodic themes. Descending into the moment, he breaks through to a new level of reality that enables him to understand, at one and the same time, the course of his own life and that of all humanity. He has no need for history as we know it.

Modern philosophers, led by Russell and Wittgenstein, may challenge Augustine's notion of time on logical grounds, but the fact remains that his existential insight derives from theology, not philosophy.[5] It is the by-product of a newfound confidence in the Incarnation that inspired him to compose the *Confessions.* We must now turn to an account of Augustine's life as reflected in the *Confessions.* This account will serve two purposes: first, it will trace the path by which Augustine rejected the classical ideal of contemplative ascent and embraced the *now;* second, it will show, through Augustine's view of his own life, that he did not conceive of his past as distinct from his present. Central to both his intellectual development and his view of it in the *Confessions* is a Pauline notion of sin and redemption that emphasizes the reality and immediacy of the Incarnation. In *The City of God* Augustine would seek to preserve the immediacy of the Incarnation despite the ever-receding promise of a Second Coming. The strange persistence of the material world in the face of this divine decree would eventually transform Christian "presentness" into something the early Christians never intended—an orientation in the present that would set the stage for the emergence of the past.

Breakthrough to the *Now*

The roots of Augustine's notion of temporality extend back to Judaism, which situated all actions, both divine and human, in an endless flow of time. Strictly speaking, the Hebrews divided this flow into the age before Creation, the present age, and the age following the advent of the Messiah, though they sometimes expressed this threefold division in a twofold way, distinguishing between the present age (before the Messiah) and the future age (after the Messiah). The important point for our purposes is that all these ages existed in time. The Hebrews did not make the Greek distinction between time and eternity (which recalls Aristotle's distinction between the contingent and the universal); instead, they regarded even the ages before Creation and after the Messiah as partaking of the "unending duration of God's time."[6] Primitive Christians modified this temporal scheme only slightly. Their assertion that the Messiah had actually come simply heralded the imminence of a new phase of "God's time," which would begin soon thereafter with the Parousia, or Second Coming.

As Primitive Christian conceptions became increasingly Hellenized—in part under the influence of Gnostic blends of Greek philosophy and Eastern mysticism—"God's time" after the Parousia became equated with eternity, the timeless beyond. There also developed a tendency, known as Docetism, to deny the humanity of Christ and hence the significance of the Incarnation as an event. Further, Gnostic Christians generally discounted the Old Testament, with its history of God's actions in time. Under the press of these influences Early (as opposed to Primitive) Christians downplayed the historicity of the Incarnation and, consequently, distinguished more starkly between the world of time and the timeless beyond. As long as the Incarnation symbolized something more spiritual than historical, the world of time paled in significance before the timelessness of eternity.

As we will see, Augustine dabbled with a form of Gnosticism in his youth, and he converted to Catholicism by way of Platonism. Indeed, his earliest extant writings, composed soon after his conversion, are dialogues of Christian philosophy designed to foster contemplative ascent toward a timeless, immaterial God conceived along Platonic lines. Yet in the decade following his conversion to Catholicism, Augustine took an even more fundamental turn, this time toward the Pauline view of sin and redemption. He subsequently questioned the very possibility of contemplative ascent and, instead, asserted the radically fallen nature of a humanity so alienated from God that it needed an intermediary—Christ, God-made-man. Augustine thus began to take the reality of the Incarnation more seriously. This event highlights not only the Fall but also the Parousia, illuminating the ever-growing expanse of time between Christ's Resurrection and the Second Coming. From his perspective in the present, Augustine could anticipate the Second Coming and the promise of eternal salvation, but the expanse of time between present and Parousia still remained fundamentally alienated and alienating. Trapped in the ongoing present of his consciousness, Augustine yearned for a God he could not reach, in an almost romantic longing that rendered him a pilgrim, a stranger condemned to wander in time.

THE POWER OF AUGUSTINE'S INSIGHT INTO the nature of the temporal pilgrimage stands in direct proportion to the power of the timeless, contemplative ideal it supplanted, a classical ideal that permeated all of Augustine's previous conversions—to Ciceronian wisdom, to Manichaeism, to neo-Platonism, to the Catholic Church. Lest the much-converted Augustine appear feckless, however, we must begin our review of his intellectual odyssey by establishing that he always remained at heart a Christian. His mother, Monica, herself a baptized Catholic, raised him as a catechumen. This status relegated him, literally and figuratively, to the vestibule of the church, outside the inner sanctum. Whatever went on inside remained closed to the uninitiated. To cross that threshold, one had to accept baptism, which constituted foremost a pledge to live by the moral strictures of the church. Without a sacrament of penance to alleviate this burden, initiates risked expulsion from the Christian community for repeated moral lapses. Baptism thus entailed a commitment Augustine naturally hesitated to make, despite Monica's urgings. Relegated to the vestibule, he did eventually stray outside, seeking wisdom in a Gnostic form of Christianity, only to be pulled back toward orthodoxy by Platonic philosophy.

A reading of Cicero's now lost dialogue *Hortensius* ignited the nineteen-year-old Augustine's love of wisdom and desire for intellectual ascent toward timeless truth: "These were the words that excited me and set me burning with fire" (*Confessions*, 3.4). The youthful Augustine had moved from his North African hometown of Thagaste to Carthage two years earlier—in 371—to complete his studies in rhetoric, at which he already excelled, and to undertake the study of law as prelude to a career in the imperial administration. Like many an adolescent gone off to college in the big city, Augustine quickly sank into what he would later decry as a dissolute life. We moderns tend to emphasize the fact that he took a "concubine," though he lived with her faithfully for fifteen years—and fathered a child—in a form of second-class marriage common to upwardly mobile young men, who reserved first-class marriage for the purpose of career enhancement in their maturity. Hardly less sinful than concupiscence was his passion for the theater, whose attractions nourished an adolescent sense of drama.

The *Hortensius* lifted the nineteen-year-old's mind to higher things, and it had an enduring influence on his subsequent development. As Garry Wills observes, "Cicero's dialogue embodied a paradox that Augustine would later live out himself, of the great rhetorician rhetorically dismissing rhetoric" (27). As best we can tell from fragments preserved by Augustine and others, Cicero enjoined his readers to renounce worldly things and love wisdom for its own sake. The young Augustine took this injunction to heart and, as a Christian catechumen, turned naturally to scripture as the fountainhead of wisdom (he found the lack of any mention of Christ in the *Hortensius* off-putting). To his dismay, though, he encountered an Old Testament full of seemingly irrelevant stories and a rambling and sometimes contradictory New Testament that began crudely by plugging the name of Christ into a Hebrew tribal genealogy. No echo here of Cicero's refined call for wisdom!

Recoiling from the rudeness of scripture, Augustine took refuge in an early form of quasi-Christian rationalism, the sect of Mani. This third-century Persian sage/martyr blended Zoroastrian dualism with a mix of Babylonian, Buddhist, and Christian elements—rigidly excluding from the latter any reference to the Old Testament—to produce a Gnostic faith that offered salvation through knowledge of the true condition of humanity. Mani preached of a cosmic struggle between Good and Evil—Light and Darkness—that left humankind (once formed of Light) imprisoned in the Darkness of the terrestrial world. Through knowledge of this struggle, "the soul—admonished and restored to pristine memory—recognizes the source from which it derives its existence . . . [securing] for itself the merit of reconciliation with God."[7] This teaching guaranteed salvation to the fully initiated "elect"—who led lives of ascetic renunciation—and held forth its promise to as yet uninitiated "hearers" like the young Augustine. He thus found a faith that renounced worldly things, echoing Cicero's call, while retaining the name of Christ (the second person of the Manichaean trinity, whose third was Mani himself). The sect also enabled him to discount the stories of the Old Testament and to rationalize his youthful incapacity for sagelike asceticism. He could readily impute his inevitable moral lapses to the forces of Darkness, much as (notes Garry Wills perceptively) we moderns might ascribe our own impulses to the power of a Freudian subconscious that defies our best intentions (29).

Augustine flirted with Manichaeism for at least nine years and, not surprisingly, became an effective spokesman for it, converting friends and acquaintances less dialectically skilled than he. But along the way he began to doubt the very dualism he had once found so satisfying. It ran counter to the prevailing cosmologies of the natural philosophers—which sought to explain the physical universe in more material terms—and his rhetorical training inclined him to examine both sides of the cosmological issue in the skeptical manner of the Ciceronian orator. The more he did so, the more he leaned toward traditional cosmology. Seeking to rescue himself from growing doubt, he only ended up further disillusioned after his encounter with Faustus, the foremost Manichaean preacher in Africa, who proved personally charismatic but intellectually shallow. Writing in the *Confessions* from the perspective of his maturity, Augustine notes, "If I had been able to conceive of a spiritual substance, all [Manichaean] inventions would at once have been disproved and rejected from my mind" (5.14). But the young man remained ignorant of such abstractions.

He nonetheless began to philosophize during this period with the composition of his first book, *De pulchro et apto* (On beauty and proportion) around 380, at the age of twenty-six or twenty-seven. Augustine ultimately disdained this work for its Manichaean qualities—and that's probably why he managed to lose all copies of it—but from his account of it in the *Confessions*, we can infer the beginnings of a desire for some form of intellectual ascent from the material to the spiritual. Although he still thought dualistically of an aesthetic opposition between the beautiful and the ugly, he conceived of the former as a unity, a "monad," and the latter as a disunity, a "dyad" (4.15). Further, he distinguished between a lower extrinsic beauty and a higher intrinsic beauty: "And this idea gushed forth into my mind from my innermost heart" (4.13, my translation). We can sense here intimations of an intellectual ascent, from the ugliness of disunity to the appearance of extrinsic beauty to the reality of intrinsic beauty. The young Augustine even regarded intrinsic beauty as the seat of rationality, truth, and goodness. Though still under the influence of Manichaeism, he had clearly begun to wriggle free of its dualistic straitjacket, gaining leverage with an ideal of aesthetic hierarchy.

Complete liberation came with his conversion to neo-Platonism around 386. He had left Carthage for Italy in 383, using his Manichaean connections to establish himself as a teacher of rhetoric in Rome, though he quickly tired of his students' evasions whenever he tried to collect his tuition. Networking further, he drew the attention of the influential pagan poet, orator, and senator Symmachus, who had been charged by the emperor with choosing the next professor of rhetoric for the city of Milan, where the imperial court resided. This figure would become in effect the imperial "minister of propaganda," charged with delivering panegyrics on court appointments and policies. Symmachus—fighting in the rearguard of paganism against the advances of his Catholic cousin Ambrose, bishop of Milan—no doubt delighted at the thought of ensconcing a Manichaean heretic in the imperial court. Augustine did not disabuse his benefactor. Although increasingly skeptical of the sect, he welcomed the appointment as the crowning achievement of his career and moved to Milan with his common-law wife and child in 384, to be joined by his mother, Monica, the following year.

As an increasingly supple rhetorician, Augustine had already come to question Manichaeism's dualistic rigidity. But that very dualism still retained for him some residual appeal because it offered a more sophisticated conception of divinity and a more straightforward explanation of evil. Instead of the crudely anthropomorphized deity that Augustine had associated with the teachings of Monica's African church, the Manichaeans elaborated a vision of the godhead as a force or light diffused throughout the cosmos. And this light was (by definition) distinct from darkness, so that it could not be directly implicated in the existence of evil.

In Milan, however, Augustine found himself drawn into the circle of Christian neo-Platonists that gravitated around Ambrose, where he encountered an idea of "spiritual substance" that offered a still more sophisticated conception of divinity. Although the Manichees did not anthropomorphize the god of light, they still conceived of it in material terms: the imagination apprehends light, no matter how ethereal, with reference to the senses. By contrast, the neo-Platonists conceived of the deity as a spiritual substance apprehended through a process of intellectual abstraction that left the material world far behind—their god was a substance entirely other than that of man. They also affirmed Augustine's vision—first glimpsed in *De pulchro et apto*—of existence as a continuum emanating from the "higher" spiritual realm to the "lower" material one. This vision explains darkness as the absence of light, rather than as an independent cosmic force, thus obviating the problem of evil.

In his pioneering work on the *Confessions* Pierre Courcelle contends that Augustine's ultimate conversion was to philosophy rather than religion. Indeed (as James O'Donnell notes in his commentary on the text), Augustine first mentions "the books of the Platonists" in the ninth chapter of book 7, in the middle of the middle book of the *Confessions*—hardly a coincidence for a rhetorician so finely attuned to compositional rhythms. Yet a number of factors—not all of them spiritual—conspired to push Augustine beyond the way station of philosophy toward religion. Even before reading the books of the Platonists, he had already become a catechumen in Ambrose's church. This move may have begun as much out of convenience as conviction. Ambrose was a powerful figure in an increasingly Catholic city. And after her arrival in Milan, Monica contracted for her son a first-class marriage with a Catholic heiress, which no doubt further inclined him toward orthodoxy. (He sent his common-law wife home and—a confirmed serial monogamist—took another concubine while awaiting his bride-to-be's coming-of-age.)

Instrumental motives notwithstanding, Augustine also derived genuine spiritual benefit from his return to the Catholic Church. Over time Ambrose's sermons revealed to him a new allegorical way of reading scripture that made even the intractable stories of the Old Testament yield hidden meaning. And Ambrose's preaching about the immaterial nature of God and the soul's transcendence of the body dovetailed with neo-Platonism, fostering a more fully spiritualized form of Catholicism than Augustine had previously known. He now began reading scripture with new eyes, largely under the influence of the Christian Platonist Simplicianus, Ambrose's mentor and eventual successor as bishop.

It was Simplicianus who first suggested the catechumen reread Paul's epistles. Augustine had previously dismissed the apostle's writings as inconsistent and even contradictory, but he now found in the Pauline contrasts between "spirit" and "flesh," between "inner" and "outer" man, a confirmation of the contemplative ideal of spiritual transcendence: "Whatever truth I had found in the Platonists was set down here as well" (7.21). The esoteric "wisdom" of the Manichees—limited to the absorption of a single truth—now gave way to a vision of wisdom as ascent toward God, conceived of as a substance entirely distinct from man.

Paul not only confirmed the insights of the neo-Platonists but linked their intellectualized spirituality to the heartfelt piety of Catholicism, via the intercession of Christ, who lifted man from the depths of earthly existence to the highest spiritual plane. Augustine would indeed need Christ's help to break the chains of habit that enslaved him. Although he yearned to lay worldly ambition aside and seek contemplative withdrawal, he still found the way to transcendent spirituality barred by indecision, by the natural reluctance to let go of his accustomed life. Like many of his contemporaries, he viewed the turning toward God as a turning away from all forms of worldliness. Baptism was thus incompatible with even a first-class marriage, necessitating that he renounce not only concupiscence but everything he had worked so hard to achieve.

The perverse civil war within his will, between a yearning for God and an attachment to earthly things, climaxed in the summer of 386 with his famous conversion in the Milanese garden. In a moment of heart-wrenching struggle and anguish he opened a volume of Paul's epistles at random to a passage (Romans 13:14) that concludes, "Arm yourselves with the Lord Jesus Christ; spend no more thought on nature and nature's appetites" (*Confessions*, 8.12). Augustine suddenly felt himself released from indecision and infused with confidence by a Pauline surrender to Christ. Reason had proven incapable of ascent toward God, but now Augustine realized that he need no longer fight alone.

His surrender to Christ presaged the demise of the classical ideal of wisdom by dramatizing the incapacity of unaided human reason to transcend spiritual indecision. But Augustine did not yet regard himself as consigned to an earthly pilgrimage, for he still assumed that with God's aid reason could attain spiritual heights. In preparation for baptism he and a circle of friends and family withdrew to a borrowed villa at Cassiciacum and pursued the contemplative life of Christian philosophizing. A deluge of writings testifies to the intellectual release afforded by his conversion. In barely five months Augustine completed four philosophical dialogues and had sketched out others. His blueprint for Christian erudition, *De ordine (On Order)*, epitomizes this period of productivity. Here he attributes the apparent "evils" of the world to the failure of human beings to understand the intrinsic order of God's creation. We can apprehend this order and thereby approach God through a program of systematic study grounded in the liberal arts and culminating in philosophical contemplation. Wisdom and Christianity thus conjoin in a vision of philosophical ascent toward God.

After baptism by Ambrose in the spring of 387, the band at Cassiciacum dispersed. Augustine planned to return to his hometown of Thagaste in Africa, along with his son and mother, where they hoped to duplicate on family property the Christian retreat of Cassiciacum. Civil war, though, closed the sea lanes and left the trio stranded at Ostia, where Augustine and Monica—for the first and only time—shared the fruits of Christian contemplation. Standing at a window of their lodging that (significantly, as we will see) overlooked a peaceful garden, they conversed serenely and joyously about the happiness of the saints. "As the flame of love burned stronger in us and raised us higher towards the eternal God, our thoughts ranged over the whole compass of material things in their various degrees, up to the heavens themselves," and far, far beyond, arcing toward the truly transcendent wisdom of the divinity. "For one fleeting instant, we reached out and touched it," only to fall back reluctantly, sighing, into the material world

(*Confessions,* 9.10). The promise of this ascent would remain unfulfilled, for Monica died of a fever two weeks later, leaving Augustine stranded in mundane reality.

WE HAVE THUS FAR RECONSTRUCTED AUGUSTINE'S LIFE from his account of it in the *Confessions,* which culminates with the vision at Ostia. At this point the so-called autobiographical books conclude, giving way to the so-called philosophical ones on memory, time, and hermeneutics. The sudden switch in subject matter presents us with a stunning anomaly, for Augustine omits his most seminal conversion from the account of his spiritual odyssey—a conversion away from the neo-Platonic Paul and toward a much harsher reading of the apostle, with a starker contrast between sin and redemption. This conversion occurred some ten years after Monica's death, and it had such a powerful effect on Augustine that it actually inspired him to write the *Confessions.* Of this seminal event there is not a word, even though its repercussions resound throughout the work, in his denial of the possibility of contemplative ascent and in his radically reflexive turn toward the *now.*

One might try to explain away this anomaly by saying that Augustine's new reading of Paul was anticlimactic, that it simply amounted to a more refined understanding of an apostle whom he had already embraced, especially during his anguish in the Milanese garden. Or one might claim that what I am calling a "conversion" was really a more gradual, and therefore less noticeable, change of heart. Yet in his *Retractationes (Retractations),* the retrospective on his writings composed toward the end of his life, Augustine recounted his struggle in writing the piece that inspired his new view of Paul—a piece in response to some knotty questions of scriptural exegesis posed by Simplicianus, his friend and mentor from Milan. While pondering these questions, Augustine actively fought against the view he would ultimately espouse, only to be won over at last by "the grace of God," which revealed the true meaning of Paul's words (*Retractations,* 2.1). Augustine thus found himself converted—in the literal sense of "turned"—away from the ideal of contemplative ascent that had previously guided him and toward the view of humanity's alienation in time, the ramifications of which he would elaborate in the *Confessions.*

We can partially explain why Augustine omitted this event from the account of his life by reiterating that he was not writing an autobiography but rather confessing. As witness to this activity the reader—that unacknowledged presence in the room—need only know that Monica had successfully seen her wayward son returned to the fold. She personifies the omnipresent grace of God, in praise of which Augustine confesses. In advancing this explanation, however, we must also concede that the press of the ongoing activity—its very presentness—obscured for Augustine the crucial event that had inspired him to supplant contemplation with confession. In other words, preoccupation with the *now* precluded the perception of his past as a reality distinct from his present, as marked by something seminal. The "autobiographical" portions of the *Confessions* reveal the omnipresence of God, showing how he continually operates in Augustine's life—in his infancy, in his boyhood, in his adolescence, in his manhood . . . in his recollection of a past whose superficial "reality" has obscured this essential truth. God's omnipresence thus collapses all distinctions between past, present, and (for that matter) future. It is as if, with the account of Monica's death, Augustine has reached a natural stopping point in a demonstration that has become tedious, and he now turns, in books 10–13, to engage the logos more directly. These latter books are his true meat, though it seems to us moderns as if he has suddenly changed the subject, abandoning the account of his spiritual odyssey in midjourney.

MUCH OCCURRED IN THE TEN YEARS between Monica's death and Augustine's new insight into Paul, making it all the more surprising that we should have to reconstruct this eventful time from writings other than the *Confessions*. Although Augustine eventually returned to his property in Africa in 388, and even managed to continue writing dialogues on Christian philosophy, the rhythm of his life had decisively changed. He found himself increasingly tugged from his retreat into the orbit of the African church, which—assailed by Manichaean heretics and Donatist schismatics—sorely needed the aid of dedicated laymen like himself. After the deaths in quick succession of his son and a dear friend, Augustine surrendered to this pull, perhaps to distract himself from his grief. In 391 he moved to the town of Hippo, ostensibly to found a monastery, but he ended up dragooned into the priesthood by the local bishop, whom he eventually succeeded in 395.

As an illustrious ex-Manichee the new priest was immediately pressed into combating this heresy, an effort that drew him back into a reconsideration of the problem of evil and, via this avenue, into a rethinking of Paul's epistles. During a two-day debate with the arch-Manichee Fortunatus in the summer of 392, Augustine forcefully asserted that we sin of our own free will rather than at the behest of a cosmic force of darkness: "He who sins not voluntarily, sins not at all" (*Acts or Disputation against Fortunatus*, 20). Against this bold assertion Fortunatus cited the apostle himself, who had declared that "the flesh lusteth against the spirit and the spirit against the flesh, so that ye may not do the things that ye will." And again the apostle: "I see another law in my members, warring against the law of my mind" (ibid., 21). Augustine's retort attributed these so-called involuntary actions to the power of habit *(consuetudo)*. Look within yourselves, he says, and see the effects of our willingness to sin: "When by that liberty we have done something and the pernicious sweetness and pleasure of that deed has taken hold upon the mind, by its own habit the mind is so implicated that afterwards it cannot conquer what by sinning it has fashioned for itself." Habit thus constitutes "the mind of the flesh" (ibid., 22).

Ready in his rejoinder to Fortunatus, Augustine had obviously been thinking about the power of habit for awhile. In the dialogue *De musica (On Music)*, perhaps sketched out at Cassiciacum and begun in 387 (though not finished until around 391), Augustine suggests that bodily pleasures, imprinted on the soul by habit, preserve their force in memory, where, with each reactivation, they become increasingly difficult to suppress (6.5; 6.14). Although the power of habit did not yet preclude the project of contemplative ascent—music was one of the liberal arts that could prepare the mind for God—Augustine would eventually build an interpretation of its overweening power on this foundation. In his *De sermone Domini in monte,* or *Commentary on the Lord's Sermon on the Mount* (c. 394), he explains—with remarkable psychological acuity—that a physical craving is extinguished by the act of sinning, but the memory of that act kindles an even more intense pleasure that itself calls for satisfaction, engendering over time a habituation to sin so powerful that it can be overcome only with the aid of Christ (1.12). How ignominious that the classical sage with his vaunted reason should succumb to the lowly power of habit!

Although he had already been tilling the soil in which his ultimate conversion would take root, that event awaited his response to Simplicianus's above-mentioned exegetical questions of around 396, which forced Augustine into a final reevaluation of human reason and will. His friend's most perplexing question concerned the meaning of God's words as quoted by Paul in Romans 9:13: "Jacob I loved, but Esau I hated." What had Esau done to merit God's hatred? In his response, *De quaestionibus ad Simplicianum* ("To Simplician—on Various Questions"), Augustine interprets this passage in the light of the entire epistle, which circumscribes human with divine will—specifically with a notion of election by which divine grace enters the will, inspiring its turn toward God. Human beings can do absolutely nothing to merit this gift; election depends solely upon God; "otherwise grace is not grace" (bk. 1, quest. 2.2). From seeing human will as enslaved by overweening habit, Augustine has now come to see man as totally dependent on God's grace, without which he is helpless. Does this mean that God is unjust? (For surely the infant Esau did nothing to merit God's judgment.) Here Augustine reiterates Paul's comment, that by softening some hearts while leaving others hardened, God demonstrates the power of his love.

This new reading of Paul utterly eclipsed the previous neo-Platonic one, completing the destruction of the contemplative ideal that had underlain Augustine's prior conversions. Now, though, he confronted a new problem: how to reach out to a God who has placed himself beyond human grasp? "Who can rightly call upon thee, that is yet ignorant of thee? How shall they call on him, in whom they have not believed? And how shall they believe without a preacher?" The anxious questing that opens the *Confessions* arises from a man who has no choice but to search within himself for the presence of God. Incapable of ascending, he must descend; he must bring philosophy down to earth, down into the self, into the mind of the knower, into memory, into the fallen heart of the soul. In Peter Brown's trenchant words, "The writing of the *Confessions* was an act of therapy."[8]

MOST EXTRAORDINARY IN THIS SELF-ANALYSIS was Augustine's steadfast refusal to jettison the prior selves of earlier conversions. He remained acutely aware of the weight of his past. Even during the act of confessing, as he directly experiences God's working within him "a feeling quite unlike my normal state, an inward sense of delight"—even then, in the very midst of rapture, "my heavy burden of distress drags me down again to earth: again I become a prey to my habits, which hold me fast" (*Confessions,*10.40). A man so exquisitely sensitive to the power of memory could not discard a past that was all too present. So radical a cure would not have been radical enough. Instead, he attempted something even more extreme and far more difficult. He explored the mysterious integration of past sinfulness and future blessedness—of human will and divine grace—operating in a dynamic present, in the very diachronic nature of his actual being. He searched for the presence of God in the act of recollecting his past.

Hence the nine so-called autobiographical books of the *Confessions* culminate with the remarkable tenth book on memory, where Augustine delves into the locus of his temporality, the source of the actual being whose confessings in the previous books have traced the outlines of a life. (Spurious arguments that this book was a late addition to the text are repudiated in O'Donnell's exhaustive commentary.) "Let me know thee, my knower, let me know thee as I am known" (10.1, my translation). With this prayer—this *confessio laudis*—Augustine descends within himself to find God. "What, then, do I love when I love God?

Who is this Being who is so far above my soul? If I am to reach him, it must be through my soul" (10.7). The descent into the self becomes an ascent toward God, one whose stages (not coincidentally) mirror those of the ascent at Ostia, the crucial difference being that Augustine is now *within* rather than beyond himself: "I have learned to love you late! You were within me, and I was outside myself *[intus eras et ego foris]*" (10.27, my translation).

Augustine's search for God leads him beyond his sensate being into the vast storehouse of his memory, home to everything he has ever experienced or could possibly imagine. "In it are the sky, the earth, and the sea, ready at my summons" (10.8). As he explores the wonder of this capacious faculty lying within the confines of his mind, Augustine finds himself drawn inexorably beyond himself: "Although it is a part of my nature, I cannot understand all that I am. . . . The mind is too narrow to contain itself entirely. But where is that part of it which it does not contain?" (10.8). The mind apprehends the liberal arts—say, the rules of grammar or arithmetic—by means other than the senses, acknowledging truths somehow implanted deep within memory. How did they get there? Likewise, the mind recognizes incorporeal feelings—emotions like sadness and joy—whose originals could only have entered the mind by some mysterious means. The paradox of forgetfulness epitomizes this puzzle, for it is by definition the absence of memory, yet somehow we manage to recognize things we had forgotten.

Straining with intellectual effort—"Oh Lord, I am working hard in this field, and the field of my labors is my own self" (10.16)—Augustine probes deep within his mind seeking the origin of that sense of "blessed happiness," the *beata vita,* for which he yearns. Where does it come from? Is it something imagined, or faintly remembered, or "forgotten," only to be recognized when found? These possibilities suggest a Plotinian subtext to the *Confessions,* whereby the transcendent soul of humanity—fragmented by the Fall—retains some imprint of its former state and seeks to recapture its prelapsarian unity. Augustine, though, turns this desire for neo-Platonic transcendence inward and discovers the unity of his temporal being in his search for God. The mind's descent into memory enacts the mortal soul's pilgrimage toward God, a quest that holds present in mind both the memory of past sinfulness and the promise of future blessedness.

Augustine's exploration of memory naturally embroils him in the problem of time, the subject of the next book. "What, then, is time? I know well enough what it is, provided that nobody asks me" (11.14). Again bending to the heavy task and inching forward laboriously, Augustine concludes—everyday usage notwithstanding—that "past" and "future" exist only within the soul attending to them in the ongoing present. "The present of past things is the memory; the present of present things is direct perception; and the present of future things is expectation" (11.20). The unity of the soul resides in this ongoing present, which Augustine illustrates by analyzing an instance of remembering:

> Suppose that I am going to recite a psalm that I know. Before I begin, my faculty of expectation is engaged *[tenditur]* by the whole of it. But once I have begun, as much of the psalm as I have removed from the province of expectation and relegated to the past now engages my memory, and the scope of the action which I am performing is divided *[distenditur]* between the two faculties of memory and expectation, the one looking back to the part which I have already recited, the other looking forward to the part which I have still to recite. But my faculty of attention is present all the while, and through it passes what was the future in the process of becoming the past *[praesens tamen adest attentio mea, per quam traicitur quod erat futurum, ut fiat praeteritum]*. (11.28)

Consciousness, *attentio,* lies "distended" between the expectation of the future and the memory of the past, creating the appearance of time's passage, whose duration conforms to our assumptions about the subject at hand: "What is true of the whole psalm is also true of all its parts and of each syllable. . . . It is true of a man's whole life, of which his actions are parts. It is true of the whole history of mankind, of which each man's life is a part." Regardless of the time scale, future and past are functions of our consciousness in an ineffable, ongoing present. Thus, notes Garry Wills, "The mind brokers this odd interplay of times in a no-time" (91).

Confessing defuses the power of habit. In the midst of this ongoing act Augustine's consciousness is distended between past sinfulness and future blessedness. Expectation of the *beata vita* enables him to attend to the past without reactivating the sins stored in memory. By holding God's promise ever-present in his mind, Augustine gains a critical perspective on the past, transforming his "distention" into "intention": "I look forward, not to what lies ahead of me in this life and will surely pass away, but to my eternal goal. I am intent upon this one purpose, not distracted by other aims *[non distentus, sed extentus, non secundum distentionem, sed secundum intentionem]*" (11.29). In the books on memory and time Augustine brings philosophy down to earth, into this life-as-he-lives-it, where the presence of God in his mind integrates his scattered self, unifying his personality. The omnipresent God had always been within, beckoning to him—

even when he was least capable of hearing—and has patiently brought him along to the point where he can now delight in the call.

THE *CONFESSIONS* ASSERTS THAT LIFE is a continual pilgrimage toward God. When he denied the possibility of intellectual ascent, Augustine relegated Christians to the ongoing act of confessing their unattainable yearning for God in this world. The act takes place in, and focuses attention on, an ineffable moment, conjoining past, present, and future. In the trinity of memory, attention, and expectation, the future outweighs the past, for the promise of the *beata vita*—of blessed happiness beyond time—transforms the soul's distention into intention, simultaneously unifying it and liberating it from the power of habit. These benefits notwithstanding, expectation remains by definition unfulfilled, leaving the Christian radically alienated in and from the world. As H.-I. Marrou observes, time is characterized by "ambivalence."

Although the *Confessions* tells the story of how Augustine came to recognize himself as a pilgrim, that story is secondary—and indeed incidental—to the ongoing act of confessing. Hence his ultimate conversion—so hard fought, so crucial, so unprecedented—passes without mention. Confessing precludes sustaining an idea of anachronism that would highlight the differences between one's past and present, for that idea would have left the soul scattered rather than unified. In effect, Augustine's focus on the present did not permit the existence of an autonomous past. The latter occupied his mind only as an *exercitatio animi,* an exercise of the soul in pilgrimage toward God. In this regard, notes Weintraub, "the analysis of the past is never simple remembrance" (39). Or, to phrase the matter differently: when he regarded his past, Augustine looked not beyond or outside but rather within himself. The past, as we use the term, had no independent existence for him.

AUGUSTINE'S TENDENCY TO ILLUMINATE HIS LIFE by means of scripture intensified the coexistence and intermingling of temporal states. On one level he read scripture as literal truth. Thus Adam really lived in the Garden of Eden, he really ate the forbidden fruit, and, as an immediate consequence, he really experienced shame at his nakedness. Unlike some of his contemporaries, Augustine insisted on the literal meaning of scripture, lest one diminish God's majesty by relegating his actions to a merely symbolic realm. But Augustine also insisted that one should not mistake the literal for the principal sense of scripture, that the factual account constituted "the base and not the crown."[9] For example, the simple fact that Abraham had two sons, one by the slave Hagar and then one by his wife, Sarah, correlates with the fact that there are two testaments, Old and New, and this correlation illustrates that Christians rather than Jews are the true heirs of Abraham. The facts conveyed by scripture designate other realities that become apparent only in retrospect.[10]

This specific form of retrospective analysis is known as the "figural" or "typological" interpretation of scripture, from the Latin *figura* or the Greek *typos*. According to this reading of events, the two sons of Abraham "prefigure" the two testaments, and the testaments "fulfill" the figure of the sons, or (in typological language) the sons stand in relation to the testaments as "type" to "antitype." We will have occasion to examine this mode of scriptural analysis in greater detail later. Suffice it to say here that Augustine's figural way of interpreting the interplay between New and Old Testaments accustomed him to think retrospectively in general about the interplay between his life and scripture.

Oliver Wendell Holmes may have thought it a "rum thing to see a man making a mountain of robbing a pear tree in his teens," but for Augustine that act (to which he devoted the second book of the *Confessions*) replays the Fall, right down to the fruit tree.[11] Similarly (in the same book), he replays Adam's shame at his nakedness when he describes a trip to the public baths with his father, who delighted in the manifestations of his son's manhood. And (as noted above) gardens—especially the ones in Milan and Ostia—feature prominently in the *Confessions*. Indeed, themes from *Genesis* resound throughout a work whose penultimate book analyzes the biblical account of creation.[12]

Were we to regard such resonances as "merely" symbolic, we would miss a fundamental feature of Augustine's thought. His deeds not only symbolize the Fall but also derive their primary reality from it—and vice versa. The current flows both ways: the Fall derives its reality from these deeds, from the recognition that *he* is fallen. The deeper meaning of the scriptural account—beyond its mere literal truth—becomes intelligible when viewed in the context of his theft of pears, which dramatizes the significance of the events in the Garden of Eden. That drama occurs in the present, not the past, in the act of retrospection that connects the two. The past thus draws its reality from the present, not its "historical" but its "real" reality, its essential Christian truth as something lived and felt by a believer. We ought to take Augustine quite literally when he speaks of "a present of past things." The presence of the past within him takes precedence over the past as something outside himself. Indeed, past draws its significance from present in a Christian consciousness that transects these temporal states.[13]

In this form of consciousness scripture illuminates the connections between temporal states. When modern commentators emphasize the linear narrative of

Augustine's life—focusing on the by-product of his confessing rather than the activity itself—they lose sight of the fact foremost in Augustine's mind, that present memory constructs personal past. Without the illumination of scripture, memory would have been hopelessly lost. Its fundamental weakness rendered it incapable of making sense of an existence full of seemingly (and literally) forgettable occurrences, the least of which—a boyhood prank, a comment in the baths—might prove dramatically important. Scripture illuminated his life by rescuing from oblivion those apparently inconsequential things that convey the truth Augustine so urgently sought; and in turn, his life illuminated scripture by revealing the meaning embedded in its surface account, a meaning that might otherwise remain inaccessible. Thus, as one scholar says of Augustine's method of biblical interpretation, "We do not learn intelligible things from Moses or Paul or the Evangelists; we learn them by seeing them for ourselves in the eternal Truth. But the words of scripture are signs that direct our attention to what we could, but rarely would, see without them." In the *Confessions* past, present, and future conjoin in a Christian consciousness enlightened by the eternal Word.[14]

The Idea of the *Sæculum*

P aradoxically, Augustine's form of Christian consciousness—rooted in the *now*—coexisted with a notion of temporal progress. His sense of alienation from God was tempered by a peculiar form of optimism for the future. "Peculiar" because the space between present and Parousia remained profoundly ambivalent. In his sermons he decried it as a time of slow-motion death—moment by moment, breath by breath—and in the *Confessions* he bemoaned it as burdened with an almost unbearable longing. Yet it was also filled by the triumphal advance of the Catholic Church. For all his talk of pilgrimage, Augustine remained a lifelong Platonist with a deep love of philosophy, whose teachings had become the property of Catholic thinkers like Ambrose and Simplicianus. Augustine regarded the Catholic Church as the vessel of an intensely inward spirituality, disseminating the once esoteric truths of philosophy to the broadest possible audience.

This idealized view of Catholicism dovetailed with a more general conceit, that the conversion of the empire marked the onset of the *tempora christiana,* a "Christian era" witnessing the contemporary fulfillment of biblical prophecies. Early Christians had coined this expression as a value-free way of denoting the time after the advent of Christ, but by the fourth century it had begun to acquire ideological content, especially after the emperor Constantine legitimated Christianity. In his pathbreaking ecclesiastical history, Constantine's court bishop, Eusebius, asserted that the Roman Empire was divinely ordained for the spread of Christianity, as demonstrated by the birth of Christ during Augustus's *pax romana.* Subsequent ecclesiastical historians elaborated this providential view, seeing the swift spread of Christianity as the contemporary fulfillment of biblical prophecies. The notion of the *tempora christiana* thus became identified with the triumphal progress of Christianity in the fourth century.

Augustine initially resisted the ideological implications of this notion. In his early sermons and dialogues he expressly denied that one could comprehend the nature of God's plan for humanity beyond what was revealed in scripture; the space between biblical times and the present remained blank to human understanding. Of course, God had not ceased to operate in that space, but he had ceased to broadcast his intent. Around the time of the *Confessions,* though, Augustine began to loosen this stricture against identifying God's plan in recent events, largely because of the apparent triumph of Christianity, which culminated in the early 390s with the Theodosian decrees outlawing paganism. Swept up in the enthusiasm of the moment, Augustine belatedly added his voice to the chorus of the *tempora christiana,* despite an earlier reluctance to proclaim knowledge of God's postbiblical plans. In the heady days of an emergent Catholic Church and a triumphal Christianity, he found himself drawn toward an idea of progress potentially incompatible with a Christian consciousness rooted in the *now.*

THE VISIGOTHS' SACK OF ROME IN 410 called into question assumptions about the *tempora christiana* and the advance of Catholicism, revealing to Augustine the disparity between the ideology of progress and his avowed form of consciousness. Before this event he could readily and unthinkingly situate the personal act of confessing within a general framework of spiritual advance. But the sack of Rome confronted him with the necessity of finding a new context for Christian consciousness, one that better corresponded to the reality of a calamitous world. In *The City of God* he articulated a historico-theological conception of existence that extended his personal vision of temporal alienation to society as a whole, now conceived of as the *sæculum.*

In his magisterial study of Augustine's theology of history and society— entitled *Sæculum*—Robert Markus defines this term loosely as "the world of men and of time" (viii). It derives from the classical Latin word for "age," "generation," or "century," though it acquired a broader association with "the world" and "worldliness" in Latin translations of the Bible. It appears only infrequently in the *Confessions*, where it retains its classical and biblical meanings. In *The City of God* Augustine's usage of the term and its derivatives mushrooms—perhaps understandably, given his historical concerns—but it also acquires a more nuanced meaning. Instead of denoting the secular, as distinct from the sacred, it came to define the space in which sacred and secular intertwine, forming a braid that would only be untangled on Judgment Day. Or, described another way, the *sæculum* encompasses the mortal lives of all the descendants of Adam—past, present, and future—both saved and damned. Although time still retained its ambivalence for Augustine, and Christians still remained pilgrims within it, the circumstances of their alienation received much more subtle treatment once the lives of the saved and the damned were seen as intermixed in the same temporal vessel.

The idea of the *sæculum* realized on a historical scale the existential consequences of Augustine's radical reflexivity. In the *Confessions* he had described time as a distention of the self, as the ineffable point between expectation and memory, regardless of whether the object of the mind's attention was a psalm, a human life, or history in general. The notion of the *tempora christiana* had superficially complemented this personalized standpoint, enabling Augustine to fit his urge to confess within the pattern of Christian progress. When the sack of Rome forced him to discard this framework, he confronted a curious problem inherent in his personalized view of time. Whereas his mind existed within his body, which gave coherence to his consciousness, "human history had no physical body."[15] He now needed to find a principle of historical coherence to supplant that of the ideology of progress. The idea of the *sæculum* provides this principle by enclosing temporal space within an eschatological frame. "The world of men and of time" lay distended, as it were, between God and the Devil, constituting the temporal arena in which individuals choose their predestined fates—in which they continually enact their ever-present divine end. The historical analogue to Augustine's radical reflexivity, the *sæculum* exists both in and beyond time, enclosing transactions that are, to paraphrase Garry Wills, ultimately brokered in a no-time. The *sæculum* is the space where the *now* transpires.

Augustine's new principle of historical coherence addressed several issues obscured by the Christianization of the empire and now raised in high relief by the sack of Rome. The notion of the *tempora christiana* had provided a convenient providential interpretation for the ever-growing expanse of time between Incarnation and Parousia. Some even claimed that their age was witnessing the

establishment of God's thousand-year kingdom on earth, which would immediately precede the Second Coming. Providential views of history, and related
millenarian fantasies, obviated the need to consider further the nature of the
historical period after the Incarnation, even though that period was continually
lengthening. The sack of Rome shattered these pretenses, requiring an explanation for the strange persistence of time.

The period after the Incarnation was especially noteworthy for the dominance of the Roman Empire and, ultimately, for the triumph of Christianity.
Both these developments had been readily explained as the realization of biblical prophecies. In the wake of the sack of Rome, however, Christians needed to
reevaluate their relationship to the empire, lest they tie their faith too closely to
its fate. By the same token, debates about the nature of the institutional church
intensified once it became apparent that the heavenly kingdom was not at hand.
Was the church a devout community held to the highest standards of religious
purity, or was it a universal church open to people whose faith might fall short
of those standards? If the latter, how would one distinguish between the worldly
institution and its heavenly counterpart? Augustine addressed these issues in
The City of God, where he articulated, in Robert Markus's apt expression, "a
theology of the *sæculum.*"[16]

ALTHOUGH THIS MASSIVE WORK WAS OCCASIONED by the sack of
Rome, its gestation precedes that event, for Augustine had previously conceived
of writing on the theme of the heavenly and earthly cities, which had been explored by earlier church fathers like Tertullian. Augustine's personal interest in
this theme may have owed its origins to his practical experience as bishop of
Hippo, where his idealized Catholicism inevitably collided with a more carnal
Christianity. Here he also confronted the obdurate sect of the Donatists, who
claimed to constitute the only true African church, unpolluted by those who
had betrayed the faith during the last of the great persecutions. The exclusionary
church of the Donatists—who initially outnumbered Catholics in Hippo and
rivaled them in Africa—called into question the progressive advance of Catholicism and the philosophical ideal it embodied. These social realities may have
inspired Augustine to begin reconsidering the relation between the earthly and
heavenly cities, but the sack of Rome led him to incorporate this theme within
an entirely different project, an apology for Christianity that defined it over and
against classical culture. The sack of Rome necessitated this apology, both to
defend Christianity against the criticisms of a resurgent paganism and to stiffen
the resolve of Christians themselves, who now felt bereft of God's favor.

Augustine began writing *The City of God* around 412 and took nearly fifteen years to complete it, though he had a general conception of the entire work in mind from the very start. At the close of book 1 he sketched the broad structure of the work and detailed that of the first ten books, which defend Christianity against its pagan critics by reevaluating classical culture from within. Despite the advance of Christianity in the fourth century, paganism still claimed powerful and vocal adherents, like the poet/senator Symmachus, who had elevated Augustine to the chair of rhetoric in Milan. Such men even staged an impressive pagan revival in the late fourth century, targeting the culturally literate with an urbane defense of traditional Roman values. They drew their main support from the great authors of the late republic and early empire, including Cicero, Sallust, Livy, Virgil, and especially Varro, Rome's foremost antiquarian scholar. Augustine saw this cultured appeal to Roman traditions as a dangerous threat to Christianity, whose own idealized view of itself had suffered a serious setback. In the first ten books of *The City of God* he met this attack head-on and turned it at every point, using arguments drawn from classical authors like Varro to undermine the very traditions they had upheld. He aimed his disquisition at both educated pagans and the Christian elite, whom the sack of Rome had rendered more susceptible to the allure of pagan nostalgia.

Having done his learned best to demolish pagan cultural pretense in the first ten books, Augustine turned to the construction of a new theory of human existence in books 11 through 22. Here he tells the story of the origin, intertwining, and end of the heavenly and earthly cities, with the term *city* denoting a "society" or "association." Augustine embellished this story with lengthy digressions attending to various philosophical and theological issues, digressions that took on a life of their own as he buttressed the biblical account of humanity and its history against the weight of the classical tradition. The outlines of the biblical account as expounded by Augustine reveal his broader purpose, that of substantiating a Christian consciousness rooted in the *now*.

He describes how Adam and his ilk were originally created to inhabit the heavenly city, along with the angels, who would all bask eternally in the radiance of their Creator (books 11–12). But contumacious angels led God to cast them into hell, where they constituted the city of the Devil, and from whence they enticed Adam to sin. Being made of human rather than angelic stuff, Adam's sin landed him not in hell but in the corruptible, material world—"Earth thou art and onto earth thou shall return" (books 13–14). Here Adam's sons, Cain and Abel, constituted the "city of men" and the "city of God" respectively, as characterized by two loves, "the earthly city by the love of self, even to the contempt of

God; the heavenly by the love of God, even to the contempt of self" (14.28). Abel regarded himself as a "pilgrim" on earth and disdained any permanent habitation. Envious of his younger brother's devotion to God, Cain slew Abel and founded the first town, progenitor of the earthly city that would culminate in the work of another fratricide, Romulus (book 15). Augustine traced the history of the two cities, starting with the development of the city of God from Noah to Abraham to David to Christ (books 16–17). Similarly, he followed the course of the city of men through the great empires of antiquity, synchronizing these chronologically with events in the Bible (book 18). The last four books deal with the end of the two cities on Judgment Day, when the two loves will receive their respective rewards, with eternal damnation awaiting the lovers of self in the city of men and eternal salvation for the "saints" of the city of God.

"Heavenly city," "city of God," "city of men," "earthly city," "city of the Devil"—Augustine didn't always keep his terms straight over the many years, and many hundreds of pages, of composition. (Had he done so, he doubtless would have ruined a brilliant set of metaphors.) The phrases *heavenly city* and *city of God* are generally interchangeable and have either an eternal or a temporal referent, the latter designating those destined for eternal life. The phrases *earthly city* and *city of men* are more ambiguous; Augustine often uses them interchangeably, though they can have different temporal referents, and he occasionally obfuscates matters further by equating them with the "city of the Devil." Strictly speaking, though, the cities of God and the Devil are not of this world. They exist as eschatological entities, becoming fully manifest only at the end of time, when the citizenry of each will become known by its eternal reward. The "earthly city" is best conceived of as the temporal arena where the saved and the damned enact their divinely allotted fate; thus, we might in theory distinguish it from a more unabashedly pagan "city of men," with the caveat that Augustine did not always sustain this distinction in practice. (His lack of clarity reflects the fact that Christianity was arising within—and transforming—an age-old pagan culture, rendering its status ambiguous.) The Devil and his minions appear in the earthly city as demons—the pagan gods of the material world—luring people into idolatry. Whereas pagans love material existence as an end in itself, Christians treat it as a means to a higher end, the love of God. To the extent that their goal lies beyond this world, Christians are pilgrims—would-be citizens of the heavenly city—but they have long since lost Abel's luxury of shunning settled habitation, becoming instead involved in the life of the earthly city, as Augustine's account details. Thus their ultimate estrangement from that city does not preclude their immediate engagement with it. Indeed, they willingly attend to it as a temporal manifestation of their heavenly allegiance. For example, they uphold human laws and institutions conducive of earthly peace, which exists for them not as an end in itself but as a reflection of the eternal peace for which they yearn. The lives of Christians and pagans thus intertwine in the earthly city, even though they are lived for different purposes. This intertwining constitutes the *sæculum,* the arena in which the saved and damned work toward their respective ends.

Augustine's notion of the *sæculum* enfolds the temporal alienation of individual existence within a broader historical framework, conceived as finite and linear but not progressive. The *sæculum* originates with the earthly city of Adam's fall, culminates with the Incarnation of Christ, and concludes with his Second Coming. The first two events encompass the period of humanity's preparation for the gospel, as God has revealed in scripture. The final period, between Incarnation and Parousia, constitutes a *tempora christiana* only in the original, value-free sense of the term. Although scripture portends the ultimate outcome of history, which will end with the Second Coming, the immediate pattern of postbiblical events remains obscure. This period contains—indifferently—the rise of the Catholic Church, the Christianization of the empire, the sack of Rome, and whatever else God has ordained for humanity. The pattern of events is triumphal and progressive only in the restrictive sense that it ends by populating the cities of God and the Devil with their predestined citizenry.

In his "theology of the *sæculum*" Augustine resolved the major issues raised by the sack of Rome. First, he explained the ever-lengthening period after the Incarnation as the time designated by God to fill out the two eschatological cities, utilizing the divinely ordained instrument of individual human choice. Second, he established that Christians would necessarily remain engaged in the life of the state, despite recent setbacks, because they saw in its aims a pale reflection of the divine goal, though the gross imperfection of human law underscored the misery of their alienation from God. Third, he distinguished the visible, institutional church here on earth from the gathering of saints in heaven. Although he described the visible church as the City of God in worldly pilgrimage, Augustine nonetheless insisted that it included many not destined for salvation. In effect, he maintained only a loose connection between the population of the heavenly city and the spread of Christianity in the Roman world. His theology of the *sæculum* narrowly restricts the meaning of history, thereby insulating the faith from the unpredictable nature of events. Since the course of events lies beyond our understanding, we should fix our eye only on the ultimate end of human existence and live out life accordingly.

The City of God works out the consequences of Augustine's radical reflexivity on the grandest possible scale, applying it to humanity as a whole. The earthly city lies distended between God and the Devil, populated by citizens who will end up in either heaven or hell come Judgment Day. Were this distention between polarities of equal power—as in Manichaeism—time would be meaningless. But for Augustine the Platonist, evil is merely the absence of good; thus, humanity's distention becomes—for both the saved and the damned—the means of conveyance toward the divine end. Distention is merely the circumstance of humanity's continual passing away—from future to past—while the divine end is constantly enacted, ever-present in time's passage. The theme of the two cities transposes to history as a whole Augustine's personal view of time as an ineffable present circumscribed by memory and expectation, where the trinity of memory, attention, and expectation symbolizes the eternal amid the temporal. Augustine has simply shifted his perspective, viewing the human scene not from within but from without, from the God's-eye view afforded by scripture, where humanity's temporality is circumscribed by an ever-present eternity.

We should beware the modern tendency to regard temporal existence as constituting a continuum, for this notion bequeaths an intrinsic meaning to events that Augustine expressly denied. He insisted that events had no discernible meaning beyond what was revealed in scripture. This principle held true for all events, those of his personal life as well as broader, historical ones. Although the *Confessions* constructs a life, that story is utterly incidental to the ongoing act of confessing that serves as a continual acknowledgment of and surrender to the glory of God. Confession precludes autobiography. Similarly, although *The City of God* posits a linear historical scheme that begins with the Fall and ends with the Parousia, postbiblical events are not amenable to causal analysis on anything other than a trivial level. The real meaning of history is eschatological; only God has the key. This perspective devalues everything we regard as "historical," even though Augustine's scheme encompasses a linear expanse of time. He fixed his eye not on the expanse itself but on the fateful transactions occurring within it. The *sæculum* constitutes not so much a temporal continuum as the space of an ongoing transaction, the purpose and fulfillment of which is known only to God.

Commentators debate whether *The City of God* offers a "philosophy of history," a "theology of history," or a "theological interpretation of history."[17] All this hair-splitting misses the point because the term *history* assumes (on the part of these commentators) an idea of the past that Augustine didn't have. The notion of the two cities is not historical in any conventional sense: it does not trace the evolution from earthly to heavenly, from past to future; indeed, it does not imply any kind of evolution at all. Instead, it offers an antidote to the ideology of progress inherent in the notion of the *tempora christiana*. In response to this illusion Augustine sought to refocus attention on the ineffable moment of existence, now reconceived as the inextricable fusion of sacred and secular. All humanity lies distended between the two cities, with the right kind of love transforming distention into intention.

This insight into the nature of the human condition builds on the *exercitatio animi* that yielded Augustine's personal vision of time in the *Confessions*. Modern readers tend to pass over this *exercitatio* as unduly quaint or academic. Augustine, however, intended it not as a mere academic exercise but as a heartfelt expression of the interpenetration of past, present, and future. It confirmed the sense of integration he experienced while reading scripture. Just as scripture compensated for the weakness of personal memory, guiding the process of recollecting one's past, so, too, it guided any consideration of human history as a whole, revealing the eternal amid the temporal. Although this biblical perspective generated a vision of history as a self-contained entity with a beginning and an end, the immediate connections it fostered between past, present, and future—connections transecting these temporal states—precluded any sustained idea of anachronism by which to distinguish past from present.

The *Sæculum* Reconfigured

I t was Augustine's great misfortune to have an influential disciple who misunderstood him . . . or so the story goes. Sometime around 414, Paulus Orosius journeyed from his native Spain to Hippo, in Africa, most likely drawn by Augustine's reputation for Christian learning. After a yearlong stay with his mentor, and another year of additional study with Jerome in Palestine, Orosius accepted Augustine's commission to write what would become the *Historiarum libri VII adversus paganos*, or *The Seven Books of History against the Pagans*. Augustine had envisioned this work as an extended apology for Christianity, substantiating the argument—sketched chiefly in book 3 of *The City of God*—that the events of pagan Roman history were no less calamitous than those of Christian Rome and that Christianity thus bore no special blame for the recent sack of the city. Orosius promptly executed this commission with the tediousness of a dutiful student; but in so doing, he contaminated the *sæculum* with a notion of progress, setting forth the steady amelioration of civilization's woes after the coming of Christ. He thus admitted through a back door the very idea that his mentor had barred from the front, imparting to Augustine's aimlessly ongoing *now* a presumptuous sense of direction and purpose. Since medieval historians were far more likely to read *The Seven Books of History* than *The City of God*—thinking the former offered a shortcut to the latter—they unwittingly acquired a very un-Augustinian view of the *sæculum* as a linear, directional space where God makes his will known through the sequence of events.

This conventional story presents Augustine as the injured party, whose refined sensibilities got trampled in a clumsy disciple's rush to sacralize the *sæculum*. That Orosius exceeded his brief is undeniable, but this fact should not blind us to Augustine's own complicity in the demise of the *sæculum* as an autonomous space, neither sacred nor secular. To understand how he helped undermine his own idea, we must return to Augustine's figural view of scripture, a subject I briefly touched upon above, in my discussion of the *Confessions*. In theory Augustine attempted to restrict the range of the figural view by sharply distinguishing between biblical and postbiblical events, reserving the figural mode of interpretation for scripture only. But in practice he extended the figural beyond biblical events to encompass the Parousia, using it to circumscribe all of human history from start to finish. This extension of the figural enabled subsequent thinkers to sacralize the *sæculum* by interpreting recent events as prefiguring God's final judgment.

Augustine's reconfiguration of the figural to encompass all human history had momentous consequences not only for the nature of the *sæculum* but also for the emergence of a unitary conception of the past. As an indeterminate space the *sæculum* was simply the ongoing *now* of existence, where the meaning of events lay beyond human comprehension. But when he extended the figural mode to encompass the Parousia, he enabled his successors to conceive of the *sæculum* increasingly as a temporal rather than spatial entity, characterized by cause-and-effect relations that distinguish between past and present. The complete transformation from a spatial to a temporal conception, though, could not be effected as long as the figural mode remained the key to understanding the *sæculum*, for the cause-and-effect relations it revealed were not always governed by chronology. In the reconfigured *sæculum* the future had a peculiar way of reaching back into the past.

AUGUSTINE PLAYED A CRUCIAL ROLE in the development of the figural or typological view of scripture.[18] Derived from the Latin *figura* or the Greek

typos—as noted above—this way of reading the Bible constitutes a form of retrospective analysis connecting actors or events in the New Testament to their
"figures" or "types" in the Old. To use one commonplace example, Adam stands
as the figure or type for which Christ is the "fulfillment" or "antitype." In this
pairing, both Adam and Christ are real men, creatures of flesh and blood who
walked the earth, but the full significance of Adam in the divine plan cannot
be understood unless viewed from the perspective of Christ, whose Incarnation completes or fulfills the figure. This example pairs person to person, but
figural parallels can exist in every conceivable combination, between people
and events, people and institutions, events and events, events and institutions,
and so forth. The figural view traces back at least to the Pauline epistles, where
the apostle interpreted the books of Moses typologically in order to make Jewish history relevant to the Gentiles. In Galatians, for example, Paul retold the
story of Abraham's sons by the slave Hagar and his wife, Sarah, as prefiguring
the birth of the true church in Christ, which freed humanity from its enslavement to Jewish law. Paul's unsystematic pairings later gave way to a more thoroughgoing analysis of the parallels between Old and New Testaments by the
church fathers. Of the latter, Tertullian, in particular, resisted the tendency to
interpret figures allegorically as symbols. Instead he insisted (to quote Erich
Auerbach) that "*figura* is something real and historical which announces something else that is also real and historical."[19] In this way he preserved the full
reality of Old Testament accounts, which might otherwise have been reduced
to mere shadows of the New.

Tertullian was an early convert (c. AD 190) to an embattled church whose
recent emergence and struggle for survival testified to the imminence of the Second Coming. The new age heralded by the Incarnation was but the final confrontation before Truth's ultimate triumph, anticipation of which obviated any
need to consider the possibility of an extended "postbiblical history." For all
practical purposes, figural pairings of type with antitype circumscribed the to-
tality of events from creation to the present; Christians needed no further form
of historical explanation in a world that was about to end. All this changed—
gradually, with the stubborn persistence of the world after the Incarnation, and
suddenly, with Constantine's legitimization of Christianity. Indeed, as Robert
Markus has argued, "The conversion of an emperor, followed by the large-scale
christianization of society within a few generations, seemed to transform the
conditions of Christian existence dramatically, and certainly more visibly than
the great divide of the Incarnation."[20] No longer an embattled minority whose
very struggle for existence symbolized the "last days," Christianity had triumphed

so suddenly as to threaten its sense of identity as a beleaguered faith. A Christian idea of progress helped reconnect the present church of the emperors to the past one of the martyrs, but it rested on a fragile conceit, that the current age constituted the *tempora christiana* witnessing the fulfillment of God's prophecies. The sack of Rome would shatter this illusion and the sense of continuity it fostered.

At this critical juncture Augustine reconfigured the figural view of reality so as to encompass postbiblical history, creating a new kind of connection between past, present, and future that affirmed God's promise despite the vicissitude of events. Although he remained open to allegorical readings of scripture, Augustine always insisted on the underlying actuality of biblical accounts, which he elaborated figurally in the realist manner of Tertullian. *The City of God* abounds with commonplace figural parallels: between Noah's Ark and the church, Moses and Christ, Hagar and the Old Testament, Sarah and the New, Jacob and the Christians, Esau and the Jews. In these relations Augustine insists on the real, concrete nature of both figure and fulfillment, but he adds a new element to these commonplace parallels by asserting that a figure's earthly fulfillment itself stands as promise of a heavenly fulfillment come Judgment Day: "The Holy scripture, even when prophesying of things that are already done, outlines in a certain manner a figure of future things *[figuram deliniat futurorum]*."[21] A heavenly future thus parallels the earthly dyad of the Hebrews in the Old Testament and the Christians in the New.

This tripartite view of figural relations lay implicit in Tertullian and other early church writers—who had recognized that past, present, and future were all one in God—but Augustine made it explicit, especially after 396, when Simplicianus's prodding inspired the final, Pauline conversion that led him to write the *Confessions.* In the *De quaestionibus ad Simplicianum* Augustine espoused an idea of divine predestination that highlighted the tripartite unity of time in God: "For what is foreknowledge but knowledge of the future? But what is future to God who transcends all time? If God's knowledge contains these things, they are not future to Him but present; therefore it can be termed not foreknowledge, but simply knowledge."[22] The tripartite view of the figural constitutes the perfect analogue to God's (fore)knowledge, as we can see in *Contra Faustinum (Answer to Faustus)*, where Augustine penned one of his clearest expressions of figural relations: "For we are all aware that the Old Testament contains promises of temporal things, and that is why it is called the Old Testament; and that the promise of eternal life and the kingdom of heaven belongs to the New Testament: but that in these temporal figures there was the promise of future things, which were to be fulfilled in us, on whom the ends of the world are come, is no fantasy of mine, but the interpretation of the apostles, as Paul says, speaking of these matters."[23] In this expression of figural relations God foreordains everything, rendering past, present, and future as one.

The above passage from *Contra Faustinum,* which dates from around 398, clearly implies that the end is near, a conviction consistent with Augustine's newfound adherence to the idea of Christian progress, that the success of the religion points toward an inevitable climax. After the sack of Rome put paid to the illusion of the *tempora christiana,* the tripartite view of the figural assumed new importance for Augustine as a means of circumscribing the ever-lengthening expanse of postbiblical time, which he tethered to God's promise in the ever-receding Incarnation. Regardless of the vicissitude of events, God would fulfill the promise of the Incarnation in the Parousia, the reality of which—the ecstasy of the saved and the agony of the damned—Augustine detailed in the closing books of *The City of God.* In his mind the Parousia was as real an event as the Incarnation, even though it lay in the future. The concrete reality of this future for Augustine offers yet a further demonstration of the simultaneity of time in the *sæculum,* the space circumscribed by a divine will where past, present, and future coexist and commingle. This perspective renders the ebb and flow of events inconsequential to a Christian, for whom God's promise remains ever-present in the *now.*

The tripartite view of the figural fit so well into Augustine's theology of history that he overlooked its logical shortcomings.[24] How could the Christ of the Parousia be said to "fulfill" the Christ of the Incarnation if they are one and the same? (Typological relations are between *different* entities.) How could the Incarnation be said to "prefigure" the Parousia? (The former is normally described as "inaugurating" or "announcing" the latter.) How would the Parousia make the full significance of the Incarnation clear to Christians? (By definition, they already believe and trust in Christ.) Finally, how could the Incarnation remain "unfulfilled" until the Parousia? (The significance of the former is self-evident to believers.) Perhaps Augustine could have responded to any one of these questions in isolation, maintaining for instance that the Christ of the Parousia *is* different from the Christ of the Incarnation (though surely such an assertion would have opened a theological mare's nest). Taken together, however, these anomalies begin to overwhelm the tripartite system, raising legitimate doubts about whether Augustine has stretched the figural too far. In all likelihood his emphasis on the concrete reality of the Parousia obscured these anomalies, enabling him to extend the figural view into the future without a qualm.

By expanding the scope of the figural to encompass all of human history, Augustine unwittingly enabled his successors to transgress his own boundary between the biblical and postbiblical realms. He had reaffirmed the separation between the two after the sack of Rome—asserting that one cannot know God's will outside of scripture—in part because the Incarnation had trivialized the meaning of postbiblical events. Even the most cataclysmic of upheavals merely served as the backdrop for the individual's actions in the *now*: "And thus it is that in the same affliction the wicked detest God and blaspheme, while the good pray and praise" (*The City of God*, 1.8). The extension of the figural into the future, however, sometimes inclined Augustine to see these individual actions as prefiguring the final outcome. With an unremitting sternness, he claims in book 1 of *The City of God* that those who lost their lives and livelihoods in the sack of Rome may have had themselves to blame: "Some were tortured who had no wealth to surrender. . . . These too, however, had perhaps some craving for wealth, and were not willingly poor with a holy resignation" (1.10). This attitude borders on a providential interpretation of events. Although Augustine scrupulously stayed to his side of the divide—avowing that one could not know the will of God aside from scripture—he walked such a fine line that those attempting to follow his lead inevitably slipped to the other side.

IN HIS *SEVEN BOOKS OF HISTORY AGAINST THE PAGANS* Orosius fashioned a providential interpretation of history from a Eusebian notion of Christian progress and an Augustinian view of figural relations. In writing his history Orosius relied heavily on the works of Eusebius, especially his *Chronicle*, which Jerome had revised and extended. Eusebius had employed a literal (rather than figural) interpretation of scripture for the polemical purpose of establishing the antiquity of Christianity. He began his *Ecclesiastical History* by asserting that Christ (as Logos) oversaw creation and that he manifested himself to the Hebrew patriarchs (Abraham, Isaac, Jacob, Moses, Joshua), who worshiped him as Lord. The true religion of the Hebrew patriarchs eventually became perverted by a misguided emphasis on Jewish law, which brought down the wrath of God upon the Jews and their kingdom. Out of incessant war and discord, Rome eventually emerged to establish universal peace and a worldwide audience for the (re)proclamation of the one true religion. The Incarnation led to the immediate dissemination and success of the religion throughout the empire. Eusebius explained the subsequent Roman persecution of Christians as God's punishment—prophesied in Jeremiah and the Psalms—for dissension among the faithful, who had grown lax in their success. He concluded with an estimation of Constantine as the new Moses, who gained Rome (the new promised land) after God drowned his opponent, Maxentius (the new pharaoh), in the waters of the Tiber. For Eusebius biblical events literally foretold contemporary ones.

Orosius borrowed from Eusebius not only the identification of Christianity with Rome but also the willingness to connect biblical and contemporary events. Whereas Eusebius interpreted these connections literally, however, Orosius (dutiful student of Augustine) tended to regard them figurally. To some extent this tendency was inherent in Augustine's commission, which encouraged Orosius to look for parallels between pagan and Christian times to prove that the latter had no monopoly on calamity. But Orosius sometimes went beyond this simple task to give the parallels a distinctly figural "feel." In book 2, for example, he elicits a divine message from parallels between the sacks of Babylon and Rome:

> Thus Babylon, almost one thousand one hundred and sixty-four years after it had been founded, was despoiled of its wealth by the Medes and their king, Arbatus, moreover their prefect, and was deprived of the kingdom and king himself; yet the city itself remained unsubdued for sometime afterwards. Similarly, Rome also after the same number of years, was invaded by the Goths and their king, Alaric, also their count, and was despoiled of her riches, not of her sovereignty. She still remains and rules unsubdued, although between both cities by hidden decrees [of God] the order of the whole parallelism was so preserved that in the one case its prefect, Arbatus, seized the power and in the other its prefect, Attalus, tried to rule; yet in Rome alone was the impious attempt frustrated with the aid of a Christian emperor. (2.3)

The relation between these two events is more figural than literal. The sack of Babylon does not foretell the sack of Rome; but when the two are compared, the latter fills out the meaning of the former by showing how God ameliorated barbarian outrages after the advent of Christianity. Of course, Orosius has exceeded Augustine's brief by injecting a note of progress into his account, but even Augustine would have had to admire (perhaps grudgingly) the ingenious parallels his disciple drew between the two events, culminating with the similarity between the names of the two so-called prefects. Among believers, who generally found this kind of forced evidence compelling, only an Augustine could steadfastly deny that the hand of God was well and truly at work.

Technically, the above example is not figural, if only because it does not involve scripture; but one can readily see how the search for parallels could become explicitly figural when it included biblical events. In book 6, for example, Orosius describes Augustus Caesar's triumphal return to Rome in 29 BC, after he had defeated Antony in the last of the republican civil wars. On the day of his entry into the city, January 6, the Romans closed the doors of the temple of Janus, signifying that Rome—and hence the world—was finally at peace. This event recalled for Orosius God's promise of eternal peace through Christ: "There is no believer, or even one who contradicts the faith, who does not know that this is the same day, namely in the 6th of January, on which we observe the Epiphany, that is, the Apparition or the Manifestation of the Sacrament of the Lord. . . . It was proper to have recorded this event faithfully for this reason, that in every respect the Empire of Caesar might be proven to have been prepared for Christ's coming." The conclusion Orosius drew from this parallel is typically Eusebian— namely that God ordained the Roman Empire for the spread of Christianity— but he drew it by figural rather than literal means. The full significance of the closing of the temple doors only emerges when seen from the perspective of the Epiphany.

The Seven Books of History reflects the powerful influence of Eusebius, especially his willingness to connect biblical and postbiblical events. But Orosius established this connection by figural means, revealing the equally powerful influence of Augustine. Of course, Orosius's reliance on the figural may also derive from Jerome, his other mentor, who often utilized this mode of analysis; but Jerome did so in a less thorough and systematic way than Augustine. The latter not only established the Bible as the key to history, and the figural mode of analysis as the key to the Bible, but he also extended the figural to encompass the Parousia, thus using it to circumscribe all human events. Who could blame the disciple, when charged by the master with comparing pagan and Christian times, for employing the master's own methodology to explore the connection between sacred and secular events?

The nature of Orosius's commission necessarily limited his opportunities for figural interpretation. For the most part he had to content himself with cataloging the succession of wars and miseries in pre-Christian antiquity. The decline of the Roman Empire in the West, however, expanded the opportunities for figural analysis of contemporary events, which increasingly came to resemble biblical ones. In the late fourth and early fifth centuries, one could still cling to the illusion of a universal Roman rule endorsed by the birth of Christ; but by the sixth century even the illusion had vanished. Justinian's mighty efforts to reconquer Italy in the name of Rome made hardly any impression on the historian Gregory, bishop of Tours, whose world was dominated by a host of competing Frankish kings and kinglets. In the mind of a man thoroughly schooled in the Bible and patristic literature the jealousies, conspiracies, and conjurations of the kings of the Franks resembled nothing so much as the travails of the kings of Israel. Gregory simply could not resist the urge to understand contemporary events with reference to biblical stories about kingship; thus, he readily drew figural parallels between his own world and that of the Old Testament. A century and a half later, the Venerable Bede would entirely detach the figural mode from its anchor in scripture. In so doing, he would transform the *sæculum* from a spatial entity containing all human activity into a temporal entity charting God's purposive action in the world.

Gregory of Tours and the *Sæculum*

Historical writing languished in the Latin West from the time of Orosius until Gregory of Tours (c. 539–94), who has the distinction of authoring "the first Christian narrative of a Christian era."[25] Unfortunately, this salient work has been for centuries grossly misrepresented, right down to its supposed title—*The History of the Franks*—which Gregory himself would have disavowed. The work concludes with a list of his writings, where Gregory refers to the text as "*decem libros Historiarum*," which translates literally as *Ten Books of Histories* or, more colloquially, as *Ten Books of History*. In his exacting study of this work, Martin Heinzelmann favors the more colloquial rendition, arguing that Gregory used versions of the term *historia* to refer both to *books* of history and to *history* as the course of events; in effect, the ten books constituted for him a "continuous history" in the more abstract sense of the term.[26] Gregory thus deviated from classical usage, where *historia* simply denoted a body of literature written by historians, with no reference to any more expansive meaning. Our philological curlicue is not without a larger point, namely that his broader use of the term indicates that Gregory conceived of the field of human action as an integrated whole. Do not be seduced, though, by the sound of the word *history* into regarding the unity as temporal, deriving from chains of cause and effect that link past to present. Rather, the unity is still spatial. Gregory's *History* is nothing less than the realization of what Augustine meant by the *sæculum,* the space where sacred and secular intertwine, where past, present, and future coexist in the *now*. To entitle this work a "history of the Franks" is to distort it utterly.

Why, then, was this first Christian narrative of a Christian era so thoroughly misunderstood? Despite Gregory's closing plea to his episcopal successors that "you never permit these books to be destroyed, or to be rewritten, or to be reproduced in part only with sections omitted" (10.31), Carolingian propagandists beset the text in the mid-to-late seventh century, slashing it from ten books to six in order to fashion from it a history of the Frankish kings. The text subsequently circulated in both six- and ten-book versions until the twentieth century, when scholars finally concluded that the longer was indeed the original version. (The path to this conclusion may have been obscured by the standard assumption that old texts started out shorter and tended to get longer over time with later additions.)

Progress toward resurrecting Gregory's true intentions has also been slowed by a modern tendency to sell him short, to see him as a crude and credulous writer mirroring a "dark" age. Perhaps Gregory has himself to blame for this impression. In his preface to the work he famously laments the loss of learning in his day, as reflected in his own rustic style of writing. If he intended this statement as a rhetorical conceit—designed to confer trustworthiness to his account—it succeeded all too well. This and other instances of self-deprecation evoke the picture of him as a simple chronicler, recording events (to quote Lewis Thorpe's translation) in the "muddled and confused" order in which they occurred. "Muddled and confused"—this rendition of Gregory's barbarized Latin, *mixte confusequae* [sic], in the opening line of book 2 both summarizes and validates our reaction to the narrative. Yet we are so far removed from Gregory's mental world that we translate as an admission of authorial simplicity what he intended as a description of historical reality, of the *sæculum* where the heavenly and earthly cities intermingle.[27] Only by portraying this mixture could Gregory clarify the role of the city of God in human affairs.

BOOK 1 OF THE *HISTORY* BEGINS, significantly, with a confession of faith, "so that whoever reads me may not doubt that I am a Catholic." Those who greet Gregory's extended recitation of the Nicene Creed with either indulgence or impatience—waiting for him to be done with this silly ritual and get on with the show—miss the point. Herein lies the very purpose of historical writing for Gregory, to reveal the *ecclesia Christi*, the city of God in earthly pilgrimage. Though the lives of the saved closely intertwine with those of the damned—constituting a field of human action that is *mixte confuseque*—Christians must always remember that the "saints" compose an actual, distinct community, to which all should aspire to belong. For Gregory the city of God is not just an eschatological entity but a real one here on earth—existing not only in the future but in the past and the present as well—and the Nicene Creed delineates its boundaries.

This city is foreknown and foreordained by he who made the heaven and the earth "in his own Christ, that is in His own Son, who is the origin of all things." Gregory's rhetoric here is purely Eusebian, but the latter's argument for the antiquity of Christianity has lost its literal quality, becoming entirely figural. Christ presides over creation as God-made-man, as something more than just a disembodied logos, and prelapsarian Adam stands in relation to Christ as type to antitype (*Adam, antequam peccaret, tipum Redemptoris domini praetulisset* [1.1]). Similarly, just as Eve was made from Adam's rib, so, too, the Church (*ecclesia*) flowed from the wound in Christ's side. Figural relations, expressed and implied, come fast and thick in the opening chapter of book 1, conjoining Christ, Creation, Adam, Eve, and church in a dense web of meaning that transcends temporal distinctions.

The same figural pattern recurs throughout book 1, which covers the 5,596 years from the Creation to the death of St. Martin: Noah's Ark is the "concept" (*tipum*) of the Mother Church (1.4); Joseph, with his visions, stands as "forerunner" (*typum*) of the Redeemer (1.9); the parting of the Red Sea is a "symbol" (*tipum*) of baptism (1.11); the Babylonian Captivity is a "symbol" (*typum*) of the enslavement of the soul by sin, and Zerubbabel, who freed the Jews and restored the Temple, implicitly prefigures Christ (1.15). The seventh chapter epitomizes this figural mode, when Christ reveals himself to Abraham: to this Eusebian claim Gregory conspicuously adds a figural touch, that Abraham had reportedly been prepared to sacrifice Isaac on the site of Mount Calvary. The Incarnation and Resurrection occupy the central chapters of the book, which concludes with the death of St. Martin, the third and most illustrious bishop of Tours. Exactly midway between the accounts of Christ's ascension and Martin's death lies a chapter on Martin's birth. Here Gregory relates how it occurred during the reign of Constantine and coincided with the discovery of the remains of the true Cross. He thus implies a typological relation between Martin and Christ—as well as between the reigns of Constantine and Augustus—signified by the discovery of the true Cross and the chapter's theme of nativity. In his use of figural imagery Gregory has clearly erased the Augustinian distinction between biblical and postbiblical times.

Not only does Gregory's history abound with figural references, but it is figural in its very structure, as Heinzelmann reveals through a painstaking analysis of the chapters placed prominently at the beginning, middle, and end of each book. The prefatory chapter to book 2 establishes the fundamental typology—between the Franks and their kings and the Hebrews and theirs—that informs the entire work. Here Gregory introduces five antithetical pairings of priests, kings, and prophets drawn from the historical books of the Old Testament: between the righteous king/priest Samuel and the sacrilegious priest Phineas, between King David and the Philistine "king" Goliath, and between the godly prophets Elisha, Elijah, and the good king Hezekiah on the one hand, the Jewish people on the other. In the remaining books Gregory reveals the contemporary fulfillment of these biblical figures. The preface to book 3 pairs the blessed bishop St. Hilary with the heretical priest Arius, and the orthodox King Clovis with the heterodox Alaric, thus fulfilling the figural antitheses announced in the previous preface, between Samuel and Phineas and between David and Goliath. In subsequent books the bishops of the church—including Gregory himself—emerge in their relations with the kings of the Franks to fulfill the figure of the Old Testament prophets, showing the path toward righteousness. The overarching typological structure of the *History* reveals the fundamental parallel between the kings and prophets of Israel and the kings and bishops of the Franks.

This synchronicity serves a moral purpose. Far from naively chronicling the deeds of the Franks, Gregory's carefully structured work depicts the reality of the *ecclesia Christi* in a *sæculum* where the actions of saints and sinners lie *mixte confuseque*. One needs a guide through this thicket, lest one lose sight of God's plan and purpose. That plan is revealed not only by typological relations between the Hebrews and the Franks but also by the pattern of "miracles and slaughters" (in Walter Goffart's evocative phrase) common to both biblical and contemporary kingdoms. Thus, holy deeds "mix" with monstrous ones in a pattern that only seems "confused" when viewed in isolation, apart from God's archetypal actions in the Old Testament. Gregory consistently highlights this divinely decreed pattern at the expense of the narrative flow and historical coherence of his account. He freely breaks causal chains, disrupts plotlines, omits crucial details, and leaves events hanging—sometimes for chapters or even books—all for the sake of juxtaposing instances of good and evil. Indeed, God intended this "mixed and confused" pattern so that life in the *sæculum* would impart a spiritual lesson, which the continuity of fortune might otherwise obscure.

Two examples should illuminate the divine lesson Gregory sought to illustrate. Sandwiched between accounts of the birth and death of St. Martin, the penultimate chapter of book 1—"The Chaste Lovers"—seems like a digression. Despite its unusual length and conspicuous detail, modern readers dismiss it unthinkingly as a credulous tale inserted by a rustic author amid more important material. It recounts how a young bride on her wedding day lamented not being able to dedicate her body to Christ; how the groom—touched by her devotion—acceded to her wishes; how they slept in perfect chastity side by side throughout their long marriage; how, after her death, the wife spoke lovingly to her husband from her bier as he offered her unsullied body to the care of Christ; how, the morning after the husband's own death and burial, their tombs (which had been placed along separate walls of a chamber) were found lying side by side.

This story recalls what Gregory had written earlier about the parting of the Red Sea—a symbol *(tipum)* of baptism—where he likened the *sæculum* to a sea *(hoc saeculo, quod figuraliter mare dicitur)* that parts in different ways for different people. Some (like the virginal wife) pass through in the first hour: "These are they who are reborn by baptism, and are thus able to remain unsullied by any defilement of the flesh until they reach the end of their life here below" (1.10). Others (like the abstemious husband) "are hired to work in the Lord's vineyard" at later hours of life, depending on when they are converted from the flesh. The story of the chaste lovers illustrates the different paths to holiness, while demonstrating that the saints live among us. Christ, Martin, the virginal wife, the abstemious husband, and innumerable others still walking on this earth all belong to the same godly community, the *ecclesia Christi,* whose heavenly presence in the here-and-now is attested by divine miracles.

The story of the death of St. Salvius, bishop of Albi, further illustrates that the city of God coexists in heaven and on earth. This story stands conspicuously at the beginning of book 7, the crucial juncture between the account in books 5 and 6 of the godless king Chilperic and his evil queen, Fredegund, and the account in books 7 through 9 of the reign of the good king Guntram. (Gregory, who as bishop of Tours had confrontations with Chilperic and Fredegund, implicitly likens himself in books 5 and 6 to Elijah prophesying against Ahab and Jezebel; and Guntram fulfills the role of Hezekiah in books 7 through 9.) The demise of Chilperic's dynasty—forecast by St. Salvius at the end of book 5—occurs at the end of book 6, clearing the way for the great narrative transition from the story of a godless king to that of a righteous one. Yet in the first chapter of book 7 Gregory conspicuously (and typically) interrupts the narrative flow with a lengthy account of the two deaths of St. Salvius.

Like the virginal wife in the "Chaste Lovers," Salvius had resolved as a layman to dedicate his body to Christ. Ultimately, though, he chose to abandon secular life altogether and enter a monastery, where he so devoted himself to God that he eventually became abbot. Far from taking pride in his new office,

Salvius withdrew even farther within the monastery, while not ceasing to pray fervently for others. Time and again the sick went away healed after his intercessions. When he finally died, his fellow monks spent the night in vigil over his body; but come morning it stirred, and he came back to life. Despite the beseeching of his brethren, he remained silent for three days, taking neither food nor drink, before he finally spoke of his experience in heaven. He described how he had stood among the saints—angels, martyrs, and holy men—how they had all basked in the radiance of a luminous cloud brighter than any light, and how they had required no further nourishment than the sweet perfume in the air they breathed. Then a voice announced from the cloud, "Let this man go back into the world, for our churches have need of him." Against his protestations— but assured of his eventual return—Salvius was transported to the land of the living, where he was sustained for three days by the perfume of heaven, until he finally broke his silence. Gregory concludes with an account of Salvius's later life, as abbot and then as bishop of Albi, where he counseled others always to act in such a way "that if God should decide to recall you from this world, you may enter not into His judgment but into His peace."

Bishop Salvius died a holy man in the same year as the wicked king Chilperic, whose end he had prophesied. Let one ponder their contrasting fates at one's leisure, never forgetting that the city of God is *now*. Though they have their place in heaven, the saints walk among us, and some may even be sustained on this earth (if only for a few days) by heavenly perfume. Who can in good conscience defy such holy men? The story of St. Salvius—a seeming digression— really sets the stage for the account of the good king Guntram, who, in respecting his bishop/prophets and following the will of God, demonstrates his devotion to the *ecclesia Christi*.

GREGORY'S *SÆCULUM* IS LESS A TEMPORAL ENTITY than a spatial one. True, his account of contemporary events moves year by year, and the entire *History* encompasses (by his tally) 5,792 years. That's quite a long time . . . almost as long as the wanderings of Odysseus! The point is that Gregory, like Homer and Herodotus, thinks of a long expanse of time as duration, as an indeterminate continuum with no chronological reference points. But (one might object) what about the Incarnation? Doesn't the prominence of that event distinguish Gregory's continuum from Homer's? True, the Incarnation and Resurrection occupy the central chapters of book 1, but Christ also appears prominently at the beginning and end of the book. Indeed, Christ is present at Creation, Christ is prefigured by Adam and Eve, Christ reveals himself to Abraham,

Christ is prefigured in Joseph's visions, Christ is prefigured by Zerubbabel. . . . Christ is everywhere—even (and especially) in the birth of St. Martin, "our new luminary" of holiness (1.39). In effect, the ubiquity of Christ obliterates the prominence of his coming as a landmark event.

But (one might continue to object) surely men like Clovis, Chilperic, and Guntram represent prominent figures giving distinctive shape to their world. True, Gregory presents vivid stories about recent and contemporary kings and bishops, who appear in much higher relief than their biblical counterparts. Their importance, however, lies not so much in their actions—the account of which Gregory freely sacrifices to his moral aims—but in the fact that they parallel biblical lives. Contemporary figures serve to illustrate the continuity of an ongoing biblical pattern, in which God intended good and evil to lie *mixte confuseque,* so that one would not lose sight of him and his *ecclesia* here on earth. Gregory's 5,792 years thus constitute a spatial rather than a temporal expanse, a field of human action bound together and rendered homogeneous by the figural view of reality.

Augustine could hardly have foreseen this outcome when he extended the figural view to encompass the Parousia, but his instinct to separate biblical from postbiblical history was right on the mark. When Gregory openly violated this boundary—when he began using scripture as a guide to understanding contemporary developments—he unwittingly undermined the distinctive reality of biblical events, which were relegated to the status of mere symbols. What we fail to realize—because we are blinded by the modern distinction between past and present—is that this effect works both ways: contemporary events became no less symbolic for Gregory than biblical ones. The extension of the figural view into postbiblical times drained *all* events of their distinctiveness, even the ones Gregory recorded with such characteristic vividness.

Ironically, the homogeneity of Gregory's historical outlook enabled him to approximate best what Augustine meant by the *sæculum.* Unlike Orosius, whom he read and admired, Gregory did not contaminate the *sæculum* with an idea of progress. To some extent the tumultuous world of the successor states could not have accommodated this rosier view of Christianity. But once Gregory discovered the connection between the kings and people of the Franks and the kings and people of Israel, he rendered all history meaningless, at least as a sequence of events. His figural parallels eliminated the idea of progress from the *sæculum* and reasserted the fundamental vicissitude of events, which God intended as a reminder of human vanity and a test of human devotion. Like Augustine, Gregory maintained that this indeterminate pattern would continue until Judgment Day, intimations of which appear in the tenth and final book of the *History*.[28] Only then would God reveal the meaning of events.

Gregory tethered contemporary events to biblical ones. To my knowledge, he did not conceive of figural relations as existing between pairs of postbiblical events. Of course, he did parallel the age of Constantine with that of Augustus, but the latter is still arguably biblical (albeit associated with the New rather than Old Testament). And he did conceive of a relationship between himself and St. Martin, but the latter does not so much prefigure as precede Gregory in a line of episcopal succession akin to those established by Eusebius in his *Ecclesiastical History*. Finally, he did sometimes list contemporary events out of chronological order—which (as we will see) can be an index of figural relations—but he does so only for dramatic effect and not to establish some figural tie between otherwise unconnected events.[29] For Gregory, figural relations had to be anchored in scripture, in the truth of God's word.

Bede would loose this anchor, freeing the figural from its hermeneutical moorings and enabling it to become a self-contained view of the world. Of course, it would still serve the theological purpose of revealing the workings of God's will in time. Augustine had limited that knowledge to what is revealed in scripture, and Gregory had connected these revelations to contemporary developments. Following the path first trod by Gregory, Bede would connect English history to scripture, but then he would go on to show how one recent event prefigured another, giving rise to a new sense of God's purposive action in the world. In so doing, he furthered the transformation of the *sæculum* from a spatial to a temporal entity. Ironically, though, Bede's Christian notion of time freely violates our modern notion of chronology, scrambling the temporal distinctions between past, present, and future by allowing the future to reach back into the past.

Back from the Future
Bede and the Figural View of Reality

Of the early narrators of barbarian history, Gregory of Tours and St. Bede are frequently compared, much to the advantage of the latter. Bede (673–735)—entitled "Venerable" since the ninth century—lived all his life in Benedictine monasteries in the Anglo-Saxon kingdom of Northumbria, first at St. Peter's in Wearmouth and then, from boyhood on, at

St. Paul's in nearby Jarrow. The commonplace portrait of him as a cloistered monk writing in contemplative seclusion has sufficed to explain the scholarly and narrative virtues of his *Ecclesiastical History of the English People,* which provides a much more coherent and gripping account of the Anglo-Saxons than Gregory's *Ten Books of History* does of the Franks. This commonplace confirms and reinforces our modern bias that narrative coherence—characterized by clearly plotted lines of cause and effect—is the norm toward which historical accounts naturally evolve. From this perspective Gregory's history appears "primitive" in comparison to Bede's because of the less settled times and condition of the Franks and their chronicler. By now (hopefully) one senses at least a whiff of tautology in this explanation, which devolves upon a judgment about the proper narrative standard of historical accounts. This judgment ignores the fact that Gregory achieved exactly what he set out to do, namely depict the *sæculum* as God intended one to experience it, *mixte confuseque.* Modern notions of historical coherence have no place in Gregory's world, a fact that makes Bede's subsequent approximation of these standards appear all the more unnatural and anomalous. What enabled him to construct, by our lights, such a coherent narrative?

To answer this question, we must revisit Augustine's vision of the figural, which he had expanded to encompass the Parousia. This innovation rendered Augustine's historical viewpoint firmly eschatological—one could know the meaning of postbiblical events only on Judgment Day, when God would dispense eternal reward and punishment for human action. Neither Eusebius nor Orosius shared this eschatological view, for they regarded God as having made his judgment evident in this world, through the conjoined success of Christianity and the Roman Empire. Orosius even declared prominently, at the beginning of book 2 of his history, that one didn't need scripture to perceive God's will in human affairs: "Therefore, that all power and all ordering are from God, both those who have not read feel, and those who have read recognize." God revealed his will in events as well as in scripture, as the coming of Christ during the age of Augustus clearly indicated.

Gregory of Tours did not share this assurance—which was based on a fragile conceit that went the way of the Roman Empire in the West—and he closed his history with somber references to the approach of Judgment Day. For Gregory, the nature of the last judgment could not be predicted from events, in part because it was known only to God and in part because it was subject to change. In one of the most horrific passages of his entire history, Gregory describes how

King Lothar consolidated his power by remorselessly killing his two nephews, mere boys who begged their uncle in vain for mercy as he personally butchered them (3.18). Ten short chapters later, Gregory recounts how Lothar found himself hopelessly surrounded by hostile armies, put his faith in God, and was saved by divine intervention (the storm that flailed the surrounding armies with hail left his encampment dry and untouched). Clearly, it's never too late to repent, as Lothar again demonstrates when, in the fifty-first and final year of his reign, he confessed all his evil deeds before the tomb of St. Martin. Gregory reiterates the theme of timely repentance at the opening of the last, eschatological book of his history, which begins with an exhortation by Pope Gregory I to the plague-stricken people of Rome: "None of you must despair because of the enormity of your sins." Although the end is near, the outcome remains up for grabs until the final moment of life.

Bede shares Gregory's eschatological outlook but not its indeterminacy. The finality of God's judgment is readily apparent to Bede from the outcome of events. He interprets the history of the English people and their church figurally: much like Gregory's Franks, Bede's Anglo-Saxons are a chosen people, the new Israelites, but the resemblance of approach ends here. Gregory tethers recent events to biblical ones in binary pairs, whereas Bede creates figural chains that extend outward, from scripture to one postbiblical event after another. These chains—which follow a narrative but not always a chronological order—account for the greater coherence of Bede's historical vision. He interweaves events so seamlessly as to obscure the points where the narrative flow parts company with chronology—where the future reaches back into the past, giving added impetus to the course of events. Bede's eschatological viewpoint makes this retrogressive move possible, for he sees the Last Judgment as the fulfillment in eternity for actions taken in time, where earthly outcomes prefigure divine rewards. Admittedly, this vision goes far beyond what Augustine intended when he extended the figural view to encompass the Parousia; but without Augustine's innovation, Bede's eschatological perspective on the figural would have been inconceivable.

BEDE BEGINS HIS HISTORY IN THE MANNER of Orosius, with a geographical overview of his subject that establishes Britain's position in the known world; but this traditional opening leads almost immediately into figural territory: "At the present time there are in Britain, in harmony with the five books of the divine law, five languages and four nations—English, British, Irish, and Picts. Each of these have their own language; but all are united in their study of God's truth by the fifth—Latin—which has become a common medium through the study of the scriptures" (1.1). From the five books of Moses to the five languages of Britain, the figural parallel is unmistakable—God has special plans for the people of this island. And, as if to drive the point home, Bede composes his history in five books. These provide an account of the English people and church in particular—of the Anglo-Saxons who established themselves on the island, converted to Christianity, and quickly became one of the leading lights of the Catholic faith. In Bede's figural interpretation of history the English are God's new chosen people.

They were invited to the island by the feckless British, the original inhabitants who had earlier submitted to Roman rule and converted to Christianity. Bede's stirring tale of the martyrdom of St. Alban notwithstanding (1.7), he judged the British unreliable Christians, susceptible to every kind of heresy because of their readiness "to listen to anything novel, and never hold firmly to anything" (1.8). After the Romans abandoned the island, the British threw off the yoke of Christ and lived wantonly until struck by a terrible plague: "But not even the death of their friends or the fear of their own death was sufficient to recall the survivors from the spiritual death to which their crimes had doomed them" (1.14). They consequently incurred further punishment at the hands of the Irish and the Picts, who began to raid their land. Hard-pressed by these incursions, the British called for aid from the peoples of Germany—the Saxons, Angles, and Jutes. "This decision, as its results were to show, seems to have been ordained by God as a punishment on their wickedness" (1.14).

Bede has clearly adopted a biblical tone here: God rewarded the faithless British as they deserved—with the plague, the raids of the Irish and the Picts, and the coming of the Anglo-Saxons. But he casts this story of divine retribution in a figural mold shaped by eschatology. His interpretation of events works backward from Judgment Day, from the above-mentioned "spiritual death" to which the British had doomed themselves through their wickedness. (Note, by comparison with Gregory's account, how Lothar's wickedness does not necessarily presage his eternal punishment.) Bede's greater assurance about divine intentions derives from his eschatological viewpoint, wherein the extension of the figural to the Parousia transforms earthly actions into prefigurations of their ultimate fulfillment in eternity.

This eschatological viewpoint becomes explicit in Bede's description of St. Augustine of Canterbury's mission to Britain. Eventually known as the "Apostle of the English," Augustine had been sent to the island by Pope Gregory

I to preach to the Anglo-Saxons after the British had neglected to convert them to Christianity. Bede sees this negligence as final and irrefutable proof of the wickedness of the British, whose laxness would have condemned the Anglo-Saxons to eternal damnation, had not God remembered his chosen people and inspired Gregory to send them an apostle in 596. The account of Augustine's mission, beginning in chapter 22 of book 1, follows hard on the heels of the fall of the Roman Empire in the West (1.21) and marks the true beginning of Bede's history of the English and their church.

Augustine's mission culminates in the second chapter of book 2, with Bede's account of events leading up to the battle of Chester in 615, which resulted in the slaughter of the faithless British. After his arrival on the island, Augustine and his fellow missionaries had established themselves in Kent, where they lived such exemplary lives as to inspire the conversion of the local king, Ethelbert, in 597. Pope Gregory subsequently consecrated Augustine as bishop of the English. In this capacity, and with the aid of Ethelbert, Augustine summoned the leaders of the British church to a conference in 603, intending to cure them of heresy (they did not celebrate Easter on the proper date) so that they could pursue the conversion of the Anglo-Saxons in unity with the Catholic Church. Despite miracles attesting to the truth of the Catholic position, the British remained obdurate, whereupon Augustine uttered a prophecy: "If they refused to accept peace with fellow-Christians, they would be forced to accept war at the hands of enemies; and if they refused to preach to the English the way of life, they would eventually suffer at their hands the penalty of death." This prophecy came true in the battle of Chester, when Ethelfrid, the pagan king of the Northumbrians, crushed not only the British but their false priests, massacring the monks of Bangor almost to a man: "Thus, long after his death, was fulfilled Bishop Augustine's prophecy that the faithless Britons, who had rejected the offer of eternal salvation, would incur the punishment of temporal destruction."

Bede's figural relations reach back to the Old Testament, to the Hebrews who prefigure the English; but unlike Gregory, Bede does not content himself with binary parings of figure and fulfillment. Instead, he creates causal chains: the failure of the British to preach to the new chosen people (brazenly abandoning the Anglo-Saxons to spiritual death) prefigures the actual death in battle of the British at the hands of those they would have consigned to hell, which itself prefigures God's final judgment on the British, "who had rejected the offer of eternal salvation." The chain's anchor lies in the future rather than the past, in God's final judgment. This eschatological perspective makes the chain perceptible, despite the twelve years separating the battle of Chester from the events that prefigured it. Bede—ever sensitive to chronology—notes the temporal gap between the events in question but only after having established their figural connection in a way that leaves no narrative gap. The future thus guides the course of events, in the specific sense that the judgment of history reflects the Last Judgment.[30]

Bede's narrative flows not only from past to future but from future to past. By allowing the future to reach back into the past, Bede gives added impetus to his figural interpretation of events. One might be tempted to attribute this feature of the narrative to chronological naiveté were it not for Bede's very evident skill in this area. The author of two treatises about chronology—*On Time* and *On the Reckoning of Time*—Bede always knew when he was inverting the order of events, as indicated by his circumlocutions. In chapter 16 of book 1, for example, we encounter the story of a Roman, Ambrosius Aurelianus, who led the British to their "first" victory over the Angles, who soon thereafter suffered a decisive defeat in the battle of Badon Hill (recall that the dispirited British had sought Anglo-Saxon aid in fending off the Irish and Picts). The chapter ends with a chronological reference: "This took place about 44 years after their [the Anglo-Saxons'] arrival in Britain, but I shall deal with this later." The next chapter—which begins with the line, "A few years before their arrival . . ."—inaugurates the story of the Bishops Germanus and Lupus, who journeyed from Gaul to help the British combat the Pelagian heresy and ended up leading the British to victory over the combined forces of the Saxons and the Picts. The battle—detailed in chapter 20—was won by prayer, when Germanus and Lupus led the British army in shouts of "Alleluia," whose echoes frightened off the pagans. "So the bishops overcame the enemy without bloodshed, winning a victory by faith and not by force."

The narrative flow in these chapters progresses from a bloody victory achieved by human means to a bloodless victory achieved by divine means. To establish this narrative, however, Bede has had to reverse the chronological order of events: Germanus and Lupus came to Britain *before* the arrival of the Anglo-Saxons, whereas the battle of Badon Hill occurred forty-four years *after* their arrival. Bede has knowingly reversed the order of events so as to cast them in a figural light. The accomplishments of Ambrosius, culminating with the victory at Badon Hill, prefigure those of Germanus and Lupus, whose divine victory—won solely by faith—fulfills the meaning of the human one. An eschatological perspective makes this reversal wholly legitimate in Bede's eyes, for past, present, and future lie bound together in God's judgment.[31]

FOR OUR PURPOSES BEDE COMPLETES the transformation of the *sæculum* from a spatial to a temporal entity. The former encompassed the seemingly aimless vicissitude of human events, whereas the latter detailed a narrative of God's purposive action in the world. Yet the figural view of reality that held Bede's *sæculum* together rendered its temporality of an entirely different sort than we moderns would expect. We read his figural chains as if they were chains of cause and effect, despite the fact that Bede sometimes allowed the "effect" to precede the "cause." Even when we become aware of these temporal inversions, we tend to regard them as anomalies, as quaint lapses in an otherwise coherent chronological narrative. But we should really regard them as windows onto an underlying, eschatological reality, which enabled Bede to look backward from a Parousia that lies in the future. This eschatological perspective determines the true relationship between events in Bede's narrative, one that is temporal without being chronological.

Although Bede's grand historical narrative remained without any successor until the later Middle Ages, other kinds of historical writing came to the fore in the interim, most notably the chronicle in its many manifestations. This form, too, is characterized by an eschatological viewpoint that reveals itself in figural relations. Medieval chroniclers showed great precision in establishing the order of events and great ingenuity in developing parallel dating systems to distinguish events occurring simultaneously in different realms. Nonetheless, the chroniclers also felt free to detach people and events from their carefully elaborated temporal contexts and pair them with others, from widely different contexts. As Hans-Werner Goetz observes, "A typological way of thinking enabled the chroniclers to detect (or even construct) a correlation of events that was widely separated in place and time"; this form of "detemporalization" derived from an eschatological perspective, "based on the conviction that all history was God's revelation of the process of salvation."[32]

The typological habit of mind—which had already become second nature by the twelfth century—reached its fullest expression in Dante's *Divine Comedy*. The details of Dante's figural view of reality need not detain us; Erich Auerbach, among others, has described them at length in several famous studies. Suffice it to say that Dante's depiction of sinners in the *Inferno* acquires its remarkable vividness from a figural perspective, whereby the defining characteristics of the individual in life are amplified in hell, becoming the defining aspect of the sinner's torment. In other words, the individual in hell fulfills the character of the individual in life, whose earthly existence prefigures his eternal state. What better expression of the eschatological perspective that looks back from the future!

WE HAVE COME A LONG WAY from Augustine's *Confessions,* but the sensibilities he expressed there had an enduring afterlife. Augustine gave voice to a Christian consciousness rooted in the *now* that most of his contemporaries could only feel inchoately (that it resonated deeply with them accounts for the popularity of the work). While this form of consciousness devalued the linear and episodic "pasts" of classical antiquity, it also left no room for the development of "the" past. Not only did his existential stance preclude this idea, but so, too, did his figural mode of scriptural analysis, which was augmented informally by his tendency to seek the parallels between his life and scripture. These tendencies reveal the coexistence of past, present, and future in the *now,* leaving no room for a past distinct from the present. What better proof of this contention than the fact that Augustine omitted his most significant conversion from the account of his spiritual odyssey? From his standpoint in the *now* he did not perceive the past as an autonomous conceptual entity.

In *The City of God* Augustine transmuted his personal standpoint in existence to a social level, via the notion of the *sæculum.* This notion marks an important development in the birth of the past, for it enabled Christians to conceive of human action as an integrated whole; it gave them the potential to transcend the fragmented pasts of classical antiquity. But the *sæculum* still remained rooted in the *now,* for Augustine conceived of it as a spatial rather than temporal entity—the place where sacred and secular actively intertwine. Ironically, though, he gave his successors a means of subverting this space—of sacralizing the *sæculum*—when he expanded the figural view of reality to encompass the Parousia. This move made it possible for them to interpret the whole *sæculum* figurally, including not only biblical but postbiblical events. Orosius first recognized this possibility, and Gregory of Tours transformed it into the organizing principle of his history, which drew figural parallels between the Franks and the Israelites.

With Bede the figural mode of analysis came fully into its own as a freestanding view of reality, detached from its anchor in scripture. Although Bede drew figural parallels between the English and the Israelites, he also drew figural parallels between contemporary events, without any direct reference to scripture. These figural chains give his account its extraordinary narrative coherence as the story of God's action in the world, thus transforming the *sæculum* from a spatial to a temporal entity. But Bede's conception of temporality bears little resemblance to our own, for it takes its start from the end of time and works backward. This characteristic reflects the persistence of Augustine's vision of Christian consciousness as rooted in the *now,* where past, present, and future come together as one. Although Augustine, Gregory, and Bede could refer to the past colloquially as the time before the present, they could not conceive (in Janet Coleman's terms) "the pastness of the past," as something systematically different from the present (294). No "pastness" . . . no past.

PART THREE

Renaissance

What is all history but praise of Rome?

—Francesco Petrarca, *Against a Detractor of Italy*

Every example is lame.

—Michel de Montaigne, *Essays*

The Living Past

An icon of High Renaissance art, Raphael's *School of Athens* adorns a room in the Vatican's papal apartments, the Stanza della Segnatura, or "Room of the Segnatura," so named for the papal tribunal that originally met there. By the time Raphael began decorating this room around 1508, it was intended to house Pope Julius II's library and serve as his personal study. The pope commissioned from Raphael four frescoes that together would illustrate the general theme of wisdom as the union of truth, beauty, and goodness. Raphael reserved the two largest walls for the depiction of sacred and secular truth. His first effort, the *Disputation of the Holy Spirit,* symbolizes sacred truth in the church's marriage of heaven and earth. Directly opposite it stands his second effort, the *School of Athens,* which portrays secular truth as a gathering of great philosophers. Along the side walls he placed *Mount Parnassus* (embodying beauty in the form of the muses and poets clustered around Apollo) and *The Cardinal and Theological Virtues* (representing goodness). Although the young Raphael conceived of this quartet (and its complement of ceiling frescoes) as a thematic whole, he gained artistic confidence as he worked, manifesting his full genius in the *School of Athens* (see illustration on cover).

In Leonard Barkan's succinct judgment this fresco presents "the quintessential image of the chronological encounter between Renaissance and antiquity."[1] A monument to Renaissance humanism and its rediscovery of the classical past, the *School of Athens* depicts the great ancient philosophers in a manner we may describe as "historically correct," with each figure suitably clothed, standing in the proper company, and bearing the book or instrument that best characterizes his work. At the very center, framing a vanishing point that recedes between them through a succession of arches, stand Plato and Aristotle, the teacher bearing a copy of his *Timaeus* and pointing upward toward the eternal Ideas that inform the corporeal world, the pupil holding his *Ethics* and gesturing outward toward the corporeal world from which all knowledge derives. To either side of these contrasting figures, others stand or sit in various circles, each cluster intent on its own discussion. Only two figures remain apart. One, traditionally identified as Diogenes—the Cynic who disdained social convention and material wealth—lies alone in a scant robe, sprawling indecorously in the middle ground; the other, gloomy Heraclitus, sits in the foreground, brooding in downcast thought. The painting gathers all these figures together in an idealized Athenian *stoa* that both symbolizes the space of classical discourse and encompasses the collective wisdom of the ancients.

Upon reflection, though, one may consider the setting a bit incongruous. Raphael arrays his sages on steps that rise toward a succession of massive arches, two of which uphold between them an airy dome, whose pillared window frames a bit of cloud floating in the blue sky. This would-be *stoa* owes more to the soaring vision of Bramante—recalling his plan for the reconstruction of St. Peter's— than to a classical Athenian portico. Indeed, one of the clustered figures in the right foreground—whether Euclid or Archimedes—bears Bramante's likeness. And Heraclitus bears Michelangelo's, Plato Leonardo's, Apelles Raphael's (staring straight out at us)—with the host of other presumed and possible transpositions having spawned a small scholarly industry. Tributes to contemporaries are, of course, commonplace in Renaissance painting—where patrons in particular often end up commemorated in the works they sponsor—but Raphael's transpositions serve to elevate himself and his fellow artists to the status of philosophers and sages. In so doing, he evokes an ideal community that transcends temporal and geographical limits. In the circle to the left of Heraclitus/ Michelangelo, a turbaned Averroës stands near the shoulder of Pythagoras, despite the thousand plus years—and thousand plus miles—that separate the medieval Spanish Arabian from the (presumed) pre-Socratic Greek. And beside Apelles/Raphael stand Zoroaster and Ptolemy—three figures (or maybe we should say four) separated by a considerable expanse of time and space. Indeed, as one's eye moves outward from the center of the painting, the geographical and chronological proximity of teacher and student gives way to an improbable scene and setting, gathering together figures from diverse times and places who could not possibly have met each other, visited Athens, or stood in a *stoa*. The transposition of ancient figures and modern faces partakes of and accentuates a general tendency to blend together historical figures from widely different contexts.

Of course, the other frescos in the room display a similar kind of blending. The *Disputation of the Holy Spirit,* for example, is a bilevel painting, with heavenly figures arrayed on a semicircular cloud floating above and paralleling an arc of earthly ones around an altar in adoration of the Holy Sacrament. The heavenly circle brings together figures from the Old and New Testaments, and the earthy one comprises saints from different eras. Similarly, the *Parnassus* depicts a circle of ancient and modern poets gathered around Apollo and the Muses. In each of these cases, though, we expect this kind of blending from a divine communion—whether Christian or pagan—that by definition transcends the modalities of time and place. By contrast, Barkan notes, the *School of Athens* purports to occupy "a real space in which there are real interactions whose meaning depends on up-to-the-minute scholarship"; the fresco celebrates Pope Julius as a second Augustus, who "inspires a gathering of *all* of antiquity in a genuine, present space, indeed *this* space of Bramante's own St. Peter's" (14). It thus expresses a vision of the past that manages to be both historical and atemporal, that celebrates the greatness of antiquity while obliterating the distance between it and modernity. Instead of relegating the past to a place far removed from the present, the fresco heightens its presence in what I will term "the living past."

THE ATTENTIVE READER MAY RECALL that I employed the term *past-made-present* in Part One to denote the way Homer and the *logioi* made the past immediately accessible to the present by representing the two as fundamentally the same. Raphael's living past, however, is something entirely different. It is ancient to its core, with an antiquity more thoroughgoing and genuine than Homer's instrumentalist "olden days"; it is at one and the same time both "past" (different from the present) and "alive" (immediate and vital). This condition raises a curious question: how can something be simultaneously both past and present?

Atavisms, of course, spring to mind—those obvious holdovers from or throwbacks to the past. True, some holdovers are not so obvious, such as the often-heard admonition that children should behave like young "ladies" and "gentlemen," advice that references (when one stops to think of it) a long-dead chivalric world. But once they stand revealed for what they are, atavisms are perceived as harkening to something recognizably remote and anachronistic, in the specific sense of being historically out of place. In the Renaissance, however, the idea of anachronism defined the "pastness" of the past, not to distance it from but to propel it into the present, such that the two could actively cross-fertilize. In the light of this dynamic—which I will analyze in detail later—one can say that we have posed the above question improperly, utilizing a framework that automatically and instinctively separates past from present. Instead, we should conceive of the living past as constituting a synchronous space that preserves temporal differences while annihilating time.

Leonard Barkan helps us visualize this strange kind of space by means of an analogy from Freudian psychology, one that (like Raphael's painting) also reflects a deep love of classical culture. Freud based his psychology on the principle "that in mental life nothing which has once been formed can perish" (17). In *Civilization and Its Discontents*—which links the history of the psyche with the history of culture—Freud articulates this principle with reference to the archaeology of Rome, his quintessential symbol of the past. He begins by describing the modern city, site of successive archaeological strata. He then contrasts this historical Rome with an imaginary one in which all the archaeological layers coexist simultaneously. In this imaginary Rome, for example, one can see the original rude settlement atop the Palatine hill existing alongside the palaces of the caesars. Not only would structures from different time periods exist side by side, but different states of the same structure would be superimposed upon each other, as if in a hologram: "In the place occupied by the Palazzo Caffarelli would once more stand—without the Palazzo having to be removed— the Temple of Jupiter Capitolinus; and this not only in its latest shape, as the Romans of the Empire saw it, but also in its earliest one, when it still showed Etruscan forms and was ornamented with terra-cotta antefixes" (18).

Freud ultimately abandons this analogy for the permanence of psychic life because the chimera of superimposed structures proves impossible to visualize (there were no holograms in his day). Before he lets go of the analogy, however, he reveals in his detailed knowledge of ancient and modern Rome a deep love for this city, the mother of European culture. Barkan notes that a nineteenth-century Moravian-born Jew felt as cut off from what this city represented as Raphael did from the ancient one; Freud's Rome was at least as symbolic as it was historical. Thus, not surprisingly, he chose it as a model for a synchronous space in which past and present coexist, a space that annihilates time.

Having come this far at some intellectual peril, let us risk a further explication of the living past with reference to the "contemporaneity of the noncontemporaneous," the formulation I introduced at the close of Part One to epitomize the experience of multiple pasts in antiquity. Recall how Reinhart Koselleck employed this expression to capture an aspect of the premodern experience of time, in which (say) all the stages of the Polybian historical cycle lay immanent within any given stage. Also recall how we extrapolated from this formula to epitomize the ancient experience of multiple pasts characterized by different measures of time, all of which lay immanent in the minds of the historian and his audience, precluding any single perspective on "the" past. To this ancient experience of synchronicity we can now add the Renaissance experience, in which the different pasts are all recognizably "past" while still remaining present.

Whereas an ancient historian like Thucydides had treated the multiple time frames of different pasts serially—in a foregrounded way that eliminated the perception of temporal depth and historical distinctness while retaining a sense of narrative flow—Renaissance readers of ancient histories experienced these works in their temporality and historicity, but with little narrative connection between them, such that each historical account appeared freestanding. They did not think so much of studying "Roman history" as of reading Roman historians; similarly, they thought less about "classical poetry" than about, say, Virgil and Horace. Furthermore, as we will see, they digested Roman historians and classical poets in collections of commonplaces that consisted of discontinuous bits and pieces of ancient culture, all lovingly restored to their original purity. These intellectual habits fostered a Renaissance version of the contemporaneity of the noncontemporaneous, characterized by a synchronic collection of historically distinct pasts. In this mental world a Raphael could portray himself as Apelles and position this composite alongside historically accurate representations of Zoroaster and Ptolemy without engendering any incongruity. To our modern mind, however, this living past is a strange beast indeed!

Its strangeness derives from its origins in a humanist educational curriculum characterized by an eclectic form of reading and writing, which exploited diverse classical models in an attempt to revive ancient literature and culture. We will examine the rise of Italian humanism later, but for now let us simply contrast it with another new curriculum, scholasticism, imported to Italy from northern Europe at around the same time, starting in the early fourteenth century. In the hot competition that eventually developed between these two movements, the humanists proclaimed the superiority of the *studia humanitatis,* or "studies worthy of human beings," comprising grammar, rhetoric, history, poetry, and moral philosophy—grammar and rhetoric (instead of scholastic logic) because they improve one's capacity to communicate (whereas logic merely provides techniques of analysis); history, poetry, and moral philosophy (instead of metaphysics and natural philosophy) because they elevate one's thought and action (whereas metaphysics and natural philosophy merely describe man and nature in the abstract). This educational system proceeded by means of *imitatio,* the imitation of classical models, for the ancients were perceived as having perfected the art of eloquence, with which they had presented the most outstanding examples of human thought and action in the most compelling way. The humanists believed their program of imitation would revive not only the brilliance of classical language and literature but also the glory of classical civilization, which was encapsulated in and conveyed by the words and style of ancient writings. That their scholastic rivals derided them as woolly-headed moralists only added polemical fervor to their adoration of all things ancient, from which they felt separated by a "dark age" that had lost the light of classical eloquence, an age epitomized by the barbarity of scholastic neologisms.

When one reads for the purposes of imitation, one reads with an eye for the exemplary. Something is exemplary when it stands out as a model or as a striking instance of a universal truth; it thus potentially embodies a paradox, for it is at one and the same time unique and general. Scholastic logicians, of course, would be the first to recognize that something could be both unique and general in a hierarchical ordering of knowledge, but the humanists eschewed logic in favor of practical truths, thus heightening the potential paradox at the heart of their notion of exemplarity. This potential was not realized in antiquity because the foregrounded nature of classical literature had immersed an ancient audience in each richly detailed scene at hand, which vividly illustrated the social and moral norms the community took for granted. Although the rich detail of each scene—comprising stories within stories—rendered it brimful of examples, each one eclipsed its predecessor and thus managed to appear both unique and universal.

Renaissance readers of the assembled body of classical literature encountered a wealth of striking anecdotes and narratives, which they tended to absorb in the same way they encountered them—piece by piece, story by story, text by text. Because they valued these examples precisely for their classical style and subject matter, for their difference from modernity, they tended to conceive of each example—and the text from which it derived—as historically distinct. The distinctiveness of a text inevitably evokes that of its context, calling the whole notion of exemplarity into question. As a classical text comes to be seen as specifically Greek or Roman—and, even more so, as referenced to Athens or Ionia, or to republican or imperial Rome—it loses its exemplarity, which dissolves in the solvent of historical and cultural relativism. Indeed, the process of dissolution begins almost immediately on the discovery of difference; in other words, it began at the very beginning of the Renaissance and continued throughout this period. From our modern perspective this process appears dislocating and disorienting—and surely it was for some—but it offered others an extraordinary opportunity to bridge the gulf between past and present by means of *imitatio*. The period of the Renaissance is defined by the viability of this project, which progressively undermined itself as it advanced, until it reached a point where it was no longer viable.

We turn now to an analysis of the humanist movement and the idea of anachronism it inspired. This movement sought to recover a lost classical culture by means of a program of reading designed to facilitate imitation. Once we have laid out the principles underlying the humanist program of imitation, we can go on to consider its actual practice as implemented by Francesco Petrarca (anglicized as Petrarch), one of the first and most influential humanists. For Petrarch the living past was inseparable from—and inconceivable without—the exercise of *imitatio* that animated it. We can see in Petrarch's writings how the commingling of past and present opened up creative possibilities for self-expression, heightening his awareness of his own historical uniqueness. Over time the habit of reading he helped instill began to undercut the possibility of imitating classical models, whose remoteness from modernity weakened their exemplarity. Classical texts came to be viewed in their classical contexts, accentuating the sense of historical and cultural relativism. In the wake of this development, humanistically trained thinkers—such as the jurist Jean Bodin—began to conceive of new representations of the symbolic space in which past and present cohere, representations that constitute a literary analogue to Raphael's *School of Athens*. Bodin's more "literal" treatment of this space, however, reified it in a process that gradually drained it of its symbolic meaning.

The Birth of Anachronism

This book is premised on the thesis that a sustained awareness of anachronism emerged only with the Renaissance. The novelty of this thesis lies merely in the starkness with which I have presented it and the conclusions I've drawn from it; otherwise, its lineaments derive from the major interpretations of the period, starting with the epochal work of Jacob Burckhardt. In his *Civilization of the Renaissance in Italy* (1860) Burckhardt identified the defining characteristic of the Renaissance as the "development of the individual," by which he meant most broadly the rise of a sense of individuality, or uniqueness, as it applied both to people and to their understanding of the world. In *Renaissance and Renascences in Western Art* (1960) Erwin Panofsky further refined this notion as the "reintegration of form and content in art," whereby Renaissance artists came to depict a subject like Virgil as a classical poet clad in a toga rather than as a medieval schoolman dressed in monk's robes. This development epitomizes the growing awareness of anachronism. A multitude of recent scholars have further explored the manifestations of this awareness in a wide range of activities—in the rise of philological scholarship, in literary and artistic creations, in political and historical thought.[2]

From this thesis I have drawn a simple, logical conclusion: the first stirrings of an idea of the past—defined as not simply prior to the present but fundamentally different from it—originated in the Renaissance with the birth of a sense of anachronism, although the living past thus engendered hardly resembles our modern notion of a past "back there" in time. We are now about to consider this point of origin, but we cannot explore it in detail without first examining the notion of anachronism a little more closely so that we can specify exactly what was emerging. For our purposes the idea of anachronism has two aspects. On the one hand, it signifies the positioning of a historical entity outside its historical context; on the other, it represents an awareness of this positioning as being out of place. It is this latter "awareness of anachronism" that I seek to trace, but it takes on a variety of forms that are related to the former "commission of anachronism." So let us begin by considering the different ways one can produce an anachronism.

The literary critic Thomas M. Greene, perhaps the foremost modern scholar on this subject, has elaborated a typology encompassing five categories of anachronism: (1) "naive" anachronism, which characterizes "a culture lacking a strong historical sense," as epitomized by (say) medieval depictions of Virgil as a cloistered scholastic in a monk's cowl; (2) "abusive" anachronism, which singlemindedly adheres to a model that clashes contemptuously with contemporary usage—"The habit of the strict Ciceronian to refer to the Christian God as 'Jupiter Optimus Maximus' is abusive because the writer wants to repress history, not out of ignorance but out of a misconceived, rigid, and inappropriate decorum"; (3) "serendipitous" anachronism, which also attempts to control history but by adhering to a model improperly or incompletely understood—thus the Renaissance vogue for constructing "grottoes" in presumed imitation of the ancients always rendered them cavelike because the models for these once-above-ground structures were all found buried; (4) "creative" anachronism, apparent in the highest forms of imitation, which utilizes the awareness of differences between past and present as a springboard for self-expression, as we will see when we examine the works of Petrarch; and (5) "pathetic" or "tragic" anachronism, which evokes the inevitability of change that renders all human creations "dated." One can sense in Greene's typology a certain permeability of the boundary between the commission and the awareness of anachronism that may have helped stimulate artistic and literary creativity.[3]

The awareness of anachronism itself predates the Renaissance. I have already noted how ancient authors utilized a local, instrumentalist sense of anachronism when they referred—casually and sporadically—to the olden days and to customs no longer in use. This limited awareness evident in writing found its counterpart in reading, especially as articulated by the Alexandrian critics of the second century BC. Chief among these was Aristarchus of Samothrace, whose thoroughgoing stylistic knowledge of the *Iliad* and the *Odyssey* enabled him to determine when a word or usage seemed out of place. Such precision in reading, however, bore hardly any fruit in antiquity, for it was submerged by an authorial tendency to draw literary inspiration from as many different sources as possible. Ancient literary eclecticism thus precluded the possibility of a more systematic, sustained awareness of anachronism.[4]

When it finally did begin to emerge, the more systematic sense of anachronism became colored by a range of sensibilities, as Greene's typology makes clear. Of his five categories, three clearly manifest themselves as different kinds of awareness of anachronism, as distinct from its unwitting commission. The abusive, creative, and tragic types of anachronism all seek consciously to exploit the differences between past and present in distinct ways. To these categories we must add one of our own, which, in fairness to Greene, lies implicit in the other three: the awareness of anachronism as "error." In the final analysis this last sensibility will grow to overshadow the other three, largely (but not entirely) supplanting the synchronic encounter between past and present with a diachronic one.

A SUSTAINED DISTINCTION BETWEEN PAST AND PRESENT developed from the study of classical antiquity in the Renaissance. The reasons for this development are complex, but we can briefly caricature one of the major historical dynamics. The prolonged struggle between the papacy and the Holy Roman Empire from the eleventh century to the thirteenth created a power vacuum in northern and central Italy, in which there arose a multitude of small, self-governing city republics. Each of these "communes," as they were known, constituted a political hothouse, with a relatively small number of families and their allies competing for power in a struggle that exploited feudal relations and kinship ties. But the term *commune*—which probably originated from the expression for taking "common counsel" or holding deliberations "in common"—also signals an emergent countervailing interest in the public good and the community in general. So, alongside the hothouse competition between individuals and families there also arose a sense of public-mindedness and civic pride that animated civil institutions. Both these factors (among others) contributed to the revival of classical culture.

The intensity and complexity of civic life in the communes spurred an interest in rhetoric—the art of persuasion in speech and writing—unmatched elsewhere in Europe. Its practitioners emphasized the notarial art of public letter writing— the *ars dictaminis*—which served a wide range of diplomatic, commercial, and political purposes. At first, the *dictatores,* or teachers of letter writing, remained content with medieval manuals and models, but eventually they began to gravitate toward classical ones. In part, they became increasingly aware that classical Latin was a more supple and sophisticated language than contemporary (medieval) Latin—that it was better suited to their complex political and social environment. And in part, they became increasingly aware that classical culture was an urban one like their own and that they could look to it for enduring civic norms. From these twin spurs toward the study of classical language and literature there emerged a sustained sense of the differences between antiquity and modernity—that the modern (medieval) world had lost the light of classical eloquence, and the civic ideals underlying it, and that by reviving classical Latin one could resurrect the glories of classical culture.

The past thus constituted had none of the "pastness" we moderns commonly associate with it; it was not relegated to a space in time remote from the present, for such a space did not yet exist. Rather than pastness, its defining quality might best be described as an awareness of things "not present," with all the multivalence of this expression. The past was not present in the sense of being "unlike the present"—an unlikeness apparent in the differences between classical and medieval Latin and literature—but it was also not present in the sense of "absent," since the quality of "unlikeness" was conveyed by disparate texts (themselves often corrupted, fragmentary, and fragmented) suggesting a larger absence. In the parlance of postmodern literary criticism, this absence was present in the texts of classical literary works, which embodied the traces of something lost. Humanists sought to revive this lost thing through the program of *imitatio*—the imitation of classical models.

At the heart of this enterprise lay the sense of loss that defined the thing recovered as unlike the present, but the humanists did not contextualize this lost thing as part of a past culture or civilization in the way we moderns would, even though they prided themselves on living in close proximity to ancient ruins. In *Unearthing the Past*—about the Renaissance reaction to sculpture dug from these ruins—Leonard Barkan describes how such discoveries evoked a "gap":

"Not just the space between ancient and modern or between objects and the discourse about them but what we might call the energy gap—the sparking distance—that exists between an artistic source and its destination" (xxxi). The fragmentary nature of these remains stimulated a variety of responses, whose vital quality is prominently illustrated by reactions to the *Pasquino*, a Hellenistic marble consisting of the battered remnants of two joined torsos—one helmeted but literally defaced, the other barely hinted at by a small portion of chest. Sixteenth-century Romans indulged in the practice of clothing this fragment (which stood in front of the Palazzo Orsini) in satirical verses, as if it were haranguing passersby. (They thus gave rise to the European tradition of the "pasquinade"—the open display of poems lampooning public officials.) Barkan likens the *Pasquino* to a figure that not only speaks but invites response: "In the most fundamental way Pasquino is dialogic. He speaks to the viewers, and the viewers speak to him" (223). The *Pasquino* thus sparks the gap in a way that illustrates the living quality of the past in the Renaissance.

We moderns miss this living quality because we assume that such dialogues harken to a past "back there" in time. Images of the exiled Machiavelli—kicking off his muddy farmer's boots and donning his curial robes—spring to mind. Properly attired, he feels fit to discourse with the ancients, to leave his humdrum country existence behind and recall the glories of the past. If he had conceived of himself as going back in time, however, he wouldn't have bothered changing his clothes, for the discourse would have been a monologue addressed to the dead. Yet, as I have pointed out, Machiavelli's letter of 10 December 1513 makes abundantly clear that the ancients respond to his questioning: "I am not ashamed to speak with them and to ask the reasons for their actions, and they courteously answer me."[5] In this dialogic space—delimited by the texts where the ancients live—he must dress appropriately, lest they mistake him for a peasant. The *Pasquino* and a copy of Livy could thus evoke similar responses.

In the Renaissance, texts took on a life of their own, apart from their historical contexts, because their readers were (at least initially) ignorant of these contexts. The Middle Ages identified Pliny as both a natural historian and a literary figure; not even Petrarch knew (as Veronese scholars would eventually reveal) that "Pliny" was really two men, uncle and nephew. One of the defining moments of Petrarch's life occurred in the city of Verona in 1345, when he discovered a collection of Cicero's letters to his friend Atticus and his brother Quintus, letters that revealed his beloved Cicero as not just an orator and philosopher but one of the great politicians—and hypocrites—of his age. (Indeed, these letters have since become the standard primary source for the last days of the Roman republic, casting vital light on the serpentine politics of that crucial period.) And despite the limitations of his historical knowledge, Petrarch stands far in advance of "a certain famous man"—the Florentine canon lawyer Iohannes Andree—who thought the epitomizer Valerius Maximus the greatest of moral philosophers, who regarded Plato and Cicero as poets, who had never even heard of Plautus, and who had thoroughly scrambled the chronology of Roman literature.[6] At its inception the humanist program of imitation targeted classical texts apart from their contexts, knowledge of which emerged only gradually as several generations of humanists poured over these texts.

Of course, when he chides a contemporary for lack of historical knowledge, Petrarch points to the importance of that knowledge, imperfect though his own may have been. But he did not attach the same importance to it that we do. The humanist program of imitation was less concerned with the recreation of antiquity than with its creative emulation. In *The Light in Troy* Thomas M. Greene identifies four hierarchical types of imitation: (1) the slavish kind that ploddingly follows a single model, (2) the eclectic kind that alludes to several models, (3) the "heuristic" kind that highlights the differences between text and model, and (4) the "dialectical" kind that evokes a dialogic interplay between text and model (38–48). The last two kinds are closely related, with authors exploiting the sense of historical anachronism—of the differences between past and present—to define themselves in relation to their models. The sense of anachronism inherent in the highest forms of imitation thus impelled the most capable authors away from the mere recreation of antiquity and toward its use as a springboard for self-expression. In the hierarchy of imitation, recreation is the lowest form of compliment, a mere preliminary step toward a fuller engagement with the living past.

IN THE WAKE OF THE SEMINAL SCHOLARSHIP of Paul Oskar Kristeller, the term *humanism* has lost its vague associations as a "philosophy of man" in opposition to scholastic theology and has taken on more precise meaning as the *studia humanitatis*, the literary curriculum comprising grammar, rhetoric, history, poetry, and moral philosophy. Despite its precision, though, this designation says little about the process of imitation by which the curriculum was implemented and exploited. Part of the genius of Barkan's *Unearthing the Past* is that Barkan renders visible the actual practice of imitation—"when material goes in ancient and comes out modern"—through an analysis of drawings made in artistic academies and studios, where students learned their art from masters, with both student and master imitating ancient models (287). Tracking this process in literary creations is much more difficult, but we can begin to do so by viewing humanism less from the outside, as a literary curriculum, and more from the inside, as a method of reading. The complement to writing, reading opens a window onto the living past.[7]

In his *Plato in the Italian Renaissance* James Hankins has attempted a preliminary classification of reading strategies in the later Middle Ages and Renaissance, identifying seven kinds of reading, comprising five fully developed forms—"meditative," "doctrinal," "scholastic," "allegorical," and "imitative"—and two emergent forms—"critical" and "aesthetic."[8] Of the developed ones, imitative reading is the type specifically associated with humanism. It constitutes (according to Hankins) a revival of the ancient form of "ethical criticism," which "sought to transmit the accepted *ethos* or values of the educated classes in society by selecting a canon of texts thought to embody those values and establishing them as the loci of imitation" (1:22). This form of reading coexisted with earlier, medieval forms—meditative, doctrinal, scholastic, and allegorical—of which the doctrinal in particular nicely complements the imitative. Doctrinal reading uses an authoritative text as "an armature upon which to hang moral lessons and an encyclopedic knowledge of all the arts and sciences" (1:19). The heavy glossing of an authoritative text would thus transform it into a "memory palace," and when that text was a canonical, classical one, the information displayed would constitute both *res*, or "things" (the content of humanist discourse), and *verba*, or "words" (the best examples of style).

The tendency for reading to trail off into what we would today regard as note taking was further accentuated by the other three developed forms of reading. Meditative reading took passages out of context, discouraged critical analysis, and, instead, encouraged the reader to allow the passage to "dissolve in the mind like a lozenge" (1:18), thus revealing its divine implications. These meditative passages, when further compressed and refined, found their way into *florilegia*, the "collections of flowers" utilized by medieval preachers in search of subject matter for their sermons. Scholastic reading distilled the key texts of the professions—law, theology, and medicine—into summaries and propositions easily taught by professors and easily remembered by students. And allegorical reading, which sometimes shaded into doctrinal reading, tended to decode each element of the text in relation to a subtext. All of the five developed forms of reading encouraged a reception of the text that we moderns would regard as fragmented and disjointed.

Of the seven types of reading identified by Hankins, only the two emergent forms correspond to what we would today recognize as "reading" per se. A nascent type of critical reading, which highlighted the historical differences between texts, began to emerge in the late fifteenth century; it utilized an idea of anachronism to establish accurate classical texts, along with their contexts (we can here see the debut of the sensibility that marks anachronisms as errors). And aesthetic reading—what we would today call "reading for pleasure"—began to make its appearance in the sixteenth century. Hankins emphasizes that all these forms of reading—and especially the first five—coexisted in the Renaissance, with any given reader engaging in all the fully developed forms of his or her day. The humanist encounter with the texts delineating the living past was thus different from what we moderns might expect, given our own reading habits. In particular, the first five forms of reading all tended to break the text down into discrete packets of information, which generally ended up as the subject of marginal notations and separate manuscript notebooks. In the Renaissance, reading was essentially indistinguishable from note taking.

THE FUSION OF READING AND NOTE TAKING REINFORCED the humanist program of *imitatio* by emphasizing the exemplary nature of a classical culture full of models to be both imitated and excerpted. Of the *studia humanitatis,* grammar and rhetoric provided the means of expression, while history, poetry, and moral philosophy constituted its substance. The humanists thus sought to rehabilitate the classical discursive structure known as the *exemplum,* for they regarded "example" as a form of rhetorical proof superior to logic in its ability to move the human will toward responsible action in a complex world. The writings of classical historians, poets, and moral philosophers embodied the ideal content of humanist discourse. They were literally "exemplary," both for illustrating discourse at its best and for embodying the most enduring examples of virtues to emulate and vices to avoid. The "rhetoric of exemplarity" (to borrow an expression from Timothy Hampton) eclipsed the medieval, typological habit of mind, whose figural view of reality bound past, present, and future together in the will of God. Instead, the rhetoric of exemplarity tended to focus attention more on the world of human action, which humanists distilled into a multitude of universally valid moral norms, as reflected by the subject headings of their notebooks. In essence, each excerpt represented an instance of the living past, authorized by antiquity and applicable to modernity.

Ironically, the urge to imitate carried within itself the seeds of its own undoing. As they read—always on the alert for striking examples—humanists learned to view the exemplary deed from the perspective of the exemplary life and to place that life in a broader historical context, in what Hampton calls a narrative of "long term intentions."[9] Whereas the medieval, typological habit of reading emphasized a divine purpose transecting time, the humanist habit ultimately drew attention to the otherness (what critics like Hampton call the "alterity") of a past that appeared increasingly different from the present. Ultimately, the awareness of these differences would undermine the exemplarity of classical culture, calling into question the whole program of *imitatio* and, along with it, the very possibility of a living past.

My thumbnail sketch of the history of humanism—circumscribing a movement that began in the early fourteenth century and ended in the late sixteenth—appears neater than the reality. Humanism did not so much "end" as trail off into philology—the scholarly reconstruction of classical texts—while the *studia humanitatis* evolved into the "humanities." The emergence of philology—predicated on the notion of anachronism as error—did not immediately overshadow other conceptions of anachronism, which continued to inspire major literary efforts (as they still do today). Thus, what appears to us moderns as a "crisis of exemplarity" may not have been experienced as such by the humanists and their offspring.[10] (Humanistic note taking remained a widespread practice well into the eighteenth century, as Thomas Jefferson's efforts attest.) Indeed, the birth of anachronism coextensive with humanism engendered a long period of creative interplay between alterity and exemplarity. Far from inducing an enervating relativism, the awareness of anachronism provided humanists with an artistic occasion whose opportunities variously masked, dissipated, or heightened the tension at the heart of their movement. We now turn to the creative tension born of anachronism and its substantiation of the living past.

Petrarch's "Copernican Leap"

For all practical purposes the living past originates with Petrarch, the fourteenth-century Italian poet and scholar who championed the *studia humanitatis* and its program of imitation. Although he is the seminal figure in the early humanist movement, one cannot say—as Arnaldo Momigliano did of Herodotus—that there was no Petrarch before Petrarch. In the intense caldron of Italian civic life, thirteenth- and early fourteenth-century lawyers and notaries had begun awakening to the expressive power of the classical Latin language and its literature. Perhaps the earliest of these figures, the Paduan lawyer Hieremias de Montagnone (d. c. 1320), assembled a compilation of quotations, the *Compendium moralium notabilium* (Compendium of memorable sayings), which included a wide range of classical authors, some virtually unknown in the Middle Ages. He also tried to determine the real words of ancient sayings (rather than being content with their gist), and he divided the classical portion of his collection into two rudimentary periods (before and after Augustus) instead of lumping them together as a whole. Two other Paduan lawyers, Lovato dei Lovati (1241–1309) and Albertino Mussato (1261–1329), had absorbed enough of the distinctive spirit of ancient literature that they attempted to revive it by imitation, Lovati as a poet and Mussato as a tragedian. The efforts of these Paduan scholars have been described variously as constituting a form of pre- or early humanism.[11]

Such early efforts, however, do not prepare us for Petrarch's transformation of the study of antiquity. Whereas his predecessors could imitate ancient models only crudely and imperfectly, Petrarch had a more highly developed sense of classical Latin style, enabling him not only to follow his models more closely (the lowest form of imitation) but also to understand and internalize their spirit—to ascend from imitation to emulation. In this process he came to conceive of ancient authors as emissaries from another world, one vastly different from his own. Thomas M. Greene marvels at this "Copernican leap," which he finds all the more incredible considering that Petrarch accessed the ancients through contemporary illuminated manuscripts, written in gothic script and filled with illustrations depicting classical figures in medieval garb.[12] What makes Petrarch so distinctive is his startling intuition of the differences between antiquity and modernity, his remarkable ability to delve beneath the surface appearance of these texts and grasp not only their alterity but that of their authors. The ancients thus popped into three-dimensional focus for him; they ceased to be medieval disciplinary placeholders—such as "The Philosopher" or "The Rhetorician"—and became instead personalities, individuals who authored classical works of history, poetry, philosophy, and rhetoric.

Yet Petrarch's was a Copernican leap, not a Keplerian or a Newtonian one. Like the Polish mathematician, he retained much of the earlier worldview, even as he laid the foundation for its overthrow. His sense of the differences between past and present coexisted with a countervailing tendency to seek underlying unities. The tension between these two tendencies animated the program of imitation, with its emphasis on the singularity of general models. As Petrarch knowingly and actively exploited this tension, probing the limits of *imitatio*, he also established the boundaries of the living past. We will explore this creative tension in three of his more famous works. His first letter to Marcus Tullius Cicero reveals the coexistence of historicizing and universalizing impulses, and it shows how Petrarch exploits them by means of *imitatio,* creating an atemporal engagement with the past. Another famous letter, about his ascent of Mount Ventoux, demonstrates the limits of *imitatio* and shows how Petrarch defines himself over and against his models, asserting the uniqueness of his own personality. And the dialogue *Secretum* (or *The Secret Conflict of My Cares*) points toward the central role of exemplarity in humanism, which transforms reading into note taking, an activity that constitutes the living past. All three cases demonstrate that the living past originates in, and remains inseparable from, the humanist program of imitation.

PETRARCH WAS BORN IN 1304 of a recently banished Florentine family living in nearby Arezzo. (The family had fallen prey in 1302 to the same internecine strife that landed Dante in exile.) His father, a notary, subsequently sought employment in the papal bureaucracy, moving the family to Avignon in 1311, after the papacy had relocated there. Urged onto his father's career path, Petrarch studied law at Montpellier and then (along with his brother Gherardo) at Bologna. Legal training, based on the study of Roman law, may have stimulated a broader interest in things classical; and during his time at Bologna he may have also tried his hand at poetry, writing in the vernacular. Ultimately, he felt unsuited to a legal-notarial career and abandoned it after his father's death in 1326. Returning to Avignon, he eventually took minor clerical orders and attached himself to a wealthy patron, serving as Cardinal Giovanni Colonna's "household chaplain." This was the first of many such sinecures by which he supported himself in his literary efforts, writing poetry first in Italian and then, increasingly, in a classical Latin style, as well as deepening his knowledge of classical literature and refining his Latin prose. By the time he left the cardinal's employ in 1337, he had become a famous and sought-after poet. Ultimate recognition for his literary achievements came on 8 April 1341, when he was crowned poet laureate in a ceremony on the Capitoline hill, in the ancient name of the Senate and People of Rome (SPQR). This ceremony—the first of its kind in more than a millennium—symbolized his pivotal role in the revival of classical Latin literature.

Petrarch was not only a poet but also a scholar. Among his earliest scholarly achievements is what might be termed the first "critical" edition of Livy's history of Rome. In Petrarch's day the first, third, and fourth "decades" of this work were extant—a decade being a collection of ten books—and these were circulated and read in no particular order. Petrarch not only arranged them chronologically, so that they formed a narrative, but he also compared different manuscript copies—a difficult undertaking in the age before printing—in order to determine the most accurate version of the text. As a classical Latin stylist, he most wanted to recover Livy's real words. This desire to know the actual words of the ancients opened a window onto their personalities and, ultimately, their world.

The same impulse that led him to recover Livy's words also inspired Petrarch's lifelong search for lost classical manuscripts. He made his greatest discovery in the cathedral library of Verona in May 1345, when he stumbled across a volume containing the sixteen books of Cicero's letters to Atticus, as well as his letters to his brother Quintus and to Brutus. These letters had long been rumored to exist, but not even the Veronese knew what treasures they had in their possession. Petrarch immediately set himself to the immense task of copying the letters even as he first read them. Whereas the Middle Ages had known Cicero as a disembodied author of rhetorical and philosophical treatises, Petrarch had already begun to revive and internalize Cicero's ideal of the orator, whose eloquence personified wisdom: "O great father of Roman eloquence, not I alone but all who bedeck themselves with the flowers of Latin speech are grateful to you."[13] But these letters revealed a different Cicero, more personal, more human, less savory. Instead of the golden-tongued sage, Petrarch discovered Cicero the inveterate gossip, the rumor monger, the political opportunist, the ambitious schemer.

He registered his disappointment in a famous letter to Cicero (24.3) dated 16 June 1345, the first of two addressed to this figure. On the surface the purpose and meaning of the letter seem transparent: when Petrarch's idol reveals himself as a hypocrite, Petrarch immediately takes him to task for failing to live up to his own ideals. "I who had known the kind of preceptor that you were for others now recognize the kind of guide that you were for yourself." Late in his retirement Cicero had forsaken philosophical withdrawal for political engagement and subsequently suffered a death that belied his life: "What false luster of glory led you, an old man, into wars with the young, and into a series of misfortunes that then brought you to a death unworthy of a philosopher?" Petrarch sounds the theme of contemplative withdrawal from worldly affairs again toward the end of the letter: "Oh, how much better it would have been, especially for a philosopher, to have grown old peacefully in the country, meditating, as you write somewhere, on that everlasting life and not on this transitory existence." The whole letter is pervaded by this philosophical ideal, whose universality Petrarch takes for granted.

At the same time, though, there emerges a countervailing sense of historicity. In his betrayal of his own ideals, Cicero revealed himself as a Roman mired in the politics of his day; and Petrarch struggles to understand the motivation for the shifting allegiances and attitudes disclosed in his letters. Perhaps, writes Petrarch, one can excuse Cicero's inconstancy toward family members (praising them in one letter only to criticize them in another), and perhaps one can even understand his equivocations about Pompey and Caesar (both of whom aimed at despotism), but what possessed him to attack Antony while embracing Octavian if both were tyrants, only to then turn on his erstwhile ally? This relentless questioning and probing confronts Petrarch with the "real" Cicero, with the personality of the man behind the words; and as he struggles to understand this Roman, he perceives the vast distance between antiquity and modernity. The letter's coda solemnizes the unbridgeable gulf separating Petrarch from the man he so desperately seeks to understand: "But these words indeed are all in vain. Farewell forever, my Cicero. From the land of the living, on the right bank of the Adige, in the city of Verona in transpadane Italy, on 16 June in the year 1345 from the birth of that Lord whom you never knew." How Petrarch yearns to communicate his disappointment to this man he still dearly loves!

The closing passage in particular and the letter as a whole recall Panofsky's famous caricature of the Renaissance: "The Middle Ages had left antiquity unburied and alternately galvanized and exorcised its corpse. The Renaissance stood weeping at its grave and tried to resurrect its soul" (113). Petrarch's first letter to Cicero seems to present us with a nascent sense of historical perspective, born of the author's bereavement. But appearances are deceiving, for the loss Petrarch feels does not engender a sense of the past as something dead and buried. Rather, the letter's historicizing tendency coexists with a universalizing one that affords him a critical foothold, a pushing-off point for an exercise in *imitatio* that commingles past and present. Petrarch's harsh judgment of Cicero the man is inseparable from his imitation of Cicero the model—the former has no existence without the latter. Petrarch's Copernican leap thus constitutes, at one and the same time, his perception of the difference between past and present and his jumping of that gap. The living past born of imitation becomes apparent when we examine Petrarch's bereavement a little more closely.

"Now it is your turn, wherever you may be, to hearken not to advice but to a lament inspired by true love from one of your descendants who dearly cherishes your name, a lament addressed to you not without tears *[non sine lacrimis]*." Thus Petrarch launches into his criticism of Cicero, with tears of anger at the would-be sage's hypocrisy and tears of frustration at his inaccessibility. But these lamentations obscure the presence of another tearful emotion—joy. Petrarch's discovery in the cathedral library revealed to a man initially schooled in medieval notarial arts a whole new and exciting dimension of letter writing. For the first time he realized that letters—far from being mundane missives or desiccated documents—might constitute a separate literary genre, a vehicle for revealing the personality of their author. And how did he respond to this discovery? He wrote a letter! To whom? Cicero? Or was he really writing to us, his readers? In this letter Petrarch communicates to posterity his "spontaneous" feelings—the image of his personality—just as Cicero had communicated his to Petrarch. Already, though, one might begin to suspect that the letter is not so spontaneous and that behind the appearance of artlessness lies great art. Did Petrarch really write the letter on 16 June 1345? He surely wrote something on that date; but like virtually everything else from Petrarch's pen, this letter may have been reworked in whole or in part, as probably were his subsequent letters to the ancients—Seneca, Varro, Livy, Quintilian, Pollio, Horace, Virgil—most of which also bear specific dates. This gallery concludes one of Western literature's great epistolary collections, the 350 "letters"—some fictitious—that constitute Petrarch's *Familiarium rerum libri XXIV,* his twenty-four books of "familiar" letters. This monument to the author's inner and outer life might never have existed were it not for that fateful day in Verona, when he discovered his hero had feet of clay.

Not only does Cicero's hypocrisy provide a pretext for self-portraiture, but so, too, does his temporality, the fact that he lived in a pre-Christian world. Petrarch utilizes this awareness of anachronism as a literary device to reveal his innermost feelings, specifically the yearning that accompanies a deep personal loss. He mourns for Cicero and, more so, for all of classical antiquity; this mourning defines Petrarch, both as a person and as an author: "The discovery of antiquity and simultaneously the remoteness of antiquity made of Petrarch a double exile, neither Roman nor modern, so that he became in his own eyes a living anachronism."[14] His sustained sense of the differences between past and present inspired an attempt to conjoin the two through the imitation of ancient models. Petrarch sought to make this imitative dimension of the letter clear in ways large and small: "O wretched and distressed spirit, or to use your own words, O rash and ill-fated elder." The letter in imitation of Cicero's letters is itself a tissue of borrowings from Cicero and others, both acknowledged and unacknowledged. "Like a wayfarer at night carrying a lantern before him, you revealed to your followers the path where you yourself stumbled most wretchedly." One wonders—as Petrarch perhaps intended—from whom he borrowed this striking image. (And what greater delight than to beguile his readers into thinking his own words those of an ancient!) Petrarch's letter to Cicero not only solemnizes the divide between past and present but—to recall Leonard Barkan's automotive analogy—playfully sparks that gap.

In Petrarch's letter the past has no objective existence outside this creative tension, where the awareness of anachronism subverts itself. Historians tend to overlook this tension because they seize on the content of the letter while ignoring its epistolary form. Of course, one can hardly overestimate the importance of Petrarch's insight into the differences between antiquity and modernity. Yet this Copernican leap entails that other one, the heartfelt desire to jump over the "middle age" that had lost the light of classical eloquence and tap directly into the (ancient) wellspring of culture. The sense of distance and the desire to vault it constitute different sides of the same coin—Petrarch did not perceive the past per se, independent of *imitatio*. Indeed, what made the past conceivable for him was its living quality, its existence not in a temporal realm but in a symbolic one that annihilates time, where the sustained awareness of differences between past and present simultaneously occasions their commingling.

The scholastics, of course, were right to criticize the humanists: the notion of *imitatio* underlying their moralistic outlook does indeed admit of a certain woolly-headedness. The tension in Petrarch's letter between the universal ideal of the sage and the awareness of historical anachronism is merely the surface manifestation of a deeper tension inherent in the paradox of exemplarity—combining singularity with generality—which itself animates the whole humanist program of imitation. As Charles Trinkaus so cogently observes, "The humanists ordinarily opted for a taking of position in the broadest of terms, avoiding what they called subtleties and disputation; perhaps it might even be called a predilection for vagueness or for an untroubled inconsistency."[15] The most prominent reflection of this untroubled inconsistency is the coexistence of their universalizing and historicizing tendencies, which underlay their conception of the living past. We sometimes lose sight of this inconsistency in our scholastic urge to tidy up after the humanists, to spell out fully the logical consequences of what they first perceived, the historical ramifications of which the humanists blithely ignored.

ANOTHER "FAMILIAR" LETTER—ON PETRARCH'S ASCENT of Mount Ventoux (4.1)—reveals a dialogic quality in the creative tension between past and present, a quality that characterizes the highest form of *imitatio* and the fullest extent of its attendant notion of past.[16] Dated 26 April 1336, the letter is addressed to Dionigi da Borgo San Sepolcro, a learned theologian of the Augustinian Order whom Petrarch had met around 1333, after returning to Avignon from Bologna. Dionigi had gifted the amorous Petrarch with a *vade mecum*—a small-sized copy of Augustine's *Confessions*—in the hopes of stiffening his spiritual resolve. On account of Dionigi's good offices, Petrarch wrote him this letter in imitation of Augustine's life and work. Throughout the letter Petrarch appears to identify with his model. Like Augustine he yearns for spiritual ascent (allegorized by the mountain climb); like Augustine he feels mired in carnality (they both fathered illegitimate children); like Augustine he admires monastic withdrawal (his climbing companion and brother, Gherardo, would soon become a monk); like Augustine he feels the contrary pull of worldly ambition (both excelled as men of eloquence); like Augustine he experiences a seminal encounter with a book (his little copy of the *Confessions*); and like Augustine he believes in the power of allegory to reveal hidden truth.

These parallels, both implicit and explicit, help structure a letter that begins, interestingly, with reference to a work from pagan antiquity. Although Petrarch had long contemplated climbing this mountain near Avignon, he drew his immediate inspiration from a passage in Livy's history of Rome, where King Philip of Macedon ascends Mount Haemus because he thought it would afford a view of the Adriatic and Black seas. Petrarch bends this classical inspiration toward a Christian purpose, which lies implicit in his finicky choice of a climbing companion—that no ordinary company will do signifies that this is no ordinary climb. His brother and future monk, Gherardo, proves the ideal choice; and as the two set off, the climb quickly becomes an allegory for ascent toward "the blessed life" *(vita beata)* that contrasts Gherardo's spiritual resolve (he heads straight for the summit) with Petrarch's more lax ways. When he finally obtains the summit after several detours, Petrarch turns his gaze first toward Italy and then inward, in contemplation of his life and what the future may hold. It had been exactly ten years to the day since he had abandoned his legal studies and left Bologna. Looking back on the intervening years, he confesses (in Augustine's words) "the carnal corruption of my soul": "What I used to love, I love no longer. But I lie *[mentior]*: I love it still, but less passionately. Again I have lied *[iterum ecce mentitus sum]*: I love it, but more timidly, more sadly. Now at last I have told the truth; for thus it is: I love, but what I should love not to love, what I should wish to hate" (42). This Augustinian winnowing of truth reminds him of Dionigi's efforts to stiffen his will with the gift of the *vade mecum.* He resolves to commemorate the spiritual progress gained during his physical ascent by opening the little copy of the *Confessions* at random—much as Augustine had opened his copy of Paul's epistles in the Milanese garden. And like Augustine his eyes fall on a passage that leaves him transfixed: "Men go to admire the high mountains, the vast floods of the sea, the huge streams of the rivers, the circumference of the ocean, and the revolutions of the stars—and desert themselves" (44; *Confessions*, 10.8). As he descends in the declining light, Petrarch meditates on the spiritual meaning of this message: "How intensely ought we to exert our strength to get under foot not a higher spot of earth but the passions which are puffed up by earthly instincts" (46). When he returns to the little rustic inn from which he had embarked, he hurriedly puts pen to paper "on the spur of the moment," lest inspiration evaporate.

This synopsis does little justice to the complexity of the letter, which repeatedly shifts between spatial and temporal perspectives and exploits a wide range of pagan as well as Christian sources. The central model, though, is the *Confessions;* and at first glance one cannot avoid the impression that Petrarch identifies with Augustine and directly imitates his climactic conversion. Yet a closer examination of the ultimate moment of identification reveals a fundamental disjunction between author and model. Unlike Augustine's reading of Paul's epistles, which resolved a spiritual crisis and lent new meaning to his life, Petrarch's reading of Augustine's *Confessions* leaves him disquieted: "I was stunned, I confess *[Obstupui fateor]*." Whereas Augustine felt spiritually renewed and openly shared his experience with his friend Alypius, whom he encouraged to find his own salvific oracle in Paul's text, Petrarch closes his copy of the *Confessions,* turns his back on Gherardo, and begins to berate himself for admiring earthly things—a point driven home, significantly, by a passage from Seneca ("Nothing is admirable besides the mind; compared to its greatness nothing is great"). And as he makes his way down from the summit—distracted from the roughness of the path by the "storm in my breast"—he periodically glances back over his shoulder and wonders (in essence) what possessed him to climb that mountain.

The answer, of course, is that Livy inspired him to imitate the example of King Philip: "It seemed to me that a young man who holds no public office might be excused for doing what an old king is not blamed for" (37). This rationale is immediately followed by Petrarch's deliberations about a climbing companion. Thus, right from the start of the letter, he assumed that a pagan example could inspire a Christian purpose—much as he would later use the above passage from Seneca to reinforce the fateful one from the *Confessions*—and that a physical climb could advance a spiritual goal. In other words, he assumed that his life could enact an allegory, too—just like Augustine's. But events didn't turn out as he had intended, and his troubled descent bespeaks (in Robert Durling's phrase) "the crisis of allegory," a crisis induced by reading Livy.

The crisis of allegory reveals not only the distance between Petrarch and Augustine—between author and model—but also between the modern Christian world and the ancient pagan one. Ideally, allegory should overcome this distance by disclosing the eternal amid the contingent, but the truth revealed to Petrarch on the mountaintop is that he should have stayed at home to contemplate God—that the example from Livy could not be Christianized. In this regard the fateful quotation picked at random from the *Confessions* stands dialogically as a rebuke, one that seems to leave Petrarch isolated in time by calling into question any attempt at imitation, whether of Livy or of Augustine. His account of the day's events takes an epistolary form that confirms and reinforces this sense of isolation: "While the servants were busy preparing our meal, I withdrew quite alone into a remote part of the house to write this letter to you in all haste and on the spur of the moment *[solus ego in partem domus abditam perrexi, hec tibi, raptim et ex tempore, scripturus]*. I was afraid the intention to write might evaporate, since the rapid change of scene was likely to cause a change of mood, if I deferred it." The image of the author alone in a remote corner of the inn—hurriedly writing a "spontaneous" letter in an effort to capture an evanescent moment—epitomizes what Thomas Greene has termed Petrarch's "historical solitude," the alienation of a "living anachronism."

As with his first letter to Cicero, however, Petrarch transmutes this solitude into a literary pretext—an occasion to write us about himself—and for Petrarch such pretexts are rarely spontaneous. Did he really compose this long letter—with all its careful symmetries and contrasts—on the night of 26 April 1336, in the few spare moments before his evening meal? One of the letter's most obvious contrasts is between Gherardo's spiritual resolve and Petrarch's moral laziness, a contrast no doubt grounded in Gherardo's unexpected decision to become a Carthusian monk around 1343. This decision suggests that Petrarch may not have put pen to paper until at least seven years after the purported date of the letter, by which time its reputed recipient, Dionigi, would have already been dead for a year. That Dionigi resided in Avignon in 1336—and that Petrarch therefore had no need to write him—argues further against the genuineness of the letter's date. The specificity of that date may simply reflect Petrarch's desire to highlight certain compositional symmetries. He claims to have attained the summit—and a perspective on his life—ten years to the day after he had left Italy, abandoning the law for what would become a literary career. And in that year he was thirty-two, the same age Augustine had been when he experienced his famous conversion. In view of these contrivances one might question not only the date but whether Petrarch ever really climbed Mount Ventoux at all. This famous "letter" might thus be one of those fictional epistles invented to fill in some personal or chronological gap in the *Familiari;* indeed, recent scholarship dates the composition of the letter at around 1352–53.

The invention of a literary pretext does not discredit the genuineness of Petrarch's "historical solitude"—which holds true regardless of whether and when he actually climbed the mountain—but it does underscore a distinction between his sense of the past and our own, a distinction rooted in the practice of imitation. His feeling of solitude is simply the flip side of the sense of individuality that impels him to write us about himself. In "The Ascent of Mont Ventoux" he pushes off against the intractable otherness of his models—his inability (try as he might) to identify with them—in order to establish his own uniqueness. Christian allegorizing no longer works for him; the irreducible nub of his personality obtrudes into the Augustinian presentation of himself as an "everyman." The realization that he can't simply copy his model opens the way toward the highest form of imitation, a dialogical interplay between author and model that Greene labels "dialectical." This form of imitation reveals the peculiar nature of the sense of historical and cultural relativism accompanying the humanist awareness of anachronism.

According to Greene, dialectical imitation is closely related to "heuristic" imitation, which we have already encountered in Petrarch's first letter to Cicero. Heuristic imitation advertises its models (Petrarch openly imitates Cicero's letters) only in order to distance itself from them (Petrarch laments Cicero's inaccessibility by way of establishing his own identity). Dialectical imitation moves beyond the one-way pathos of inaccessibility to open a dialogical interchange between text and model. On the one hand, the awareness of anachronism renders any model questionable, no matter how venerable and revered. On the other hand, this same awareness privileges neither text nor model but rather renders them both equal, such that the model can stand in criticism of the text. In "The Ascent of Mont Ventoux" the model not only proves inappropriate to Petrarch's situation, but it also reaches out across the centuries to actively defy him: the message of the *Confessions* is that Petrarch shouldn't have bothered climbing the mountain. This message leaves him shaken in large part because it reveals an inconsistency in the relation between antiquity and modernity, between paganism and Christianity. Whereas he had once assumed that a passage from Livy could inspire a Christian act, he's no longer so sure, and this uncertainty calls into question both his literary and religious aspirations while, at the same time, providing Petrarch with a golden opportunity to make himself known to us.

Dialectical imitation reveals most fully the humanist sense of historical and cultural relativism, but we must beware the temptation to separate this relativism from its literary source in the program of imitation and to reify it into a free-standing principle of historical knowledge. It emerges from an exercise in *imitatio* that privileges neither text nor model but establishes the uniqueness of both. In the creative tension between the two, the text not only defines itself over and against its model but also opens itself to aggression from the model. As the past intrudes into the present, "anachronism becomes a dynamic source of artistic power."[17] It creates a living past in which model and text—past and present—freely commingle, energizing each other.

THE "CRISIS OF ALLEGORY" APPARENT in "The Ascent of Mont Ventoux" is part of a larger phenomenon, which some critics have labeled a "crisis of exemplarity." We have already noted that the humanists championed argument by example rather than precept as the most efficacious means of moving the will toward responsible action in the world. In the humanist curriculum, works of classical history, poetry, and moral philosophy provided the most outstanding examples of actions either to imitate or to avoid. The humanists encouraged one to identify with these stories of exemplary action, to internalize the timeless truths they illustrate, and to understand, in each instance, how they embody these truths. In his first letter to Cicero, for example, Petrarch identifies with the ideal of the sage that Cicero had espoused in his philosophical writings but failed to uphold in his personal life. Petrarch accepts without question the relevance of the ideal and explores the specific ways Cicero fell short of it. Although this exploration reveals Cicero as a man—and, indeed, a Roman—rather than a philosopher, Petrarch never loses sight of the guiding ideal. In "The Ascent of Mont Ventoux," however, exemplarity becomes more problematic when Petrarch tries to appropriate the story of Augustine's conversion for his own life. His inability to do so highlights the distinctiveness of his own personality and temporal situation, which undercuts his attempt to find allegorical meaning in his actions. In the *Secretum,* a famous dialogue written around the same time, Petrarch further explores the complex relationship between his own distinctiveness and the examples with which he tries to identify, putting the whole humanist curriculum to the test. In so doing, he most fully reveals the potential flaws in the rhetoric of exemplarity that shaped the humanist program of reading and note taking. When Petrarch's successors adopted his program, elaborating it into a system of commonplaces that structured the living past, they would be building on an unstable foundation.

The *Secretum* opens with a prologue in which the figure of Truth reveals herself to Petrarch—with Augustine by her side—in an effort to lead him from error and set him on the right path of life. This auspicious beginning has inspired the traditional interpretation of the text as Petrarch's response to a spiritual crisis after being crowned poet laureate in 1341. According to this interpretation Petrarch first drafted the dialogue in 1342–43, revising it until at least 1353; and he used the interchange between its interlocutors, "Augustinus" and "Franciscus," to represent the conflict between his Christian and humanist selves. Although elements of such a conflict do appear in the text, this interpretation has been called into question by the redating of the first draft to around 1347. Without dwelling on these scholarly controversies, we can move beyond the traditional interpretation and—following the perceptive lead of Carol E. Quillen in her fine study of Petrarch and Augustine, *Rereading the Renaissance*—assert that the *Secretum* highlights the issue of imitation and how an author should exploit his readings.[18] This issue is apparent from Franciscus's first startled words upon encountering the apparition of Truth—"By what name should I call you, maiden? For your face is hardly mortal, and your voice is not that of a human being."—the very words spoken by Aeneas when, after landing in Africa at Dido's Carthage, he first encountered the figure of Venus. What better illustration of the principle of *imitatio* than this remarkably resonant line from the *Aeneid*, a work of special significance for a poet who had won his laurel for a Virgilian epic (the *Africa*) about the Second Punic War?

The prologue introduces a three-part dialogue that takes place over three days, in which Augustinus, at Truth's behest, tries to show Franciscus the error of his ways. Augustinus spends the first day encouraging Franciscus to shed his tendency toward self-deception and recognize the mortal danger confronting his soul, which finds too much gratification in the seductions of this world. At first Franciscus doesn't even recognize that he has a problem, but eventually he confesses to being drawn—against his will—toward earthly things. At this point Augustinus encourages Franciscus to identify with the example of his own conversion in the Milanese garden: "I am not surprised that you find yourself entangled in these complexities, by which once I myself was tormented. . . . I remained the same man I was, until deep meditation at last heaped up before my eyes all my misery. And then after I desired completely to change, I was also instantly able, and with miraculous and most welcome speed I was transformed into another Augustine, whose life story, unless I am mistaken, you know from my *Confessions*" (55–56).

Petrarch fully intends for us to see the contrast between his Augustinus (who converts himself by an act of will) and the "real" Augustine of the *Confessions* (who is converted by the grace of God). Augustinus has much more in common with the Stoic philosophers of pagan antiquity than with the early church father; he embodies not so much the historical Augustine as the ideal of exemplarity itself. Indeed, he caps off the example of his conversion with a choice verse from the *Aeneid* that succinctly captures Franciscus's inability to will what he desires: "The mind remains unmoved, fruitless tears pour down." Augustinus then elaborates on his choice of this line: "Although I could have gathered many illustrations about this, nonetheless I was content with this single example that is particularly familiar to you." Franciscus responds: "You have chosen wisely. For your case did not need more, nor could another example have penetrated more deeply into my heart." Franciscus comments further on the effect of this example: "This is all the more true because, although we are separated by the greatest distance, as great as that between a shipwrecked person and one who possesses a safe port, or between a happy person and a miserable one, still somehow within my inner turmoil I recognize a vestige of your wrenching struggle" (56). Aside from the irony that a pagan verse has illuminated Franciscus's reading of the *Confessions,* we should also note that this verse has enabled him instantaneously to bridge the spiritual and temporal gulf separating him from Augustinus. At this point Franciscus surrenders all opposition and gives himself over to the full force of Augustinus's argument, thus further exemplifying the power of a well-chosen example to move the will toward action.

THE SECOND DAY'S DIALOGUE CONTINUES THIS THEME, exploring the utility of examples and how to glean them from one's readings. Augustinus begins by measuring Franciscus against the traditional Christian yardstick of the seven deadly sins. Although Augustinus admits that envy, gluttony, and anger hold little sway with Franciscus, he indicts him for lust, pride, avarice, and sloth. Franciscus openly confesses to lust—Petrarch had fathered an illegitimate son in 1337 and a daughter in 1343—and then lets the matter drop. Against the charge of pride he defends himself more adamantly, and this time Augustinus (desirous of moving on) lets the matter drop. Augustinus presses Franciscus harder on the matter of avarice, eventually forcing him to admit that the desire for wealth has led him to forsake the healthful solitude of rural life for an urban existence full of noise and distraction. Sloth, though, presents the ultimate challenge (Petrarch found himself subject to periodic fits of melancholia—what

Franciscus calls *accidia* or *aegritudo*—whose enervations he subsumed under this traditional moral label). Franciscus and Augustinus circle inconclusively round and round this stubborn problem, with Augustinus ultimately offering what sounds to our modern ears like lame advice: exploit the power of positive thinking by writing down all the helpful maxims you encounter in your readings. Commenting on this recommendation, no less astute an observer than Karl Weintraub remarks, "Augustine tries to give all sorts of 'reasonable' advice, but frankly sounds a bit helpless—if not actually a bit silly" (104). And on this apparently lame note about note taking, the second day's dialogue ends.

Despite our modern reactions, however, the second day's dialogue does not trail off into silliness over an intractable problem; instead, it builds to a climax about the salubrious effects of reading. Recall that reading is the basis for imitation, and imitation is the means of internalizing and applying the universal truths best exemplified in classical works of history, poetry, and moral philosophy. Also recall that in the Renaissance reading intertwines with note taking: all of the five developed forms of reading—imitative, meditative, doctrinal, scholastic, and allegorical—emphasize the distillation of truths from texts. Indeed, from our modern perspective this way of reading actually represents a double or triple distillation: Renaissance readers extracted truths from stories, which they had in turn distilled from texts, which they had read with an eye for the universal rather than the contextual.

Petrarch explicitly discusses this form of reading/note taking several times in the *Secretum*. During the above exchange about Franciscus's *accidia*, for example, Augustinus argues that one must have salutary maxims embedded in one's memory, ready at hand to combat the passions, whose sudden onslaught can overwhelm the citadel of reason without warning. Franciscus demonstrates to Augustinus that he has indeed internalized this truth about reason's need for vigilance:

> And to show that I have taken this truth not only from the philosophers but also from the poets, I have often thought that Virgil, when he describes the fury of the winds lying in deep caves and mountains rising above them, and King Aeolus sitting on high and restraining the winds with his power, could be describing anger and other impulses. Those passions burning deep in the breast that, unless they are restrained by the bridle of reason, as we read in the same poem, "would in their fury carry off the seas and the earth and the depths of the sky and drag them off through the air."

Not content with this analogical reading, he goes on to allegorize it: "By 'earth' Virgil means nothing other than the earthly material of the human body. By 'seas' he means the moisture through which we live. By 'depths of the sky' what else does he mean but the soul dwelling deep within . . . ?" Of course, Virgil means nothing of the sort, as Petrarch well knew, but he had Augustinus approve of this exegesis, regardless of "whether Virgil himself intended these meanings when he wrote, or whether they were the farthest thing from his mind and he meant to describe a storm and nothing more" (99–100). True eloquence can and should avail itself of any appropriate example to move its intended audience.

The above passage illustrates three different kinds of reading, which all conduce to note taking. In addition to the "allegorical" there is (obviously) the "imitative" form of reading, whereby Petrarch uses the *Aeneid* to dramatize the relationship between passion and reason. And the prominence of the *Aeneid* here and throughout the dialogue indicates the presence of "doctrinal" reading, in which an authoritative text—and nothing could have been more authoritative for Petrarch than the *Aeneid*—becomes (to reprise Hankins) "an armature upon which to hang moral lessons and an encyclopedic knowledge of all the arts and sciences." Note taking inevitably follows from these combined forms of reading. When Augustinus advises Franciscus to deploy helpful maxims in his fight against melancholia, he encourages him to take notes on his readings as a means of embedding them in his memory. The second day's dialogue culminates with this recommendation: "During your readings . . . when you come upon such things, put marks next to the useful passages. Through these marks, as with hooks, you can hold in your memory useful things that wish to fly away." With maxims thus ready to hand, Franciscus can beat back the sudden onslaughts of melancholia. As Augustinus elsewhere declares, "What good is it to know a lot if you do not know how to use this knowledge to address your needs?" (126).

Many commentators regard Petrarch's allegorical interpretations of the *Aeneid* here and elsewhere in the *Secretum* as medieval anachronisms, as Christian holdovers inappropriate to the understanding of classical texts. This judgment, though, has the effect of dismissing one way of reading in favor of another, whereas they all coexist and mutually reinforce an inherent tendency toward exemplarity—to detach a text from its context, to distill from it illuminating anecdotes and scenes, and then further to distill from them timeless, universal truths. Note taking results from this triple distillation, either through the transformation of authoritative texts into encyclopedias by heavy glossing and indexing or through the creation of separate manuscript notebooks. Far from being a curious by-product of the humanist program of imitation, note taking and notebooks embody its essential point—to distill and deploy examples of truth capable of moving the will toward action. Note taking constitutes the visible trace of the living past in the activity of reading.

THE *SECRETUM*'S ADVOCACY OF *IMITATIO*, EXEMPLARITY, and the humanist art of reading culminates in the second day's dialogue with Petrarch's observations about the importance of note taking. Day three's dialogue puts these observations to the test, along with the whole purpose of the humanist curriculum, when Augustinus probes the twin source of Franciscus's erroneous ways, namely his misguided love of Laura and of the poet's laurel. Petrarch claimed to have first glimpsed Laura at a church service in Avignon in 1327, soon after abandoning his legal studies, and—whether real or a figment of his imagination— she became his lifelong muse. Horrified by Augustinus's accusation that he might be lusting in his heart for Laura, Franciscus defends his love as pure and virtuous—indeed, as the propaedeutic for his love of God. "But that perverts the order of things," retorts Augustinus (112). Franciscus, however, remains unmoved, so Augustinus pulls out the big guns: "On this topic of love, you know that there have been written not only remarkable treatises by outstanding philosophers but also whole books by illustrious poets. . . . Perhaps you would not consider it unfriendly for me to advise you how these things that you have read and understood can be directed toward your salvation" (119). He then deploys examples from Cicero and Ovid to highlight the need to flee "the plague of love," but Franciscus confesses that he has already tried and failed to follow this advice, so strong is his attachment to Laura. Echoing Seneca, he declares, "I have fled, but I carry my evil with me wherever I go," to which Augustinus responds, "Unless the patient is well-disposed, the power of the physician is ineffective." Franciscus's comeback exposes a fundamental issue at the heart of the program of imitation: "Now I am really confused. You offer me the prescription of flight for a recuperating and healing soul, yet you simultaneously proclaim that my soul must be cured and healthy before it can flee" (121).

The program of imitation underlying the humanist curriculum is based on the assumption that one can directly identify with classical examples, easily internalizing the universal truths they represent. Franciscus's exasperated comeback calls this assumption into question, and the interlocutors proceed to tussle over the issue, with Augustinus attempting to advance against Franciscus's determined opposition. As they spar, they reveal how the same example can mean different things to different people, illustrating the extent to which context determines exemplarity, potentially undermining the universality of classical examples. At one point Augustinus recommends that Franciscus flee Avignon, and the close proximity of Laura. Citing Seneca—"For one who is trying to put off love, every reminder of bodily pleasure must be forbidden"—Augustinus argues that even a soul cured of error should avoid temptation. Franciscus rejects this example, claiming that Augustinus has misapplied it: "These words are said not of one who *has already* put off love, but of one who *is trying* to put off love." Augustinus, though, defends his application by suggesting a different context for the line: "If the healthy must guard against these things, how much more careful must be those whom sickness has not yet deserted!" (123–24). Clearly, the choice of a context for *imitatio* is dependent on the interpreter and the interpretation, which (in turn) relativizes the meaning of the example.

As if to drive home this lesson, Petrarch follows this exchange with a scene where the interlocutors talk past each other. Hoping to urge Franciscus to reflect on his own mortality, Augustinus asks him what he thinks when he beholds his graying temples in the mirror, to which Franciscus responds by recalling a host of classical examples about gray hair, all mitigating the fear of aging. These examples have exactly the opposite effect than intended by Augustinus. To his frustrated retort—"If I had talked about your baldness, I guess you would have trotted out Julius Caesar"—Franciscus blithely responds: "It is a great consolation to be surrounded by such famous companions; and so I confess that I do not reject the use of such examples, which I use as I use the material goods I rely on every day." Just as Augustinus had turned the tables on him over the interpretation of Seneca, Franciscus has now turned the issue of gray hair around, forcing Augustinus to concede the utility of his opponent's view: "To be honest, this library of examples is fine with me, as long as it doesn't lead to laziness but rather only dispels fear and sorrow" (128–30). If the exemplarity of an example is relative, then so too is the ideal of exemplarity itself, thus undermining the whole humanist program of imitation.

The *Secretum* further exploits this point when Augustinus segues from the error of loving Laura to that of loving the laurel—the enticements of literary renown. He accuses Franciscus of seeking to charm his readers by merely compiling classical examples, "seizing little pearls of wisdom here from poetry, there from histories, indeed from all kinds of literature" (136). Although Franciscus vigorously denies this accusation—claiming that such compilers are "butchers of literature"—Augustinus argues that these efforts to win favor have culminated in two enormous unfinished projects, the epic poem *Africa* (celebrating the life of Scipio Africanus) and the biographical collection commemorating the heroes of ancient Rome, *De viris illustribus.* "Writing about others, you forget yourself. How do you know that, with both works unfinished, death will not snatch the exhausted pen from your hand?" Perhaps this is every author's worry—I write these words cloistered in my study on a beautiful summer's day—but it takes on Christian relevance with Augustinus's insistence that Franciscus's time is better spent preparing to meet his maker rather than on literary efforts soon forgotten. Franciscus disdainfully dismisses Augustinus's accusation that he seeks immortality through literature: "Human glory is enough for me." To his claim that one must pursue human glory while here on earth, Augustinus retorts with equal disdain, "You are truly an idiot! *[Stultissime homuncio]*" (140).

The *Secretum* ends at this impasse, with Franciscus pledging (in Augustine's famous line from the *Confessions*) to "collect the scattered fragments of my soul," but only after having attended to his earthly obligations as a writer. The great irony in day three's dialogue—which undermines the whole three-day exchange—is the reversal in Augustinus's stance. In the first and second days' dialogues he championed the humanist curriculum as a panacea for what ailed Franciscus, whose moral resolve could be strengthened by his readings. But what purpose does all this reading serve, if not to enhance one's writing? Once this goal becomes clear in day three's dialogue, the conflict between the pursuit of eloquence through imitation and the Christian transcendence of worldly concerns becomes starkly apparent. Despite Petrarch's repeated assertions, here and elsewhere, that pagan examples can inspire Christian virtue, he reluctantly confronts the same fact encountered in "The Ascent of Mont Ventoux," that Livy can't lead him up the mountain toward God. Not even an Augustine can mediate the differences between the classical and Christian worlds, and Augustinus ends up jettisoning the humanist program of reading he had previously championed. Franciscus's valedictory, however, stands as the last word on the subject: "I cannot restrain my desire for the world" (148). With this confession he takes refuge in the (vain) hope that the world's siren call will eventually subside on its own.

THE *SECRETUM* ENACTS THE LIVING PAST as a dialogue, but the ambiguous nature of its interlocutors dramatizes that this dialogue is not between the past and the present as we conceive of them. Augustinus and Franciscus are transtemporal composites, the literary equivalent of Apelles/Raphael. They symbolize an interchange between past and present that transcends our arid, modern distinction between the two, an interchange in which the past stands as a creative force in the present. Herein lies the beating heart of the "Renaissance discovery of classical antiquity"—to echo Roberto Weiss's book title of a generation ago. An eminent and accomplished scholar, Weiss treated his subject in a highly refined and technical way as the pre- and early history of archaeology, thus taking for granted the existence of our conception of the past in the Renaissance. Back then, however, the past was no dead thing but "vital" and "alive," adjectives that do not simply modify "the past" as a preexistent given but rather constitute its very substance.

It is hard for us moderns to wrap our minds around this living past. I have tried to show how it emerges in and through the humanist program of imitation. Even here, though, we may experience an almost unavoidable tendency to think of the humanists as imitating "the past," thus positing as a given something that did not exist for them. (Had it existed, Petrarch's "Augustinus" would have had much more in common with the historical Augustine—and the *Secretum* would be a much less involving and intimate work.) Instead of imitating the past, the humanists imitated examples, which combined historicizing and universalizing aspects. And the process of imitation was no mere copying of a prior thing (a modern conception that evokes the distinction between past and present) but rather a complex interchange between text and model that affirms the vitality of both.

The first letter to Cicero, "The Ascent of Mont Ventoux," and the *Secretum* all demonstrate Petrarch's awareness of the paradox inherent in the humanist program of imitation. The more the humanists succeeded in resurrecting the ideal of classical literature and culture, the less relevant it became to their world. This issue plays itself out forcefully in the *Secretum,* where (writ large) *imitatio* is both a moral panacea and a spiritual distraction, and (writ small) examples shine as fixed moral beacons while, at the same time, reflecting the diverse assumptions of their beholders, which relativize their lessons. In typical humanist fashion Petrarch remained untroubled by these inconsistencies or— to modify Trinkaus's caricature of the movement's tendency toward vagueness—he deftly turned these inconsistencies into literary occasions for the presentation of his authorial self. He remained throughout his life, first and foremost, a writer in the classical mode, who had internalized a wealth of examples from ancient literature, making them his own. To echo Franciscus's valedictory, he could not restrain his desire for the world, a desire that manifested itself in and through imitation. He thus remained a powerful advocate for the humanist curriculum, despite his uncertainties, and his advocacy helped guarantee its success, along with the habit of reading/note taking it instilled.

We turn now toward a consideration of the system of note taking spawned by the humanist curriculum. This system, and the moral ideals that underlay it, substantiated the living past born of imitation, embodying the symbolic space epitomized by Raphael's *School of Athens*. The vitality of this space depended on the humanists' ability to negotiate the tension between universality and historicity in their use of examples. The best humanists—such as Erasmus—managed this tension by means of an exquisite sense of *decorum,* an ability to pick only the most appropriate examples from the immense diversity of those stored in their notebooks. Eventually, though, this diversity overwhelmed the means of storage, creating a sixteenth-century version of information overload. The resulting attempts to create new forms of information management would ultimately sap the vitality of the living past in the attempt to organize and control it.

The Commonplace View of the World

P etrarch's living past existed in and through the humanist program of imitation, of which he was the chief early proponent. *Imitatio* engendered a synchronous space in which past and present intertwined creatively—defining, reinforcing, and offsetting each other—in an ongoing interchange that simultaneously established and revealed Petrarch's authorial self. His immediate successors—men like Coluccio Salutati (1331–1406), Gasparino da Barzizza (1360–1430), Leonardo Bruni (1370–1444), Guarino da Verona (1374–1460), and Vittorino da Feltre (1378–1446), to give only a smattering of names—increasingly advanced beyond Petrarch in their knowledge of ancient culture, their mastery of classical Latin style (to which they added a knowledge of Greek), and their command of ancient literary models. They generally did not match his literary brilliance, however, even though Salutati and Bruni in particular were highly regarded stylists.

Perhaps the lesser light of their literary talent facilitated their ability to translate Petrarch's innovative use of *imitatio* into a fairly standardized educational curriculum. In so doing, they helped develop Petrarch's informal suggestions about reading/note taking into a more rigorous system of commonplace notebooks. During the fifteenth and sixteenth centuries, humanist notebook techniques became the chief support and instrument for the exercise of *imitatio*. In place of Petrarch's supple exploitation of a relatively small number of classical models—with a heavy emphasis on Cicero and Virgil—humanist students and readers filled their notebooks with a much wider array of material, utilizing Greek as well as Latin sources, and medieval and contemporary ones too, especially as all these found their way into print in the course of the sixteenth century. They stored and accessed all this material through a system of commonplaces representing accepted truths, the social and moral norms they took for granted in their everyday lives. They used this material to construct rhetorical arguments *in utramque partem,* on both sides of a question, in order to arbitrate between contrasting possibilities and choose the most likely course of action. In contrast to their scholastic contemporaries, the humanists maintained that the skeptical weighing of possibilities best suited practical life in a complex world where logical certainty was rarely attainable.

As Petrarch's general recommendations about note taking were translated into actual commonplace notebooks, the living past became less a product of *imitatio* than a preliminary to it. Instead of creating the living past by testing their examples and being tested by them, Petrarch's successors learned how to deploy them as modes of proof in rhetorical set pieces. I have perhaps overstated this point in order to make it: Petrarch's practice of *imitatio* was not always innovative, nor was that of his successors consistently unimaginative. He obviously deployed examples in set-piece rhetorical arguments on both sides of a question—utilizing commonplace truths that he took for granted—and many of his successors fully opened themselves to the dialogic interplay between past and present, which is the highest form of *imitatio.* But as this program became routinized in a system of education, it inevitably lost much of its subtlety, and the living quality of the past came to be located more in the commonplace headings of one's notebooks, representing universal truths that would remain forever and always meaningful, than in the supple practice of *imitatio* that might call those truths into question. At the same time, though, the examples subsumed under these headings became more historically and culturally diverse, especially as knowledge of antiquity deepened. The growing disjunction between universality and historicity increasingly highlighted the paradox of exemplarity, which ultimately not even the most refined practice of *imitatio* could redress.

PETRARCH'S RECOMMENDATIONS ABOUT NOTE TAKING found a ready audience among the next generation of humanist pedagogues. In "De studiis et literis" ("The Study of Literature"), a short educational treatise written for the daughter of the Count of Urbino around 1405, Leonardo Bruni recommends that she mine the works of the best classical and Christian authors, in an exhaustive analysis that presumes the practice of detailed note taking: "With them she will train and strengthen her taste, and she will be careful, when she is obliged to say or write something, to use no word she has not first met in one of these authors" (99). With this treatise, concludes R. R. Bolgar in his classic assessment of humanist education, "the age of mnemotechnical aids has begun" (269).

But the humanists remained surprisingly reticent about describing the actual practice of note taking. The greatest educator of his day, Guarino da Verona, had his students keep two kinds of notebooks—the *methodice* (containing rhetorical forms and idioms) and the *historice* (containing general information). Contemporary descriptions of his classroom practices, however, say nothing about the structure and organization of these compendia. Perhaps this silence reflects the disdain many of his aristocratic charges must have felt for this menial activity. Indeed, for the young aristocrat who balked at taking notes, Guarino even recommends hiring "some suitable and well-educated lad" to do it for him.[19]

Humanist note taking in fifteenth-century Italian schools primarily aided in the acquisition of a Ciceronian Latin, but as this practice spread to northern Europe in the sixteenth century, it acquired a broader, more philosophical justification that elevated its importance in the eyes of both teachers and students. This development resulted from the fifteenth-century fusion of rhetoric and dialectic. In the traditional Aristotelian hierarchy of knowledge, dialectic occupies a position midway between logic and rhetoric. Whereas logic demonstrates truths that can be known with certainty through syllogisms, and rhetoric proposes likelihoods that can be established with probability by arguing on both sides of a question, dialectic employs commonly accepted opinions as premises in proofs that cannot be established with certainty but that can nonetheless serve as a basis for informed judgment. Dialectic is thus sometimes regarded as the "logic" of rhetoric. In his treatise on dialectical disputations—*Dialecticae disputationes* (first written in 1439 and revised repeatedly)—Lorenzo Valla (1406–57) expanded the realm of dialectic into that of logic, claiming greater legitimacy for propositions made in the "ordinary language" of literate discourse (i.e., proper, Ciceronian Latin) than in the specialized language of scholastic philosophy, whose obscurities created rather than resolved logical problems.

In attempting to win back for humanist rhetoric ground lost to scholastic logic, Valla laid one of the cornerstones for what we may term the "commonplace view of the world." He effectively fused the dialectical and rhetorical "places" where one searched for arguments framed in the language of ordinary discourse. As the influence of humanism spread northward from Italy, these places—or "seats" of arguments—would eventually evolve from analytical categories into moral and social norms, represented by the headings of student notebooks, also known as "commonplace books." Students learned to deploy this commonplace material by means of arguments *in utramque partem* in order to establish probability in a world where (humanists claimed) truth could not be ascertained. This skeptical mode of reasoning was anchored by a normative view of the world, in which diverse examples converged to demonstrate social and moral assumptions that enabled one to arbitrate between contrasting positions. By the sixteenth century, as we will see, the commonplace headings of one's notebooks had become identified with these assumptions, embodying the sites of the living past. Commonplaces preserved classical material in all its historical distinctiveness for the purpose of applying it to the practical problems of modern life, which resembled those of antiquity.[20]

THE TERMS *PLACE* (in Greek *topos,* or Latin *locus*) and *commonplace (koinos topos,* or *locus communis)* have a long and extremely complicated history, as recently attested by Francis Goyet's weighty and ironically titled tome, *Le sublime de "lieu commun"* (The sublimity of the "commonplace"). For our purposes, though, suffice it to say that Aristotle distinguished in his *Rhetoric* between "common" and "special" places—common ones contained ways of framing arguments applicable to all forms of knowledge, whereas the special ones applied only to specific forms of knowledge. He subjected the common places to extensive analysis in his *Topics,* which serves as the dialectical counterpart to his *Rhetoric,* showing how to use commonly accepted assumptions and categories to construct convincing arguments on both sides of a question. Cicero (and later Quintilian) subsequently muddied these clean Aristotelian distinctions, in part because the practical-minded Romans prized rhetoric over philosophy, thus devaluing special places in favor of common ones. In framing his rhetorical arguments, Cicero distinguished between *loci,* the dialectical places where one searched for different kinds of arguments, and *loci communes,* the ideas and expressions applicable to all arguments. He thus distorted Aristotle's distinction, while thinning the boundary between the two kinds of places. Whereas Roman orators deployed *loci* and *loci communes* chiefly in the service of forensic rhetoric, Christian rhetoricians used them to address moral as well as legal concerns. The moral thrust of Christian oratory gradually transformed the *loci* from categories of argumentation into collections of virtues and vices and the *loci communes* from embellishments for any argument to expressions of traditional wisdom. By the Renaissance, the terms *loci* and *loci communes* had become virtually indistinguishable, paving the way for Valla's fusion of rhetoric and dialectic.

Following in Valla's wake, Rudolph Agricola (1444–85) offered one of the first detailed descriptions of a humanist notebook, whose places mirrored those of the new humanist dialectic. Born in the Low Countries, Agricola had sojourned extensively in Italy, where he studied in Ferrara with Guarino's son Battista. While in Italy, he composed the bulk of his *De inventione dialectica* (On dialectical invention), written in the spirit of Valla's treatise. Agricola defined dialectic as the art of finding "whatever can be said with any degree of probability on any subject."[21] Dialectic thus encompassed a very wide range of arguments, from informally demonstrated likelihoods to more rigorously deduced proofs; it aimed to establish the "places" these different kinds of argument have in common.

The "common headings" *(capita communia)* of his dialectic bear intentional resemblance to the "commonplaces" *(loci communes)* in his model for a humanist notebook. These he described in a short educational treatise, *De formando studio* (On the shaping of studies [1484]), written immediately after completing the treatise on dialectic. His system of note taking builds on the tradition of medieval *florilegia,* the "collections of flowers" culled from sacred and secular literature that preachers consulted when composing sermons. From these he borrowed the scheme of moral headings—"virtue," "vice," "life," "death," "love," "hate," and so on—under which quotations were stored. But he subjected this scheme to greater systematization, creating antithetical pairings—"virtue and vice," "life and death," "love and hate"—that reflected the primacy of rhetorical arguments *in utramque partem* and the humanist dialectic that underlay them. Indeed, he encouraged students to exercise their ingenuity in storing any given example under as many different headings as possible in order to facilitate its use in arguments on both sides of a question.

Agricola's *De formando studio* only circulated in manuscript during his lifetime, but its recommendations at the very least resemble—if they did not actually influence—those Erasmus made in two famous educational treatises: *De ratione studii* (On the right method of instruction [1511]) and, most important, *De copia verborum ac rerum (On Copia of Words and Ideas)*. First published in 1512 and repeatedly revised, *De copia verborum ac rerum* became the most influential textbook of the first age of printing, with more than one hundred editions published in the sixteenth century alone. Erasmus's recommendations on note taking occur in book 2, concerning the abundance of *res* (or "things"), the ideas and examples for use in one's compositions. Here he declares the necessity of reading classical literature with pen and notebook at hand, "for he who wishes to be considered learned must do that thoroughly once in his life" (87). He advises keeping a *liber locorum rerum*—literally a "book of the places of things"—divided into three groups of *loci.* The first group consists of paired virtues and vices, such as piety and impiety, which he in turn divides into subheadings, such as piety and impiety toward God, the fatherland, the family, and so on. The second group consists of what he terms *exempla,* unusual examples—such as extraordinary longevity, vigorous old age, senile youth, and so forth—again paired with their opposites. The third group consists of what he terms *loci communes,* maxims or proverbs derived from the previous *loci* and noted alongside them.

Erasmus sought to derive moral examples from even the most unlikely sources, such as mathematics and geometry. "No learning is so far removed from rhetoric that you may not enrich your classifications from it. . . . For example, a wise man, happy in his wealth, not dependent on anyone else, constant and unmoved in his own virtue whatever way the winds of fortune may blow, is compared with a sphere everywhere similar to itself" (90). The classifications of the *liber locorum rerum* represent not arbitrary categories but the moral substratum of reality, apparent in the normative assumptions everyone takes for granted. These anchor the skeptical mode of reasoning *in utramque partem.* In their predilection for vagueness and for an untroubled inconsistency, the humanists could afford to disparage logic in favor of rhetoric because theirs was merely a limited skepticism. They never doubted their ability to recognize truth—or, better yet, verisimilitude—whenever they encountered it.

Whereas Erasmus's analysis of rhetorical dilation treats *verba* (vocabulary, idioms, and expressions) before *res,* Philip Melanchthon (1497–1560) reverses this order in his highly influential treatment of the topic, *De locis communibus ratio* (On the method of commonplaces). (This handbook—lifted in its entirety from a section of his 1519 treatise on rhetoric, *De rhetorica libri tres*—received wide distribution in a special volume on note taking, *De ratione studii* [1531], which also included Agricola's *De formando studio* and Erasmus's recommendations, excerpted from *De copia verborum ac rerum.*) His reversal of emphasis reflects his belief that the things of the world correspond to certain sets or "patterns" *(formae),* which can serve as the basis for one's *loci.* Indeed, he even goes so far as to say that the *loci* used in one's note taking reflect the innermost foundation of nature *(ex intimis naturae sedibus eruti, formae sunt seu regulae omnium rerum).*[22] Melanchthon—Luther's right-hand man and the foremost humanist among the early Protestants—had almost as profound an influence on early modern education as Erasmus, and his elevation of the *loci* from topic headings to representations of the substance of reality sets the seal on the fusion of rhetorical and dialectical places that began with Valla.

The *liber locorum rerum* was the largest and most important of the humanist notebooks, which might also include other volumes, such as a *liber styli* devoted to proper Latin style and a *liber sermonis* for eloquent classical expressions.

Taken together, these substantiated a commonplace view of the world that stored information from diverse times and places—with each entry preserving the distinctive style of its original—under headings of normative value for use in arguments on both sides of a question. During the course of the sixteenth century this commonplace mentality was reinforced by printing, with the publication of otherwise blank notebooks divided into preselected topic headings, of editions of classical works with extra space between each line to facilitate note taking, and of a host of dedicated commonplace books organized by a variety of schema (alphabetical, topical, antithetical, or whatnot). Indeed, the prevalence of printed commonplace books minimized, if it did not actually eliminate, the need to take notes on one's own. All these compendia, of whatever sort, provided humanistically trained writers with raw material for exercises in *imitatio,* by which they deployed "historically correct" instances of the living past in skeptical arguments anchored by universal truths.

THE RENAISSANCE CAREER OF THE CICERONIAN maxim *historia magistra vitae* best illustrates the fate of the living past as it became bound up with the commonplace view of the world. Even in antiquity, Cicero's praise of history—"the witness of time, the light of truth, the life of memory, the teacher of life *[magistra vitae],* the herald of ancient days" (*De oratore,* 2.9.36)—had epitomized its value as philosophy teaching by example. The roots of this "exemplar theory of history" extend back to Polybius, who punctuated his interminable account of occurrences with periodic digressions on the utility of history. Indeed, declares George H. Nadel in his seminal essay on early historical thinking, "to have read Polybius is to have read most of the advocates of exemplar history, ancient and modern" (65). For Polybius, the utility of history lies in its ability to provide a wealth of vicarious experience, such that "those who study history are, we may almost say, provided with a method for dealing with any contingency that may arise" (*The Histories,* 9.2.5). This method hinges on two requirements: that the account be truthful and that it be thorough—that it provide not just the facts but the causes underlying the facts, causes best discerned by historians with personal experience in political and military affairs. Polybius and his successors in antiquity never thought to question the utility of one age's lessons for another—or even to frame the issue in this way—because they did not have a systematic and sustained idea of anachronism. In the absence of this sensibility, *historia magistra vitae* became an instant commonplace, almost as soon as Cicero voiced it.

Prizing instruction by example rather than precept, the humanists made this truth their own, according history a special place in their curriculum. Paolo Vergerio (c. 1370–c. 1444) captures their attitude toward history in his widely read educational treatise *De ingenuis moribus et liberalibus studiis* (On good manners and liberal studies): "We come now to the consideration of the various subjects which may rightly be included under the name of 'Liberal Studies.' Amongst these I accord the first place to History, on grounds both of its attractiveness and of its utility, qualities which appeal equally to the scholar and to the statesman.... History ... gives us the concrete examples of the precepts inculcated by philosophy. The one shows what men should do, the other what men have said and done in the past, and what practical lessons we may draw therefrom for the present day."[23]

In its attractiveness and utility, history served both scholar and statesman as a form of political education. The common attitude expressed by Vergerio around 1400 informed a whole genre of humanist literature, the *ars historica,* or art of history, which flourished in the sixteenth and seventeenth centuries. Virtually all *artes historicae* replay, with some variation, the Ciceronian theme of *historia magistra vitae.* If anything, it had become by the Renaissance even more of a commonplace than it had been in antiquity. Viewed from the perspective of Erasmus's note-taking system, it was what he would have termed a *locus communis*—a maxim or proverb expressing traditional wisdom—representative of his third group of *loci,* to be entered in his *liber locurum rerum* alongside the examples from which it derived. Regardless of whether one actually went to all this trouble, one undoubtedly registered the commonplace whenever one encountered a noteworthy example. In effect, the humanist habit of note taking served to confirm the truth of the commonplace—again, and again, and again.

This truth was further reinforced by the humanist habit of reading, especially in the age before printing. When one had relatively few histories available, one mined each extensively for its lessons, in a process that naturally enriched the ore. Thus a former student of Vittorino da Feltre's, Frederico da Montefeltro (1422–82)—one of the great *condottieri* of his day, who by craft and force made himself duke of Urbino—customarily dined in his ducal palace while listening to Latin recitations of Livy. Although one could hardly claim that Livy was the key to his success, Frederico's leisurely and reiterated progress though the text left him free not only to savor the gravity and richness of Livy's prose but also to explore the wealth of possible connections between ancient Roman and modern Italian events, connections (whether real or imagined) that might only become apparent through a long, slow, close reading . . . and rereading. The important point for our purposes is that Frederico not only assumed the existence of such connections, but he further assumed that to reveal them was both to substantiate and confirm history as the *magistra vitae*. (Otherwise, why spend long hours listening to Livy?) The commonplace thus had a circular aspect—because it was true, one found lessons in the past, and the lessons one found affirmed its truth.

Humanist habits of reading and note taking made for a remarkably durable notion. The Ciceronian commonplace reoccurs with mind-numbing frequency in *artes historicae,* from the inception of this genre around the time of Giovanni Pontano's *Actius* (1499) to its close around the time of Lord Bolingbroke's *Letters on the Study and Use of History* (1738). Repeatedly encountering variations on this old saw, modern readers of the genre skip over them with a yawn, as if those who generated all this verbiage didn't really believe in it. Yet the commonplace survived innumerable blows—both political and philosophical—in part because those who mouthed it were reluctant to let go of the living past.

Perhaps the greatest blow came with the French invasion of Italy in 1494. Aided by the innovation of mobile siege artillery, the French army advanced through Italy with startling speed, demonstrating the weakness of Italian city-states when confronted with the economic and military might of a European kingdom. Thereafter, Italy became a battleground between France and Spain, and once-proud princes like Frederico da Montefeltro became pawns in a larger struggle. Machiavelli, in particular, lamented this development, especially in the introduction to his *Discourses on the First Ten Books of Titus Livius,* where he declared that Italians universally admire the ancients but everywhere fail to imitate them: "And yet to found a republic, maintain states, to govern a kingdom, organize an army, conduct a war, dispense justice, and extend empires, you will find neither prince, nor republic, nor captain, nor citizen, who has recourse to the examples of antiquity!" (104). The problem for Machiavelli lay in the need to systematize the lessons of history, to assimilate them to general rules, because the ways of conducting a war, dispensing justice, or extending an empire varied according to whether one commanded a principality or a republic, or whether one was a captain or a citizen. In both *The Prince* and *The Discourses* he showed how the material of history is situational and thus needs not only to be mined but refined—processed—in order to yield its lessons. In the final analysis, then, events challenged but did not overturn the notion of *historia magistra vitae.* Machiavelli subjected the text of Livy to a scrutiny at least as close as it received in Frederico's dining hall, secure in the assumption that its material—when properly refined and assayed—would confirm the value of history as a form of political education, perhaps even enabling Italians to reassert control over their homeland.

The philosopher Francesco Patrizi (1529–97), however, tackled the theoretical underpinning of this assumption head on, hammering it repeatedly in his *Della historia diece dialoghi* (Ten dialogues on history [1560])—one of the most disquieting of all the *artes historicae*. Until Patrizi, historical skepticism had been limited largely to hypercritical exercises, like that of Cornelius Agrippa (c. 1486–1535), who attacked history in passing in his declamation on the vanity of all learning. Patrizi's criticisms posed a much more serious challenge by questioning the logic of the Ciceronian commonplace itself. Feigning ignorance in the first dialogue, Patrizi asks his interlocutors to define the study of history. Did it include Aristotle's history of animals, Theophrastus's history of plants, or Pliny's natural history? When they sought to limit history to the memory of human events, Patrizi responded by questioning whether accounts of contemporary events, trivial events, or personal events could count as history. When they sought to limit history to public lives lived in politics, Patrizi accused them of ignoring the significance of inventors and explorers. Confronted with such logic—concludes Anthony Grafton in his lively account of this exchange—"the best-loved bromides of Cicero and Livy fall like dandelions before a sickle."[24]

Patrizi's questions reflect the impact that printing had on a highly critical mind that now had at its disposal a wide range of texts—political and military narratives, natural histories, biographies, travel accounts, memoirs, diaries, legal documents—which might actually constitute a new kind of history. This expansion of historical horizons threatened the coherence of the rhetorical conception of history, which had been grounded in a few beloved authors. Not content with this logical deconstruction of Cicero's commonplace, Patrizi also offers a methodological one in his fifth dialogue—the most famous of the ten. Here he denies the possibility of finding a worthwhile historian. He reasons that the best historians had witnessed the events they described, either as participants or as neutral observers; but participants always wrote biased accounts, while neutral observers—ignorant of either side's secrets—always wrote superficial ones. The structural flaws inherent in historical writing thus give the lie to the notion of *historia magistra vitae*.

Most surprising, though, is not Patrizi's attack on the commonplace but his inability to dispense with it. Time and again, as Giorgio Spini notes perceptively, he lets in through the window what he has just swept out the door. In the first dialogue he raises the possibility of a broader definition of history—one that might rescue it "from the marshes of rhetoric"—only to let it sink back

again into the exemplar theory.[25] Even the withering skepticism of the fifth dialogue serves not to invalidate the study of history but rather to place it on a
firmer footing. In subsequent dialogues he argues for the composition of narrative histories grounded not in partisan politics but in the impartial analysis of
customs, laws, and institutions, which can explain the true causes and outcomes
of events. Reinforced by this critical underpinning, narrative history can still
function as the *magistra vitae*.

The persistence of the Ciceronian commonplace might appear to us moderns
as an atavism, a classical holdover in an early modern world where printing had
expanded the body of literature called "history," where philology had lent exactitude to the study of texts, where antiquarian scholarship had unearthed a host
of new historical materials—coins, inscriptions, and documents of all sorts.
Were it not for the prevalence of this tired commonplace (we might think) the
early modern world would seem almost modern, at least from a historiographical perspective. Yet were we to ignore the durability of this commonplace—
focusing instead on the coming "historical revolution" that would lead to the
modern discipline of history—we would overlook the fundamental tautology
that rendered *historia magistra vitae* so durable. It was a commonplace because
people believed it was true, and they believed it was true because they found its
truth wherever and however they looked. The humanist habit of reading/note
taking guaranteed this result. Thus, people could define history as broadly as
they pleased, and the commonplace would still be true; they could employ the
most refined scholarly techniques, and (again) it would still be true.

The commonplace would retain its potency as long as the past remained a
living thing, as long as it continued to speak directly to the present. But the venue
for this interchange had evolved in the course of the Renaissance, from the activity of *imitatio* to the pages of a commonplace book, and this shift ultimately
sapped the vitality of the living past. I have used Petrarch's writings to show how
the past lived in and through the activity of imitation, yet we should take care not
to canonize him. Erasmus and Montaigne (to name but two figures) proved
equally skilled at this activity, thus demonstrating that the highest forms of
imitatio flourished throughout the Renaissance. The itinerary from Petrarch to
Erasmus to Montaigne, however, also traces the course of humanist note taking
forward to its ultimate outcome. Petrarch recommended it, Erasmus implemented
it, and Montaigne survived it. As a young student in the 1540s at a progressive
humanist school in Bordeaux, the Collège de Guyenne, Montaigne learned how
to keep a *liber locorum rerum*, a *liber styli*, and a *liber sermonis*. Similarly schooled,
most readers of the first edition of his *Essays* (1580) greeted it as a standard com-

monplace collection, which gathered illustrative examples under chapter titles that served as topic headings. They saw what they expected to see—what they were trained to see. It took the exceptional reader to note that in virtually every chapter, Montaigne discoursed upon examples that defied systematization, thus transforming the anticipated rhetorical set piece into an unexpected search for truth.

Montaigne surely ranks among the intellectual giants of his age, if only because he transcended the limits of his education. Most of his contemporaries, though, conformed to the commonplace view of the world. They remained accustomed to using examples to identify and support established truths. But as Patrizi clearly demonstrates, radically diverse examples—drawn from so many different kinds of sources—threatened to overturn the truths they were supposed to support. Faced with this challenge, most humanistically educated thinkers sought to reinforce the commonplace view of the world by further systematizing it, in a process that eventually devitalized the living past.

Jean Bodin and the Unity of History

The impact of printing redoubled the effect of a peculiar feature of Renaissance consciousness that stands as a necessary consequence of the living past. Recall that in Freud's conception of the psyche nothing ever dies; the same holds true for the living past. In the Renaissance mind all pasts persist in all their specificity; the space of the living past—imagine Raphael's portico—can thus become rather crowded as knowledge of antiquity grows. This possibility would have posed little difficulty for Petrarch. Although he treasured a manuscript of Homer, it served largely as a talisman; Petrarch did not read Greek, nor did he have a precise knowledge of the different phases of classical Latin style, his practice of *imitatio* being more eclectic than purely Ciceronian. The living past for him consisted of relatively few entities, whose distinctiveness did not so much set them apart from each other as from the present. But as the humanist movement matured, as its command of classical languages and cultures broadened and deepened, the space of the living past began to fill with more and more entities, all equally unique and alive—all bearing immediate meaning in and for the present.

The development of humanist notebook techniques is, at least in part, a response to this growing press of entities. The *liber locorum rerum,* in particular, served its compiler as a personal storehouse of classical learning, one specifically geared to the requirements of rhetorical composition. Over time, though, the humanists had to adapt this notebook to the task of organizing an ever-increasing body of knowledge. The habit of arranging commonplace topics in antithetical pairs eventually became unwieldy, calling forth more innovative means of controlling this information, especially as commonplace books found their way into print. The simplest expedient was to append an alphabetical index of topics to such antithetical collections, enabling one to cross-reference diverse information (this innovation necessarily awaited the invention of printing, which made possible the accurate reproduction of long lists of page references). Another expedient was to abandon antithetical arrangements for analytical ones, based on (for example) Aristotle's ten predicaments, his categories of knowledge. One of the most successful printed commonplace books, Theodor Zwinger's *Theatrum vitae humanae* (Theater of human life), which was first published in 1565 and continually expanded in dozens of editions, maintains the use of antithetical *loci* but emphasizes the logical and analytical connections between them. And last but not least there was the expedient of ordering topics alphabetically, an arrangement that had the advantage of being infinitely expandable, though knowledge stored in this way did not automatically lend itself to arguments *in utramque partem*. Indeed, the more analytical the collection, the more akin to an encyclopedia it became, and the less suited to the imperatives of rhetorical composition that had originally inspired the humanist habit of note taking.

All these methodologies for storing and organizing information tended to utilize normative categories, reflecting prevalent moral assumptions about the fundamental nature of human reality. (Even purely alphabetic listings followed moral themes.) In a living past where nothing ever dies, the manifold distinctiveness of entities stored by these means began to call into question the very means of storage itself, as moral *loci* filled to bursting with ever more diverse information. Montaigne's *Essays* epitomizes this development, as we can see from the opening chapter of his work. Although it is among the last chapters he composed for the first edition of the *Essays,* he placed it at the beginning specifically to highlight the problem of diversity.

The title of this chapter, "By diverse means we arrive at the same end," is clearly a commonplace, a maxim that Montaigne attempts to apply to his age of religious and civil war. The issue examined in the light of the commonplace— whether he who falls into the hands of his enemies should seek to save himself by submission or defiance—was a practical one for a prominent Catholic living in the midst of a Protestant stronghold. Montaigne tries to flesh out the commonplace by showing how stouthearted captors would likely esteem their prisoners' expressions of courage and defiance, while weakhearted ones would probably favor meekness and submission. But an array of examples from different times and places—about Epaminondas and Pelopidas of Thebes, Pompey and Sulla of Rome, Edward of Wales, Conrad of Germany, and Scanderbeg of Albania— ultimately thwarts this anticipated conclusion, demonstrating instead how stouthearted captors might just as likely ignore the courage of their prisoners. These examples overturn the commonplace title and end up showing (ironically) that by the same means we can arrive at diverse ends. Subsequent editions of the *Essays* expand the chapter with additional examples of capricious and unpredictable behavior, thus further illustrating Montaigne's ultimate conclusion: "Truly man is a marvelously vain, diverse, and undulating object. It is hard to found any constant and uniform judgment on him" (5).

Montaigne's *Essays* dramatize an exceptional thinker's awareness of the effect of information overload on the commonplace view of the world. Most of his contemporaries, however, dealt with the surfeit of information by attempting to reinforce and extend this view. As commonplace norms became overburdened, educated people had natural recourse to metanorms; they simply climbed to a higher conceptual perch, seeking a broader perspective from which to organize the diversity and variety of the world. This reaction was only to be expected from those for whom Aristotelian hierarchical thinking formed the standard of common sense. The metanormative approach to the problem of diversity is especially apparent in the transformation of the study of law during the Renaissance. When Roman law began to lose its normative value as the universal standard of jurisprudence, legal theorists attempted to articulate a new kind of universal law, fabricated from the best statutes of the most noteworthy peoples. This project necessarily embroiled them in a detailed study of history, for "in history the best part of universal law lies hidden."[26] Jean Bodin, one of the foremost legal theorists of his day, made this claim; and in seeking to substantiate it, he designed a would-be *liber locorum historiarum* from which to distill his legal metanorms. We will now examine the transformation of the study of law during the Renaissance, which culminates with Bodin's plan for a historical commonplace book.

UNTIL THE SIXTEENTH CENTURY the *Corpus juris civilis*—a sixth-century digest of Roman legal practices commissioned by the Byzantine emperor Justinian—held a privileged position in Europe as the most thoroughgoing and systematic statement of civil jurisprudence. It essentially constituted a body of universal law, immediately applicable to modern legal problems. It had initially owed this status to its revival in the West by the medieval Italian "glossators," who recovered the text in the late eleventh century and added layers of commentary to it over the next two hundred years. In these commentaries they applied Roman law directly to the circumstances of their political and social world, bending these circumstances to fit the letter of the law. They thus identified the prerogatives of the medieval German emperor with those of the Roman emperor as stated in Justinian's code. This literal reading of the text became harder to sustain in the thirteenth and fourteenth centuries, as the power of the German emperor dwindled, especially in Italy, where city-states customarily ignored imperial decrees. By the fourteenth century, a group of Italian "postglossators" had emerged, who abandoned the literal interpretation of Roman law for a more flexible one that better conformed to their political situation. The most illustrious of these men, Bartolus of Sassoferrato (c. 1313–57), proved remarkably adept at freely interpreting Roman law for contemporary use, molding its principles to conform to contemporary realities far from any Roman practice or intention. By revitalizing and preserving Roman law as universal law, he lent his name to an entire school of jurisprudence.

During the course of the Renaissance, humanists began to study the text of Roman law as they would any revered classic, with the intent of purifying it of scribal errors. Already in the mid-fifteenth century, Lorenzo Valla had argued for the need to understand the actual words of the *Corpus juris* before grasping its principles and applying them to contemporary legal problems. Although Valla indicted Bartolus for ignorance of classical Latin, he did not himself undertake a philological study of the *Corpus juris*. Toward the end of the century Angelo Poliziano (1454–94) did undertake such a study, comparing medieval versions of the text to its oldest extant copy—the sixth-century *Codex Florentinus* in the Medici library—but his efforts were fragmentary and unsystematic. It remained for a French scholar, Guillaume Budé (1468–1540), to implement the program of legal humanism advocated by the Italians. In 1508 he published his annotations on the first twenty-four books of the *Pandects*—the chief portion of the *Corpus juris*—in which he demonstrated that Bartolus and his successors had worked from defective manuscripts. An Italian professor of law sojourning in France, Andrea Alciato (1492–1550), subsequently adapted Budé's philological analysis of Roman law to the French legal curriculum. By the time he returned to Italy in 1532, he had helped establish the University of Bourges as the chief center for the new humanistic study of law, which became known as the *mos gallicus docendi*—or "French manner of teaching" Roman law—as opposed to the *mos italicus* of the Bartolists.

For Alciato, Roman law remained universal law; he used philological techniques to clarify the enduring legal principles conveyed in the *Corpus juris*. But his most famous successor at Bourges, Jacques Cujas (1522–90), used philology as a tool of historical research to illuminate the original laws from which Justinian's digest derived; he was entirely unconcerned with the relevance of Roman law to the modern world. When asked to apply his erudition to a contemporary legal problem, he is said to have replied, "Quid hoc ad edictum praetoris?" (What does this have to do with the praetor's edict?).[27] He regarded the *Corpus juris* not as a body of universal law but as a historical artifact—as the law of the Romans, pure and simple. Historical criticism thus began to corrode the norm of Roman law. This development inspired a metanormative reaction from Cujas's successor at Bourges, François Hotman (1524–90), who sought to preserve the vitality of the living past through a program of "neo-Bartolism."[28]

In his *Antitribonian* (1567) Hotman combines a critique of the *Corpus juris* with a proposal to establish a new, more inclusive body of universal law. Through a detailed analysis of the categories of civil law, Hotman shows that the terminology of the *Corpus juris,* and the practices based on this terminology, are relevant only to the historical circumstances of Rome and have no bearing on French law, with its feudal precedents. Indeed, he exclaims, a jurist trained solely in Roman law would, on finding himself in a French court, no doubt feel as if he had landed among the savages of the New World. Hotman combines this critique of the study of Roman law with a critique of Tribonian, the sixth-century editor selected by Justinian to compile the digest of Roman law. A sycophant of the Byzantine court, Tribonian was morally unfit to understand the civic virtue that had animated Roman law, and his assistants were not even native speakers of Latin but Greeks incapable of interpreting very obscure and difficult Latin texts. The *Corpus juris* thus embodies not the grandeur of Roman civilization but the decadence of its own age, and Hotman implies that it is useless even for understanding Byzantine law and history.

No sooner does he demolish the *Corpus juris* than Hotman unexpectedly gives it pride of place in the proposal for legal reform that concludes the *Antitribonian.* The time is now ripe, he declares, to assemble a commission of jurisconsults and statesmen to distill from the best laws of the most noteworthy peoples a new body of universal law. In this undertaking the *Corpus juris* will be like a "priceless treasury," where one can find "all the best and most admirable things." Indeed, it will provide not only some of the best examples of "natural equity" but also the principle for the organization of the new legal code. Hotman thus preserves the primacy of the *Corpus juris* for a new metanormative body of universal law. In a turnabout worthy of Patrizi, Hotman's neo-Bartolism lets in through the window what he has just swept out through the door.[29]

The "pro-Tribonian" conclusion of the *Antitribonian* demonstrates that historical and universal conceptions of Roman law coexist for Hotman in the synchronous space of the living past. He understands the *Corpus juris* historically, as the product of a Roman world different from the French one, a world with its own distinctive linguistic and legal styles—Republican, Imperial, Byzantine. But he does not relegate the *Corpus juris* to a place on a temporal continuum where it could be regarded as essentially dead and buried. Instead, it retains its vitality in a space full of many such entities—Greek law, Persian law, Hebrew law, Egyptian law—a synchronous space in which all historical entities reside on the same plane.

This synchronous space admits of no dichotomy between historicizing and universalizing tendencies; indeed, the two coexist without one diminishing the other. The *Corpus juris* thus stands as the text of a specifically *Roman* law and as a "priceless treasury" of universal value. It is very hard for modern historians to conceive of a historical entity as having universal value. We naturally tend to assume that the perception of its contingency undermines the possibility of its universality. This assumption has led scholars to regard Hotman's pro-Tribonian conclusion as a paradox, an inconsistency explained away as an oversight or dismissed as a quaint anomaly. But I submit that the paradox of the *Antitribonian* is our paradox—not Hotman's—born of our historical assumptions, which distort Hotman's conception of the living past.

In this synchronous space philology reveals the distinctive nature of historical entities without relegating them to a distant past. Indeed, rather than clarifying the past by organizing it chronologically, philological criticism simply clutters it up. The synchronous space where nothing ever dies tends to become overfilled, not only with a bewildering variety of different entities but also (as if in Freud's holographic vision) with different states of the same entity. In Hotman's neo-Bartolist proposal Roman law must share the stage with other bodies of law; and Roman law itself breaks down into its Republican, Imperial, and Byzantine manifestations, each of which has its own forms, such as the republic's Twelve Tables, praetors' edicts, and Justinian's Digest. In a synchronous space where nothing ever dies, the press of entities threatens to become overwhelming.

IN HIS *ARS HISTORICA,* the *Methodus ad facilem historiarum cognitionem* (*Method for the Easy Comprehension of History* [1566]), Jean Bodin aimed to clean up all this clutter. While pursuing his goal, Bodin imposed a structure on the synchronous space of the past that had the effect of reifying it, of fixing it in such a way that it began to lose its vitality. In place of the immediacy of the living past, Bodin substituted a concern with its "unity," a concern that ultimately points toward what Reinhart Koselleck terms "history itself," as distinct from "histories."[30] The latter are accounts of events, whereas the former is more than the sum total of these accounts; it is the arena in which events transpire—it is the past "back there" in time. Although Bodin conceived of himself as writing a "method for the easy comprehension of *histories*," his enterprise reveals growing anomalies within the traditional notion of history as a body of literature, anomalies that point beyond the living past and toward the emergence of "history itself" in the eighteenth century.

Perhaps the foremost political, legal, and economic theorist of his day, Jean Bodin (c.1529-96) remains an elusive figure. About his early life we know hardly more than that he studied law at the University of Toulouse in the 1550s, where he was exposed to the *mos gallicus*. Although he retained a scholar's sensitivity to the historical varieties of law, he nonetheless rejected the "grammatical pest" that had infected the study of law, where philology undermined the universal principles of equity.[31] These he attempted to reestablish in the *Methodus* and the *Juris universi distributio* (Table of universal law [1578]), two works that represent complementary halves of a single undertaking. The *Distributio* seeks to establish a new body of universal law—supplanting the *Corpus juris*—by classifying the art of jurisprudence in a hierarchy of topics and subtopics; and the *Methodus* seeks to fill in the topics of universal law through a systematic study of history. Bodin's was the most thorough attempt to bring the neo-Bartolist project to fruition. By contrast, Hotman merely contented himself with a brief outline of the project, which enabled him to articulate a synchronous conception of the past without having to concern himself with the actual disposition of entities within that space. Bodin, however, found himself forced to organize the synchronous space of the living past, an imperative that began to sap its symbolic meaning.

Although the *Distributio* was published twelve years after the *Methodus*, Bodin actually began writing it first, as is evident from references to it in the dedicatory letter of the *Methodus*. Here he apologizes to a fellow jurist for interrupting his work on the classification of universal law in order to write about the study of history. In the dedication Bodin never explains why he felt obliged to turn from one work to the other, but his description of his progress toward the classification of law suggests that it highlighted the need for a systematic study of history in order to clean up the clutter of the past, a clutter made apparent by the demise of Roman law as the universal standard of jurisprudence:

I disregard the absurdity of attempting to establish principles of universal jurisprudence from the Roman decrees, which were subject to change within a brief period. It is especially absurd, since almost all the laws of the Twelve Tables were supplanted by an infinite multitude of edicts and statutes, and later by the Aebutian Rogation also; repeatedly the old regulations were replaced by new ones. Moreover, we see that almost all the legislation of Justinian was abrogated by following emperors. I pass over how many things were absurd in the statutes which remain—how many were declared outworn by the just decrees of almost all peoples and by long disuse. The fact remains that they have described the laws of no people except the Romans, and these, indeed, in the wrong order. (2)

Instead of "Roman law," as set forth in the *Corpus juris,* one could now perceive "Roman laws"—the Twelve Tables, the Aebutian Rogation, and a host of other statutes—each of which had to be reconstructed and assessed for its contribution to a new body of universal law. In the dedication to the *Methodus* Bodin described how this process of historical criticism would apply not only to the laws of the Romans but also to those of the Persians, Greeks, Egyptians, Hebrews, British, Turks, and Germans, to name only a few. In the *Distributio* he intended to analyze each body of law by breaking it down into its constituent parts, assigning each part to a place, or *locus,* in his classificatory table of law. By comparing and contrasting the entries under each *locus,* one could derive the universal principles relevant to that aspect of jurisprudence.

Instead of making the study of law easier by historicizing it—and thereby relegating the Twelve Tables and the Aebutian Rogation to a past remote from the present—philology had made it more complicated. Philology revealed the existence of a multitude of Roman statutes that all merited a place in the table of universal law; and it would do the same for other bodies of law, deconstructing them into their own distinctive statutes, each of which merited study. In other words, philology had the effect of cluttering up a synchronous conception of the past in which nothing was ever regarded as dead and buried. No doubt, as Bodin began to confront this prospect, he realized that the task of classifying universal law was secondary to that of arranging the historical materials from which it derived, a realization that led him to shelve the *Distributio* in favor of working on the *Methodus.* In a synchronous space that included all historical entities, ordering the record of these entities was equivalent to making sense out of the past.

THE SYNCHRONOUS SPACE WAS SYMBOLIC IN NATURE, with temporal entities referencing transcendent ideals, and as such it could not bear too much historical scrutiny. It was born of a disjunction between past and present—the Petrarchan sense of anachronism—which gave rise to the yearning for a new connection between the two, an unfulfillable yearning that rendered the space of the past fundamentally utopian. It was the space within which Petrarch wrote letters to classical authors, within which Machiavelli donned his curial robes to converse with the ancients, within which Raphael gathered together all the great sages of antiquity. The neo-Bartolist vision was no less utopian, seeking as it did to reunify the law after the historical deconstruction of the *Corpus juris,* to reconstitute the wisdom of ancients—whose reach the neo-Bartolists (like Raphael) had expanded to include the Middle Ages, as well as antiquity. This utopian vision was necessarily fragile, resting on a delicate balance between exemplarity and historicity. Bodin's attempt to systematize this relationship did not so much dispel the living past as devitalize it, reducing it to a husk.

The *Methodus* begins like a typical *ars historica,* with a preamble about the meaning of the commonplace, *historia magistra vitae,* the traditional starting point for all discourse about history as a body of literature. Although modern readers tend to skip over these well-worn platitudes, Bodin based his effort to organize the record—and space—of the past on this commonplace. The notion of history as philosophy teaching by example illustrates the fragility of the utopian space of the past, in which the search for universal lessons could potentially undermine the sense of historical distinctiveness. In practice, though, the exemplar theory coexisted with and even complemented the synchronous conception of a past full of uniqueness, as long as one did not try to elaborate the Ciceronian commonplace systematically. Indeed, what Leonard Barkan has described as Raphael's collection of "greatest hits" from antiquity—Plato! Aristotle! Ptolemy! Heraclitus!—has its parallel in the exemplar theory, which cast the great historical figures of antiquity in high relief, turning each one into a unique instance of exemplarity.[32]

Bodin's perception of the clutter of historical entities, however, forced him to elaborate the commonplace systematically. He begins in his preamble by discoursing in a traditional way about the ease and pleasure of history, which are surpassed only by its utility for inculcating rules of moral, political, and military conduct. But he then goes on to express doubts about the ability to apply its lessons: "On account of the inexpressible advantage of such knowledge, I have been led to write this book, for I noticed that while there is a great abundance and supply of historians, yet no one has explained the art and method of the subject. Many recklessly and incoherently confuse the accounts, and none derives any lessons therefrom" (14). The diversity of historical examples is almost too bewildering for one to profit from them. On this account Bodin announces that the subject of his *ars historica* will not be the traditional theme of how to write histories but rather how to read them. He thus commits himself to working out the truth of the commonplace systematically for the audience of history, a task not previously attempted.

Bodin describes his method of reading in the second chapter, which aims at organizing the wealth of historical information in order to create a "universal history of all peoples." One should begin the study of history by reading a general chronology of the major peoples and events from Creation to the present. Then, one should supplement this chronology with another one—more detailed but still brief—that fills in all the remaining peoples, "such that one can see almost at a glance what was the established form of each state." From this now complete overview—which establishes the relationship of the particular to the universal— one can proceed first to read about each people and stage of events in detail and then to study the lives of the most illustrious individuals of each race (21).

The order of reading is less chronological than analytical, as Bodin's analogy between history and cosmography makes clear. The cosmographer begins with a small map of the universe that positions the earth in its portion of the cosmos. He then divides the earth into its continents, subdivides each continent into regions, and further subdivides each region into its topographical characteristics, each of which has its own distinctive geometry. Cosmography simply provides a model for what Bodin calls "analysis": "This, in general, shows how to cut into parts and how to redivide each part into smaller sections and with marvelous ease explains the cohesion of the whole and the parts in mutual harmony" (20). Bodin's habit of dividing and subdividing his subject matter is often said to reflect the bifurcating logic of the humanist educational reformer, Peter Ramus, but it is also indicative of the more general classificatory assumptions of his age, when Aristotelianism provided the standard of common sense.

The process of analysis reaches its fullest expression in the third chapter of the *Methodus,* concerning the arrangement of information derived from one's readings. If history is to remain the teacher of life, one must not only read it systematically but organize its lessons: "Such is the multiplicity and disorder of human activities, such the abundant supply of histories, that unless the actions and affairs of men are confined to certain definite types *[ut nisi certis quibusdam generibus hominum actiones ac res humanae distribuantur],* historical works obviously cannot be understood, or their precepts long retained in mind" (28). To reduce the mass of historical materials to "certain definite types," Bodin advocates expanding humanist notebook techniques to create a would-be *liber loco-*

rum historiarum that would organize the material contained in histories: "What scholars, then, are accustomed to do to assist memory in the other arts should, I think, be done for history also. That is, similar instances of memorable matters should be placed in a certain definite order, so that from these, as from a treasure chest, we may bring forth a variety of examples to direct our acts *[id est, ut loci communes rerum memorabilium certo quodam ordine componantur, et ex iis, ve-lut è thesauris, ad dirigendas exemplorum varietatem proferamus]*" (28).

The general framework for the notebook derives from philosophical assump-tions about the nature and purpose of human activity. Following Aristotle, Bodin divides this activity into a hierarchy of levels, starting with the need for self-preservation, moving on to encompass the acquisition of material comforts, and culminating with the desire for contemplation. For example, activities relating to self-preservation are hunting, agriculture, animal husbandry, construction, and medicine. The next level of human activity concerns the acquisition of riches through trade, navigation, weaving, and mechanical arts. The next level con-cerns the maintenance of society through the governing of oneself, one's family, and one's state, culminating with the performance of civic duties through a va-riety of public offices. Service to the polity constitutes the most important level of activity, for it is within the well-run state that individuals can cultivate the moral and intellectual excellence toward which human life tends.

Bodin recommends subdividing each class of activity into *loci* for note tak-ing. For instance, under the class of activities concerning the governing of the state, one might establish *loci* on the forms of taking counsel, the organization of assemblies, and the nature of public speaking. In general, though, Bodin pre-fers to establish pairs of contrasting *loci,* on such topics as the promulgation and annulment of laws, the roles of magistrates and private citizens, modes of de-claring war and peace, reactions to defeat and victory, systems of reward and punishment, and so on. This arrangement follows the traditional pattern of hu-manist note taking recommended by Agricola, Erasmus, and Melanchthon.

Lest this antithetical arrangement become unwieldy, Bodin proposes to gloss the contents of the *loci* with brief marginal notations specifying the relationship between each entry and the class of human activity it illuminates. (These glosses are akin to what Erasmus in *De copia* terms *loci communes,* his third group of *loci,* maxims extracted from the examples of the second group and listed along-side them.) In particular, Bodin suggests adopting a system of abbreviations to indicate the moral significance of each entry. For example, under the heading for taking counsel in the state one might (following the distinction of the Stoics) note in the margin of the entry whether the plans discussed were honorable, base, or indifferent, signifying them as such with a system of abbreviations—like "C.H." to denote *consilium honestum* (honorable counsel). Examples of other types of activity would be reduced to other kinds of moral qualities, with their own abbreviations. Taken together, these marginal notations constitute an index to the lessons taught by history.

This index enables one to establish metanorms, derived from many examples of human behavior, with which to guide one's actions. All one need do is flip through the *liber locorum historiarum,* using the abbreviations to compare different examples of a particular kind of behavior in order to distill its universal qualities from its many particular instances. These metanorms would supplant the norms that history had traditionally supplied. As the *magistra vitae,* history customarily served as a storehouse of lessons for living, the presumption being that one had access to this storehouse simply by reading a history whose subject matter was appropriate to one's own concerns. From this perspective, each history potentially had normative value. But after printing had dramatically multiplied the number of available histories, and after philology had demonstrated the historical contingency of their lessons, one could no longer read a history with the same confidence. The *liber locorum historiarum* offered a way around this problem by enabling one to distill metanorms from diverse histories—it offered a means of systematizing history as the *magistra vitae.*

This project was fundamentally neo-Bartolist. Indeed, the relativization of the lessons of history exactly parallels that of the *Corpus juris,* leading one to question the relationship of a once normative past to the present. The automatic response to this relativism was not to reject the existence of universal norms but rather to derive them more abstractly, as metanorms. A famous episode in an ancient history, for example, might no longer be regarded as providing *the* example of "honorable counsel," though it could still provide an instance of such behavior, which, when combined with other such instances, would illuminate a universal rule of conduct. Bodin's method for the easy comprehension of histories is thus not simply an art of reading a specific body of literature, any more than neo-Bartolism can be reduced to an art of reading legal codes. Rather, both are parallel attempts to organize a more complex experience of the world, a world filled to bursting with historically distinctive figures and entities—the living past. This organizational effort ended up devitalizing the synchronous space of the past by literally reifying it in the pages of a commonplace book.

A GROWING CONCERN FOR THE "UNITY" of history accompanies the devitalization of the past as a symbolic space. As long as the symbolic nature of the past remained intact, one did not need to concern oneself with its unity, for the nature of the utopian space was such that past and present coexisted *as* a unity. But Bodin's attempt to bring the neo-Bartolist project to fruition broke the utopian spell by more fully revealing the clutter of the past and, thereby, necessitating the kind of practical housekeeping destructive of a symbolic space that could not bear too much analysis. The more devitalized the space became, the greater the need to find the "unity" of history.

This concern emerges at the very beginning of the very first chapter of the *Methodus,* where Bodin outlines the three parts of history—human, natural, and divine—which form a whole: "In accordance with these divisions arise history's three accepted manifestations—it is probable, inevitable, and holy—and the same number of virtues are associated with it, that is to say, prudence, knowledge, and faith. . . . From these three virtues together is created true wisdom, man's supreme and final good." Bodin argued that the scholastics err in basing the search for wisdom on divine history alone: "They should first notice the goodness of God and His pre-eminence in human affairs, then in manifest natural causes, then in the arrangement and splendor of the heavenly bodies." The only problem with this inductive approach is that "human history mostly flows from the will of mankind, which ever vacillates and has no objective," so readers of history have a hard time discerning its underlying meaning. He regarded his task in the *Methodus* as that of cutting through this morass to reveal the truths of human history that point toward those of natural and divine history (15–17).

Bodin aims to achieve this goal through analysis. The chronological overview he recommends in chapter 2 simply serves to divide and repeatedly subdivide the topics of history into ever smaller parts—starting with major peoples and events, moving on to lesser peoples, and ending with the lives of the most illustrious individuals of each race. And the *liber locorum historiarum* of chapter 3 carries this process even further, dividing all historical information into the species and subspecies of human activity. A notion of unity is implicit in this process of analysis, for all the topics of history belong together as species of the same genus. But the analytical nature of the process proceeds by means of a principle of division that distinguishes one species from the next, one subspecies from the next, and so on. In other words, the very process of analysis itself tends to obscure the unity on which it is based by emphasizing the discreteness of each entity under consideration, thereby calling forth the need for greater assertions of unity.

The tendency for analysis to obscure unity is inherent in Bodin's *liber locorum historiarum*. The very act of gathering together diverse historical examples under a single *locus* highlights the differences between them. Hence, after describing the arrangement of historical materials in chapter 3, Bodin moves on in chapter 4 to establish standards for determining which historians merit close reading—lest one read indiscriminately, filling one's *loci* with too many misleading examples. Here Bodin comes close to the distinction between primary and secondary sources that characterizes modern historical scholarship. He establishes a hierarchy of historians, ranked according to their proximity to the events they describe and according to their qualifications as interpreters of those events. The best historians have participated in the events they recount and are generally well versed in public affairs. Such men, however, necessarily betray some partisan spirit, so one must learn to weigh their judgments. For example, one may question a historian's effusive praise of friends and allies, but his praise of enemies will more likely represent an honest assessment.

Despite the careful choice of historians, however, one's notebook could still become unmanageable, for even good historians sometimes contradict themselves, and they often disagree with each other. On this account Bodin elaborates a further means of evaluating worthwhile histories in chapter 5. Drawing on contemporary theories about the relationship between climate and bodily humors, Bodin provides a "scientific" means of arbitrating between divergent historical accounts, one that establishes a connection between human and natural history. For example, the peoples of the Southern Hemisphere are characteristically cruel because they have a preponderance of "black bile," due to a hot climate that draws out the other humors. Therefore one may believe, for instance, accounts by Roman historians attributing acts of incredible cruelty to the Carthaginians during the Punic Wars. And should a historian contradict himself, attributing cruelty to a people in one part of his history and compassion in another, one can use climate and humor theory to set the record straight.

Ultimately, though, Bodin could not derive the unity of history from a program of analysis, as we can see from a reading of the pivotal sixth chapter, "The Type of Government in States." He intended this long chapter to demonstrate the fruits of his method of reading, namely its ability to distill operative truths from a wide range of histories. Through an exhaustive analysis of this body of literature, he sought to explain "what is the best kind of state"—the state most in accord with natural and divine reason. Modern scholars study this chapter for its contribution to an emerging theory of state sovereignty. Bodin defined sovereignty as residing either with the people, the aristocracy, or the monarch—a definition necessitating that he overturn the Polybian notion of the mixed constitution as the best form of government. As Bodin pursues this argument—culminating with the assertion that limited monarchy is the best form of government—the moral categories of the *liber locorum historiarum* disappear entirely from view; a whole dimension of reading, treated extensively in his historical commonplace book, has become irrelevant to the search for meaning in history. Indeed, it is hard to see in this chapter how his conclusions emerge from his method. Far from following a systematic program of reading, Bodin culls from histories only the information that serves his point, which culminates with the parochial assertion that France has the best form of government, for its kings are restrained by an ancient constitution: "No empire has been more lasting than that of the Gauls or less given to civil wars" (267). Some ten years later in his *Six livres de la république (Six Books of the Commonwealth)*, when France seemed on the verge of disintegrating amid religious civil war, Bodin would draw from history a different point, that the sovereign is above the law and that the best form of government is absolute monarchy. So much for reading methodically. As Anthony Grafton concludes, "The notebook could not determine the results of the analysis."[33]

By highlighting the diversity of historical examples, the *liber locorum historiarum* revealed contradictions in history as a body of literature, contradictions that intensified Bodin's need to find the unity of history. This need arose in direct relation to the devitalization of the past, as historical entities became increasingly detached from the universal truths they supposedly illustrated. The greater the need to breathe new life into the synchronous space of the past, the more thorough the subdivision and reification of this space in the pages of the commonplace book, thus furthering the desire for unity. Bodin ultimately broke this vicious circle only by imposing an order upon history rather than by finding one intrinsic to it.

BODIN'S PERVASIVE CONCERN WITH "UNITY" REPRESENTS a search for the meaning of history that points beyond its role as the *magistra vitae*. By arbitrating between contrasting histories, his method serves implicitly to distinguish between events and the accounts of them. Histories could no longer provide practical guidance in human affairs without offering detailed access to the events themselves. The demand for accuracy in historical accounts tends to corrode the exemplar theory, in which the lessons derived from the past had traditionally overshadowed the actual events recounted. Ironically, then, the notion of *historia magistra vitae* falls prey to its own systematic application in the effort to clean up the clutter of the past.

The search for meaning in the *Methodus* leads away from the conception of history as a body of literature and toward a conception of "history itself," the arena where events transpire. Climate and humor theories—and (elsewhere in the *Methodus*) astrology and numerology—are suggestive of this arena, but they do not actually constitute it; they remain typologies consonant with the analytical framework of the *liber locorum rerum*. Climate and humor theories, for example, simply provide abstract means of categorizing information about human behavior—they are purely classificatory. Bodin did not conceive of these static typologies for the organization of information as forming the dynamic "causes" of events. By shifting attention from the accounts of events to the events themselves, however, his typologies advance the classificatory view of history to its farthest limit, beyond which lies "history itself."

Before this new view of history could come into being, the synchronous conception of the past had to break down—the living past had to die before a dead past could be born. As Bodin's *Methodus* demonstrates, the demise of the living past owed largely to factors internal to the humanist habit of reading and note taking. The more systematically Bodin attempted to apply this habit of mind to the task of preserving the unity of history, the more thoroughly he drained the living past of its symbolic meaning, thereby necessitating the further search for unity to hold it together. Although this search points toward a vision of "history itself," Bodin could not break free of his classificatory habits. The ever-intensifying search for unity increasingly ossified the synchronous space of the living past, which became ever more cluttered with unique entities, each distinct from the next. The living past born of the Petrarchan sense of anachronism thus languished amid a growing intellectual congestion that makes the late Renaissance mind seem, in the light of our modern sensibilities, so claustrophobic.

PART FOUR

Enlightenment

Laws, taken in the broadest meaning, are the necessary relations deriving from the nature of things; and in this sense, all beings have their laws: the divinity has its laws, the material world has its laws, the intelligences superior to man have their laws, the beasts have their laws, man has his laws.

—Montesquieu, *The Spirit of the Laws*

Presence and Distance

In Montaigne's rambling essay "Of Coaches," which (among other topics) entails a famous denunciation of Spanish cruelties in the New World, we find a remarkable estimation of the Aztecs and their encounter with Cortés and his conquistadors. Montaigne begins with a relatively short sentence that frames Aztec virtue in classical and European terms, but this estimation gives way—in the long-exhaled breath of an immense run-on sentence—to a series of destabilizing perspectives that switch back and forth between European and Aztec points of view:

As for boldness and courage, as for firmness, constancy, resoluteness against pains and hunger and death, I would not fear to oppose the examples I could find among them to the most famous ancient examples that we have in the memories of our world on this side of the ocean. For as regards the men who subjugated them, take away the ruses and tricks that they used to deceive them, and the people's natural astonishment at seeing the unexpected arrival of bearded men, different in language, religion, shape, and countenance, from a part of the world so remote, where they had never imagined there was any sort of human habitation, mounted on great unknown monsters, opposed to men who had never seen not only a horse, but any sort of animal trained to carry and endure a man or any other burden; men equipped with a hard and shiny skin and a sharp and glittering weapon, against men who, for the miracle of a mirror or a knife, would exchange a great treasure in gold and pearls, and who had neither the knowledge nor the material by which, even in full leisure, they could pierce our steel; add to this the lightning and thunder of our cannon and harquebuses—capable of disturbing Caesar himself, if he had been surprised by them with as little experience and in his time *[et à cett'heure]*—against people who were naked (except in some regions where the invention of some cotton fabric had reached them), without other arms at the most than bows, stones, sticks, and wooden bucklers; people taken by surprise, under color of friendship and good faith, by curiosity to see strange and unknown things; eliminate this disparity, I say, and you take from the conquerors the whole basis of so many victories *[contez, dis-je, aux conquer-ans* [sic] *cette disparité, vous leur ostez toute l'occasion de tant de victoires].*[1]

Implicitly, Montaigne frames this great gush of indignation within a transcendent ideal of *honnêteté*—the honor, virtue, and integrity that mark true nobility of spirit in all ages. What the Aztecs embody in the opening sentence, the conquistadors lack by the end of the long, run-on one, which attributes their so-called victory to "ruses and tricks." Within this broadminded framework, though, Montaigne's perspective shifts disconcertingly back and forth between Aztec and European points of view.

The initial shift is announced by the arrival of "bearded men"—as if this were some kind of oddity, as indeed it proved to be for the Aztecs—"mounted on great unknown monsters." With this last phrase we see the conquistadors as they were seen—in all their strangeness. With the further observation that the Aztecs had no beasts of burden, we reenter the European perspective, only to leave it again when we encounter (in the manner of the Aztecs) "men equipped with a hard shiny skin and a sharp and glittering weapon." From the "miracle of a mirror or a knife," we make our way back into a European perspective, when Montaigne has us consider how the Aztecs, even in full leisure, did not have the means to pierce "our" steel. From this observation we turn to the fusion of two perspectives in one, when he refers to the "lightning and thunder of our cannon and harquebuses." That these were "capable of disturbing Caesar himself" recalls the comparison between Aztec and ancient virtue in the opening sentence but with an unexpected shift to a Roman viewpoint—even this most valorous general would have responded to firearms as the Aztecs did "if he had been surprised by them with as little experience and in his time." And, were all these shifting points of view not destabilizing enough, Montaigne crowns them with a surprising double shift that splits the European perspective in two. Utilizing the second-person-plural pronoun (rarely employed in the *Essays*), he declares, "recount to the conquerors this disparity" and "you" disabuse them of their "victory." He thus distinguishes between the conquistadors (and presumably the Spanish in general), who gloried in their success, and those Europeans like himself who had come to understand its true "occasion."

The conquistadors owed their success to ruses and tricks, and the greatest trick of them all was occasioned by their very being. This startling realization derives from something still more startling, Montaigne's imaginative engagement with the Aztec point of view. As we will see, he often tried to put himself in another's shoes—speculating about the feelings or thoughts of an Alexander, Cato, Caesar, or Socrates—but he did not presume to see the world directly and immediately through their eyes, as he purports to do with the Aztecs. This imaginative engagement with the Aztec point of view contrasts with his earlier, more mediated treatment of New World peoples in the essay "Of Cannibals" (1.31). Here he begins by discussing the quality of his informants—how he maintained in his employ a man who had lived among the Brazilian cannibals ("a simple, crude fellow—a character fit to bear true witness"), whose testimony he carefully supplemented with that of visiting sailors and merchants. And the composition culminates with the description of his personal interview with a Brazilian cannibal during his visit to Rouen in 1562. He thus openly acknowledged his sources, reporting and commenting on what they had said. In "Of Coaches," by contrast, he throws himself into the Aztec point of view and alludes to his chief source of information—Lopez de Gomara's account of the Spanish conquests—only once at the conclusion of the essay, where he simply mentions Gomara in passing and anonymously as "my author."

In the manner of Newton's third law, presence entails distance. When he viewed the conquistadors through Aztec eyes, Montaigne gained a perspective on them that reduced their success to something ignoble. This perspective was neither "European" nor "Spanish" but "French," as Timothy Hampton has shown in his *Literature and Nation in the Sixteenth Century*. Montaigne's French identity was rooted in his tendency toward seasickness, his aversion to the kind of rocking motion characteristic of ships—and coaches—that forever relegated him to his side of the Atlantic. His French perspective thus devolves into a personal one. In the very act of putting himself in the position of the Aztecs, Montaigne reveals his own, personal point of view as the "right" one, at least by contrast to that of the Spanish. In other words, the play between presence and distance enabled Montaigne to view events in the New World from a privileged perspective.

WE HAVE NOW ARRIVED AT AN INTELLECTUAL CROSSROADS, on the other side of which lies modernity, with its systematic distinction between past and present that renders the past dead and buried. The Renaissance awareness of the differences between past and present had engendered a program of *imitatio* designed to bring the past back to life. For all practical purposes, this living past constituted an undifferentiated collection of entities, all equally relevant to the present. As scholarship both elaborated on and multiplied these entities, the space of the living past became increasingly cluttered and choked. Rather than seek a unity underlying this diversity, Montaigne chose to embrace its complexity, upon which he exercised his judgment. In the process of thus essaying himself, he revealed his self as his point of orientation amid diversity, an orientation that he further stabilized and solidified through his imaginative engagement with other forms of being human. This engagement entailed the kind of perspective distance that could potentially relegate the past to a place "back there" in time.

Montaigne himself was very aware of the historiographical import of his reflections in "Of Coaches," where the interplay of Old World and New World perspectives resonates with that between ancients and moderns. Timothy Hampton has explored the manifold and subtle ways in which "the novelty of the New World disrupts the discourse of history" (208). We can see some of this effect in our opening quotation, which references the traditional view of history as the *magistra vitae,* the teacher of life. Montaigne evokes the exemplar theory of history in the first sentence, about Aztec virtue: "I would not fear to oppose the examples I could find among them to the most famous ancient examples." Lest one lose sight of this ideal of exemplarity in the long sentence that follows, Montaigne draws attention to it again in his remarks about Julius Caesar. Whereas the first reference confirms the traditional view of history by comparing Aztec to ancient virtue, however, the second reference destabilizes the first by reversing the comparison—equating Romans to Aztecs—and thereby casting a previously unquestioned ideal in a relativistic light. (Imagine a terminally befuddled Caesar!) This unsettling implication sits like a droplet of acid, which pools together with other droplets (detailed by Hampton) to form a corrosive bath that progressively dissolves the ideal of exemplarity and, along with it, the traditional view of history that buoyed the living past.

The empathy that dissolved exemplarity would seem to open a direct path toward our modern understanding of the past. Yet Montaigne did not take this path because, for him, it wasn't the straight one. The tension between presence and distance born of empathy did not so much open as foreclose the possibility of obtaining a sustained perspective on the past. True, imaginative empathy enabled Montaigne to gain the "right" perspective on the conquistadors, but this mere local victory yielded no global vantage point. Indeed, the very existence of a New World—populated by inhabitants so far removed from European experience that they regarded horses, mirrors, and firearms as monstrous, miraculous, and awesome—invalidated the pretense of ever obtaining such a vantage point. Might there be other strange new worlds left to discover? And even

if there weren't, the past would still contain an infinitude of worlds long forgotten, worlds far different from the European one: "Even if all that has come
down to us by report from the past should be true and known by someone, it
would be less than nothing compared with what is unknown" (3.6.692). Amid
this vast ignorance, Montaigne chose to essay his judgment on the little he did
know and thereby to affirm his own vantage point, which was "right" for him but
nonetheless relative. The empathy that dissolved exemplarity thus leads straight
to the essay, to the constant shifting of perspectives by which Montaigne established his point of orientation in a diverse and complex world, a shifting of
perspectives that precluded the possibility of obtaining a single, sustained one.

Our examination of the birth of the past, then, must explain not only how
Europeans obtained a sense of perspective distance on themselves and others
but also how they learned to sustain it. The search for the answers to these questions will take us from the humanist habit of reading, which ultimately schooled
its practitioners in empathy, to an analytical view of the world characteristic of
the French Enlightenment, which schooled its practitioners in relational thinking. This analytical innovation contributed to our modern historical view of
the world by encouraging the notion that any given point in time and space was
constituted as such by a nexus of factors existing in measurable relation to each
other, much as any given point on a graph can be described as a nexus of the x
and y axes. In other words, each historical phenomenon consisted of relations
that, by their very nature, defined the phenomenon and fixed its position relative to other historical phenomena. The French Enlightenment thus spawned a
relational point of view that served to sustain the sense of perspective distance
born of Renaissance humanism.

THERE WERE MANY ENLIGHTENMENTS—French, English, Scottish,
German—and the closer one looks, the more Enlightenments one finds. (In his
massive study of Edward Gibbon, *Barbarism and Religion*, J. G. A. Pocock even
details an Arminian Enlightenment in Lausanne that influenced Gibbon during his stay there.) But the best-known strain of Enlightenment—the one sometimes misidentified as *the* Enlightenment—runs through France, and especially
Paris, around the mid-eighteenth century. At its heart lies an analytical vision
of the world whose roots extend back to Descartes, who had himself sought to
dispel the skeptical relativism popularized by Montaigne in the "Apology for
Raymond Sebond," the massive central chapter of his *Essays*.

In his epochal *Discourse on the Method* Descartes founded intellectual certainty upon "clear and distinct ideas" that left no room for doubt. From these he

extended thought outward via "long chains of reasonings" that proceeded systematically, from simple to complex observations. Unlike previous philosophical systems that classified concepts hierarchically according to their genera and species, Descartes's long chains of reasonings express proportional relations among entities—designated by the terms *greater, lesser,* and *equal*—that (he assumed) characterize all forms of human knowledge, such that they could be linked together like a "series of numbers." In other words, Descartes supplanted qualitative with what amounts to quantitative thinking. His breakthrough discovery of analytical geometry seemed to confirm this new intellectual vision, for he was able to combine the previously separate genera of arithmetic (the number genus) and geometry (the spatial genus) by positing that numbers can designate points on a line, with each number expressing a ratio, a relationship between two numbers (just as any point on a graph can be designated as a ratio of the x and y axes). This integration of arithmetic and geometry heralded for Descartes the reintegration of all knowledge on an analytical basis. The Cartesian insight into relational thinking thus presented an alternative to the traditional, classificatory view of the world that had broken down for Montaigne, an alternative that offered the possibility of finding new order amid diversity.[2]

While many French enlighteners preferred Bacon's inductive method over Descartes's deductive one, they nonetheless remained implicitly Cartesian despite themselves. This paradox owes largely to the pervasive influence in the seventeenth and eighteenth centuries of Descartes's greatest disciple, Nicholas Malebranche (1638–1715). Although the invention of analytical geometry had presaged for Descartes the unification of all natural and moral sciences, he never made good on his avowed promise to elaborate a new tree of knowledge. Malebranche, however, tried to accomplish this goal in his philosophical writings, beginning with his *De la recherche de la vérité (The Search after Truth)*, which offered the possibility of unifying science and religion in a Cartesian relational system based on mathematical assumptions. Regardless of their uneasiness with Descartes's purely deductive method, French enlighteners found Malebranche's vision of intellectual unity tremendously seductive. No less astute an observer than David Hume sees its influence at work in the above-quoted epigraph—the opening lines from Montesquieu's *The Spirit of the Laws*—and it bore its ultimate fruit in the great mid-eighteenth-century project of the *Encyclopedia*, where the organization of all knowledge derived from the operational methods of mathematics.[3] Cartesianism thus remained a powerful undercurrent in eighteenth-century French thought, impelling enlighteners to extend its relational way of thinking to all aspects of human knowledge. As they did so, the relations they described began to express a sense of historical distance that systematically sustained the distinction between past and present.

The foundational figure in this development—Charles de Secondat, baron de Montesquieu (1689–1755)—has many affinities with Montaigne. Both hailed from Gascony; both were noblemen; both trained in the law; both served on the Parlement of Bordeaux; both abandoned legal pursuits for literary ones; both used these pursuits to cast contemporary practices in an ironic light; and both did so through acts of authorial empathy. But in the *Essays* the light of Montaigne's empathic pretense flickers off and on as he shifts attention from object to object, whereas in Montesquieu's first great literary effort—the *Persian Letters* (1721)—he sustains that light, creating the extended simulacrum of a non-European point of view. Behind this sustained empathic pretense one catches glimpses of relational assumptions at work, as in the passage in Letter 83 where Montesquieu has one of his Persian correspondents write, "Justice is a relation of suitability *[un rapport de convenance]*, which actually exists between two things." (This comment anticipates the opening line of *The Spirit of the Laws*, where Montesquieu describes laws as "necessary relations *[rapports nécessaires]* deriving from the nature of things."[4]) Indeed, the relational perspective pervades the *Persian Letters* as a whole, where the extended contrast between Persian and French practices offers Montesquieu a privileged point of view from which to judge both cultures. Modern readers miss the significance of this relational perspective because they have become accustomed—largely through the very success of the *Persian Letters*—to viewing it largely as a satirical device.

As we will see, the relational perspective informs all of Montesquieu's thought. In the *Persian Letters* he exhibits a broad interest in matters of historical causation. Whereas ancient historians had treated causation as a series of occurrences—"this happened, then this, then this"—Montesquieu describes it as a nexus of factors, as a set of relations between things. Thus in Letters 112–22 he shows how demographic trends in Europe and Asia depend on various moral and physical factors that derive from and intertwine with different religious practices—pagan, Christian, Muslim—creating in each case a complex web of causation. Behind the facetious exterior of these letters lies a relational view of culture, which he would later attribute to the "infinite chain of causes that multiply and combine from century to century," forming the distinctive character of each society.[5] Just as Descartes's "long chains of reasonings" describe the order of the sciences, Montesquieu's "infinite chain of causes" depicts a human science. He attempts to lay out the operation of these causal chains explicitly in his second pioneering work, *Considerations on the Causes of the Greatness of the*

Romans and Their Decline (1734). Here causes emerge clearly as historical vectors abstracted from the sequence of events, with each vector being constituted by a nexus of factors. And, as we will see in his culminating work, *The Spirit of the Laws* (1748), he not only describes laws as relations, but he also reveals the "spirit" of the laws as the relations of these relations, from which he distills a comprehensive science of human society.

MONTESQUIEU'S WRITINGS REPRESENT A SEA CHANGE in historical thinking, despite the fact that he was neither a historian nor much interested in the temporal dimension of things. Basically, he showed how to deploy Cartesian analysis beyond the logical (and theological) realm, using it to grasp the relations between distinctively human entities. In so doing, he distinguished between these entities by holding them at a remove from each other and measuring the distances between them. This procedure established not only a systematic distinction between past and present but also between one past and another, with each entity being defined by its own nexus of relations. In other words, his analytical view of the world provides the basis for our contextualized one.

Modern historical understanding—usually designated in English by the term *historicism*, a neologism derived from the German *Historismus*—has been traditionally regarded as originating from late eighteenth-century and early nineteenth-century romanticism, which bequeathed the notion that each culture should be understood relative to its own context. Scholars have customarily contrasted romanticism with a caricature of "the Enlightenment" that dismisses French thought in particular as so excessively rationalistic that it discounted the importance of historical and cultural context. In addition to this crude dichotomy between Enlightenment and romanticism, there has also emerged a more subtle pairing between Renaissance and romanticism, in which recent scholars have traced the origins of nineteenth-century historicism back to developments in fifteenth- and sixteenth-century humanism, with its attendant sense of anachronism. Proponents of this view regard historicism as emerging from early modern antiquarianism, which in turn emerged from Renaissance philology.[6]

By now it should be clear that I am offering a corrective to both views. I do not contest the importance of nineteenth-century historicism, with its impulse to understand all human entities relative to their own contexts; however, the commitment to understanding any given entity from *within* its context derived from an analytical view of the world that contextualized from *without,* by gauging the differences between entities. And this analytical view ordered the profusion of entities born of antiquarian and philological scholarship, revealing measurable (rather than idealized) relations between them. In this regard Montesquieu stands at the point where humanism and Cartesianism converge, providing a foundation for historicism that has hitherto been obscured by our tendency to separate quantitative from qualitative thinking. We will now trace the path leading from Renaissance humanism to this critical Enlightenment juncture.

Biography as a Form of History

To understand the origins of Montaigne's bursts of empathic imagination—of the kind that Montesquieu would later sustain by means of relational thinking—we must revisit the humanist habit of reading. Already in Petrarch's association with the ancients one can see empathic processes at work, as he struggled to understand Cicero the politician and as he defined himself as a Christian in relation to Augustine. By the fifteenth and sixteenth centuries, this kind of personal engagement with the ancients—which would always remain the hallmark of the greatest humanists—had become depersonalized and routinized in the pages of student commonplace books. Indeed, the widespread practice of note taking encouraged readers to view any given text from the perspective of what they could extract from it rather than what its author had to say. Bodin's *Methodus* epitomizes this development, in which readers searched for information to fill out the preselected categories of their notebooks.

The practice of note taking underscores a mode of "intensive" reading—as distinguished from an "extensive" mode—characteristic of the Renaissance. Although Bodin's plan of systematically plowing through the history of all humanity with pen and notebook at hand may seem unrealistic to us moderns, it was less so in the sixteenth century, when the supply of books and the store of knowledge was considerably more manageable. Nonetheless, most people did not have the time and resources necessary to devote to this kind of programmatic study. Recall how the fifteenth-century pedagogue, Guarino da Verona, had recommended that his aristocratic charges hire the note-taking services of their less fortunate peers; similarly, there arose in the sixteenth century a class of professionals skilled at the craft of intensive reading. In a pathbreaking article, "'Studied for Action': How Gabriel Harvey Read His Livy," Anthony Grafton and Lisa Jardine reveal how one such professional functioned in the household of the Earl of Leicester, where Gabriel Harvey's (1550–1630) successive readings of Livy in the service of his patrons helped prime them for action in the world by providing guidance in political and military affairs. In one instance, for example, Harvey read Livy's account of the war with Hannibal with Sir Thomas Smith's son (Thomas junior), as a prelude to the latter's military expedition to Ireland.

The marginal notations in his copies of Livy and related texts—all written in the same clear, steady hand with very few excisions—suggest that Harvey worked his way through multiple books in tandem, closely cross-referencing them, rather than reading one book at a time from cover to cover. Grafton and Jardine speculate that this mode of slow, deliberate, intensive reading might have been facilitated by an early modern invention, the book wheel—a kind of small Ferris wheel for books—which would have enabled the reader (seated at its base) readily to read and cross-reference a dozen books or more at a session. Thus when Harvey read Livy with the younger Thomas Smith, the Roman history stood at the center of a collection of texts chosen to illuminate it in a variety of ways. Indeed, to engage in this kind of reading, one need not be a professional with a book wheel but a leisured amateur with a large desk. The point for our purposes is that intensive, directed reading, whether by professionals or amateurs, encouraged the extraction of information from multiple texts at the same time, for the expressed purpose of applying it to practical problems. Bodin's *Methodus* presumes this model of reading.

Of special interest is the effect of repeated, intensive readings. Harvey's copy of Livy, dense with annotations, bears the traces of successive perusals, each undertaken with different companion texts and a different aim in mind. As he read, reread, and re-reread his Livy in different contexts, Harvey did more than simply extract practical information from the text; he developed a view of the Roman past as "highly colored and in three dimensions" (69). Grafton and Jardine find their chief example of this multidimensional understanding in Harvey's annotations on the third decade of Livy's history, about the Second Punic War, where Harvey expresses impatience with Hannibal's failure to attack the city of Rome itself after his crushing victory at Cannae. In Livy's accounting, Hannibal's cavalry commander, Maharbal, had urged him to march directly on Rome after the battle, but Hannibal prevaricated. In his marginalia Harvey observes, "Maharbal's excellent advice could have made Hannibal as great as Alexander. But Hannibal, intent on lesser goods, lost his one chance for the greatest success. Now or never" (72). In Harvey's counterfactual imaginings, Grafton and Jardine see a bit of "sympathy for the devil," as Harvey frees himself from the orbit of Livy's text, written expressly to glorify Rome, and begins to consider

Hannibal's actual predicament. Harvey accomplished this shift in perspective "with an ease and dexterity that one might not expect from a humanist" (73).

To some extent Harvey's mental dexterity derived from his association with an aristocratic house intent on urging Queen Elizabeth toward a more aggressive foreign policy. Given these circumstances, he naturally felt impatience with Hannibal's indecision. But one can also sense in these marginal notes the frustration of a man who, however briefly, has managed to put himself in Hannibal's position. Harvey's deep and detailed understanding of the text of Livy seems to take flight through biography, through a focus on ancient lives and personalities. This focus provided a field for the kind of empathic identification that fashions from the text—and its ancient context—an imagined life. If histories provided a storehouse of practical lessons for the present, the personal portraits contained in histories and biographies offered the potential for something altogether different, an imaginative engagement with bygone lives that emerged almost unbidden from the text. In this sense biography opened a window onto what we would today regard as historical understanding.

THERE WERE DIFFERENT ROUTES TOWARD the understanding of what Koselleck has called "history itself," as distinct from "histories." Intensive reading, focused on specific objectives, could have the effect of illuminating historical personalities, who would come all the more vividly to life through the details that emerged when one read a central text slowly and repeatedly, in tandem with an array of critical analyses and supporting materials. But there were other forms of reading as well, which we might describe loosely as "extensive" rather than intensive, encouraging a less focused and more eclectic appreciation of texts. D. R. Woolf has analyzed some of these in his fascinating study *Reading History in Early Modern England*. The image of the book wheel—or of a study table overflowing with opened texts—obscures the fact that much (if not most) reading was performed aloud, generally to an audience. We have already encountered this practice in the Duke of Urbino's dining hall, where Frederico da Montefeltro listened to daily recitations of Livy, and (as Woolf points out) the practice of reading aloud was common in many kinds of venues, both large and small. Unfortunately, it leaves little trace, though one presumes that repeated hearings of texts (classical or otherwise) would have accustomed the ear to particular literary styles and turns of phrase, inculcating a taste for certain kinds of rhetoric.

In contrast to reading aloud to an audience, private reading (whether silent or aloud) leaves its traces in marginal notes, in commonplace books, and in diaries, as well as in literary works. Woolf's analysis of this material indicates a growing tendency in the early modern period to read histories casually rather than intently. Henry Prescott and Samuel Pepys often read with a history in one hand and a pint in the other, and the lovelorn Dudley Ryder read history in particular as a social lubricant—"studying" for a different kind of "action" from that intended by Gabriel Harvey and his patrons. Woolf observes, though, that early modern readers shared a common tendency "to read their histories for the example, the isolated episode, the portable anecdote, rather than end to end for a complete sense of the work" (106). Although this tendency accords with Harvey's practice of intensive reading, it also complements a more eclectic approach, in which the reader followed a theme through multiple texts rather than plowing through a central text with attendant ones at hand. Nowhere is this practice of extensive reading more apparent than in Montaigne's strange little essay "Of Thumbs" (2.26), where he extracts odd tidbits of information about his stated subject from a wide range of Greek and Roman texts. One can well imagine him standing at his library shelves, flipping through book after book, as he exercised his ingenuity on this trivial theme, which did not have the wherewithal to sustain more than the briefest inquiry.

Montaigne's manner of extensive reading also illustrates how biography became for him, too, a form of history, as repeated encounters with key historical figures ever deepened his appreciation of them. The figure of Cato the Younger had a special appeal for Montaigne, who had retired to his estate in 1571 to live the remainder of his life in pursuit of sagelike constancy, an ideal epitomized by Cato's suicide. After the fall of the Roman republic Cato had resolved to die a free man rather than live enslaved to Caesar. On the chosen day he enjoyed a philosophical meal with friends, took a nap, arose refreshed, and thrust a sword into his abdomen, only to have his servants discover his unconscious body and bind up his wounds—whereupon he regained consciousness and disemboweled himself with his bare hands. Even in antiquity Cato's fortitude in death served as a model of Stoic virtue.

In the process of essaying his mind on a wide range of historical and moral topics, Montaigne had many occasions to revisit the life and death of Cato, as described by Plutarch and other classical authors. In addition, he read and reread extensively about the lives of Cato's contemporaries—especially Caesar and Cicero—and about the demise of the republic. As he did so, his understanding of Cato took a profoundly psychological turn, away from the traditional praise of Cato-the-sage (characteristic of Montaigne's earlier essays) and toward a more nuanced appreciation of the man's distinctive personality. Writing in a later essay, "Of Cruelty" (2.11), Montaigne progressively strips away the commonplace interpretations of Cato's virtuous end to reveal the singular wellspring of his final act:

> When I see him dying and tearing out his entrails, I cannot be content to believe simply that he then had his soul totally free from disturbance and fright; I cannot believe that he merely maintained himself in the attitude that the rules of the Stoic sect ordained for him, sedate, without emotion, and impassible; there was, it seems to me, in that man's virtue too much lustiness and verdancy to stop there. I believe without any doubt that he felt pleasure and bliss in so noble an action, and that he enjoyed himself more in it than in any other action of his life. . . . And if his goodness, which made him embrace the public advantage more than his own, did not hold me in check, I should easily fall into this opinion, that he was grateful to fortune for having put his virtue to so beautiful a test and for having favored that brigand [Caesar] in treading underfoot the ancient liberty of his country. I seem to read in that action I know not what rejoicing of his soul, and an emotion of extraordinary pleasure and manly exultation, when it considered the nobility and sublimity of its enterprise. (2.11.308–9)

And this insight about Cato spurs one about Socrates, another traditional model of constancy: "By that quiver of pleasure that he feels in scratching his leg after the irons were off, does he not betray a like sweetness and joy in his soul at being unfettered by past discomforts and prepared to enter into the knowledge of things to come?" Indeed, the natural ease of Socrates's death belies the arduousness of Cato's: "Cato will pardon me, if he please; his death is more tragic and tense, but this one is still, I know not how, more beautiful" (2.11.310). The extensive mode of reading fostered these associations between diverse figures, enabling Montaigne to transcend his sources, gradually forming his own unique interpretation of these figures from repeated readings about them, their contemporaries, and their world.

This quality of insight reaches its fullest articulation in Montaigne's imaginative engagement with the Aztec point of view. In "Of Coaches" the biographical approach to historical understanding has morphed into something broader, as he ceases to focus on individual lives and, instead, imagines the experience of an Aztec everyman confronted with the unexpected appearance of the conquistadors. A number of factors underlie Montaigne's transcendence of the biographical form of history. First, and most obviously, he didn't have the same quantity or quality of information about individual Aztecs as he did about individual Greeks and Romans. Second, and no less important, he had ceased to view the lives of ancient heroes and sages as exemplary, regarding them instead as inimitable in their uniqueness. Third, and related to the decline of exemplarity, he had begun to portray himself as an everyman, as someone whose humble and inglorious life was as worthy of presentation as anyone else's. And finally, as he portrayed himself as an everyman, he had come to recognize the sustaining role of habit and custom in his life, which formed him as surely and definitively as his primary, human nature. Indeed, in a late essay, "Of Husbanding Your Will" (3.10)—written around the same time as "Of Coaches"—Montaigne flatly declared that "habit *[l'accoutumance]* is a second nature, and no less powerful" (772). He thus regarded himself not only as an everyman but also as a Frenchman, a Gascon, and an individual with his own personal idiosyncrasies— endowed qualities that served to sustain as well as to shape him, providing a sturdy, supple, natural frame for his existence. This self-avowed Gascon everyman found himself well and truly primed to imagine the experience of his Aztec counterpart.

Montaigne's act of historical imagination proceeds via the unusual means of cultural contrast, firmly rooting the Aztec perspective in a New World context defined over and against that of the Old World. Thomas More had tried something similar in his *Utopia* (1516), locating his "nowhere" in the New World. But he conceived of it simply as a mirror image of the Old World—a kind of Europe-in-reverse—whereas Montaigne attempted to conceive of the New World in its own terms. The strangeness of the Aztecs and the stunning collapse of their civilization called forth an unprecedented imaginative leap, requiring that he empathize not with some well-known classical figure but with a multitude of remote, inaccessible ones.

Montaigne was able to intuit Cato's joy at disemboweling himself because he had been raised on the mother's milk of ancient culture—having learned classical Latin before his native tongue, having communed with the great heroes of antiquity from childhood on, and having long revered the Stoic ideal of the sage. Although the Aztec everyman proved as virtuous as any Roman, this shared moral quality did not provide Montaigne with a meaningful standpoint for understanding the fate of Aztec civilization; indeed, it only made that fate appear all the more inexplicable. Montaigne's only recourse was to reconstruct the unfamiliar by contrast to the familiar, to imagine how Europeans must have appeared to Aztecs, starting from the material differences between the two peoples—in clothing, metallurgy, animal husbandry. This impulse derived from his insight into habit as a second nature. From an appreciation of the accustomed ways of the Aztecs, he evoked a picture of the conquistadors—hirsute, encased in shiny hard skins, atop huge monsters, babbling nonsense, commanding the power of lightning and thunder—that makes them seem so strange as to not even appear human. Such is the tremendous power of habit!

Montaigne transcended the biographical form of history to the extent that his picture of the Aztec mentality stands in high relief against the background of Aztec habits and customs. It is thus more thoroughly contextualized than his biographical understanding of individuals like Cato, Caesar, and Cicero. Of course, Montaigne was intimately familiar with the Roman context for these lives. Indeed, he often claimed that "to judge a man really properly, we must chiefly examine his ordinary actions and surprise him in his everyday habit" (2.29.533). Of the ancient Romans he wrote, "I like to reflect on their faces, their bearing, and their clothes. . . . I would enjoy seeing them talk, walk, and sup" (3.9.763). In his mind's eye these men wore togas, spoke a refined Latin, and dined while reclining on couches. But in the final analysis his conception of their personalities did not emerge from these contextual details. Montaigne had communed with them so long and so closely that he had absorbed their culture along with the very air he breathed—indeed, along with the classical language he had learned as his mother tongue. With the Aztecs, however, it was different. They were remote enough from his experience to require that he reconstruct their mentality from the habits and customs they took for granted, which stood out against the background of European assumptions. In this way Montaigne self-consciously viewed them in relation to their historical context.

It makes no difference for our estimation of the historical nature of his reasoning whether Montaigne accurately reconstructed the context of Aztec life. In fact, Lopez de Gomara—his chief source of information about the Aztecs and conquistadors—had never visited the New World, and some of his own contemporaries contested the accuracy of his account. Nonetheless, it enabled Montaigne to engage with another form of being human to the fullest of his capabilities. In this regard we should distinguish between his act of historical imagination and the scholarship that facilitated it. We cannot expect Montaigne's understanding of Aztec life to approximate that of a modern historian, as if the latter constitutes some elusive "gold standard" of objectivity (a point to which we will soon return). For our purposes it is entirely sufficient that he attempted to reconstruct the mentality of a people from the context of their civilization—a civilization that, in full ripeness, had been obliterated by brutal conquest.

The Politics of History

Montaigne's condemnation of the conquistadors accords so completely with our own contemporary view of the New World "holocaust" that we hardly think to question the nature of his judgment. Indeed, his willingness to entertain an Aztec point of view makes his judgment appear all the more objective, especially when contrasted with the cultural imperialism (and worse) of the Spanish. But our receptiveness to Montaigne's contextualizing viewpoint in "Of Coaches" blinds us to its anti-Spanish instrumentality. He first composed the essay between 1585 and 1588 and subsequently revised it until his death, in 1592. During this period Spanish interference in French affairs precipitated a civil war in which Montaigne found himself personally involved as a political actor. "Of Coaches" embodies his growing antipathy toward Spain, not only as a Frenchman but also as a Gascon, a native of the region in southwestern France bordering the Pyrenees, a region long jealous of its own identity. Montaigne's contextualizing viewpoint derives not from some nascent anthropologico-historical urge to understand a remote people but rather from a sophisticated political agenda to denigrate his kingdom's mortal enemy.

The death of the last Valois heir to the throne of France in 1584 had left a Protestant prince, Henry of Navarre, next in line of succession. The specter of a French Protestant king arose at the very time when the Spanish conceived of sending an armada to conquer Protestant England, as the prelude to ending once and for all the stubborn rebellion of the Dutch Protestants in the Spanish Netherlands. To advance their anti-Protestant campaign against the English and Dutch, the Spanish resolved to destabilize France and (if necessary) install a puppet government, using as their agents the treacherous brothers, the duke and cardinal of Guise. By the terms of the secret Treaty of Joinville, concluded in December 1584, the Spanish agreed to subsidize the Guises, enabling them to revive a dormant extremist coalition, the Catholic League, with which to exterminate the Protestant heresy in France. The resulting War of the Three Henrys (1585–88) pitted the leader of the French Protestants, Henry of Navarre, against the head of the Catholic League, Henry Duke of Guise, who dragged in his train a reluctant king of France, the childless Henry III.

Montaigne found himself in the thick of these developments. Although an avowed Catholic, he was also a well-known *politique*—a moderate for whom political stability trumped religious orthodoxy—and he thus maintained close ties with both Henry III and Henry of Navarre. In 1577 Navarre (king of a small principality astride the Pyrenees) had appointed Montaigne a gentleman of his chamber; and in 1581 Henry III had nominated him as mayor of Bordeaux, the principal city in the royal province of Guienne—a sensitive appointment in a province that had become a hotbed of Protestant resistance to the crown. During his two terms as mayor, from 1581 to 1585, Montaigne earned the trust of both Navarre and Marshal Matignon, the royal governor of Guienne, smoothing over friction between these two opponents and thereby sustaining a shaky peace in the province.[7]

The War of the Three Henrys culminated in Guienne on 20 October 1587 at the Battle of Coutras, when Navarre's retreating forces turned unexpectedly and defeated a larger Catholic League army at a village near Bordeaux. Only three days later Navarre hastened to spend the night at Montaigne's chateau—surely no social call—for he now had an opportunity to detach the reluctant Henry III from his nominal ally, Henry of Guise; he needed Montaigne's services both to restrain Marshal Matignon in Guienne and to broker a deal with the king. After meeting with both Navarre and Matignon in subsequent weeks, an aging Montaigne—severely afflicted with gout and kidney stones—mounted his horse in January 1588 for a long, painful ride to Paris, through a countryside infested with brigands. Ostensibly, he undertook this arduous journey to oversee the publication of a new edition of his *Essays,* but contemporary political observers— most notably the Spanish ambassador and Guise paymaster Bernardino de Mendoza—suspected his true purpose was to mediate between Navarre and the crown.

We know nothing of these presumed negotiations, other than that they would have been preempted by Henry of Guise's seizure of Paris in a virtual League *coup d'état* on 12 May 1588, the infamous "Day of the Barricades." Guise subsequently had a severely ill Montaigne rousted from his Parisian sickbed and thrown into the Bastille, only to have to release him a few hours later when the Queen Mother herself—the redoubtable Catherine de Medici—interceded on his behalf. Montaigne eventually followed the king's entourage to the year-end meeting of the Estates General at Blois, and he may have even been there when the king—desperate to reassert his authority—had the duke and cardinal of Guise assassinated. The king's own assassination some nine months later led to Navarre's accession as Henry IV, which precipitated the Spanish invasion of France in 1590. To judge by his letters and by comments in the *Essays,* Montaigne had by then become a confidant of the new king. As he openly declared in his last extant letter—addressed to Henry—Montaigne planned to join the royal court; and he undoubtedly would have but for his failing health and final illness.

Despite all his artful protestations in the *Essays,* Montaigne was no everyman but an esteemed and influential nobleman embroiled in the highest politics of the realm. At his level of involvement there could be no mistaking the dire nature of the Spanish threat to the integrity of the French crown. If the Spanish ambassador could suspect political motives for Montaigne's trip to Paris and track his movements in dispatches to Madrid, so too could Montaigne readily perceive Spanish influence over the Catholic League in general and the Guises in particular—whose treachery was, in any case, little more than an open secret. Montaigne thus had a considerable anti-Spanish axe to grind while composing and later revising "Of Coaches," and he made it all the sharper and more deadly for wielding it from an Aztec angle. By means of this unique perspective he aimed to expose the vaunted "triumph" of Spanish arms in the New World as an outright fraud.

IN FRAMING THE ABOVE ANALYSIS, I have done what historians do—I have interpreted a text from the perspective of its context. Montaigne did something similar when he evoked an Aztec point of view from an Aztec context, defined by contrast to a European one. Although both he and I have made similar kinds of contextualizing moves, his is all the more impressive for being such an early and unusual use of this technique, which makes the motivation behind it stand in even higher relief. Montaigne's dramatic exercise of historical imagination is at heart the highly political expression of his antipathy toward Spain. This insight casts a revealing light on my own contextualizing move, suggesting that what historians commonly regard as an objective interpretative tool may be rooted in partisan impulses.[8]

That "all history is political" is a commonplace, but it takes on special relevance for the Renaissance, when scholarship routinely served anything but disinterested purposes. Consider, for example, one of the most famous cases of humanist scholarship, Lorenzo Valla's exposure of the "Donation of Constantine" as an early papal forgery. This document established the papacy's claim that Constantine had granted territorial oversight of the western empire to the popes when he moved his capital east to Constantinople. Utilizing both philological and rhetorical arguments, Valla disputed this claim by showing that the so-called Donation did not fit into a late-imperial context. He demonstrated that the document's terminology did not accord with Latin usage current at the time of its reputed date of composition and, even more conclusively, that the form and substance of the document ill-suited a late-imperial audience, which would have greeted its propositions with incredulity. The cogency and validity of these arguments tends to obscure the fact that Valla undertook this exercise at the behest of his employer—Alfonso of Aragon, king of Naples—in order to help him gain some leverage in a territorial dispute with the papacy. Valla thus exploited what we would today regard as historical arguments for political purposes.

By contrast, Montaigne did not simply use a contextualized viewpoint for a political purpose, as if employing an objective means for subjective ends. Rather, his Aztec perspective on the conquistadors was, in and of itself, the emblem and product of his anti-Spanish prejudice. In other words, his contextualizing viewpoint was political not only in its use but in its very inception. Of course, Montaigne's humanistic education had already inclined him to acknowledge the importance of context, as revealed by rhetoric and philology. Like Valla he knew that audience considerations should determine literary form and content and that the Latin language had evolved through different historical styles. Although these general insights may have inclined him toward an awareness of the importance of context, however, they did not directly influence his understanding of the Aztecs, a subject far removed from rhetorical and philological analysis. Rather, that understanding—startling in its immediacy—emanated from his French and Gascon aversion to Spain, whose imperialistic meddling threatened to ruin the French kingdom just as it had the Aztec one.

Montaigne's empathic engagement with the Aztecs illustrates the fundamentally partisan nature of the contextualizing move, which emerged in the Renaissance as an ideological weapon in what Constantin Fasolt terms the "historical revolt" of the humanists against "medieval universalism"—against the hegemonic pretenses of pope and emperor (16–22). Humanists asserted (among other things) the sovereignty of the state by contextualizing the claims for papal and imperial universalism. To the extent that both pope and emperor alleged a power universal in time as well as space, the idea of anachronism became one of the chief weapons in the humanist arsenal. Its extraordinary effectiveness is due to the fact that both papal and imperial assertions of precedence rested on ancient texts, biblical and classical. The humanists merely seemed to propose slight changes in the way of reading these texts, beginning with the ostensibly unobjectionable call to restore the texts to their original purity. Their "revolt" thus hardly appeared as such, even to the humanists themselves. The program of *restoratio*, however, proved the thin edge of the wedge, after which humanists insisted that one interpret the restored texts with reference to the contexts by which they had been restored. Even this more radical claim appeared at first unobjectionable, enabling the humanists to use historical criticism to dismantle medieval universalism in the guise of reinforcing its textual supports.

The contextualizing procedure is thus "red in tooth and claw." It evolved not as a truth ever more firmly grasped but as one species of thought struggling with another. We moderns take it for granted as the standard of objectivity because of its great utility for understanding a complex world—witness my above analysis of Montaigne's text as an anti-Spanish polemic. The utility of this perspective, though, ought not to obscure the fact that modern historical understanding triumphed at the expense of an atemporal species of thought whose extinction has left it branded as "unfit"—a label that (when we stop to think of it) might appear suspect to us moderns, now that our mode of historical understanding has evolved beyond its sanguinary origins. The very instrumentality of the contextualizing move in the Renaissance heightens the need to explain how it became the standard of common sense. The course of this evolution is inseparable from the birth of the past.

THE FULL NATURE AND IMPORT of the historical revolt revealed itself by the seventeenth century, when humanistic scholars openly assaulted the bastions of medieval universalism. In *The Limits of History* Constantin Fasolt lays bare the essential character of this assault. I cannot do justice here to the subtlety and sophistication of Fasolt's argument, which critiques the contextualizing premise of historical thought through a detailed exercise in historical scholarship. Suffice it to say that he takes as his subject the seventeenth-century German polymath Hermann Conring (1606–81), whose short but provocative treatise the *Discursus novus de imperatore Romano-Germanico* (New discourse on the Roman-German emperor [1642]) reveals the quality of intellectual violence that now passes for historical objectivity.

The *New Discourse* addresses itself to an important question, which was still being contested in the last stages of the Thirty Years' War: Did the Roman Empire continue to exist, or was it dead and gone? Conring concluded that either the empire had ceased to exist or that it had shrunk to a tiny territory centered on the city of Rome and controlled by the papacy. These conclusions rubbed against the grain of tradition. According to the medieval notion of the *translatio imperii,* or "translation of the empire," imperial authority had been transferred from Italy to Germany with the crowning of Otto the Great as Holy Roman

Emperor in 962. To prove that the Roman Empire was indeed a dead letter, Conring had to dismantle the claim, made most famously by the great medieval jurist Bartolus of Sassoferrato (c. 1313–57), that the emperor was *dominus mundi* (lord of the world), a claim backed up by both Roman law and biblical interpretation. Conring framed his argument in historical terms, first by determining the geographical extent of Roman rule in antiquity, second by considering whether the Roman emperors were actually entitled to rule the world, and third by recounting the history of imperial rule from antiquity to the present.

Although the bulk of the *New Discourse* concerns the third topic—which details the steady geographical shrinkage of the empire—Conring accomplished the real work of the discourse in the second topic, where he attacked Bartolus's claim that the emperor was *dominus mundi*. Conring began by kicking out the biblical supports for this claim, which (he argued) were not meant to be understood literally. He then dismissed the basis for the claim in Roman law, arguing that "even a child can see that the civil law of the city of Rome could not possibly have given the Romans the right to rule the world; for how could the entire world have been bound by a law that was established by a single people in their city?" (quoted in Fasolt, 159). This rhetorical question presupposes a historical viewpoint that ultimately derived from the *mos gallicus docendi*, the French manner of teaching Roman law. As we saw in Part Three above, the French pioneered a philological study of the *Corpus juris civilis* that revealed Roman law as the law of a past society. Conring used this historical perspective to render Bartolus's universalist pretensions at best quaint and at worst nonsensical.

Yet if one examines these pretensions closely—as Fasolt does—they have a logic all their own. When Bartolus claimed that the emperor was lord of the world, he did not mean that other kings were beholden to him for their power. Indeed, he insisted that the king of England and the king of France had their own realms—England and France—in which the emperor could not meddle. In Bartolus's estimation the emperor's realm was not England or France but "the world"—a unit of jurisdiction qualitatively different from that characterized by individual realms. One might almost say that "the world" in this sense is purely an intellectual abstraction, were it not for the fact that this universalist ideal was very much alive and vital for the medieval mind, speaking to an expansive notion of community that has since fallen victim to a more narrow-minded statism.

According to Fasolt, Conring both missed the point and begged the question when he cast his treatise in historical terms. Conring's opening argument about the actual extent of the Roman Empire in antiquity misses the point because Bartolus's emperor did not rule over a physical space. Conring's second argument, about the nature of the emperor's right to rule as asserted in Roman law, begs the question by interpreting Roman law historically, as the law of the Romans, rather than juridically, as a systematically conceived body of law; it leaves the juridical claim unanswered in juridical terms. Conring's historical approach thus enabled him to talk past Bartolus, rather than honestly engage with him, and thereby to subject the medieval jurist to a specious form of ridicule. Fasolt concludes that, in essence, Conring changed the subject by inventing a new one— an authorial subject (Conring the scholar) defined over and against the texts he analyzed. Unlike Bartolus, who worked from within the text of Roman law, Conring stood outside of it and mastered it historically. Fasolt's analysis thus reveals the intellectual violence inherent in the contextualizing move that now constitutes "historical objectivity," a violence all the more naked in Conring's early exploitation of historicizing techniques.

CONRING'S GLIB DISMISSAL OF BARTOLUS—he didn't even bother to read the jurist's writings themselves but based his argument on Hugo Grotius's summary of them—indicates how far the historical revolt had already progressed by the mid-seventeenth century. A widespread controversy at the close of the century, however, reveals the difficulty in sustaining the historical perspective at the heart of this revolt. The famous *Querelle des anciens et des modernes* (Quarrel between ancients and moderns) that erupted first in France and soon spread to England testifies to the ascendancy of humanistic culture, for it originated chiefly as a literary dispute over the relative merits of ancient versus modern poetry, and it evolved into a controversy about the nature and purpose of classical learning. Transpiring within the humanistic movement, the quarrel ultimately highlights how even the partisans of the historical revolt had difficulty systematically distinguishing between past and present.[9]

The secretary of the French Academy, Charles Perrault, initiated the quarrel in 1687 when he read a poem at a meeting of the academy in which he proclaimed the age of Louis XIV superior to classical antiquity. Perrault began with a nod to the achievements of modern science and technology and then moved on to his main point, a critique of Homer. The father of poetry, recited Perrault, would have been a better artist had he been born in modern France. Perrault subsequently developed this theme in his dialogue *Parallèle des anciens et des modernes* (Comparison of ancients and moderns), the first version of which appeared in 1688. The poet and scientific popularizer, Bernard de Fontenelle, seconded Perrault's opinions in his *Digression sur les anciens et les modernes* (Digression on ancients and moderns), which first appeared in 1688 as an appendix to a volume of his poetry. Fontenelle argued that nature had remained unchanged from the time of antiquity and that the moderns had the same innate capabilities as their predecessors. Indeed, in science and philosophy the moderns had clearly surpassed the ancients; and in letters, too, the moderns offered every promise of bettering the Romans, who had themselves bested the Greeks.

Supporters of the ancients—such as the poet Nicholas Boileau, the dramatist Jean Racine, the moralist Jean de La Bruyère, and the scholar Pierre-Daniel Huet, to name only a few—picked up the gauntlet. Boileau first entered the lists, having already skirmished earlier in the 1670s, when he had declared the superiority of ancient over modern poetry. In a new edition of his French translation of Longinus's *Treatise on the Sublime* (1693) Boileau defended Homer's artistry and attacked Perrault's ignorance of Greek. Other Grecophiles soon joined in, attributing criticism of Homer to an inability to read him in the original. Although this phase of the quarrel sputtered on inconclusively throughout the 1690s, it did reveal a potential conflict that would later emerge in high relief, between a reverence for ancient models and a commitment to classical scholarship that would call such reverence into question. During the French version of the quarrel, however, the defenders of the ancients usually extolled philology for facilitating the imitation of classical models.

When the quarrel crossed the Channel—to become the "Battle of the Books"—the potential for conflict between the literary veneration of classical texts and their scholarly examination became more fully realized. Fontenelle's *Digression* incited the English statesman, and man of letters, Sir William Temple (1628–99) to publish his "Essay upon Ancient and Modern Learning" in 1690. Here he defended the superiority of the ancients across the board, both in natural philosophy and in literature and learning, arguing that although nature may have remained constant since antiquity, the circumstances of human existence had degenerated, rendering modern productions inferior to ancient ones. In response the precocious classical scholar William Wotton (1666–1727) published his *Reflections upon Ancient and Modern Learning* (1694), which weighs the achievements of ancients and moderns systematically, field by field. Wotton acceded to the superiority of the ancients in poetry, rhetoric, and the fine arts, but he maintained the superiority of the moderns in natural philosophy, logic, metaphysics, and the mechanical arts. In the final analysis he temporized between the two sides, declaring that future advancement would depend on combining the strengths of both.

Despite its moderation Wotton's response intensified the battle of the books by stirring up contentions over classical philology. This was the area of Wotton's expertise, and here he maintained that the moderns knew more about antiquity than the ancients themselves, in part because of advancements in philology and in part because the moderns could survey the whole of antiquity while individual ancients knew only their own particular place in it. This argument drew the ire of classically educated men-of-affairs like Temple, who decried scholars like Wotton as "pedants." The line was thus drawn between "polite" learning and critical scholarship, even though both sides emphasized the importance of ancient culture.

Perhaps the bloodiest engagement in the battle of the books occurred over the authenticity of the so-called epistles of Phalaris, supposedly composed by a Sicilian tyrant of the sixth century BC. By legend Phalaris was infamous for his cruelty—roasting his victims alive in a bronze bull that bellowed with their screams—but in the 148 letters attributed to him, he appears as a humane ruler and refined patron. In his 1690 essay Temple seized on these letters as exemplars of the unsurpassed nobility of ancient thought, despite the fact that reputable scholars had disputed their authenticity. Sir William's imprimatur inspired demand for a new edition of the letters, which the young Oxford scholar Charles Boyle dutifully provided in 1695. In response to the error disseminated by Temple and compounded by Boyle—who actually took no position on the authenticity of the letters—Wotton prevailed on his friend and fellow philologist Richard Bentley to prove the letters a forgery; Bentley subsequently appended his "Dissertation on the Epistles of Phalaris" to the second edition of Wotton's *Reflections* (1697). Despite demonstrating conclusively that the letters could not possibly date from the sixth century, Bentley's essay—a model of chronological and philological analysis—stirred up a storm of controversy, with supporters of Temple and friends of Boyle defending the virtues of "Wit and Learning" over and against the "Dullness and Pedantry" of scholars like Wotton and Bentley.[10] The French quarrel had morphed into a contest between ancient models, esteemed for their timeless sentiments if not their historical authenticity, and modern scholarship with its more critical evaluation of classical texts.

For our purposes the most interesting aspect of this battle concerns the surprising difficulty the "moderns" had in holding back the "ancients," who nearly drove them from the field in disgrace. In part the sharpness of this struggle reflects the literary talent of the "ancients," whose number included Sir William Temple's secretary, the satirist Jonathan Swift. Against the scornful barbs and lampoons of the ancients, the "moderns" (led by Bentley) mounted a systematic, thoroughgoing, rational defense based on philology, erecting a presumably impregnable wall of scholarship. In 1699 Bentley published a revised and expanded version of his "Dissertation," which (in the estimation of that venerable histo-rian of classical erudition John Edwin Sandys) marks "an epoch in the history of scholarship." Yet, as Sandys notes ruefully, "it was long before its mastery was recognized"—more than fifty years!—so vigorous was the counterattack of the "ancients," who derided sooty scholarship that smelled of the lamplight and, instead, praised gentlemanly learning that ennobled the soul (Sandys, 2:405). Indeed, their dismissal of Bentley rises in its glibness to the level of Conring's dismissal of Bartolus—but now the shoe was on the other foot.

Despite the current (and anachronistic) assumption that the victory of the "moderns" was a foregone conclusion, "the battle of the books ended in a draw," concludes Joseph M. Levine in his spirited account of this contest (414). Although the "ancients" ceded science and philosophy to the "moderns," they held on to literature and the arts, and they split the field in history, jealously maintaining their grip on narrative while gleefully letting go of scholarship. If anything, the battle of the books demonstrates the continued vitality of the living past, even in the face of its own internal contradictions. Although the emphasis on ancient models spurred the rise of classical philology, the living past was girded with a buckler of gentility impervious to the sharpest stylus.

The Relations of Truth / The Truth of Relations

The way out of an impasse where two sides persistently talk past each other lies in transcending the terms of the debate. This is precisely what the early eighteenth-century Neapolitan scholar Giambattista Vico ac-complished in his *New Science*, first published in 1725 and thereafter extensively revised and rewritten. Of course, Vico was after much bigger game than Per-rault or Boileau, Temple or Bentley—he was gunning for Descartes—but he could hardly have ignored the noisy transalpine catfight over Homer, which erupted again in 1711 with the publication of Anne Le Fèvre Dacier's translation of the *Iliad* and her essay defending the ancient poet. This new round of the French "Quarrel between Ancients and Moderns" occurred right in the midst of Vico's twenty-year study of Homer, which would eventually yield the "master key" to his "new science," namely that Homer represented a primitive mentality utterly distinct from the modern one.[11] The very terminology of the "philologico-philosophical" method, by which he decoded this ancient "poetic" mind-set, reflects Vico's transcendence of the impasse between "ancients" and "moderns." He equated philology with awareness *(coscienza)* of the "certain" (historically contingent facts) and philosophy with knowledge *(scienza)* of the "true" (universal principles explaining why facts assume this or that particular shape) (paras. 137–40). The "new science" sought to combine the certainties of philology with the truths of philosophy, thereby establishing a new vantage point for humane wisdom, one revealing that Homeric poetry represented an early stage in the development of humanity.

We cannot do justice here to the nature and origins of Vico's stunning insight into the historicity of human consciousness, an insight that seems to materialize out of thin air. In a prescient early essay on Vico, Erich Auerbach characterized him as an "aesthetic historicist," who had chanced on Johann Gottfried Herder's principles of historical development fully fifty years before Herder himself popularized them. In Auerbach's wake a dedicated coterie of scholars has steadily unearthed Vico's intellectual roots—philological, rhetorical, legal, and antiquarian—in the soil of late humanism, revealing that his genius was not entirely anomalous. For our limited purposes, though, Vico is the exception proving the rule that Europeans needed to contextualize the distinctiveness of historical entities from *without* before perceiving that distinctiveness from *within;* they had to grasp the analytical relations between entities before they could understand each entity as the product of its own special circumstances. This analytical need helps explain—along with the obscure and sometimes even bizarre way Vico framed his precocious ideas—why he remained largely unread until the mid-nineteenth century, when he was rediscovered by the great romantic historicist Jules Michelet. Full recognition of Vico's aesthetic historicism awaited the birth of the past.

Like Vico's *New Science, The Spirit of the Laws* (1748) reflects an impulse to combine scholarship with philosophy, but Montesquieu conceived of the latter in more analytical terms, as embodying the same kind of certainty as mathematics. The quarrel between "ancients" and "moderns" leaves little trace in Montesquieu's writings—only a couple of passing jibes at both sides in the *Persian Letters* and some scattered references in his literary notebooks—but he was familiar with Vico, if only by reputation. While sojourning in Italy between 1728 and 1729, Montesquieu noted in his travel journal that he should acquire a copy of the *New Science* (though there's no proof he ever did); and he shared with Vico many of the same Italian friends and contacts. Indeed, in his exhaustive and invaluable biography of Montesquieu, Robert Shackleton notes that one of his subject's favorite churches in Naples was but a stone's throw from Vico's house, thus heightening the possibility that the two may have met. Regardless of whether they actually did so, however, we can find no overt trace of Vico's influence on Montesquieu's thought, for the Frenchman aimed at establishing a science altogether more rigorous, transparent, and accessible than that revealed by the Neapolitan's obscure "philologico-philosophical" method. In fact, Montesquieu's science even offered the possibility of transcending the impasse between Vico and his *bête noire*, Descartes, who disdained historical knowledge. By combining Cartesian standards of certainty with the most up-to-date historical scholarship, Montesquieu offered a truly analytical view of human society, providing inner assurance for a new kind of historical knowledge of value to both scholars and statesmen.

THE OPENING LINE OF *THE SPIRIT OF THE LAWS*—"Laws, taken in the broadest meaning, are the necessary relations *[rapports nécessaires]* deriving from the nature of things"—created as much confusion for Montesquieu's contemporaries as it does today. What did he mean by this strange definition of laws as "necessary relations"? Montesquieu hardly clarified matters when he went on to say that "all beings have their laws: the divinity has its laws, the material world has its laws, the intelligences superior to man have their laws, the beasts have their laws, man has his laws." Voltaire despaired of these seemingly scholastic distinctions: "Let us not play amid the subtleties of this metaphysic, let us beware entering this labyrinth." And Hume lamented the obscurity of the opening passages, which contrasted with the clarity of the rest of the work: "This illustrious Writer, however, sets out with a different Theory, and supposes all Right to be founded on certain *Rapports* or Relations; which is a System that, in my Opinion, never will reconcile with true Philosophy." Hume traced Montesquieu's *rapports* back to Malebranche, whose "abstract Theory of Morals . . . excludes all Sentiment, and pretends to found every Thing on Reason." For the skeptical Hume, Montesquieu's *rapports* are mere intellectual fantasies that remain (thankfully) irrelevant to a work of such concrete historical detail, a work affording "the best System of political Knowledge, that, perhaps, has ever yet been communicated to the World."[12]

Modern commentators are no less bemused by Montesquieu's decision to pass over accepted juridical, political, and constitutional notions of law—readily available in the writings of Grotius, Locke, and Pufendorf—in favor of an obscure, nonlegal definition from Malebranche. To explain this apparent anomaly, Shackleton scrupulously seeks the antecedents of Montesquieu's definition in a heroic survey of ancient and early modern natural law theories. While noting that his conception of natural law has a Cartesian quality—implying a mathematical dimension to the term *relation*—Shackleton ultimately emphasizes Montesquieu's empirical rather than rationalistic tendencies. In his classic biography of Montesquieu, Albert Sorel likens the opening lines to "an algebraic formula, applying to all real quantities and expressing none of them exactly," but then he quickly drops the mathematical metaphor (86–87). And in his equally classic biographical sketch, Emile Durkheim notes Montesquieu's intention "to deal with social science in an almost mathematical way" (51); but he, too, leaves this observation undeveloped.

These allusions aside, the mathematical dimension of Montesquieu's thought has remained largely ignored. In the exposition that follows, I will show how Montesquieu's "relational" definition of law betrays the presence of a submerged model of number thinking that derives from Malebranche and Descartes. In making this claim, I do not mean to assert that Montesquieu was a closet mathematician (or, for that matter, metaphysician) but rather that he was influenced by a pattern of thinking that would, by the nineteenth century, resolve itself into a theory of the "cardinal" and "ordinal" principles of number, upon which modern mathematics is based. Of course, neither Descartes nor Malebranche nor Montesquieu used these modern terms, but the relational patterns of their thought point in this direction. And Montesquieu, in particular, will use these relational patterns to sort through the complexity of human reality by means of "ideal types," measuring (as it were) the distances between them and between the manifold realities they typify. By establishing the relations between human entities, Montesquieu effectively fixed them in their contexts. In other words, he established them in their appropriate settings, from which henceforth they could not be removed without essentially dislocating them. In sum, he laid the foundation for a sustained idea of anachronism that distinguished systematically between past and present. What a great irony it is that the past as an intellectual object was midwifed by number thinking!

IN HIS ESTIMATION OF MONTESQUIEU, Hume correctly singled out the influence of Malebranche, whose Cartesian theory of truth pervades the whole of *The Spirit of the Laws*. Between the ages of eleven and sixteen (from 1700 to 1705), Montesquieu attended the famous Collège of the Oratorians in Juilly, near Paris. The Oratorians offered a progressive educational alternative to the Jesuits, and the Collège de Juilly, in particular, inculcated elements of the Cartesian method along with the more traditional subjects of a humanistic curriculum.

Renowned as "*the* Oratorian"—as well as the "French Plato"—Malebranche was Descartes's greatest disciple—with a reputation rivaling that of his master. His spirit hovered over the college—which he visited on occasion—especially during the early years of the eighteenth century, when he was most hotly engaged in defending the controversial philosophy he had first introduced in his foundational *Search after Truth* (1674–75) and developed in a host of other writings. In addition to being educated in a thoroughly Malebranchian atmosphere—where the Oratorian's ideas were very much in the air—Montesquieu also enjoyed a lifelong association with known *malebranchistes,* such as the Bordeaux mathematician d'Ortous de Mairan, Malebranche's pupil-turned-protégé; Father Pierre-Nicolas Desmolets, the librarian of the Paris Oratory; Cardinal Melchior de Polignac, who defended Malebranche against the Jesuits; and that ardent partisan of the "moderns," Bernard de Fontenelle, who composed an elegy on the occasion of Malebranche's death in 1715.[13]

Allusions to Malebranche also pervade Montesquieu's writings. The *Persian Letters,* for example, contains one of the first and most reverberant of these echoes, where Montesquieu writes, "Justice is a relation of suitability *[rapport de convenance],* which actually exists between two things. This relationship is always the same, by whatever being it is perceived, whether by God, or by an angel, or finally by man" (83.162). The opening lines of *The Spirit of the Laws* further echo these sentiments, which had originated from the first book of Malebranche's *Search after Truth,* where he distinguishes between truth and goodness: "Truth consists only in the relation between two or more things, whereas goodness consists in the relation of suitability *[rapport de convenance]* things have with us."[14] As its title clearly indicates, the bulk of the *Search after Truth* concerns relations of truth rather than suitability; but in subsequent writings, most notably the *Treatise on Morality* (1684), Malebranche developed the informal notion of suitability into a formal hierarchy of "relations of perfection," which extend as in a chain of being from less perfect to more perfect entities, culminating ultimately in God. These are the relations Hume had in mind when he criticized Montesquieu for relying too heavily in his definition of law on Malebranche's moral abstractions. And these are the relations modern commentators have in mind when they try to parse the opening lines of *The Spirit of the Laws.* They thus tend to lose sight of Malebranche's prior and more fundamental "relations of truth," which (as we will see) provide the mathematical subtext for Malebranche's theory of relations and Montesquieu's definition of law.

This subtext is obscured by the overarching philosophico-theological aim of Malebranche's writings as a whole, which sought to articulate a new *summa* that did for Cartesianism what Aquinas had done for Aristotelianism, namely reconcile it with Christian doctrine and thereby articulate a whole new ordering of knowledge. In pursuing this goal, Malebranche is commonly regarded as having subordinated relations of truth to those of perfection, whereas in reality the two were more equally balanced, as Michael E. Hobart has decisively shown in his challenging study, *Science and Religion in the Thought of Nicolas Malebranche*. Deploying sophisticated analytical tools, Hobart excavates the mathematical foundations of the relational idea of truth, disclosing the presence of a submerged idea of "number," which intertwined in Malebranche's philosophy with a more traditional idea of "substance." Number thinking would not fully surface until mathematicians clearly formulated the cardinal and ordinal principles of number in the nineteenth century, but its traces were already apparent in the work of Descartes and Malebranche, on which Montesquieu would found his new (historical) science of society.[15]

As Hobart explains, the cardinal principle of number implies a one-to-one correspondence between any two collections of things—say, between theatergoers and seats in an auditorium. When all the seats are filled and every theatergoer is seated, the two groups are said to share the same cardinal number. The ordinal principle posits that the members of a collection constitute a countable, ordered series; thus, one counts the collection of seats in an auditorium by regular intervals—"1, 2, 3," and so on—until one reaches its seating capacity. Descartes's invention of analytical geometry reveals his early intuition of these two principles, for he correlated arithmetical and linear continua, conceiving of geometrical extension as an ordered series of numbers. Imagine a triangle drawn on graph paper. Every point on the figure can be represented as the intersection of values along x and y axes, thus rendering every point a ratio of two numbers, each of which itself can be expressed as a ratio—any given number n, for example, can be expressed as the ratio of $n/1$. From this insight into the relational order of things, Descartes inferred that all knowledge beyond the direct intuition of clear and distinct ideas involved comparing mental objects and that the activity of comparison implied the existence of an underlying unity: "But I do not recognize what the proportion of magnitude between 2 and 3 is without having considered some third term, namely, the unit *[unitate]* which is the common measure of both."[16] (Note that *unitate* is the ablative of *unitas,* which Lewis and Short's *Latin Dictionary* defines as "the state of being one, oneness, unity"; although our translator here renders it as "unit"—perhaps seeking to clarify the mathematical implications of Descartes's thought—the original Latin term carries the literal force of "unity," a fact that will soon be of interest.) Whereas

Descartes tended to conceive of this "common measure" geometrically—as the continuity of lines and figures—Malebranche would articulate it mathematically, further developing what would eventually become the cardinal and ordinal principles of number.

In the *Search after Truth* Malebranche expanded on Descartes's relational view of knowledge and its underlying notion of unity. He conceived of truths as "real relations, whether of equality or inequality," and he distinguished among three kinds of truths: relations between ideas, between things and ideas, and between things. Relations between ideas constitute for him the "eternal and immutable" standard against which the other kinds of truth are measured. Relations of ideas, being either equal or unequal, reduce ultimately to relations of magnitude *(rapports de grandeur)*, with magnitude itself being nothing but a relation, a relative measure of size: "All magnitude being therefore a relation, or all relation a magnitude, it is evident that one can express all relations by numbers and represent them to the imagination by lines." According to Malebranche we readily perceive the identity inherent in relations of equality but not in those of inequality: "We know that a tower is greater than a fathom and less than a thousand fathoms but we still do not know its exact size or its relation *[rapport]* to one fathom." To compare unequal things, we need an "exact measure," a commonality underlying their relation, by which we can reduce them to identity. Malebranche called this exact measure *unité*, echoing Descartes's Latin term: "In order to compare things . . . we need a simple and perfectly intelligible idea, a universal measure that can be accommodated to all sorts of objects. That measure is unity *[unité]*." To the sixth and final edition of the *Search after Truth* Malebranche adds the following clarification of this statement: "We thus determine for each kind of magnitude the unity or common measure *[l'unité ou la mesure commune]*; for example, a fathom for length, an hour for time, a pound for weight, etc., and all these unities *[unités]* are divisible to infinity" (6.1.5.180–88).

With Malebranche's concept of *unité*, writes Hobart, "we arrive at the center of his epistemological vision" (60). More so than Descartes's Latin term *unitate*, with its literal emphasis on "unity," Malebranche's French term encompasses two meanings, expressed in English as *unit* and *unity*. Most commentators see in this double meaning an irresolvable tension between the two, between "unit" as a metaphysical notion characterized by indivisibility and "unity" as a mathematical notion characterized by divisibility (note Malebranche's addendum that fathoms, hours, and pounds are divisible to infinity). Given this tension, scholars have naturally assigned priority to the metaphysical notion of unit, which (in its indivisibility) corresponds to the clear and distinct idea of Descartes's *cogito,* and they thus assume that Malebranche's order of knowledge is based on metaphysical rather than mathematical foundations. Hobart, however, reverses this assumption by showing how the dual meaning of *unité* corresponds to the cardinal and ordinal principles of number, with a unit being a discrete, countable thing, which presumes a unity, an ordered series of things. He also shows how Malebranche's intuitive grasp of number thinking evolved, through the multiple editions of the *Search after Truth,* from an emphasis on the indivisibility of numbers to embrace their divisibility, especially as expressed in the calculus of Leibniz and Newton.

Inspired to fulfill the Cartesian dream of unifying all knowledge, Malebranche used the relational vision of truth to address a wide range of ethical, philosophical, and theological issues. In the *Treatise on Morality,* for example, he elaborated the "relations of perfection," as distinct from those of magnitude. Whereas the latter represented "scientific" truths, the former were "practical" ones concerned with the operations of the will, the imagination, and the senses rather than reason. He termed them "relations of perfection" because they constituted a qualitative hierarchy that ascended toward God, in whose mind the relations of both perfection and magnitude existed as one. Malebranche's desire to find the underlying unity of knowledge led him to fuse—and, ultimately, to confuse—number thinking with substance thinking, thus making his unwieldy skein of relations hard to unravel. At its core, though, the relational vision of truth consists of operations rooted in the cardinal and ordinal principles of number.

We will now see how Montesquieu transposed Malebranche's relational vision of truth into a view of human entities. In so doing, he fixed these entities—customs, laws, institutions, mores—in networks of relations that established the particular context for understanding each entity in question. A systematic and sustained distinction between past and present derived from this process of contextualization, but before I can demonstrate this (my ultimate) point, we must first analyze *The Spirit of the Laws* in detail, revealing the influence of Malebranche and the effects of a submerged model of number thinking. Only after we have teased out these threads—which lie tightly woven into the fabric of Montesquieu's great work—can we see how the relational view of human entities intertwines with the birth of the past.

Montesquieu and the Relations of Things

Hume can be forgiven for missing the mathematical core of Malebranche's relations and for dismissing them as mere metaphysical abstractions. Montesquieu, however, was more intimately familiar with the nature of Malebranche's teachings, whose mathematical principles shaped his own conception of a truly social science. A vast synthetic work—the product of a lifetime of reading—*The Spirit of the Laws* betrays many influences, but that of Malebranche leaps out at us from the very title: *De l'esprit des lois, ou du rapport que les lois doivent avoir avec la constitution de chaque gouvernement, les mœurs, le climat, la religion, le commerce, etc.* The term *rapport* is conspicuous, and—lest one miss its significance—it recurs at least eleven times within the brief span of the first chapter. Also prominent is the title's vexing use of the verb *devoir*, which resonates through a range of English meanings: the laws "must"/"should"/"ought" to have a relation with the constitution of each government, with mores, with climate, with religion, with commerce, and so on. Some critics dismiss Montesquieu's use of the verb here as merely ambiguous—reflecting a certain linguistic carelessness on his part—but (as we will see) it actually signifies the presence of *unités* underlying the relations of things.

The most overt references to science and mathematics in *The Spirit of the Laws* come in the central portion of the first chapter, where Montesquieu relies heavily on analytical imagery. After defining laws as "necessary relations," he insists that "blind fate" does not govern the world and that God's creation and preservation of the universe presupposes rules akin to those of modern physics: "These rules are a consistently established relation *[rapport]*. Between one moving body and another moving body, it is in accord with relations *[rapports]* of mass and velocity that all motions are received, increased, diminished, or lost; every diversity is *uniformity*, every change is *consistency [chaque diversité est* uniformité, *chaque changement est* constance*]*" (1.1.4). In its assertion of a unity underlying differences, this statement is as thoroughly Malebranchian as it is Newtonian. Montesquieu goes on to liken human laws to the eternal laws of nature, as expressions of omnipresent principles: "Before laws were made, there were possible relations *[rapports]* of justice. To say that there is nothing just *[juste]* or unjust *[injuste]* but what positive laws ordain or prohibit is to say that before a circle is drawn, all its radii were not equal *[égaux]*. Therefore, one must admit that there are relations *[rapports]* of fairness *[équité]* prior to the positive law that establishes them" (1.1.4). The astute translators of the authoritative Cambridge edition of the text note the play on mathematical words here, with the term *juste*—which means "correct" as well as "just"—setting the stage for relations of *équité*, which means "equality" in the mathematical sense, as well as "equity" and "fairness" in the legal sense. Montesquieu thus draws an implicit parallel between legal, geometrical, and mathematical relations.

After the three short chapters that compose book 1, direct references to an *esprit géométrique* diminish. On this account one might almost dismiss the initial mathematical allusions as unrelated to the rest of the text, had not Montesquieu throughout the entire work implicitly evoked the mathematical/relational imagery of ratios and inverse ratios, proportions and inverse proportions, and equivalencies expressing such mathematical properties as symmetry and transitivity. For example, in the third chapter of book 2 ("On laws relative to the nature of aristocracy") he expresses an inverse ratio: "In every magistracy, the greatness of power must be offset by the brevity of its duration" (2.3.16). And he concludes the chapter with an expression of inverse proportionality: "The more an aristocracy approaches democracy, the more perfect it will be, and to the degree it approaches monarchy the less perfect it will become" (2.3.17). The third chapter of book 5 ("What love of the republic is in a democracy") establishes a clear set of equivalencies expressing transitivity: "Love of the republic in a democracy is love of democracy; love of democracy is love of equality. Love of democracy is also love of frugality" (5.3.43). And in chapter 6 ("How laws should sustain frugality in democracy") we find an equivalency expressing symmetry: "As the equality of fortunes sustains frugality, frugality maintains the equality of fortunes" (5.6.47–48). And, in the second chapter of book 8, another inverse proportion: "The principle of democracy is corrupted not only when the spirit of equality is lost but also when the spirit of extreme equality is taken up" (8.2.112). In this chapter we also find direct proportions such as, "Corruption will increase among those who corrupt, and it will increase among those who are already corrupted" (8.2.113). And in chapter 5 ("On the corruption of the principle of aristocracy") we find another inverse proportion: "If [the nobility] are few in number, their power is greater, but their security diminishes; if they are greater in number, their power is less and their security greater; so that power keeps increasing and security diminishing up to the despot in whose person lies the extreme of power and danger" (8.5.115–16). Here Montesquieu evokes change approaching a limit, as in the calculus.

ONE CAN MULTIPLY THESE EXAMPLES at will. The ubiquity of such expressions is not merely rhetorical but reflects a deeply Cartesian habit of mind, which emerges most clearly in Montesquieu's discussion of despotism. Book 1, with its mathematical and scientific analogies and its litany of *rapports,* quickly gives way to book 2, concerning the three kinds of government: republican, monarchical, despotic. I will discuss these political types and their attendant social principles later; suffice it to say here that Montesquieu rarely casts outright judgment on the political and social forms he analyzes, preferring instead to interpret them relative to their circumstances—an impartiality that makes his overt criticism of despotism stand in high relief. Especially noteworthy is the stark two-line chapter, "The idea of despotism": "When the savages of Louisiana want fruit, they cut down the tree and gather the fruit. There you have despotic government" (5.13.59). In its brute simplicity and stupidity this action epitomizes the direct, unmediated, instinctual application of power. The despot's desires must be fulfilled immediately and without question: "Man is a creature that obeys a creature that wants" (3.10.29). In its immediacy the direct application of power admits of no relations. Despotism is thus a nullity, a nothing, a zero, and as such it evokes in Montesquieu's Cartesian mind not only moral indignation but intense aesthetic displeasure.

In book 6—"Consequences of the principles of the various governments in relation *[rapport]* to the simplicity of civil and criminal laws"—Montesquieu describes the absence of legal relations in a despotism. The despot's right to inherit all eliminates the need for inheritance laws. Similarly, because trade belongs exclusively to the despot, there's no need for laws concerning commerce; and because marriages are contracted with female slaves, there's no need for laws regulating dowries and the rights of wives. "Despotism is self-sufficient; everything around it is empty" (6.1.74). The despot does not engage with others but simply wills what he wants: "The despot knows nothing and can attend to nothing; he must approach everything in a general way; he governs with a rigid will that is the same in all circumstances; all is flattened beneath his feet" (6.1.73). Most striking here is the imagery of nothingness, emptiness, and desolation, of the nullity that is despotism.

Montesquieu describes despotism as a kind of slavery where even the master is enslaved. "A result of the nature of despotic power is that the one man who exercises it has it likewise exercised by another" (2.5.20). The prince, distracted by the allures of the seraglio, abandons public business to a vizir, "who will instantly have the same power as he," with which the vizir will further intoxicate the master. Montesquieu sums up this situation with a ratio: "The more extensive the empire, the larger the seraglio, and the more, consequently, the prince is drunk with pleasures" (2.5.20). This proportionate increase then gives way to two inverse ratios: "Thus, in these states, the more peoples the prince has to govern, the less he thinks about government; the greater the matters of business, the less deliberation they are given" (2.5.20). The greater the despotism, the fewer the relations. Elsewhere, in an implicit jab at Louis XIV—who moved his court from Paris to Versailles in order to control it more absolutely—Montesquieu rendered despotism as a reduction to the smallest common denominator: "A monarchy is ruined when the prince, referring [*rapportant*] everything to himself exclusively, reduces the state to its capital, the capital to the court, and the court to his person alone" (8.6.117).

The sole rulership of a despot ultimately reduces beyond one to a null point, to a will that, in being everything, is also nothing. In a despotic government, the vizir is not only the master of his master but also the slave of his master. "The prince's will, once known, should produce its effect as infallibly as does one ball thrown against another" (3.10.29). The billiard-ball analogy explains the strange equality that pervades despotism, in which law is none other than the will of the prince, which devolves upon the will of the magistrate or, more precisely, upon the individual wills of a multitude of magistrates. Ironically, then, all their wills are the same: "As law is only what the prince wants, and the prince is able to want only what he knows, surely there must be an infinite number of people who want in his name and in the same way he does" (5.16.66). Montesquieu sums up this situation with a transitive equation: "In despotic government, *power* passes entirely into the hands of the one to whom it is entrusted. The vizir is the despot himself, and each individual officer is the vizir" (5.16.65). But the equality that pervades despotism is an equality in nothingness: "Men are all equal in republican government; they are equal in despotic government; in the former it is because they are everything; in the latter, it is because they are nothing" (6.2.75). Implicitly, this nullity extends to the despot himself, who is enslaved by his own passions, a prisoner in his own seraglio, wanting everything, willing everything, knowing nothing. In the complete absence of relations, he is reduced to as much of a nullity as the vizir, the magistrates, the subjects—slaves all.

IF WE WERE TO GRAPH MONTESQUIEU's three kinds of government onto an *x/y* axis, with republicanism representing one axis and monarchy the other, despotism would lie at the zero point where the axes intersect. The emptiness of this point—without magnitude, devoid of relations, offering nothing for the Cartesian mind to comprehend—epitomizes the aesthetic displeasure conveyed in Montesquieu's description of despotism. Let me develop this visual analogy a bit further to see what other insights it may yield. Extending outward along the monarchical axis, one would move from the more absolute to the more constitutional form of kingship; and along the republican axis one could move either from the extreme democratic to the more aristocratic form of republic or the reverse, from the narrowest aristocracy to the broadest democracy, depending on whether one chose to define the zero point as representing the absence of equality or (in what amounts to the same thing for Montesquieu) as representing extreme equality. The farther one extends outward from the zero point, the more space one finds between the axes for the relations that constitute law. Of course, nowhere does Montesquieu suggest such a graph, but the ease with which we can diagram his thought about the three kinds of government bespeaks his *esprit géométrique*.

The visual analogy, though, would seem to break down when one considers that governments thus graphed would be a mixture of forms, with each point defined as a ratio of republican and monarchical values. How could one then speak unambiguously of republican, monarchical, and despotic forms of government? Yet here, too, the analogy still proves fruitful, for it highlights Montesquieu's sense of the complex relationship between theory and practice, between ideality and reality. This relationship emerges most clearly when we examine the interplay between government and the principles that animate it.

His designation in book 2 of the three kinds of government—republican, monarchical, despotic—diverges from previous political theory, which (following Aristotle) had identified the three basic types as democracy, aristocracy, and monarchy. Montesquieu, by contrast, subsumes democracy and aristocracy under republicanism and adds despotism (hence the republican axis of our hypothetical graph extends either from democracy to aristocracy or the reverse). Ultimately, Montesquieu's three kinds of government derive from his perception of the three principles animating them—virtue, honor, and fear—which he describes next, in book 3. Virtue is the mainspring of a republic, as manifested by the patriotism deriving from the sense of equality in a democracy and from the sense of moderation in an aristocracy; honor is the mainspring of a monarchy, as manifested in the privileges by which people and institutions maintain themselves in equilibrium with the king; and fear is the mainspring of a despotism, by which the prince makes his will felt with the directness and immediacy of one ball striking another.

Montesquieu uses the principles animating the three types of government as intellectual searchlights to illuminate salient aspects of complex political and social phenomena, which would otherwise remain obscured by the cloud of historical facts. Indeed, he makes direct reference to this intellectual tactic in his preface:

> I began by examining men, and I believed that, amidst the infinite diversity of laws and mores, they were not led by their fancies alone.
>
> I have set down the principles, and I have seen particular cases conform to them as if by themselves, the histories of all nations being but their consequences, and each particular law connecting with another law or dependent on a more general one. (xliii)

Writing of this passage, the great Ernst Cassirer concludes, "One can say of Montesquieu that he is the first thinker to grasp and to express clearly the concept of 'ideal types' in history" (210). In the manner of ideal-type thinking Montesquieu has first used the principles of virtue, honor, and fear to abstract the republican, monarchical, and despotic forms of government from the immense variety of history, and he has then imposed these principles and forms back on history as an interpretative grid. The crucial point in ideal-type thinking is not to confuse the types with reality but rather to use them in a more restrictive sense, as tools for sorting through reality. Our hypothetical graph captures the instrumentality of Montesquieu's ideal types. Despotism is in theory the zero point in human relations, but despotic governments in historical fact only approximate this point, being clustered near the zero point, where there is some limited space for relations. So, too, actual monarchies and republics only approximate their theoretical norm. They all appear on our would-be graph as complex relations that tend toward one axis or the other, but they are not so one-dimensional as to lie flat on the axis.

Montesquieu refers to these proximate tendencies in the brief concluding chapter of book 3, "Reflections on all this," which reads in its entirety, "Such are the principles of the three governments: this does not mean that in a certain republic one is virtuous, but that one ought to be *[mais qu'on devrait l'être]*; nor does this prove that in a certain monarchy, there is honor or that in a particular despotic state, there is fear, but that unless it is there, the government is imperfect" (3.11.30). He thus makes the instrumentality of his vision clear by distinguishing explicitly between the ideal types and the reality they illuminate. Most interesting here is the employment of the verb *devoir*, which captures the force,

quality, and nature of ideal-type thinking. Far from being ambiguous, Montesquieu's use of this verb in the title of his work reflects the revolutionary nature
of his thought, which (to paraphrase the title) concerns the relation that the laws
ideally have with the constitution of every government, with mores, with climate, with religion, with commerce, and so on.

WHERE DID THESE IDEAL TYPES COME FROM? Of course, the term itself
derives from the German neologism *Idealtyp,* popularized by Max Weber, a
derivation that makes Montesquieu's use of the concept 150 years *avant la lettre*
appear all the more remarkable. Recall, though, that Montesquieu was very
much a *malebranchiste,* that Malebranche espoused a relational vision of truth,
that he described "real relations" as relations of magnitude, and that he reduced
relations of magnitude to those of equality or inequality. Whenever Malebranche
encountered relations of unequal magnitude, he sought the "exact measure"
common to both, which he termed *unité.* In his nascent version of number thinking, each magnitude was a unit (akin to the cardinal principle of number) and
the exact measure common to them was a unity (akin to the ordinal principle).
This notion of *unité* lay at the heart of his epistemological vision and inspired
his attempt to find the underlying unity of all knowledge, qualitative as well as
quantitative.

In his relational vision of law, Montesquieu regarded the three principles of
government—and, by extension, the types of government they identified—as
unities underlying the seemingly random diversity of customs, laws, and institutions, which were themselves akin to units, indivisible entities that shared an
"exact measure." The republican, monarchical, and despotic principles identify
and stand for a given range of concrete social and political relations, with each
range characterized by its own particular kind of order. Although one would
search in vain through *The Spirit of the Laws* for the kinds of formulas and equa-
tions we nowadays associate with mathematics, Montesquieu's thought is at its
deepest level mathematical, shaped by a submerged model of number thinking.

This model manifests itself in the very structure of the work. Montesquieu
begins by describing the necessary relations (i.e., laws) that characterize each
of the three forms of government, as epitomized by laws establishing political
rights in republics, establishing intermediate powers in monarchies, and establishing the vizir in despotic states. These necessary relations derive from and are
reinforced by the principles of virtue, honor, and fear, which in turn shape and
are reinforced by relations within the family (as reflected in the laws of education) and between families (as reflected in laws given to society as a whole).

Montesquieu continues in this way—following "the natural order of laws less than that of these relations *[rapports]*"—to show how the manifold relations stemming from each type and principle of government themselves exist in relation to climate, geography, and the ways of life dictated by these physical factors, in relation to the degree of liberty inherent in the constitution, and in relation to religion, commerce, and mores. Finally, these laws also exist in relation to one another *[elles ont des rapports entre elles]*—to their origin, to the intention of their originators, to their historical circumstances.[17]

The *spirit* of the laws resides not in the laws themselves but in the relations these laws express and, ultimately, in the relations between these relations. This organization reflects the order of knowledge in Malebranche's *Search after Truth*, which extends from the simple to the complex in the manner of mathematics: "Relations of ideas are the only ones the mind can know infallibly and by itself without the use of the senses. But not only is there a relation between ideas, but also between relations that are between ideas, between relations of relations of ideas, and finally between collections of many relations and between relations of these collections of relations, and so on to infinity" (6.1.5.184). As Michael Hobart observes, "relations between ideas" correspond to the operations of arithmetic; "relations . . . between relations" correspond to those of algebra; and "relations . . . between relations of these collections of relations" correspond to those of the calculus.[18] Mathematics thus replaces the Aristotelian hierarchical ordering of knowledge, which classifies *things* by genera and species, with an analytical ordering, which addresses not things themselves but the *relations* between them, relations that progress toward greater and greater abstraction.

Montesquieu's integrative vision does not ascend to Malebranche's level of abstraction and generality. Instead of seeking the order of all knowledge, he seeks only to order political and social knowledge. But his more circumscribed vision emphasizes the relations between entities rather than the entities themselves. In the conclusion to book 1, where he lays out the plan of the work, he explains that he has made no attempt to distinguish political from civil laws, for "I do not treat laws but the spirit of the laws, and this spirit consists in the various relations *[rapports]* that laws may have with various things *[choses]*" (1.3.9). This relational ordering is vastly different from the order of the laws themselves, which could readily be represented by an Aristotelian classificatory hierarchy—a hierarchy of substantive entities. Instead, the relational order is one of analytical abstraction, ascending not toward a genus but toward ever more general operations of the mind, expressing ever more abstract relations between things.

Montesquieu uses the nondescript term *things (choses)* throughout the text, starting with the opening line of book 1, where he declares that laws are the necessary relations deriving from the nature of things. Perhaps we can detect here a faint echo of Descartes's *res cogitans* and *res extensa,* the thinking and extended things that form the basis of his ontology. But Descartes still conceived of these "things" as "substances" in the Aristotelian sense, whereas Montesquieu treats them as if they were measurable natural phenomena—embodied by (say) geography, climate, wealth, and population, which in their myriad combinations factored into more abstract relations governing politics, culture, and religion. The term *chose* reflects the more tangible nature of his existants, and its lack of specificity highlights their relations, for "things" in and of themselves matter less to him than the magnitude of the spaces between them. The *spirit* of the laws expressly embodies the order of these magnitudes, an order whose coherence derives from the principles of a submerged model of number thinking.

LET US EXAMINE MONTESQUIEU'S RELATIONAL VIEW of things in practice, taking as a case in point the relatively neglected book 7, "Consequences of the different principles of the three governments in relation *[rapport]* to sumptuary laws, luxury, and the condition of women." Readers commonly skip over books like this—and there are many—in their rush to get to the most famous sections of *The Spirit of the Laws,* on constitutional monarchy in England and on the effects of climate. Yet, more so than those famous books—in which most readers seek substantive truths—neglected ones like this reveal the relational means by which he arrived at his insights.

Right at the outset, in chapter 1, Montesquieu defines luxury as a relation: "*Luxury* is always proportionate to the inequality of fortunes" (7.1.96). No inequality, no luxury. He then proposes a formula for measuring the magnitude of this relation, starting from a point of equality: "Assuming physical necessities equal to a given sum, the luxury of those who have only the necessary will be equal to *zero;* he who has its double will have a luxury equal to one; he who has double the goods of the latter will have a luxury equal to three; when the next has yet again the double, he will have a luxury equal to seven; so that, always assuming the goods of the next individual to be twice those of the previous one, luxury will increase by twice plus one, in this progression: 0, 1, 3, 7, 15, 31, 63, 127" (7.1.96). In theory luxury is a relation of definable magnitude existing between two points in an ordered series.

In practice, though, this theoretical relation exists in a real world characterized by inequality between states, as well as between citizens. Luxury is thus "a compound ratio of the inequality of fortunes among the citizens and the inequality of wealth of the various states" (7.1.97). Despite great inequality between people in Poland, for example, the relative poverty of this state means that Poland does not have as much luxury as France. Even this compound ratio, though, does not suffice to capture the real complexity of the luxury relation, for "luxury is also proportionate to the size of the towns and above all of the capital, so that luxury exists in a compound ratio of the wealth of the state, the inequality of the fortunes of individuals, and the number of men gathered together in certain places" (7.1.97). Montesquieu then likens this last variable, the size of population centers, to a ratio—the larger the population, the greater the anonymity, the greater the desire to distinguish oneself. He thus treats luxury not qualitatively in moral terms but quantitatively, as a measurable theoretical relation that in practice exists in relation to other relations.

Montesquieu concludes chapter 1 with the ironic observation that in large population centers, the more people consume, the more alike they become, thus leading them to ever greater consumption to distinguish themselves. This spiral can entail "general distress," thus setting the stage for a consideration of sumptuary laws in democracy (chapter 2), in aristocracy (chapter 3), and in monarchy (chapter 4). Much like luxury itself, sumptuary laws exist in relation to their circumstances. The salutary laws establishing equality in democracies would be ill-advised in aristocracies (where the nobility ought to be allowed to distinguish itself in ways useful to the republic) and are absolutely harmful to monarchies (where luxury is a condition of their very existence). Writing in chapter 4 of the necessity of luxury in monarchies, he describes how "the rich must indeed spend in proportion to the inequality of fortunes, and, as we have said, luxury must increase in this proportion" (7.4.99). He concludes with a description of how monarchy depends on the progressive growth of luxury: "Thus, for the monarchical state to sustain itself, luxury has to increase from the laborer to the artisan, to the merchant, to the nobles, to the magistrates, to the great lords, to the principal revenue officers, to the princes; otherwise, all would be lost." This formula leads Montesquieu to conclude, "Republics end in luxury; monarchies, in poverty" (7.4.100).

Whereas chapter 4 establishes the general relation between sumptuary laws, luxury, and monarchy, chapter 5 further defines this relation, establishing that the frugality associated with democracy can sometimes serve the interests of monarchy. (Note how Montesquieu's argument follows the order of relations rather than the order of the laws themselves.) Republics are sustained by sumptuary laws enforcing an "absolute frugality" (*frugalité absolue*), but monarchies can enact sumptuary laws that enforce "relative frugality" *(frugalité relative)* when they discourage the consumption of certain expensive foreign commodities that would otherwise dangerously deplete the kingdom's resources. Montesquieu concludes this brief chapter with an elaborate formula integrating several different relations of luxury: "In general, the poorer the state, the more it is ruined by relative luxury *[luxe relatif]*, and the more, consequently, it must have relative sumptuary laws *[lois somptuaires relatives]*. The richer the state, the more its relative luxury *[luxe relatif]* enriches it, and one must be careful not to make relative sumptuary laws there *[lois somptuaires relatives]*" (7.5.101).

Most striking here is the way in which the language of *rapports* gives way to frank expressions of relativism. Indeed, when Montesquieu defines laws as "necessary relations," he simply means that they are (ideally) relative to their circumstances and that by examining these circumstances, legislators can devise appropriate laws. From this perspective, the French term *justice* loses its qualitative associations and takes on a quantitative one inherent in its root, *juste,* entailing the "correct" relation between a law and its circumstances, a relation that is (by definition) relative rather than absolute. Yet Montesquieu appears reluctant to embrace this relativism. He generally avoids explicit expressions of it in the text, preferring to emphasize the importance of relations over relativity. *Rapports* are measurable, and wherever the methodology of measurement prevails, so, too, does a vision of order. Relativity, by contrast, opens the door to chaos. Montesquieu is first and foremost a social scientist who believes that truth can be measured—in fact, to the extent that his entire system reflects a submerged model of number, he may very well qualify as the *first* social scientist. As he states unequivocally in the second paragraph of *The Spirit of the Laws*: "Those who have said that *a blind fate has produced all the effects that we see in the world* have said a great absurdity" (1.1.3). The emphasis is in the original, highlighting a point he rejects categorically. From our analysis of the first five chapters of book 7, we can say that he allows expressions of relativism to creep into the text only after he has secured the underlying relations they designate, so that what appears relative is in reality the calculable product of relations of relations. Behind the seemingly infinite contingencies of human reality, there stands a measurable order that pervades all creation, providing the ultimate basis for knowledge.

The Past Emerges

W herein lies the historiographical significance of Montesquieu's relational vision of all things human? Let us recall the intellectual crossroads reached by Montaigne in the late sixteenth century, when he viewed the conquistadors through Aztec eyes. His empathic engagement with another form of being human held forth the possibility of seeing himself and his world from a perspective distance, which would have revealed other outlooks as the product of their own circumstances, thus engendering a systematic distinction between past and present. Yet Montaigne did not sustain this perspective because he did not privilege any particular point of view. Aztecs, Romans, Spaniards, Greeks, Brazilians, Hungarians, Albanians, Gascons—to say nothing of a very particular Gascon—all these and more provide the subjects on which he essayed himself in a constant shifting of perspectives that precluded his obtaining (or, better yet, obviated his need for) a single, sustained one. Of course, as he essayed himself, he established his own unique point of orientation amid diversity, but this self remained in constant flux: "If my mind could gain a firm footing, I would not make essays, I would make decisions [*je ne m'essaierois pas, je me resoudrois*]" (3.2.611). Indeed, he especially enjoyed essaying himself on his own ever-shifting perspectives: "On an empty stomach I feel myself another man than after a meal" (2.12.425). Montaigne's brand of perspectivism had no imitators, for few could embrace such radical relativism, let alone with his aplomb!

Montesquieu seems an equally charming and genial observer of human diversity, but his equanimity derives from an altogether different source, from an insight into the intrinsic order of all things human. This order neither denies nor transcends the elemental diversity of the world but rather dwells within it, as its fundamental feature. The existence of unities amid the profusion of units—of ideal types defining the range of human entities—underscores Montesquieu's confidence in rejecting the role of blind fate in the world. When one focuses on the plethora of entities themselves, one seems to see a confusion spawned by chance; but when one focuses on the relations between entities, patterns emerge that bespeak an underlying unity, a unity that actually exists within diversity rather than despite it. In this sense the unity is not classificatory—derived by paring away the accidents surrounding an essence—but analytical, an operational feature of diversity itself, wherein entities exist in relations of "greater than," "less than," and "equal to."

The analytical perspective establishes a sustained distance between the observer and the thing observed. Montaigne's empathic identification with the Aztecs implied a distancing of himself from his European identity, but this distance depended on the feelings evoked by the person or people with whom he empathized—to say nothing of the circumstances surrounding that act—and its extent shifted from one empathic moment to the next, accentuating Montaigne's almost visceral sense of flux. Montesquieu, however, focused on the relations between things rather than the things themselves. By this means he created a sustained, operational perspective that continually gauged the intervals between things, rendering human phenomena knowable with certainty, if not precision. He could, for example, measure luxury as a theoretical relation with exactitude; and even though this relation became increasingly complex in practice, resulting in compound ratios of multiple factors, its underlying principles remained nonetheless clear. Relativity thus yielded to relations, and flux to stability.

Furthermore, this perspective was operational in a historical as well as mathematical sense. Changes in relations tracked changes in time and space, accounting for the rise and fall of nations. Rome provides the great test case for Montesquieu's insights about historical causation, as detailed throughout *The Spirit of the Laws*, as well as in his earlier *Considerations on the Causes of the Greatness of the Romans and Their Decline*. Rome's balance of predatory and republican features—where booty and the opportunities for obtaining it were shared equally—created a stable, well-managed warrior state, the success of which spelled its doom, as imperial luxury undermined the republican virtue that had facilitated world domination: "The corruption of each government almost always begins with that of its principles" (8.1.112). The political evolution of the state, from republic to monarchy to despotism, tracks the degeneration of its laws from "strictness to indolence, and from indolence to impunity" (6.5.90). The fate of Rome reveals that long-term forces underlie the accidents of history. Although these forces originate in the general principles of government—republican virtue, monarchical honor, despotic fear—they conform to the unique circumstances of each particular state: "Many things govern men: climate, religion, laws, the maxims of the government, examples of past things, mores, and manners; a general spirit *[un esprit général]* is formed as a result. To the extent that, in each nation, one of these causes acts more forcefully, the others yield to it" (19.4.310). Each of these factors constitutes a "cause," whose unique combination with other factors creates a distinctive *esprit général*: "It is unnecessary to say that moral qualities have different effects according to the other qualities united with them; thus arrogance joined to a vast ambition, to the greatness of ideas, etc. produced among the Romans the effects which are known to all" (19.9.313). The relational vision thus reveals the forces underlying the flux of events, the vectors governing the magnitude and direction of historical change. In Ernst Cassirer's considerable estimation, *The Spirit of the Laws* constitutes the Enlightenment's "first decisive attempt at the foundation of a philosophy of history" (209).

Ironically, this philosophy of history ignores the dimension of temporality. As F. T. H. Fletcher has observed in his *Montesquieu and English Politics*, "The novelty of Montesquieu's historical method really consists in its neglect of the very thing considered most fundamental to history—Time" (73). Instead of viewing human events and entities chronologically, says Fletcher, Montesquieu arrays them side by side in *The Spirit of the Laws*: "He sees history spread out flat before him, and arranged in a certain pattern, the designer of which he calls 'human Reason'" (73). The mention of "human reason" to which Fletcher referred culminates the discussion of law as relation in book 1, where Montesquieu states, "Law in general is human reason insofar as it governs all the peoples of the earth; and the political and civil laws of each nation should be *[doivent être]* only the particular cases to which human reason is applied" (1.3.8). Whereas Fletcher interpreted "human reason" as an unchanging universal principle providing the metaphysical basis for Montesquieu's "legal apologetic," we can now assert its mathematical aspect with confidence. If human law is human reason, and law is relational, then so, too, is reason. The principles of number thinking provide the key to understanding human reality in all its diversity and complexity, revealing unities amid the units of history.

Of course, Montesquieu's thought exhibits a tension between normative and individualizing tendencies—"Laws should be *[elles doivent être]* so appropriate to the people for whom they are made that it is very unlikely that the laws of one nation can suit another" (1.3.8)—and sometimes the diversity of law obscures the uniformity of its principles. But he ultimately attributes the uniqueness of a nation's laws to an array of causal factors—climate, religion, mores, manners, and so on—whose distinctive combination nonetheless shapes its *esprit général* in a measurable way. Relational thinking thus accounts for historical diversity without recourse to time, by describing each entity in terms of the relations that constitute it. And these relations, in turn, fix the entity in relation to other entities, and so on. By this means Montesquieu sustains a perspective distance not only between past and present (say, ancient Rome and modern France) but also between different kinds of past (ancient Rome and ancient Athens) each of which is defined and delimited by its own constellation of causes.

WE HAVE NOW ATTENDED TO THE BIRTH of the past. It owes its nativity to a relational vision characteristic of number thinking that thoroughly contextualizes entities. (Perhaps the baldness of the claim still jars.) Yet we have not quite arrived at the end of our labor. *The Spirit of the Laws* represents the moment of parturition, but how did the idea for this work germinate? "It originated from a Malebranchian education," one might answer, though this dry assertion desiccates the reality of Montesquieu's prolonged search for meaning amid complexity, the frustration of which he detailed in the preface to *The Spirit of the Laws:* "Many times I began this work and many times abandoned it; a thousand times I cast to the winds the pages I had written; every day I felt my paternal hands drop; I followed my object without forming a design; I knew neither rules nor exceptions; I found the truth only to lose it. But when I discovered my principles, all that I had sought came to me, and in the course of twenty years, I saw my work begin, grow, move ahead, and end" (xlv).

So great was his frustration that he even memorialized it with some verses from Virgil, a noteworthy poetic moment in so empirical a work. And after he finally found his principles, it still took him twenty years to confirm them. Twenty years! That span recalls the length of Vico's struggle to decode Homer and, even more evocatively, the length of Odysseus's absence from Ithaca. Despite the number's mythical quality, though, we may assume that the past began to crown Montesquieu's brow not long after he published his first major work, the *Persian Letters,* and that it continued its emergence through his second major (though often overlooked) work, *Considerations on the Causes of the Greatness of the Romans and Their Decline.* Indeed, fundamental similarities between all three of his major works enable us to witness the birth up close, as it were, and (by this means) to soften the jarring claim that the past originated from number thinking. In reality, the *Persian Letters* represents an intermediate stage in the birth of the past, bridging the gulf between Montaigne's qualitative outlook in the *Essays* and Montesquieu's quantitative one in *The Spirit of the Laws.*

The *Persian Letters* is one of the first literary works to sustain the kind of empathic pretense that Montaigne had evoked in the *Essays.* Montesquieu drew considerable inspiration from Giovanni Paolo Marana's immensely popular *Turkish Spy,* the first volume of which appeared in 1684. An Italian expatriate living in France, Marana composed his novel in French as a series of secret letters to the Sultan, supposedly written by a Muslim visiting Paris. As the title indicates, the book deals ostensibly with political matters, all the while exploring differences between Eastern and Western customs and beliefs. Montesquieu expanded on this epistolary pretense in the *Persian Letters,* introducing a larger cast of correspondents who treat a wider array of subjects. Through 161 fictional missives purportedly written to and by Persians, Montesquieu maintains an imagined view of Persian customs and beliefs, as well as an imagined Persian view of European customs and beliefs.

To some extent, his ability and willingness to sustain a Persian perspective reflects the eighteenth century's burgeoning interest in travel and travel litera-ture. Descartes had already popularized the intellectual benefits of travel in the autobiographical portion of his *Discourse on the Method* (1637), which recounts the dissatisfaction with humanistic education that led him to abandon the world of books for the book of the world. An outpouring of travel literature in the seventeenth and eighteenth centuries enabled readers to experience the benefits of travel without leaving home. The *Persian Letters,* in particular, relies heavily on the travel accounts of Jean Chardin (1643–1713) and Jean-Baptiste Tavernier (1605–89)—both of whom wrote extensively about Persian customs and be-liefs. The popularity of Marana's earlier novel and the growing interest in travel, though, do not suffice to explain the origin of the *Persian Letters* or its original-ity as an extended exercise in cultural relativism.

Montesquieu intended both the form and the content of the work to incul-cate an analytical outlook, although the novel's satirical and erotic elements obscure this aim. He had first published the work anonymously in Holland in 1721—perhaps to avoid censure for its caricature of contemporary French soci-ety and politics—maintaining the conceit (probably borrowed from Marana) that he had merely translated letters that had come into his possession. Contem-porary readers delighted not only in the novel's edgy satire but also in its eroticism, its prurient attention to the details of life in a Persian seraglio, where wives ardently competed for the amorous attention of their husband. This risqué subject matter, too, may have furthered Montesquieu's initial desire for anonym-ity. All in all, the *Persian Letters* gives the superficial impression of being a light-hearted frolic, yet it is anything but.

The novel begins and ends with a consideration of despotism, a theme that always lurks close to the would-be frivolous surface. Usbek, a nobleman of high standing in the Persian court, has chosen voluntary exile in the West rather than face disgrace and death at the hands of rival courtiers. The inquisitive Rica—a somewhat irreverent youth who has yet to acquire Usbek's gravity and station—accompanies him on his journey. The older man leaves behind his seraglio, which he considers "the most valuable thing that I have in the world" (2.41). The seraglio seems a splendid postadolescent male fantasy—especially as detailed lasciviously in Letter 3, from wife Zashi to Usbek—but this would-be locus of physical pleasure is in reality a symbol of political perversion, demonstrating the wanton willfulness of despotism and its monstrous consequences.

This monstrosity emerges quite clearly in Letter 2, from Usbek to his chief eunuch, the slave in charge of the seraglio. Here Usbek describes the seraglio as a bastion of virtue, though (ironically) one that needs to be defended from within as well as without. The chief eunuch oversees the virtue of the wives, as both their master and their slave: "You are in charge of my wives, and you obey them. Blindly, you carry out their every desire, and, in the same way, make them carry out the laws of the harem. You glory in doing the most degrading services for them. It is with fear and respect that you submit to their lawful commands; you serve them as the slave of their slaves. But their power is transferred, and you are master like myself, whenever you fear some relaxation of the laws of chastity and modesty" (2.42). Usbek closes with the injunction that the eunuch "humiliate" himself before his charges while, at the same time, making them aware of their own "absolute dependence," which devolves ultimately upon their status as Usbek's slaves and possessions. Other letters amplify the nature of this monstrous society, presided over by denatured men who still feel the prick of passion. This feeling they have no choice but to sublimate, taking their chief pleasure (like remorseless bureaucrats) in grinding down those they serve.

So great is the air and hand of oppression that it has become part of the accepted order of things in Usbek's household, creating a simulacrum of peace and harmony. The acquiescence of wife Roxana—raped into submission by Usbek—thus passes for love, in his eyes at least, while she privately nurtures her hatred for him. Even the more sporting Zashi is thoroughly disingenuous, though she seems attached to a system whose workings she has learned to manipulate. Her protestations of love and longing for the absent Usbek may recall for the modern reader those Soviet citizens who cried in the streets at the news of Stalin's death, oppressed for so long that they felt bereft of their oppressor. Perhaps wife Zelis expresses the perversion of will and feeling best in Letter 62: "Although you keep me imprisoned I am freer than you. Even if you were to pay twice as much attention to guarding me, I should simply take pleasure in your disquiet, and your suspicion, jealousy, and vexation are so many signs of your dependence. Continue, dear Usbek, and have me watched night and day. Do not trust even the usual precautions. Increase my happiness by guaranteeing your own, and remember that I fear nothing except your indifference" (62.129). As

Zelis clearly demonstrates, Usbek remains as much a slave in this system as his wives and eunuchs.

The farther westward Usbek travels, the more he begins to free himself from his intellectual and moral enslavement. The famous Letters 11–14, about the parable of the Troglodytes, presage his intellectual awakening, along with its inevitable end. An anarchic people, the Troglodytes behaved so selfishly toward each other and their neighbors that they all but perished. Only two families, noteworthy for their humanity and justice, flourished amid the general decline, and from this seed there eventually arose a populous and prosperous Troglodyte nation, whose members learned virtue from birth and always acted in accordance with the common good. (Contrast this community with that of the seraglio.) Alas, though, there came a day when the Troglodytes, whose natural virtue had enabled them to govern themselves spontaneously and informally, decided to chose a king, thinking that they ought to be led by the most virtuous among them. This man, knowing the inevitable outcome of their action, greeted his election with tears of grief: "Your virtue has begun to be a burden to you. In your present state, without a ruler, it is necessary for you to be virtuous despite yourselves. . . . You would prefer to be subject to a king, and obey his laws, which would be less rigid than your own customs" (14.60). (Recall Montesquieu's observation in *The Spirit of the Laws* that "the corruption of each government almost always begins with that of its principles" [8.1.112].) The parable ends with these lamentations, which augur the fate of the Troglodyte nation.

Usbek's moral development in the course of his travels follows the same arc as the parable. Leaving the wanton selfishness of his seraglio behind, he slowly comes alive to the relative liberty of French society and the freedom of inquiry it fosters. The same holds true for Rica, but even more so for his having a quick, young mind. Together they grow during their travels and learn to question the Persian customs they had previously taken for granted, in much the same way as they question Western practices. By means of comparing French and Persian ways, they learn to think analytically—they learn to take a perspective that is neither French nor Persian but that arises from a focus on the relations between the two. Usbek's judgments are the more ponderous, being freighted with greater baggage than Rica's, which sometimes seem a little glib. Yet Rica eventually sheds the burden of his accustomed ways, while Usbek ultimately succumbs to it. Upon receiving reports of disobedience and rebellion in the seraglio, Usbek resolves to return home after several years abroad. As wife Zelis had so clearly anticipated, he remains a slave to jealousy, even though it will probably cost him his life. Rica wisely declines to accompany him, and the novel climaxes in an orgy of death, as Usbek instructs the chief eunuch to make his rebellious wives pay for their disobedience, ultimately with blood. Only his beloved Roxana appears to remain loyal, but the eunuch's final letters reveal the extent of her duplicity, which she herself confirms in the novel's last missive, where she taunts and reviles Usbek as she lies dying by her own hand.

Although there's plenty of satire sandwiched between the accounts of despotism, it's hard to ignore the chilling desolation of the novel's finale, in which Usbek destroys all he cherishes, as prelude to his own destruction. (Recall Montesquieu's depiction of despotism in *The Spirit of the Laws:* "When the savages of Louisiana want fruit, they cut down the tree and gather the fruit.") Beneath its charming and erotic façade, the *Persian Letters* really constitutes the first extended meditation on the nature of despotism, which Montesquieu would later systematize in *The Spirit of the Laws.* Indeed, the word *despotism* itself was just coming into vogue in the seventeenth and eighteenth centuries as a term of abuse (note that *tyranny* and *dictatorship* had yet to acquire their modern, oppressive meanings; the former still designated illegitimate rule—regardless of its quality—and the latter a Roman republican office). To some extent (as Marana's earlier novel makes clear) interest in the subject of despotism derives from the perception of an external Turkish threat to Europe, but it also owes much to internal developments—to the notoriety of Thomas Hobbes's *Leviathan,* to the infamy of Oliver Cromwell's Protectorate, and (most important for Montesquieu) to the unpopularity of Louis XIV's absolutism, which became increasingly oppressive during the course of his long reign. Not only does the *Persian Letters* reflect a new spirit of freedom inaugurated by the death of that king but it also embodies a warning—represented by the parable of the Troglodytes and by the arc of Usbek's awakening—that virtue requires vigilance and that monarchy can always degenerate into despotism.

The epistolary form of the novel complements its political subject matter. Superficially, the book resembles a genuine collection of letters. Some correspondents appear only once or twice, and the sender's relation to the recipient often remains vague, as it would in reality. Although there's some natural difference in tone between Usbek and Rica, and between Usbek's wives, the personalities of the correspondents appear one-dimensional, as well they should in newsy missives. The letters are for the most part short, and they generally don't follow any set theme or pattern—the Troglodyte sequence and the long series of letters on demography (112–22) are noteworthy exceptions, but even these are pithy enough to appear real. All in all, it seems hardly surprising that some early readers thought the letters genuine.

But Montesquieu aimed at more than realism in the *Persian Letters*. For all the apparent artlessness of the collection, he carefully juxtaposed letters to highlight certain themes. A case in point is the initial group of letters about the seraglio (2, 3, 4, 6, 7, 9), which contrast sharply with those about the Troglo-dytes (11, 12, 13, 14), thereby defining the nature of despotic fear in relation to that of republican virtue. Lest one miss the point, Letter 15, from a eunuch in Persia to one traveling with Usbek, drives home the contrast in its opening lines: "Although I am virtually unacquainted with the relationship that they call friendship, and have been entirely wrapped up in myself, you have made me feel that I still had a heart" (15.61). Such is the quality of Montesquieu's liter-ary art that these themes seem to arise naturally, as if from a disconnected correspondence.

The disconnectedness of the letters, combined with the flatness of the char-acters, conspires to serve an intellectual purpose. By treating most subjects only telegraphically, and by switching continually from subject to subject, Montes-quieu effectively destabilizes the reader, preventing him or her from dwelling too much on the specific content of the letters. This effect is accentuated by the conceit that the correspondents are Persian, thus keeping the French reader at a critical distance from what they are saying. The flatness of the characters serves the same distancing purpose, making it hard for the reader to identify with these stick figures—an effect that Voltaire was to perfect in *Candide*. And much like Voltaire, Montesquieu intends by these means of distancing to create in the reader a philosophical perspective, one that is neither French nor Persian but comparative. This standpoint offers a consistent, sustained, analytical means of comprehending all things human by assessing the relations between them.

Despotism stands as the very antithesis of this philosophical outlook. In its selfishness, it denies the possibility of other wills, other desires, other view-points than that of the ruler; in short, it denies the very possibility of a relational perspective. So complete is this denial that Usbek—in the most primal of all relations—did not even recognize the reality of rape when he overcame Roxa-na's "modesty" as a newly acquired, young wife: "You carried the scruples of chastity too far: you did not surrender, even after you had been conquered; you defended your dying virginity at the very last extremity; you considered me as an enemy who had inflicted an outrage on you, not as a husband who had loved you. It was three months before you dared look at me without blushing." Usbek characteristically mistook the latter reaction for reticence rather than rage, and he had the blind gall to make his profession of "love" in a letter where he declaims the immodesty of French women and Roxana's good fortune at living in his seraglio, "in the home of innocence, beyond the reach of all the crimes of mankind" (26.75–76).

When thwarted, the despotic will simply destroys that which offends it, much as (in Freudian psychology) the all-encompassing infantile id seeks blindly to obliterate whatever impedes its pleasure. Fear of death—palpable in the plaintiff letters that Usbek's crackdown wrings from his wives—is thus the motive force behind despotism, and the eunuchs its ready instrument, lest they, too, incur their master's displeasure. By means of fear all wills are reduced to one in a complete and utter denial of relations. The contrast between the form and content of the *Persian Letters* thus conspires to present a consistent message about intellectual enlightenment and the chief threat to it, a threat that lay much closer to home than Persia.

IF WE TAKE SERIOUSLY MONTESQUIEU'S CLAIM that *The Spirit of the Laws* had a twenty-year gestation, then he did not discover its principles until around 1728, some seven years after the publication of the *Persian Letters*. Yet we see in this early novel a remarkable similarity to the kind of relational thinking that would emerge from Montesquieu's ultimate work, as well as a similar interest in despotism as the zero-mark on a new kind of political yardstick. Nonetheless (I would speculate), the abstract and philosophical form these interests took in the *Persian Letters* did not in the long run prove intellectually fruitful for Montesquieu, and he found himself looking for a new means of expressing and elaborating his analytical outlook.

"A thousand times I cast to the winds the pages I had written; every day I felt my paternal hands drop." We can see in his literary notebooks something of the variety of projects he picked up, only to abandon them like unwanted children. To mention merely a few, he sketched some dialogues between classical figures, took notes for a study on the "Fundamental Principles of Politics," speculated about writing a history of the Jesuits, and undertook a brief study of the political economy of Spain. This last exercise, which he picked up and discarded several times, eventually found its way into *The Spirit of the Laws* (21.22). In 1725 he read part of an incomplete "Treatise on Duties" to the Academy of Bordeaux, but we know hardly anything of this work beyond its table of contents. He also delivered a few other learned papers during this period, but aside from a couple of journal publications, only *The Temple of Gnide* (1724)—a stylish though slender and insubstantial love story—appeared in print during his lifetime.

On the strength of the *Persian Letters* he was inducted into the French Academy in January 1728, after which he embarked on a three-year tour of Europe, starting in Vienna, ending in London, and including stops in Hungary, Germany, and Italy. His longest stays were in Italy (about twelve months) and England (about twenty months). By his own reckoning, we can conclude that he found the guiding principles for his master work during this period, but we have no way of knowing whether travel inspired or merely occasioned their discovery. We do know that the sojourn in England influenced him tremendously. From a painstaking reconstruction of his movements and acquaintances in England, Shackleton speculates that Montesquieu's firsthand experience of British statesmen and their parliamentary debates probably led him to begin writing a description of the English constitution while still living there. Yet he did not complete this account until 1734—three years after his return to France—and he chose not to publish it then but rather revised it several times until 1748, when it appeared as the famous sixth chapter in book 11 of *The Spirit of the Laws.*

Surprisingly, Montesquieu's first major intellectual effort upon returning to France, and the one that most preoccupied him from 1731 through 1733, was his *Considerations on the Causes of the Greatness of the Romans and Their Decline.* (Out of an excess of political caution he first published this work anonymously in Holland in 1734.) Shackleton suggests that the popularity of Roman history in England, and the penchant for citing it in parliamentary speeches, may have drawn Montesquieu to this subject; and there might be some truth to this observation, for the English constitution—with its balance of nonaristocratic, aristocratic, and monarchical elements—may have reminded Montesquieu of republican Rome. Yet the opening line of Montesquieu's pathbreaking history harkens to an altogether different kind of comparison, suggesting a different kind of inspiration: "We should not form the same impression of the city of Rome in its beginnings as we get from the cities we see today, except perhaps for those of the Crimea, which were built to hold booty, cattle and the fruits of the field" (1.23).

Montesquieu's readers were well aware (if only from perusing Livy) that Rome had arisen from rude beginnings, but they must have been startled by his comparison of early Rome to a modern Crimean city populated by brigands and farmers. (At this time the Crimean Tatars, constituting a powerful Islamic state in alliance with the Ottomans, had a fearsome reputation throughout the Ukraine and Russia as raiders and slave traders.) The standard of comparison must have startled not only by its exoticism but also by its modernity. Following the lead of ancient authors like Polybius, commentators had compared Rome with other ancient cities—Carthage, Sparta, Athens. Yet Montesquieu brashly asserts in the very first line of his historical study that one need only look to the

Crimea to catch a glimpse of early Rome. Clearly, he has expanded his comparative viewpoint from the cross-cultural perspective of the *Persian Letters* to a cross-historical one.

Herein, I submit, lies his breakthrough. The cross-historical viewpoint accomplished two things. First, by way of comparison it brought early Rome within the compass of modern imagination as a general type of state, a predatory one in which plunder substituted for trade. Second, by way of contrast it set Rome apart from other small ignoble states, highlighting the improbability and singularity of its achievement. This duality serves as the historical corollary to Malebranche's conception of *unité,* presaging Montesquieu's ideal types. Rome is both an indivisible unit, a state with its own distinctive characteristics, and a member of an ordered series of units, a collection of similar states that includes those of the Crimean Khanate; it represents a type of polity whose own limitations it transcended as it pursued generic ends amid specific circumstances. The opening line of the *Considerations* announces how this duality will emerge from a comparative methodology that can conceivably exploit any kind of historical example—ancient, modern, European, non-European. As he proceeds to analyze Roman history—trading one comparison for another—Montesquieu creates an ever-shifting perspectival tension that focuses less on historical entities themselves than on the cross-historical relations between them, relations enabling him to separate the unique from the typical—and vice versa. By this relational means he penetrated beneath the monotonous and seemingly random surface of events—"this happened, then this, then this"—to reveal the presence of deep-seated historical forces. These "causes," as he terms them, are (like the "unities" from which they derive) both contingent and immutable; they are specific to a people, and they operate uniformly across time and space. We stand here at the threshold of Montesquieu's insight into the *esprit général* of each people that epitomizes his philosophy of history in *The Spirit of the Laws.*

Perhaps travel in general occasioned the small but subtle intellectual shift from the cross-cultural to the cross-historical, a shift with such seismic repercussions. Of course, we can already see aspects of this new orientation in the *Persian Letters.* In Letter 83, for example, he discourses on the principle of justice as an immutable *rapport de convenance,* a "relation of suitability which actually exists between two things," a relation that remains the same regardless of who perceives it. In its entirety the *Persian Letters* is an extended philosophical exercise in the relational perspective, and the letters on demography in particular (112–22) seem to bring this exercise down to earth, casting it in an explicitly historical and contingent light. Here he attempted to explain the (mistaken) impression that population had declined since antiquity by comparing contemporary Christian and Muslim marriage customs with ancient Roman ones, showing how the Romans' practice of monogamy combined with their tolerance of divorce to enhance fertility. This analysis starts off being cross-cultural and cross-historical, though the latter aspect diminishes as Montesquieu moves on to consider other factors affecting population, and the whole discussion itself is overshadowed by the novel's dreadful denouement. In general, we might say that the letter format enabled Montesquieu to introduce the reader to antithetical aspects of relational thinking—showing how it reveals immutability here and contingency there—without encouraging their combination into a single, integrated vision.

In the *Considerations* Montesquieu signalizes the intertwining of the immutable amid the contingent in a highly unusual way, by writing a historical study entirely devoid of any reference to dates or a dating system. The account still follows the chronological order of events but in short, compressed chapters that highlight a strong historical dynamic; in the benchmark Pléiade edition of Montesquieu's *Œuvres complètes,* for example, the fourth chapter of the *Considerations* covers the pivotal period of the wars against the Gauls, Pyrrhus, and Carthage in a scant nine pages—all dateless. He didn't need dates because, in his new analytical view, events reflect "general causes" that operate uniformly through time. In what is probably the most famous passage of the *Considerations,* Montesquieu distinguishes between these general causes and the particular ones that govern local events:

> It is not chance that rules the world. Ask the Romans, who had a continuous sequence of successes when they were guided by a certain plan, and an uninterrupted sequence of reverses when they followed another. There are general causes, moral and physical, which act in every monarchy, elevating it, maintaining it, or hurling it to the ground. All accidents are controlled by these causes. And if the chance of one battle—that is, a particular cause—has brought a state to ruin, some general cause made it necessary for that state to perish from a single battle. In a word, the main trend draws with it all particular accidents. (18.169)

Although he ascribed the main trend of Roman history to immutable general causes, he did not regard them as universal principles detached from events. Instead, they originated from empirically identifiable practices that were, in turn, contingent upon circumstances.

The empirical aspect of Montesquieu's project emerges right from the start, with the concrete comparison between Romans and Crimeans. Expanding on this comparison in chapter 1, he shows how Rome's early place-names betray its agrarian and predatory origins. Always at war with their neighbors, the Romans celebrated the capture of enemy crops and livestock with effusive rejoicing: "Thus originated the triumphs, which subsequently were the main cause of the greatness this city attained" (1.24). Rome was also blessed with a succession of extraordinary kings, until Tarquin seized the throne and made his power absolute. In Montesquieu's singular estimation, Tarquin "was not a contemptible man," but he unwittingly created the circumstances for a revolution when he seized absolute power: "For a proud, enterprising and bold people, confined within walls, must necessarily either shake off its yoke or become gentler in its ways" (1.25). That Rome would follow the former course was foreordained by the actions of an earlier king, Servius Tullius, who had expanded the power of the people at the expense of the nobility, "just as Henry VII, king of England, increased the power of the commons in order to degrade the lords" (1.26). Henry's actions caused the English people to grow bolder and eventually to overthrow the monarchy in the English Civil War; so, too, Servius's actions rendered Tarquin's absolutism intolerable to an emboldened people, who overthrew the monarchy and established a republic. Thus, modern history explains ancient history, "for the occasions which produce great changes are different, but, since men have had the same passions at all times, the causes are always the same" (1.26).

The above line recalls Machiavelli's *Discourses on the First Ten Books of Titus Livius,* a work that leaves a deep imprint on the *Considerations.* Starting with the very first chapter, Montesquieu draws the same kinds of normative conclusions from early Roman history as Machiavelli: "At the birth of societies, the leaders of republics create the institutions; thereafter, it is the institutions that form the leaders of republics" (1.25). So prevalent are such maxims throughout Montesquieu's text that one can sometimes lose sight of the historical nature of his study. Lest one do so, however, we should recall that Montesquieu begins, so to speak, in the Crimea, with a predatory people who outwardly resemble the Romans. The comparison places all the greater emphasis on the sheer improbability of Rome's achievement, which cannot be explained by reference to immutable principles alone.

The historical half of Montesquieu's project puts Rome firmly in its place, along with Machiavelli. On one level Machiavelli had shown how the Romans achieved greatness by following the dictates of political reason, through an implacable matching of means and ends. Yet on a deeper level he had also shown how the Romans infused this arid political calculus with a thirst for glory, with an all-or-nothing attitude that led them, time and again, to risk everything for the ultimate prize of victory—to dominate for the sake of dominating. (Failure at any point would have landed them in the relative obscurity of the Crimeans— feared but not admired—or worse.) In *Considerations* Montesquieu reveals the truly reckless and self-destructive quality of this imperialistic urge, showing through a detailed examination of Rome's historical circumstances how it survived despite itself and how its very success entailed its demise.[19]

Like the Crimeans, the Romans knew nothing of commerce and looked only to pillaging as a means of enriching themselves. When Rome became a republic, "the manner of pillaging was therefore brought under control, and it was done with much the same discipline as is now practiced among the inhabitants of Little Tartary" (1.27). The Romans regularized the equitable distribution of spoils, along with the practice of celebrating each victory with what now became known officially as a "triumph." Roman history begins to diverge from the Crimean model at this point. For the glory of a triumph, Roman consuls waged war with "great impetuosity," which imposed on them an even greater need to conquer. Discipline, steadfastness, and valor thus became the hallmarks of the Roman, to say nothing of sheer physical strength and endurance. The necessity of fighting the same enemies again and again honed these qualities. Had Rome the resources to besiege and subjugate its enemies, rather than simply beating their armies in the field, its moral and physical edge would have been dulled by luxury. The successful siege of the nearby city of Veii thus marks "a kind of revolution"—a decisive moment in Roman history—but one that ended up redoubling Roman resolve along with its resources, as the sudden expansion of the state caused its neighbors to arise in fear and its allies to abandon it (1.30). At this point in Montesquieu's account Rome diverges entirely from the Crimean model of brigandage to follow its own special course, toward world domination.

Throughout the first chapter Montesquieu uses a comparative method to isolate the generic features of a small predatory state, showing how they operated within a specifically Roman context. He continues in subsequent chapters to essay the interplay between the mutable and the immutable by means of this method, using the order of the chapters to highlight the historical dynamics at work in Roman history. Thus, he devotes chapter 2 to the foundational subject of the art of war, which schooled the Romans in moral and physical strength. In chapter 3 he distinguishes the Romans militarily from modern Europeans. Unlike the situation in modern Europe—where different peoples all share the same military arts and where disparities of power between states permanently relegate the smaller ones to relative obscurity—Rome enjoyed advantages over its enemies that enabled it to advance its power despite its small size. In chapter 4 he describes how the Gauls were a formidable adversary, equal to the Romans in valor and steadfastness, yet they suffered from technological deficiencies that ultimately rendered them weak: "The buckler of the Gauls was small, and their sword poor. They were therefore treated in much the same way as the Mexicans were treated by the Spaniards in recent centuries" (4.43). Much like the Aztecs, the Gauls proved convenient enemies, throwing themselves repeatedly against the Romans, "without ever knowing, seeking or forestalling the cause of their misfortunes" (4.43). By the time the Romans encountered Pyrrhus, an enemy of superior power and ability, they were formidable enough to survive their defeats and learn from them, adopting new weapons and tactics that enabled them to emerge from this travail even stronger—in other words, Pyrrhus could not do to the Romans what the Romans had done to the Gauls, or the Spanish to the Aztecs. And in their death-struggle with the Carthaginians, who had mastered an art of naval warfare unknown to the Romans, the latter benefited from the primitive state of ancient navigation and ship construction, arts that could be acquired by a newcomer with relative ease. Here Montesquieu highlights the singularity of Rome's historical position by comparison with modern times, when even the greatest European land power would have difficulty mastering the art of seafaring in an age of complex oceangoing vessels equipped with compass and cannon.

These cross-historical comparisons serve to explain the phenomenal rise of Rome, which would otherwise seem incredible. Without a cross-historical viewpoint, Montesquieu declares, "we would see events without understanding them, and, by not being aware of the difference in situations, would believe that the men we read about in ancient history are of another breed than ourselves" (3.39). Comparisons between past and present reveal not only the unique circumstances that favored Rome's rise but also the policies that guided its aggression. Montesquieu sketches the blueprint for Roman imperialism with a series of pithy observations in chapter 6: "Allies were used to make war on an enemy, but then the destroyers were at once destroyed"; "When the Romans had several enemies on their hands they made a truce with the weakest"; "They never made peace in good faith"; "Their constant maxim was to divide" (6.67–71). These and other guidelines constitute an identifiable pattern of Roman imperialism apparent from the very earliest days of the state, by means of which the Romans achieved world domination slowly and (as it were) imperceptibly. Spain, by contrast, acquired its empire in the New World all at once and by main force, requiring that it "destroy everything in order to preserve everything" (6.75).

Not even policy, though, could compensate for the inherent riskiness of relentless aggrandizement. Had the Greeks awakened to the reality of Roman imperialism, they would have proved invincible (chapter 5), and the example of Mithridates, king of Pontus, demonstrates what a determined enemy could achieve (chapter 7). The true danger of imperialism, however, only became apparent with its culmination, which engendered the corruption of republican principles and the slow, steady sinking of the state into civil war, monarchy, and despotism. Two causes undermined Rome: "If the greatness of the empire ruined the republic, the greatness of the city ruined it no less" (9.92). To conquer and maintain a far-flung empire, Rome resorted to the creation of professional armies, which sapped the civic spirit of soldiers by transferring their loyalty from the state to their generals. And to maintain this empire, Rome further diluted its civic spirit by extending citizenship to the peoples of Italy, foreigners who had assisted in the conquest of empire and now demanded a share in its governance. "It lost its liberty because it completed the work it wrought too soon" (9.95). Such was the price of glory that Machiavelli had memorialized in the *Discourses*. Roman history thus stands not as a model of what to imitate but as a warning of what to avoid, as an object lesson in the corruption of a state, whose short-term policies undermined its long-term health.

THE GENERAL CAUSES UNDERLYING ROMAN HISTORY emerge from the perspectival tension inherent in Montesquieu's cross-historical viewpoint. The Roman-Crimean relation reveals the predatory nature of the state; the Roman-English relation reveals its republican impetus; the Roman-European relation reveals the circumstances favorable to its expansion; the Roman-Spanish relation reveals the distinctive quality of its imperialism. Instead of looking directly at Rome and recounting the course of its events in isolation—as its own annalists had done—Montesquieu seeks its reflection in diverse cross-historical mirrors, each revealing a key feature of the state. By this means he writes Roman history afresh, much as the passage of time continually enables modern historians to grasp old topics from ever-new perspectives. This undertaking was remarkable in an age that—despite advances in antiquarian scholarship—still regarded Roman history as the collection of histories written by the Romans. Montesquieu's relational view of the past thus enabled him to conceive of "history itself," which emerged from the interplay between the mutable and the immutable.

In the *Considerations* Montesquieu's relational viewpoint has transcended the status of literary pretense or philosophical exercise to become a sustained operational perspective revealing the fundamental dynamics of history. He equated the notion of the "general causes" underlying events with the *esprit général* of each people, declaring in the penultimate chapter, "There exists in each nation a general spirit *[esprit général]* on which power itself is based, and when it shocks this spirit it strikes against itself and necessarily comes to a standstill" (22.210). This notion of the *esprit général* will bulk even larger in *The Spirit of the Laws,* where he will subject it to the closest possible scrutiny, revealing the myriad factors that impinge on and shape it—the principles and values of each type of government, the effects of climate and terrain, the types of economic activities specific to a people, their religion, manners, and mores. Indeed, the cross-historical viewpoint in the *Considerations* stands but one step removed from this more fully relational one, where relations derive from the nature of things, laws embody necessary relations, and constellations of relations constitute the "spirit of the laws." His Malebranchian education predisposed him to take this step because it offered the possibility of grounding his operational viewpoint in the same kind of certainty as mathematics. Seen in the context of its literary and historical gestation, the birth of the past from number thinking should now seem less jarring, for number thinking simply served to regularize and confirm an ad hoc comparative procedure, whose principles Montesquieu had introduced in the *Persian Letters* and concretized in the *Considerations.*

The past was born of a perspectival tension that consistently and systematically separated it from the present. The cross-historical method of the *Considerations* elucidates this tension. Think only of the difference between Roman and Spanish imperialism or (for that matter) of the similarity between Gauls and Aztecs. The former contrast makes the perspectival tension clear, but so, too, does the latter comparison, for both highlight the historical singularity of Rome, the exceptionality of its situation. (How many imperialistic states have been so fortunate in their adversaries as Rome and Spain?) And singularity itself stood in constant tension with generality, accentuating Montesquieu's perspectivism. Like the cities of Little Tartary, Rome was a generic predatory state organized for war and the acquisition of booty; the need for the equitable distribution of spoils shaped its domestic institutions, which eventually took on a distinctive, republican form that fused with the imperatives and values of a warrior society. The republican government accelerated Rome's unique rise to empire but could not survive in the more pacific environment it had created—an environment inhospitable to predation—and the monarchy that supplanted it no longer nurtured its blend of warrior/republican values, thereby ensuring the decline of the state. In this account the tension between singularity and generality explains the dynamic of Roman history, in which the state emerges from generic origins to pursue a unique course that ends up undermining its origins. To the extent that Montesquieu illustrates this dynamic by means of cross-historical comparisons, the tension between singularity and generality serves to underscore and sustain the differences between past and present, thereby establishing the past as a sustained object of thought.

NOWHERE IN THE *CONSIDERATIONS* or *The Spirit of the Laws* does Montesquieu discourse on "the past" per se; and, at this culminating point in my argument, one might well wonder why Montesquieu did not awaken to the full nature of his discovery and shout out, "Eureka! I've discovered . . .'the past'!" To some extent I have answered this question in the very process of asking it, for we can hardly expect him to refer to his discovery by means of our modern placeholder, especially given the fog of colloquial usage surrounding the term. Yet, so great was his intellectual acuity that he decisively nailed the distinction that defines and underlies our placeholder, a distinction we ourselves tend to forget—namely that the past per se is not simply *prior* to the present but *different* from it. He treats priority in time as trivial in the *Considerations,* where he dispensed with dates, and in *The Spirit of the Laws,* where he ignored temporality. Yet throughout both works he not only assiduously distinguishes past from present but past from past and present from present—the *esprit général* of Rome differed from that of Athens, just as France's differs from Spain's. Indeed, *The Spirit of the Laws* substantiates a fully contextualized view of human entities that derives not from studying the entities in and of themselves but from comparing them with other, similar and dissimilar, entities. The discovery of the past was thus inseparable for Montesquieu from a larger discovery, that of the importance of context for understanding all things human.

In the *Considerations* Montesquieu used cross-historical comparisons to demonstrate the importance of context; they reveal the "general causes" underlying the *esprit général* of each people. In *The Spirit of the Laws* he highlighted the relations inherent in these cross-historical comparisons, making them the subject of a refined and extended analysis. In so doing, he was motivated in large part by the conviction that the multiplicity of human entities existed in an operational order characteristic of number thinking (which progressed like mathematics toward more abstract, generalized, inclusive procedures) rather than the classificatory order of substance thinking (which ascended from species to genus—from specific to general—via a process of exclusion). He used ideal types as a means of searching for this operational order without imposing it on reality; they enabled him to see it as emerging from the nature of the relations themselves in all their complexity rather than stripping away that complexity in search of some underlying substance or essence. In this regard the contexts revealed by his relational viewpoint constituted an entity, distinguishing it from other entities in a natural way that accorded with the relations of things.

I will conclude my long disquisition on Montesquieu with one final example from *The Spirit of the Laws*, showing how the relational perspective sustains the contextualization of human entities. In the all-important nineteenth book—where he posits the existence of an *esprit général* for each state—Montesquieu discourses at length on some peculiarities of the Chinese, a topic that arises from an initial comparison of the characters of the Spanish and Chinese people (chapter 10). Whereas the former are scrupulous but lazy in the conduct of commerce, the latter are industrious but unscrupulous in commercial matters. From this inverse relation he goes on (following the logic of relations) to comment on the apparent indestructibility of Chinese manners and mores (chapter 13), which leads him to the further observation that Chinese manners, mores, laws, and religion are all one and the same (chapter 17). And this generalization—the product of a symmetrical equivalency—explains the astonishing durability of law in China, despite the kingdom's repeated conquest by foreigners: "As the mores of the vanquishers are not their manners, nor their manners, their laws, nor their laws, their religion, it has been easier for the vanquishers to bend slowly to the vanquished people than for the vanquished people to bend to the vanquishers" (19.18.319). The equivalency in China of otherwise distinct relations helps determine the nature of its *esprit général,* which provides the context for understanding the kingdom and its history. Indeed, without an appreciation of this context, one cannot understand China properly.

This kind of contextualizing move extends and systematizes the Renaissance sense of anachronism, transforming it into a global feature of human understanding. Fourteenth- and fifteenth-century Italian humanists had developed a local sense of anachronism—an awareness of the differences between ancient Rome and modern Italy—with which they attempted to reinvigorate classical ideals for application to the modern world. When this attitude extended northward in the sixteenth and seventeenth centuries, it expanded to include an awareness of the distinctiveness of modern states, and of modernity in general, but the flowering of the contextual impulse still languished in the shadow of a classical ideal. Montesquieu dispelled this shadow by establishing, once and for all, the importance of cultural context for understanding any human entity. By transposing the sense of anachronism from the narrow temporal realm of the Italian humanists to a much broader cultural realm, Montesquieu transformed it into a sustained and systematic feature of understanding. The past emerged from this intellectual shift, after which things taken out of context began to appear, in every sense of the word, "funny."

EPILOGUE

The Past Historicized

We live in a world we ourselves create.

–Johann Gottfried Herder, *On the Cognition and Sensation of the Human Soul*

The *Spirit of the Laws* heralds a comparative tendency in French Enlightenment thought subsequently epitomized by Voltaire's sweeping history of civilization, the *Essai sur l'histoire générale et sur les mœurs et l'esprit des nations* (1756), translated as the *Essay on Manners*. An immense labor for even so prolific an author, the seven-volume *Essay* recasts the story of universal history—which had previously been shaped around the biblical account of humanity—in a comparative mold, beginning with chapters on China, India, Persia, and Islam. We may with some justification regard this work as a chronological counterpart to Montesquieu's more analytical effort in *The Spirit of the Laws*, which Voltaire had criticized precisely because it followed the logic of relations: "I wish to know the history of the laws under which our ancestors lived; the reasons why they were established, neglected, destroyed, renewed; I seek a thread in that labyrinth; [but] the thread breaks in almost every paragraph."[1] Voltaire's universal history supplies the missing skein by using a comparative framework to present the story of Europe's rise toward civilization.[2]

The opening lines of the introduction—perhaps addressed to Voltaire's lover, Madame du Châtelet—set its overall tone: "You are at length resolved, then, to surmount your disgust from reading modern history since the decline of the Roman Empire, and to gain a general idea of the nations which inhabit and ravage *[désolent]* the face of the earth."[3] Most commentators dismiss such blatant

scornfulness as unbefitting a historian and, according to Karl Weintraub, regard the entire narrative as "little more than a *pasquinade*," yet Weintraub himself pronounces this vast synthesis "an astonishing work, especially if the title
word *essai* is taken seriously."[4] Although for the most part a standard survey of
European politics from the time of Charlemagne—Voltaire picks up the story
of universal history where his seventeenth-century predecessor, Bishop Bossuet,
had left off—the *Essay* portrays Europeans as less civilized than the Chinese,
Hindus, Persians, and Arabs, a point Voltaire reiterates by returning periodically to the affairs of these and other non-European peoples, as well as by comparing the manners of one European people to another. Not until the fifteenth
century did Europeans begin to make a distinctive contribution to the history
of civilization, which culminates for Voltaire with the great age of Louis XIV.
(The 1756 edition of the *Essay* concludes with Voltaire's previously published
masterpiece, the *Siècle de Louis XIV*, a work omitted from later editions of the
Essay, which end with the reign of Louis XIII.) The scornful tone represents less
a cheap jibe at, than a historical judgment of, Europeans, who took many centuries to equal and surpass the level of civilization attained in other parts of the
globe, parts they had ignorantly dismissed as "barbaric."

The radical nature of this judgment has been obscured by Voltaire's expressed concern with the history of "civilization" rather than "civilizations," as
if one could measure many different peoples by the same standard. The *Essay*
hence appears to sustain the verdict on Enlightenment historiography rendered by R. G. Collingwood in his classic *Idea of History* (1946): "The historical
outlook of the Enlightenment was not genuinely historical; in its main motive it
was polemical and anti-historical" (77). To understand each people properly,
according to Collingwood, one must view it from *within* its own context, a perspective that invalidates any overarching notion of "civilization." Voltaire had
insisted on measuring all earlier peoples, European and non-European alike, by
the standard of an enlightened present. Despite the breadth of his cultural field
of vision—encompassing the Chinese, Japanese, Indians, Persians, Tatars, Mo-
guls, Ottomans, and Muscovites, to say nothing of the different peoples of medieval and Renaissance Europe—Voltaire nonetheless seems to us myopic. This
impression owes much to the pervasive influence of the great eighteenth-century
Prussian philosopher Johann Gottfried Herder (1744–1803), who (among his
many other accomplishments) gave definitive shape to the historicist mentality
evidenced in Collingwood's summary verdict. In the wake of Herder's historicism the contextualizing urge apparent in Montesquieu acquired a powerful
temporal thrust that relegated the past to a place "back there" in time, invali-

dating the cross-cultural achievement of Enlightenment historiography and obscuring the role of French rationalism in the birth of the past.

TRAINED AS A LUTHERAN PASTOR, Herder studied in the 1760s at the University of Königsberg, where he encountered Immanuel Kant (1724–1804) and Johann Georg Hamann (1730–88), whom he acknowledged as his greatest teachers. To the former Herder owed his profound commitment to the power of rational analysis to comprehend the natural and human worlds, which he came to perceive as an integrated system; to the latter he owed his emphasis on the spiritual as well as rational side of existence—on the creative power of feelings and emotions—and his love for the sheer diversity of human forms, in which he found traces of divinity. Standing at the cusp between *Aufklärung* and *Sturm und Drang*—between the German Enlightenment and the "storm and stress" of the romantics—Herder also evidences other influences. He was deeply impressed by Montesquieu's view of human entities as embedded in complex webs of relations, by Rousseau's rejection of the enlightened faith in progress and his insights into the distinctive nature of childhood as a special phase of human development, and by Voltaire's evocation of the distinctiveness of the age of Louis XIV and, more negatively, his tendency to judge past ages from the pinnacle of the present.

All these influences (and more) shaped Herder's thinking as it emerged in his two seminal works on the philosophy of history, the ironically entitled sketch *Auch eine Philosophie der Geschichte zur Bildung der Menschheit* (1774) and the monumental but unfinished treatise *Ideen zur Philosophie der Geschichte der Menschheit* (1784–91). Although he intended the latter treatise as an ultimate philosophical statement, binding human history together with that of the cosmos, critics regard the former sketch as the "splendid charter of historicism" and "the most successful synthesis of historical thought he ever achieved."[5] For the limited purposes of this epilogue I will confine my consideration of Herder's historicism to a brief analysis of this work, which has been translated into English as *Another Philosophy of History for the Education of Mankind*. It combines diverse and seemingly discontinuous strands of contemporary thought, working them into a fully historicized picture of humanity.

As implied by its subtitle—"One among Many Contributions of the Century"—Herder intended *Another Philosophy of History* as a response to *philosophes* like Voltaire, Robertson, and Hume, who insisted on judging the past from the supposedly enlightened perspective of the present. By contrast, he likened the development of humanity to that of the individual—from infancy to childhood to youth to maturity—in which each stage had to be understood in its own terms, as evidencing its own internal coherence and system of meaning. In its infancy human society was pastoral, led by oriental patriarchs (like those of the Old Testament) whose word was law. Viewed from without, these first societies might appear despotic, governed by fear; but viewed from within, they take on a different hue, in which humanity in its infancy—not yet capable of reason—learned to raise itself up by the power of example, being nurtured rather than oppressed by authority. Thus does Herder use Rousseau's insights about the education of children to historicize one of Montesquieu's key ideal types.

Just as infancy gives way to childhood, so, too, did oriental pastoralism yield to settled agriculture and the rule of law with the rise of the kingdom of Egypt. It would have been as impossible for a pastoralist to live in bondage to the law as it would have been for an Egyptian to endure the authority of a patriarch. Herder demonstrates by such comparisons that one cannot judge an early stage in the development of humanity from the perspective of a later stage; rather, each has its own distinctive quality of life, which must be grasped on its own terms. As childhood gives way to youth and maturity, so, too, did Egyptian diligence yield to Greek creativity and Roman gravity. And after maturity comes death and new birth, but the subsequent history of civilization did not represent a simple return to infancy.

In bringing a decisive end to ancient civilization, the fall of Rome also cleared the ground for the emergence of the Germanic peoples, preparing the soil for a wild, new kind of growth that held oriental despotism at bay. The vast extent of the Roman Empire at its height had facilitated the spread of Christianity, which now fused with Germanic culture to create the civilization of the Middle Ages, constituting not a "dark age" of ignorance but "a singular condition of the world" (40). And from this singularity there arose the twin renewals of Renaissance and Reformation, bringing new light to art, science, and morals. Herder sees the workings of divine providence throughout the course of human history, a providence that nurtures the development of humanity by diverse and sometimes unlikely means—Roman imperialism facilitated the rise of Christianity, and the slash-and-burn destruction of classical civilization fertilized the unimpeded growth of the Germanic peoples. The full plan of history lies beyond our comprehension, but its traces can be found in the story of humanity's development, where the irony of seemingly unintended consequences reveals the operations of the divine hand.

"Development" is not "progress." One age does not represent an "advance" over its predecessor; each age is different, defined by its own circumstances. For

Herder the dawning of "enlightenment" brings with it an increase in physical, moral, and cultural degeneracy. The rise of science and technology mitigates the need for individual strength and courage; the codification of civic rights and obligations supplants the personal commitment to moral virtue; and the spread of cosmopolitan rationalism dilutes the distinctiveness of each people. In this regard—as well as in his insistence that each age be judged on its own terms— Herder's story resembles Vico's. The Neapolitan had delineated a historical cycle characterized by three ages—of gods, heroes, and men—each with its own distinctive mentality, the last of which (a rational age) entailed a collapse born of moral enfeeblement that returned humanity to its origins. Yet for Herder the temporal thrust of the story ruptures all cyclical conceptions, as Providence— picking and choosing its instruments from what men themselves have created— guides the ongoing process of human history.[6]

In effect, the developmental thrust of Herder's thinking obscures the birth of the past by historicizing the sense of anachronism. Recall that when Renaissance humanists exploited this sense, they did so in ways that encouraged the creative mixing of past and present. French enlightenment rationalism rendered this kind of mixing inappropriate, for it threatened to conceal the spirit of each people, which could emerge only from a consideration of its distinctive context, its own special web of relations. Although consistently separating past from present, the contextualizing urge did not privilege a temporal perspective over any other. But when Herder gathered together the many strands of contemporary thought— from Kant, Hamann, Rousseau, Montesquieu, Voltaire, Hume, Robertson, and others—he wove them into a new kind of pattern, portraying the diversity of human forms as the product of their process of development in relation to their circumstances. Thereafter, the sense of anachronism lost is purely comparative aspect and acquired a wholly temporal one, and the resulting form of historical understanding inextricably fused the past as *different* from the present with the past as *prior* to the present. The past now became the space "back there" in time.

Karl Weintraub's insights into the history of autobiography reveal how this temporal perception of the past has become for us the standard of common sense.[7] The term *autobiography* did not appear in English usage (or in German, for that matter) until around 1800, and its advent coincides with the flowering of a genre—distinct from memoirs, *res gestae*, letters, and diaries—which had been foreshadowed by only a handful of isolated works in Western literature, such as Augustine's *Confessions* and Montaigne's *Essays*. According to Weintraub, the subsequent avalanche of autobiographies—steadily increasing from the early nineteenth century to the present day—testifies to the prevalence of a self-conception that explains one's uniqueness as the product of a process of development in relation to one's circumstances. From this perspective one would indeed conceive of oneself differently if born ten years earlier or later, an observation that has become for us so commonsensical that we fail to realize that people before the eighteenth century did not see themselves this way. Instead of having a history, they regarded themselves as having an unchanging nature or essence, whose full realization might be impeded or impelled, but not otherwise shaped, by events. The emergence of autobiography as a literary genre testifies to the influence of Herder's developmental view of humanity, which offered a new and powerful means of understanding the individuality of all human entities—people, institutions, states, religions, civilizations.

HERDER'S THOUGHT REPRESENTS THE LEADING EDGE of what would become a nineteenth-century "romantic" reaction to Enlightenment rationalism, which further obscured the birth of the past. The romantics embraced the inner world of feeling and emotion, in which they found the mainsprings of human action. For them Voltaire's scornful tone represented an aloofness from his subject matter, a refusal to engage in real flesh-and-blood history, which entailed reimagining the lives of his ancestors rather than casting judgment on their level of civilization. Never mind that (as Mark Salber Phillips has shown) romantic empathy can be traced back to an eighteenth-century fascination with "sentiment," with private human emotions as reflected in a wide range of fictional and nonfictional writings. It sufficed for romantics to impugn all Enlightenment thinking as excessively rationalistic because its sentimentalism didn't rise to the level of a principle of historical knowledge. Although enlighteners had fully grasped the importance of historical context for understanding the distinctiveness of events and entities, the romantics nonetheless disparaged them for failing to extrapolate from this outer reality to an inner one.

The viewpoint of the romantics has subsequently colored one of the earliest and most influential narratives about the rise of historicism. In *Die Entstehung des Historismus*—a classic study first published in 1936 and translated as *Historism: The Rise of a New Historical Outlook*—Friedrich Meinecke provides a famous account of the emergence of this historicizing perspective. He gives Montesquieu his due as a prehistoricist, representing "the highest degree of historical awareness that was possible at this stage of the Enlightenment" (115), but his emphasis on the importance of context did not yet engender "a full appreciation of the wholly and genuinely individual," which would eventually emerge from the romanticism of Möser, Herder, and Goethe (122). Instead, Montesquieu tempered his sense of individuality with a countervailing tendency to rationalize diversity rather than empathize with it. Meinecke maintained that only with German romanticism did there arise an unimpeded appreciation of the individuality of historical entities, which combined with an idea of development to yield a fully historical view of the world, whereby the uniqueness of each entity appeared as the product of its historical development amid ever-changing circumstances. This nexus of the ideas of individuality and development constituted for Meinecke an intellectual "revolution" that rippled outward, historicizing virtually every aspect of human understanding—as if a stone had been thrown into the pool of human consciousness.

In its simplicity and elegance this classic formulation—which reduces the complexity of historicism to the juncture of two ideas—readily explains how developmental thinking imparted a temporal dimension to the awareness of individuality, thereafter making the two appear inseparable. Historicism thus conceived has a natural tendency to amplify our intuition that the past lies "back there" in time, that *priority* entails *difference*. When we separate out these two notions, though, we see that historicism itself rests on something even more fundamental, a systematic and sustained distinction between past and present, without which there would have been nothing to historicize. Meinecke's contrast between German romanticism and French rationalism—which serves to highlight his notion of a historicist revolution—obscures the role of relational thinking in the formation of "the past" as an object of thought.

The eighteenth-century birth of the past has been obscured not only by historicism but also by the long shadow of humanism. What Meinecke terms an idea of individuality first emerged in the Renaissance, when humanists discovered the glories of classical Latin literature and confronted the challenge of imitation. In so doing, they consistently and knowingly manipulated a sense of anachronism that had previously found only sporadic and naive expression. Ultimately, though, anachronism undermined imitation, and humanism yielded to philology in the sixteenth and seventeenth centuries, spurring an interest in "antiquities"—the artifacts of classical (and medieval) culture—including coins and inscriptions, as well as a wide range of mundane objects. When the romantics embraced the inner world of feeling and emotion, they often accessed it through the evocation of private life, as embodied in antiquities. Recent scholars have naturally turned to early modern philology and antiquarianism in their search for the origins of modern historical understanding, to a progressively widening and deepening knowledge of antiquity that increasingly rendered it dead and buried. The past thus seems to have emerged as a

natural consequence of the evolution of humanistic into philological into antiquarian into historical scholarship.

Arnaldo Momigliano stands as the progenitor of this interpretation. Dis-
trustful of Meinecke's brand of historicism, which could entail an enervating
relativism, Momigliano identified modern historical understanding with the
actual practice of historians—with modern historical scholarship per se—which
originated from the juncture of antiquarianism and Enlightenment historiography. In his seminal article "Ancient History and the Antiquarian" (1950)—as
well as in a host of other writings—Momigliano recounts the healing of an age-
old split between the study of antiquities and the writing of history, when antiquarianism rescued historiography from the threat of historical Pyrrhonism in
the eighteenth century.[8] Responding to skeptical attacks on the reliability of
historical accounts—some of which had been exposed as pure fabrications—
antiquarians came to the defense of history with tangible proof of events drawn
from coins and inscriptions, among other kinds of nonliterary evidence. According to Momigliano, Gibbon's *Decline and Fall of the Roman Empire* epitomizes the juncture of Enlightenment historiography and antiquarianism, combining an overarching narrative about "civilization" with a rigorous analysis of
historical evidence. (In *Barbarism and Religion* J. G. A. Pocock goes on to discuss
the uneasy nature of this union, showing how Gibbon's deployment of evidence
in the notes sometimes contradicts his Whiggish assumptions in the narrative.)
The narrative and scholarly modes would further meld in the nineteenth century
to form the modern discipline of history, which transcended Enlightenment
preconceptions as it appropriated antiquarian methods.

Momigliano's formulation rivals Meinecke's in its simplicity and elegance, and it has spurred widespread research into the early modern roots of
historicism—roots extending back to the likes of eighteenth-century German
university professors, seventeenth-century English antiquarians, and sixteenth-
century French philologists. This research depicts historicism less as a revolution in historical thought than an evolution in historical practice, one that eventually yielded our highly contextualized view of historical entities. The study of
early modern philology and antiquarianism has revealed the extent to which
nineteenth-century developments "depended at least as much upon the slow
and gradual accretion of information, upon the normal work of the disciplines,
as upon any sudden revelations or any large theories brought from outside."[9]
With this observation, Joseph M. Levine concludes his fascinating study *Dr.
Woodward's Shield*, which examines an instance of the early modern intersection of natural history and antiquarianism, showing how both scientific and

historical knowledge advanced not by means of revolutionary paradigm shifts but through the normal practice of everyday inquiry.

Perhaps the foremost example of this approach is Anthony Grafton's exhaustive, two-volume intellectual biography of Joseph Scaliger (1540–1609), one of the giants of early modern erudition. Although Scaliger's editions of classical authors set new standards for source criticism, and his chronological studies immensely broadened historical horizons, his work is now known only by a handful of specialists in history and literature. Yet the fields in which he labored were once of passionate interest and earnest debate for an international community of scholars that stood at the forefront of learning. Grafton evokes this lost world in remarkable detail, showing how Scaliger's critical advances emerged through his (often contentious) interaction with the work of predecessors and contemporaries. Seen in the context of these scholarly fashions and disputes, Scaliger's brilliant innovations appear more evolutionary than revolutionary; and to the extent that they approach the rigorous standards of nineteenth-century scholarship, they themselves represent the incremental steps (and missteps) in the broader development of modern historical understanding, which derived from gradual changes in the actual practice of evaluating historical evidence.[10]

It is by now unquestionable that early modern philology and antiquarianism provided historical writing with its inner assurance in the eighteenth and nineteenth centuries, enabling it to address the subject of "history itself." Yet the recent attention devoted to the rise of historical scholarship tends to obscure the crucial role played by Enlightenment historiography in its conjunction with antiquarianism. By "Enlightenment historiography" I mean none other than the kind of Whiggish narrative written by Voltaire, whose comparative viewpoint—ethnocentric though it may have been—had the effect of contextualizing the European past and thereby stabilizing it as a sustained object of thought. This innovation has been overshadowed by the notion that the past emerged inductively, through the accumulation of ever more information about it, a notion that takes the contextualizing impulse for granted. I have already demonstrated—through Montaigne's anti-Spanish exploitation of the Aztec perspective, through Conring's historicized dismissal of medieval universalism, and through the "ancients'" equally dismissive ridicule of "modern" historical pedantry—that the value of contextualization was not so much discovered as devised. And in the process of its formation it required support from outside itself in order to win and hold the field. The relational methods and mathematical principles of number thinking thus proved foundational for the development of modern historical knowledge, sustaining the distance between human entities, each of which existed in its own context, characterized by its own relations. The past emerged as an aspect of this broader relational view of things, the inherent certainty of which securely anchored a tendency to regard entities from the perspective of their historical and cultural contexts, a tendency that might otherwise have encouraged relativism.

IN ADVANCING THIS ARGUMENT, I do not mean to advocate for a historical science rooted in mathematical principles—that's Montesquieu's position. I practice history not as a social scientist but as a humanist, an assertion that no reader who's stuck with me thus far could possibly question. Yet as a humanist I've come to doubt the objective existence of the thing I've so long studied, namely "the past." Mine is not a postmodern crisis of conscience, driven by some newfangled critical theory, but a straightforward questioning of something I've always taken for granted, which has now begun to appear strange to me. Let me illustrate this strangeness with an anecdote.

Not long ago, at a dinner party in my neighborhood hosted by an insurance executive, the host asked me about my research, to which I responded, in a glib, ham-handed way, "Oh, I'm writing a history of the idea of the past." Not surprisingly, the host—an analytically minded man who doesn't suffer fools gladly— looked at me askance; and in my chagrin I quickly hit upon a way of rescuing myself in his estimation. We were sitting in the living room of his lovingly restored Chicago bungalow, one of tens of thousands constructed in a "bungalow belt" around the city during the 1920s and 1930s. His was a fine specimen of this unique architectural form, with a "Sears" addition to the second floor (a stock dormer-kit purchased from a catalog). We sat in a living room filled with Craftsman and Deco furniture and objects. The coffee table before us had, under glass, the host's colorful collection of old typewriter-ribbon tins; and along the living room walls, on a high shelf, stood his collection of lawn sprinklers—the really early kind, shaped like tractors with big wheels. On the walls of the narrow staircase to the second floor, he had hung his collection of miniature, 1930s pinball games; and in the kitchen, against the original white-tiled walls, stood a black-and-white enameled stove (of the long-legged variety) and opposite it a vintage, freestanding, stainless-steel countertop. A modern day analogue to Petrarch, who had made of himself a living anachronism, my host consciously chose to live within an anachronism. When I pointed out to him that he could not have done so without an idea of the past—and that the sense of anachronism upon which it was based originated in the Renaissance—his eyes lit up.

My host exemplifies the extent to which a systematic and sustained idea of anachronism has become second nature to us, such that we don't recognize it even when we intentionally draw on it. We simply take for granted that everything exists in its own context. Regardless of disputes about its nature and origin, historicism has accentuated this habit of thought by asserting that each entity should be understood solely from within its own unique context, thus discounting any transcendent viewpoint as inherently distorted by external preconceptions. The historicist habit of mind has become so much the standard of common sense that we fail to see that it is itself a preconception. Constantin Fasolt has tried to redress this oversight in *The Limits of History*. His effort reaches beyond previous structuralist and postmodern critiques of history, which themselves still take the contextualizing urge for granted. Michel Foucault, for example, generally began his critiques of historical knowing and its offshoots by lovingly restoring some scene, word, or book to its original context in order to establish its initial meaning, which he then used to subvert modern assumptions. As Fasolt clearly shows, even the postmodern critics of historicism stand fixedly in the thrall of its own ideal of contextualization.

This insight into our assumptions has helped me substantiate the inchoate intuition about the strangeness of "the past" that first bedeviled me more than thirty years ago. I have taken my lead not only from Fasolt's analysis of the limits of historical knowing but also from his assertion, with which I began this inquiry, that "the distinction between past and present . . . may be considered the founding principle of history." We can now see that history as a body of literature long predates this distinction and that the idea of the past—born of the perceived difference between past and present—itself has a history. My argument goes beyond the claim—congenial to historicists like Meinecke—that different eras entertained different ideas about the past; instead, I am questioning whether there always existed a mental object, "the past," about which ideas could be entertained.

We can no longer take the existence of this object for granted. "The past" has a history, and not until it came into being could we have ideas about it, ideas that have gradually transformed it into an intellectual given. I have tried to tell its story, starting from well before its origins, so that we can distinguish it from the earlier thought forms we customarily associate with it. Ancient historiography did not depict the past but rather multiple pasts that were, in essence, disassociated from one another. The difference between ancient pasts and the modern past is more than quantitative; add them all together and the sum would still not constitute "the" past. Missing from antiquity is a conception of the unity of human activity, whether directed by God or man. The Christian *sæculum*—the place where sacred and secular intertwine—provided such an arena, and the sacralization of the *sæculum* transformed it from a spatial to a temporal realm, albeit one where past, present, and future coincided in the mind of God. Renaissance humanism ruptured this figural coincidence, substituting in its place an ideal of exemplarity that harkened to a lost ancient culture, perceived for the first time as fully distinct from the modern one. As this lost culture became ever more thoroughly resurrected, the myriad examples thus engendered began to clutter and choke the imagination. Amid this congestion the principles of number thinking emerged to provide an analytical means of clarifying the relations between exemplary entities, along with the relations of their relations. This relational viewpoint ultimately served to sustain a systematic distinction between past and present—and the rest is . . . history itself.

Notes

Foreword

1. Jill Lepore, *The Whites of their Eyes: The Tea Party's Revolution and the Battle over American History* (Princeton, N.J.: Princeton University Press, 2010).

2. See Zachary Sayre Schiffman, *On the Threshold of Modernity: Relativism in the French Renaissance* (Baltimore: Johns Hopkins University Press, 1991); Michael E. Hobart and Zachary S. Schiffman, *Information Ages: Literacy, Numeracy, and the Computer Revolution* (Baltimore: Johns Hopkins University Press, 1998).

3. See especially Ann M. Blair, *Too Much to Know: Managing Scholarly Information Before the Modern Age* (New Haven: Yale University Press, 2010), and compare to Zachary S. Schiffman, "Montaigne and the Rise of Skepticism in Early Modern Europe: A Reappraisal," *Journal of the History of Ideas* 45, no. 4 (Oct.–Dec., 1984): 499–516.

4. Erwin Panofsky. "Renaissance and Renascences," *The Kenyon Review* 6, no. 2 (Spring, 1944): 201–36.

5. See, e.g., Julian Franklin, *Jean Bodin and the Sixteenth-Century Revolution in the Methodology of Law and History* (New York: Columbia University Press, 1963); Donald Kelley, *Foundations of Modern Historical Scholarship: Language, Law and History in the French Renaissance* (New York: Columbia University Press, 1970). Compare this to Schiffman's own *On the Threshold of Modernity: Relativism in the French Renaissance* (Baltimore: Johns Hopkins University Press, 1991).

6. Reinhart Koselleck, *Futures Past: On the Semantics of Historical Time*, trans. Keith Tribe (Cambridge, Mass.: MIT Press, 1985); Peter Fritzsche, *Stranded in the Present: Modern Time and the Melancholy of History* (Cambridge, Mass., and London: Harvard University Press, 2004).

7. See Daniel Woolf, *Reading History in Early Modern England* (Cambridge: Cambridge University Press, 2000), and *The Social Circulation of the Past: English Historical Culture, 1500–1730* (Oxford: Oxford University Press, 2003).

Introduction

1. The reference is to the Laud manuscript of the *Chronicle*. See *The Anglo-Saxon Chronicle*, trans. G. N. Garmonsway (London: J. M. Dent, 1953), 59.

2. This example derives from David Bodanis's lucid study, $E = mc^2$: *A Biography of the World's Most Famous Equation* (New York: Walker, 2000), 11–17.

3. Niccolò Machiavelli, Letter No. 140, trans. Eric Cochrane, in *University of Chicago Readings in Western Civilization*, vol. 5, *The Renaissance*, ed. Eric Cochrane and Julius Kirshner (Chicago: University of Chicago Press, 1986), 184.

Part One. Antiquity

1. John H. Finley Jr., *Thucydides* (Cambridge, MA: Harvard University Press, 1942); Erich Auerbach, *Mimesis*, trans. Willard R. Trask (Princeton, NJ: Princeton University Press, 1953). Auerbach's work, of course, remains a classic, though there are increasing attempts to analyze and even deconstruct his viewpoint. Finley's full-length study of Thucydides is noteworthy for being one of the first efforts to place Thucydides in his historical context, although it is only rarely cited now. The volume of essays on which it is based remains a standard in the field; see John H. Finley Jr., *Three Essays on Thucydides* (Cambridge, MA: Harvard University Press, 1967).

2. Finley, *Thucydides*, 291.

3. Virginia Hunter, *Past and Process in Herodotus and Thucydides* (Princeton, NJ: Princeton University Press, 1982).

4. Primo Levi, *Survival in Auschwitz*, trans. Stuart Woolf (New York: Simon and Schuster, 1996), 58, 87.

5. Jan Vansina, *Oral Tradition as History* (Madison: University of Wisconsin Press, 1985), 13.

6. M. I. Finley, "Myth, Memory and History," in his *The Use and Abuse of History* (New York: Viking, 1975), 16. My treatment of Greek historiography is heavily indebted to this version of Finley's article, a shorter version of which was first published in *History and Theory* 4 (1965): 281–302.

7. Aristotle, *De Poetica*, trans. Ingram Bywater (Oxford: Oxford University Press, 1946), 1451^b5–11; also, see Finley, *The Use and Abuse of History*, 11–12. All references to classical texts will be by book and chapter number and will hereafter be placed in the body of the text.

8. Vansina, *Oral Tradition as History*, 17.

9. Jan Vansina, *Oral Tradition: A Study in Historical Methodology*, trans. H. M. Wright (Chicago: Aldine, 1965), 154. Although Vansina claims to have "revised" this study in his subsequent work, *Oral Tradition as History*, the latter is a fundamentally different book that supplements but does not supersede his earlier study.

10. Vansina, *Oral Tradition as History*, 23, 168–69.

11. Vansina, *Oral Tradition*, 154.

12. Quoted in Lionel Pearson, *Early Ionian Historians* (Oxford: Clarendon, 1939; repr., Westport, CT: Greenwood, 1975), 26.

13. For the notions of linear and episodic time in antiquity I am deeply indebted to Donald J. Wilcox's *The Measure of Times Past: Pre-Newtonian Chronologies and the Rhetoric of Relative Time* (Chicago: University of Chicago Press, 1987).

14. Arnaldo Momigliano, "The Place of Herodotus in the History of Historiography," in his *Studies in Historiography* (New York: Harper and Row, 1966), 129.

15. My discussion of the Egyptian chronology, and of Herodotean and ancient time frames in general, draws heavily on Wilcox, *The Measure of Times Past*, esp. 60–64.

16. Again, I must acknowledge my debt to Wilcox's *The Measure of Times Past* for this analysis; see esp. 54–55, as well as his general discussion of episodic time in chap. 3.

17. See the analysis in W. Robert Connor, *Thucydides* (Princeton, NJ: Princeton University Press, 1984), 176–80; also see Hans-Peter Stahl, *Thukydides: Die Stellung des Menschen im geschichtlichen Prozess* (Munich: C. H. Beck, 1966), chap. 1.

18. See John Boardman, *The Archaeology of Nostalgia: How the Greeks Re-created Their Mythical Past* (London: Thames and Hudson, 2002), 11–12. Also compare Thucydides's treatment of early naval history with that in Herodotus, 3.122. In his "Myth, Memory and History" (reprinted in his *Use and Abuse of History*), M. I. Finley discusses the various chronological reference points used by Thucydides to illustrate the growth of naval power in Greece; I am much indebted to Finley's analysis.

19. Thucydides's debt to Herodotus is detailed in Hunter, *Past and Process*.

20. In *The Measure of Times Past* Wilcox analyzes the Pentecontaetia as an instance of episodic time (69–74).

21. My analysis of book 3 in particular, and Thucydides in general, is deeply indebted to Connor's *Thucydides*.

22. My analysis of Polybius and the time of the Oecumene is deeply indebted to Wilcox, *The Measure of Times Past*, esp. chap. 4.

23. My analysis of Polybius is based on F. W. Walbank, *Polybius* (Berkeley: University of California Press, 1972).

24. Niccolò Machiavelli, *The Prince and the Discourses* (New York: Random House, 1950), 271.

25. The above analysis of Livy is indebted to Wilcox, *The Measure of Times Past*, chap. 4.

26. Reinhart Koselleck, *Futures Past: On the Semantics of Historical Time*, trans. Keith Tribe (Cambridge, MA: MIT Press, 1985), 94.

Part Two. Christianity

1. Reinhart Koselleck, "The Need for Theory in History," in his *The Practice of Conceptual History: Timing History, Spacing Concepts*, trans. Todd Samuel Presner and others (Stanford: Stanford University Press, 2002), 7.

2. See Walter Goffart, *The Narrators of Barbarian History (A.D. 550–800): Jordanes, Gregory of Tours, Bede, and Paul the Deacon* (Princeton, NJ: Princeton

University Press, 1988), 174–82; we will have occasion to return to this evocative phrase later.

3. Augustine, *Confessions,* with an English translation by William Watts (1631), 2 vols., Loeb Classical Library (Cambridge, MA: Harvard University Press, 1968), 1.1. Here I have utilized the seventeenth-century translation of William Watts, which best captures the prayerful quality of the opening chapter. Unless otherwise indicated, though, subsequent translations will be from the more modern rendition of the *Confessions* by R. S. Pine-Coffin (Harmondsworth: Penguin, 1961).

4. Augustine, *Confessions,* introduction, text, and commentary by James J. O'Donnell, 3 vols. (Oxford: Oxford University Press, 1992), 2:8–9.

5. Bertrand Russell, *Human Knowledge: Its Scope and Limits* (New York: Simon and Schuster, 1948), 123; and Ludwig Wittgenstein, *Philosophical Investigations,* trans. G. E. M. Anscombe, 2nd ed. (New York: Macmillan, 1953), 42.

6. Oscar Cullmann, *Christ and Time: The Primitive Christian Conception of Time and History,* trans. Floyd V. Filson, rev. ed. (Philadelphia: Westminster Press, 1964), 62; I am also indebted to Cullmann for his interpretation of Primitive and Early Christian conceptions of time.

7. Augustine, "Acts or Disputation against Fortunatus, the Manichæan," trans. Albert H. Newman, *Christian Classics Ethereal Library,* www.ccel.org/ccel/schaff/npnf104.iv.vii.ii.html, 20.

8. Peter Brown, *Augustine of Hippo* (Berkeley: University of California Press, 1967), 165.

9. Maurice Pontet, *L'exégèse de Saint-Augustin, prédicateur* (Paris: Aubier, 1946), 171.

10. Ibid., 177.

11. Oliver Wendell Holmes to James Laski, 5 January 1921, *Holmes-Laski Letters: The Correspondence of Mr. Justice Holmes and Harold J. Laski, 1916–1935,* ed. Mark DeWolfe Howe (Cambridge, MA: Harvard University Press, 1953), 300.

12. In the commentary to his edition of the *Confessions* James J. O'Donnell makes frequent reference to these biblical resonances.

13. For this general point see Pontet (345–51), who also draws attention to John Cardinal Newman's expression of the same retrospective principle in his famous sermon, "Christ Manifested in Remembrance."

14. See Thomas Williams, "Biblical Interpretation," in *The Cambridge Companion to Augustine,* ed. Eleonore Stump and Norman Kretzmann (Cambridge: Cambridge University Press, 2001), esp. 65–66.

15. Donald J. Wilcox, *The Measure of Times Past: Pre-Newtonian Chronologies and the Rhetoric of Relative Time* (Chicago: University of Chicago Press, 1987), 124.

16. Robert Markus, *Sæculum: History and Society in the Theology of St. Augustine,* rev. ed. (Cambridge: Cambridge University Press, 1988), 133.

17. See, e.g., John O'Meara, *Charter of Christendom: The Significance of the "City of God"* (New York: Macmillan, 1961), 54–61.

18. My analysis of the figural view is deeply indebted to Erich Auerbach's essay "Figura," in *Scenes from the Drama of European Literature* (Minneapolis: University

of Minnesota Press, 1984); and to Scott David Foutz, "An Attempt to Establish an Historically Accurate Definition of Typology," *Quodlibet Journal,* www.quodlibet. net/typology.shtml (accessed 6 January 2011).

19. Auerbach, "Figura," 29.

20. Robert Markus, *The End of Ancient Christianity* (Cambridge: Cambridge University Press, 1990), 89.

21. Augustine, *City of God,* 17.8 (the translation is Auerbach's, from "Figura," 43); book 17 of the *City of God* provides numerous examples of Augustine's mode of figural analysis.

22. Quoted in Auerbach, "Figura," 43.

23. Ibid., 41.

24. These shortcomings are detailed in Foutz, "An Attempt to Establish an Historically Accurate Definition of Typology."

25. Goffart, *The Narrators of Barbarian History (A.D. 550--800),* 203.

26. Martin Heinzelmann, *Gregory of Tours: History and Society in the Sixth Century,* trans. Christopher Carroll (Cambridge: Cambridge University Press, 2001), 104–7; I am thoroughly indebted to Heinzelmann for my treatment of Gregory, as well as to Goffart. In the analysis of Gregory that follows, I will refer to his history by book and chapter number, with English translations from Gregory of Tours, *The History of the Franks,* trans. Lewis Thorpe (Harmondsworth: Penguin, 1974).

27. For this crucial point see Heinzelmann, *Gregory of Tours,* 103.

28. Heinzelmann, *Gregory of Tours,* 76–87.

29. See, e.g., ibid., 143–44.

30. For the figural aspects of this story see Robert W. Hanning, *The Vision of History in Early Britain: From Gildas to Geoffrey of Monmouth* (New York: Columbia University Press, 1966), esp. 80–81.

31. Ibid., 77–78.

32. Hans-Werner Goetz, "The Concept of Time in the Historiography of the Eleventh and Twelfth Centuries," in *Medieval Concepts of the Past,* ed. Gerd Althoff, Johannes Fried, and Patrick J. Geary (Cambridge: Cambridge University Press, 2002), 160, 164; also see Gabrielle M. Spiegel's analysis of the typological view of history in the chronicles of St. Denis and in medieval historiography in general, in her collection, *The Past as Text: The Theory and Practice of Medieval Historiography* (Baltimore: Johns Hopkins University Press, 1997), esp. chap. 5.

Part Three. Renaissance

1. Leonard Barkan, *Transuming Passion: Ganymede and the Erotics of Humanism* (Stanford: Stanford University Press, 1991), 11; my analysis of Raphael and (later) of Freud is thoroughly indebted to Barkan, 10–19. For a similar treatment of these themes see Zachary Sayre Schiffman, "Jean Bodin, Roman Law, and the Renaissance Conception of the Past," in *Cultural Visions: Essays in the History of Culture,* ed. Penny Schine Gold and Benjamin C. Sax (Amsterdam: Rodopi, 2000), 273–75. Giorgio Vasari described the fresco (somewhat incoherently) in his *Lives of*

the Artists, trans. George Bull (Harmondsworth: Penguin, 1965), 291–93; the identification of the figures (below) is traditional and extends back to Vasari's account. Raphael utilized the most up-to-date scholarship available to him to characterize the figures; because most of this scholarship is unknown to us, we still cannot identify many of these figures, and traditional attributions are sometimes disputed.

2. For a brief survey of this interpretation of the Renaissance see Zachary S. Schiffman, ed., *Humanism and the Renaissance* (Boston: Houghton Mifflin, 2002), especially my introduction to the book as a whole and to each of its parts.

3. See Thomas M. Greene, "History and Anachronism," in his *The Vulnerable Text: Essays on Renaissance Literature* (New York: Columbia University Press, 1986), esp. 220–22.

4. Ibid., 219.

5. Niccolò Machiavelli, Letter No. 140 (see introduction, n. 3).

6. For the text of this letter, and the likely identity of its recipient, see Francesco Petrarca, Letter 4.15, in Eric Cochrane and Julius Kirshner, eds., *University of Chicago Readings in Western Civilization,* vol. 5, *The Renaissance* (Chicago: University of Chicago Press, 1986), 37–41.

7. For this approach to humanism, as well as for the analysis of Petrarch below, I am thoroughly indebted to Carol Everhart Quillen, *Rereading the Renaissance: Petrarch, Augustine, and the Language of Humanism* (Ann Arbor: University of Michigan Press, 1998).

8. James Hankins, *Plato in the Italian Renaissance,* 2 vols. (Leiden: E. J. Brill, 1991), 1:18–26. Hankins was one of the first scholars to explore the subject of Renaissance reading in any depth, and his categories remain useful and instructive for our purposes. One should note, though, that subsequent scholars have begun to reveal other kinds of reading; see, e.g., *Journal of the History of Ideas* 64 (2003), which has a series of articles devoted to the subject of "Early Modern Information Overload." Of special interest is Ann Blair's incisive contribution, "Reading Strategies for Coping with Information Overload, ca. 1550–1700," which details a slightly different and less formal list of reading strategies common in the seventeenth and eighteenth centuries.

9. Timothy Hampton, *Writing from History: The Rhetoric of Exemplarity in Renaissance Literature* (Ithaca, NY: Cornell University Press, 1990), 12–13.

10. The issue of exemplarity, and whether there was a crisis of exemplarity in the Renaissance, has been addressed in a collection of articles published in the *Journal of the History of Ideas* 59 (October 1998).

11. In general see Ronald G. Witt, *"In the Footsteps of the Ancients": The Origins of Humanism from Lovato to Bruni* (Leiden: Brill, 2000).

12. Thomas M. Greene, *The Light in Troy: Imitation and Discovery in Renaissance Poetry* (New Haven, CT: Yale University Press, 1982), 35.

13. Francesco Petrarca, *Letters on Familiar Matters,* trans. Aldo S. Bernardo, 3 vols. (New York: Italica Press, 2005), book 24, letter 4 (hereafter, 24.4); also see the Latin edition, *Familiarium rerum libri,* 4 vols., ed. Vittorio Rossi and Umberto Bosco (Florence: G. C. Sansoni, 1933–42).

14. Greene, *The Light in Troy*, 8.

15. Charles Trinkaus, *"In Our Image and Likeness": Humanity and Divinity in Italian Humanist Thought*, 2 vols. (Chicago: University of Chicago Press, 1970), 1:27.

16. My analysis of this letter is indebted to Quillen, *Rereading the Renaissance;* and to Robert Durling, "The Ascent of Mt. Ventoux and the Crisis of Allegory," *Italian Quarterly* 18 (1974). All translations of this letter are from Francesco Petrarca, "The Ascent of Mont Ventoux," trans. Hans Nachod, in *The Renaissance Philosophy of Man*, ed. Ernst Cassirer, Paul Oskar Kristeller, and John Herman Randall Jr. (Chicago: University of Chicago Press, 1948).

17. Greene, *The Light in Troy*, 46.

18. In addition to Quillen's invaluable study of Petrarch one should also (in this context) consult Victoria Kahn, "The Figure of the Reader in Petrarch's *Secretum*," *PMLA* 100 (1985). All translations from the *Secretum*, and all page references, are from Francesco Petrarca, *The Secret*, ed. Carol E. Quillen (Boston: Bedford/St. Martin's, 2003); the Latin edition is in *Opera latine de Francesco Petrarca*, vol. 1: *Secretum: De secreto conflictu curarum mearum*, ed. Antonietta Bufano (Turin: Unione tipografico editrice torinese, 1975).

19. Anthony Grafton, *What Was History? The Art of History in Early Modern Europe* (Cambridge: Cambridge University Press, 2007), 208.

20. The argument that follows draws heavily on my previous treatment of this subject in Zachary Sayre Schiffman, *On the Threshold of Modernity: Relativism in the French Renaissance* (Baltimore: Johns Hopkins University Press, 1991), esp. 11–17. I am also deeply indebted to Ann Moss, *Printed Commonplace-Books and the Structuring of Renaissance Thought* (Oxford: Clarendon, 1996). Moss's work extends far beyond the study of printed commonplace books to encompass that of the whole commonplace frame of mind, and it fills in many gaps in our knowledge of this crucial subject, especially those apparent in my earlier work on commonplace thought.

21. Quoted in Moss, *Printed Commonplace-Books and the Structuring of Renaissance Thought*, 77; my analysis of Agricola is based on her perceptive treatment of him.

22. Quoted in Schiffman, *Threshold of Modernity*, 14.

23. The translation is from William Harrison Woodward, *Vittorino da Feltre and Other Humanist Educators* (Cambridge: Cambridge University Press, 1897; repr., New York: Columbia University Press, 1963), 106.

24. Grafton, *What Was History?* 130. On Patrizi also see Julian H. Franklin, *Jean Bodin and the Sixteenth-Century Revolution in the Methodology of Law and History* (New York: Columbia University Press, 1963); and Giorgio Spini, "Historiography: The Art of History in the Italian Counter Reformation," in *The Late Italian Renaissance*, ed. and trans. Eric Cochrane (New York: Harper and Row, 1970).

25. Spini, "Historiography," 102.

26. Jean Bodin, *Method for the Easy Comprehension of History*, trans. Beatrice Reynolds (New York: Norton, 1969), 8; the Latin edition is in *Œuvres philosophiques de Jean Bodin*, vol. 1, ed. Pierre Mesnard (Paris: Presses Universitaires de France, 1951). All references to the *Methodus* will be to the English translation.

27. Quoted in J. G. A. Pocock, *The Ancient Constitution and the Feudal Law* (Cambridge: Cambridge University Press, 1987), 11.

28. The account of Hotman that follows draws heavily on my previous treatment of this subject in Schiffman, *On the Threshold of Modernity*, 20–23; also see Pocock, *The Ancient Constitution and the Feudal Law*, chap. 1, which introduces the term *neo-Bartolism* and applies it to Hotman.

29. François Hotman, *Antitribonian* (Paris, 1603; facsimile ed. in *Images et témoins de l'âge classique*, no. 9 [Sainte-Etienne: Presses de l'Université de Sainte-Etienne, 1980]), 150–59.

30. See Koselleck's seminal essay, "Historia Magistra Vitae: The Dissolution of the Topos into the Perspective of a Modernized Historical Process," repr. in his *Futures Past: On the Semantics of Historical Time*, trans. Keith Tribe (Cambridge, MA: MIT Press, 1985), 26–42.

31. Bodin, *Method for the Easy Comprehension of History*, 8. The analysis of Bodin that follows draws heavily on Schiffman, "Jean Bodin, Roman Law, and the Renaissance Conception of the Past," esp. 278–87, which details how Bodin attempted to organize historical information by means of commonplace categories. In this regard also see Ann Blair, "Humanist Methods in Natural Philosophy: The Commonplace Book," *Journal of the History of Ideas* 53 (1992): 541–51; and Ann Blair, *The Theater of Nature: Jean Bodin and Renaissance Science* (Princeton, NJ: Princeton University Press, 1997), esp. 65–77.

32. Barkan, *Transuming Passion*, 14.

33. Grafton, *What Was History?* 220.

Part Four. Enlightenment

1. Michel de Montaigne, *The Complete Works of Montaigne*, trans. Donald M. Frame (Stanford: Stanford University Press, 1958), *Essays*, bk. 3, chap. 6, p. 694, hereafter referred to as 3.6.694; see also Montaigne's *Œuvres complètes*, ed. Albert Thibaudet and Maurice Rat (Paris: Gallimard, 1962), 887–88. For the analysis of this text I am thoroughly indebted to Timothy Hampton, *Literature and Nation in the Sixteenth Century: Inventing Renaissance France* (Ithaca, NY: Cornell University Press, 2001), chap. 6.

2. For a penetrating analysis of Descartes see Michael E. Hobart, *Science and Religion in the Thought of Nicholas Malebranche* (Chapel Hill: University of North Carolina Press, 1982), esp. chap. 2; also see Zachary Sayre Schiffman, *On the Threshold of Modernity: Relativism in the French Renaissance* (Baltimore: Johns Hopkins University Press, 1991), chap. 5; and Michael E. Hobart and Zachary S. Schiffman, *Information Ages: Literacy, Numeracy, and the Computer Revolution* (Baltimore: Johns Hopkins University Press, 1998), esp. chap. 5.

3. See Michael E. Hobart, "The Analytical Vision and Organization of Knowledge in the *Encyclopédie*," *Studies in Voltaire and the Eighteenth Century* 327 (1995): 147–75; Hobart and Schiffman, *Information Ages*, chap. 6; and Robert Shackleton,

Montesquieu: A Critical Biography (London: Oxford University Press, 1961), esp. chap. 11.

4. Charles de Secondat, baron de Montesquieu, *Persian Letters*, trans. C. J. Betts (Harmondsworth: Penguin, 1973), letter 83, p. 162, hereafter cited parenthetically in the text as 83.162; Montesquieu *The Spirit of the Laws*, trans. Anne M. Cohler, Basia Carolyn Miller, and Harold Samuel Stone (Cambridge: Cambridge University Press, 1989), bk. 1, chap. 1, p. 3, hereafter cited parenthetically in the text as 1.1.3. In addition to these works I will be citing David Lowenthal's translation of Montesquieu's *Considerations on the Causes of the Greatness of the Romans and Their Decline* (Indianapolis: Hackett, 1999); references to this work will be by chapter and page number. For the French edition of these texts see Montesquieu, *Œuvres complètes*, 2 vols., ed. Roger Caillois (Paris: Gallimard, 1949–51). Unless otherwise indicated, translations from Montesquieu's other writings are my own.

5. The quotation is from one of Montesquieu's miscellaneous writings, "De la politique," in *Œuvres complètes*, 1:114.

6. Some have even maintained that late Renaissance humanism was fully historicist and that sixteenth-century French scholars (in particular) had attained the contextualizing outlook characteristic of nineteenth-century romantics. For a critique of this notion see Zachary Sayre Schiffman, "Renaissance Historicism Reconsidered," *History and Theory* 24 (1985): 170–82.

7. In general see Zachary Sayre Schiffman, "Montaigne and the Problem of Machiavellism," *Journal of Medieval and Renaissance Studies* 12 (1982): 237–58.

8. For this general insight into the contextualizing move characteristic of modern historical consciousness, I am thoroughly indebted to Constantin Fasolt's *The Limits of History* (Chicago: University of Chicago Press, 2004), which explores this dimension of historical thinking with reference to the life and work of the seventeenth-century German polymath Hermann Conring.

9. My treatment of the French and English phases of the "Quarrel" is based chiefly on Joseph M. Levine's masterful analysis, *The Battle of the Books: History and Literature in the Augustan Age* (Ithaca, NY: Cornell University Press, 1991).

10. Ibid., 65.

11. Giambattista Vico, *The New Science of Giambattista Vico,* trans. Thomas Goddard Bergin and Max Harold Fisch (Ithaca, NY: Cornell University Press, 1984), paragraphs 34 and 338 (all further references will be to paragraph numbers). For a brief analysis of the text see Schiffman, *On the Threshold of Modernity,* 129–39. Because it is impossible to ignore Vico in a book about the birth of the past, but it is also impossible to deal with this complex and enigmatic figure adequately—short of writing another book—I will content myself here with explaining why I have given him short shrift. Hopefully, others will remedy this deficiency.

12. Voltaire's comment is quoted in Sheila Mary Mason, *Montesquieu's Idea of Justice* (The Hague: Martinus Nijhoff, 1975), 197; for Hume's comments see David Hume, *An Enquiry Concerning the Principles of Morals* (London: A. Millar, 1751), 54–55.

13. For Montesquieu's Malebranchian influences see Patrick Riley, *The General Will Before Rousseau: The Transformation of the Divine into the Civic* (Princeton, NJ: Princeton University Press, 1986), 139–40; Patrick Riley, "Malebranche and Natural Law," in *Early Modern Natural Law Theories: Contexts and Strategies in the Early Enlightenment*, ed. T. J. Hochstrasser and P. Schröder (Dordrecht: Kluwer, 2003), 77–78; Mason, *Montesquieu's Idea of Justice*, 8–9, 113–42; and Shackleton, *Montesquieu*, 5–8.

14. Nicholas Malebranche, *De la recherche de la vérité*, 3 vols., ed. Geneviève Lewis (Paris: J. Vrin, 1945), bk. 1, chap. 2, p. 10 (hereafter 1.2.10; note that book 1 is not divided into separate "parts" but that subsequent books are, thus resulting in references with an extra numeral after the book number). All translations from this text are my own, though I have sometimes taken my lead from Hobart's *Science and Religion in the Thought of Nicholas Malebranche*.

15. The following analysis is thoroughly indebted to Hobart, *Science and Religion in the Thought of Nicholas Malebranche*, esp. chap. 3.

16. René Descartes, *Regulae ad directionem ingenii—Rules for the Direction of the Natural Intelligence: A Bilingual Edition of the Cartesian Treatise on Method*, ed. and trans. George Heffernan (Amsterdam: Rodopi, 1998), Rule 14, p. 192.

17. See the concluding portion of 1.3, which offers a virtual outline of the entire work.

18. Hobart, *Science and Religion in the Thought of Nicholas Malebranche*, 66.

19. My interpretation here of both Machiavelli and Montesquieu is deeply indebted to Mark Hulliung, *Montesquieu and the Old Regime* (Berkeley: University of California Press, 1976), esp. chap. 6.

Epilogue

1. Quoted in Karl J. Weintraub, *Visions of Culture: Voltaire, Guizot, Burckhardt, Lambrecht, Huizinga, Ortega y Gasset* (Chicago: University of Chicago Press, 1966), 38.

2. For a recent and lively assessment of Voltaire as a historian—with special emphasis on the *Essay on Manners*—see the second volume of J. G. A. Pocock's monumental study of Gibbon, *Barbarism and Religion* (Cambridge: Cambridge University Press, 1999), 72–159.

3. Voltaire, *Essai sur les mœurs et l'esprit des nations et sur les principaux faites de l'histoire depuis Charlemagne jusqu'à Louis XIII*, ed. René Pomeau, 2 vols. (Paris: Garnier, 1963), 1:195; the translation is from Voltaire, *Candide and Other Writings*, ed. Haskell M. Block (New York: Modern Library, 1956), 313.

4. Weintraub, *Visions of Culture*, 42.

5. See Friedrich Meinecke, *Historism: The Rise of a New Historical Outlook*, trans. J. E. Anderson (New York: Herder and Herder, 1972), 340.

6. There is no indication of any direct influence of Vico on Herder. Some scholars speculate that Herder might have been introduced to Vico's *New Science* by Hamann during the early 1770s, before he wrote *Another Philosophy of History*, but there's no proof of this possibility. Herder did find confirmation for his own ideas

in Vico after reading the *New Science* around 1797, long after having completed his historical sketch and after having set aside his unfinished historical treatise.

7. See Karl J. Weintraub, "Autobiography and Historical Consciousness," *Critical Inquiry* 1 (1975): 821–48. This essay serves as the conceptual companion piece to his full-length study, *The Value of the Individual: Self and Circumstance in Autobiography* (Chicago: University of Chicago Press, 1978).

8. This essay is reprinted in Arnaldo Momigliano, *Studies in Historiography* (New York: Harper and Row, 1966). In addition to this piece one should also see the following essays in the same volume: "Gibbon's Contribution to Historical Method" (1954), "The Place of Herodotus in the History of Historiography" (1958), and "Historicism in Contemporary Thought" (1961). Also see "Historicism Revisited," in Arnaldo Momigliano, *Essays in Ancient and Modern Historiography* (Middletown, CT: Wesleyan University Press, 1977).

9. Joseph M. Levine, *Dr. Woodward's Shield: History, Science, and Satire in Augustan England* (Berkeley: University of California Press, 1977), 292. Levine further explores the gradual evolution of historical understanding from philology and antiquarianism in *Humanism and History: Origins of Modern English Historiography* (Ithaca, NY: Cornell University Press, 1987). The literature on this topic is already large and growing; for a mere sampling see (in addition to Levine's works) J. G. A. Pocock, *The Ancient Constitution and the Feudal Law* (Cambridge: Cambridge University Press, 1987); Julian H. Franklin, *Jean Bodin and the Revolution in the Methodology of Law and History* (New York: Columbia University Press, 1963); Donald R. Kelley, *Foundations of Modern Historical Scholarship* (New York: Columbia University Press, 1970); Peter Hanns Reill, *The German Enlightenment and the Rise of Historicism* (Berkeley: University of California Press, 1975); Francis Haskell, *History and Its Images: Art and the Interpretation of the Past* (New Haven, CT: Yale University Press, 1993); and Anthony Grafton, *The Footnote: A Curious History* (Cambridge, MA: Harvard University Press, 1997).

10. For another study that evokes the now-forgotten world of early modern scholarship see Peter N. Miller, *Peiresc's Europe: Learning and Virtue in the Seventeenth Century* (New Haven, CT: Yale University Press, 2000). Miller has also edited a collection of essays whose title—*Momigliano and Antiquarianism: Foundations of the Modern Cultural Sciences* (Toronto: University of Toronto Press, 2007)—aptly expresses the complex relationship between the practice of early modern antiquarianism, the modern study of that practice, and the *Kulturwissenschaften*. Of special interest in this volume is Miller's essay, "Momigliano, Benjamin, and Antiquarianism after the Crisis of Historicism," which shows how the precision of antiquarian research served, for Momigliano and Benjamin, as an antidote to historical relativism.

Selected Bibliography

Introduction

The Anglo-Saxon Chronicle. Translated by G. N. Garmonsway. London: J. M. Dent, 1953.

Bodanis, David. $E = mc^2$: *A Biography of the World's Most Famous Equation.* New York: Walker, 2000.

Fasolt, Constantin. *The Limits of History.* Chicago: University of Chicago Press, 2004.

Machiavelli, Niccolò. Letter No. 140. Translated by Eric Cochrane. In *University of Chicago Readings in Western Civilization.* Edited by Eric Cochrane and Julius Kirshner. Vol. 5, *The Renaissance,* 182–85. Chicago: University of Chicago Press, 1986.

Meinecke, Friedrich. *Historism: The Rise of a New Historical Outlook.* Translated by J. E. Anderson. New York: Herder and Herder, 1972.

Part One. Antiquity

Adcock, F. E. *Thucydides and His History.* Cambridge: Cambridge University Press, 1963.

Aristotle. *De Poetica.* Translated by Ingram Bywater. Oxford: Oxford University Press, 1946.

Auerbach, Erich. *Mimesis.* Translated by Willard R. Trask. Princeton, NJ: Princeton University Press, 1953.

Barkan, Leonard. *Unearthing the Past: Archaeology and Aesthetics in the Making of Renaissance Culture.* New Haven, CT: Yale University Press, 1999.

Boardman, John. *The Archaeology of Nostalgia: How the Greeks Recreated Their Mythical Past.* London: Thames and Hudson, 2002.

Cawkwell, George. *Thucydides and the Peloponnesian War.* London: Routledge, 1997.

Cogan, Marc. *The Human Thing: The Speeches and Principles of Thucydides' History.* Chicago: University of Chicago Press, 1981.

Collingwood, R. G. *The Idea of History.* Oxford: Oxford University Press, 1946.

Connor, W. Robert. *Thucydides.* Princeton, NJ: Princeton University Press, 1984.

Conte, Gian Biagio. *Latin Literature: A History.* Translated by Joseph B. Solodow. Baltimore: Johns Hopkins University Press, 1994.

Cornford, Francis MacDonald. *Thucydides Mythistoricus.* London: Edward Arnold, 1907.

Eliade, Mircea. *Patterns in Comparative Religion.* Translated by Rosemary Sheed. Cleveland: World Publishing, 1963.

Evans, J. A. S. *Herodotus.* Boston: Twayne, 1982.

———. *Herodotus, Explorer of the Past.* Princeton, NJ: Princeton University Press, 1991.

Finley, John H., Jr. *Three Essays on "Thucydides."* Cambridge, MA: Harvard University Press, 1967.

———. *Thucydides.* Cambridge, MA: Harvard University Press, 1942.

Finley, M. I. *The Use and Abuse of History.* New York: Viking, 1975.

———. *The World of Odysseus.* New York: Viking, 1965.

Fornara, Charles W. *The Nature of History in Ancient Greece and Rome.* Berkeley: University of California Press, 1983.

Gould, John. *Herodotus.* New York: St. Martin's, 1989.

Green, Geoffrey. *Literary Criticism and the Structures of History: Erich Auerbach and Leo Spitzer.* Lincoln: University of Nebraska Press, 1982.

Gross, David. *Lost Time: On Remembering and Forgetting in Late Modern Culture.* Amherst: University of Massachusetts Press, 2000.

Herodotus. *The Histories.* Translated by Aubrey De Sélincourt. Revised by John Marincola. London: Penguin, 2003.

Hobart, Michael E., and Zachary S. Schiffman. *Information Ages: Literacy, Numeracy, and the Computer Revolution.* Baltimore: Johns Hopkins University Press, 1998.

Hopkins, Keith. *Conquerors and Slaves.* Cambridge: Cambridge University Press, 1978.

Hornblower, Simon. *Thucydides.* Baltimore: Johns Hopkins University Press, 1987.

Hunter, Virginia. *Past and Process in Herodotus and Thucydides.* Princeton, NJ: Princeton University Press, 1982.

———. *Thucydides: The Artful Reporter.* Toronto: Hakkert, 1973.

Huxley, George. *Pindar's Vision of the Past.* Belfast: The author, 1975.

Immerwahr, Henry R. *Form and Thought in Herodotus.* Cleveland: Press of Western Reserve University, 1966.

Koselleck, Reinhart. *Futures Past: On the Semantics of Historical Time.* Translated by Keith Tribe. Cambridge, MA: MIT Press, 1985.

Kubler, George. *The Shape of Time: Remarks on the History of Things.* New Haven, CT: Yale University Press, 1962.

Lateiner, Donald. *The Historical Method of Herodotus.* Toronto: University of Toronto Press, 1989.

Lerer, Seth, ed. *Literary History and the Challenge of Philology: The Legacy of Erich Auerbach.* Stanford: Stanford University Press, 1996.

Levi, Primo. *Survival in Auschwitz.* New York: Simon and Schuster, 1996.

Livy. *The Early History of Rome: Books I–V of "The History of Rome from Its Foundations."* Translated by Aubrey De Sélincourt. London: Penguin, 2002.

Luraghi, Nini. *The Historian's Craft in the Age of Herodotus.* Oxford: Oxford University Press, 2001.

Machiavelli, Niccolò. *Discourses on the First Ten Books of Titus Livius.* In *The Prince and the Discourses.* New York: Random House, 1950.

Marincola, Mark. *Authority and Tradition in Ancient Historiography.* Cambridge: Cambridge University Press, 1997.

———. *Greek Historians.* Oxford: Oxford University Press, 2001.

Mellor, Ronald. *The Roman Historians.* London: Routledge, 1999.

Miller, Joseph C., ed. *The African Past Speaks: Essays on Oral Tradition and History.* Folkestone: Dawson, 1980.

Momigliano, Arnaldo. "The Place of Herodotus in the History of Historiography." *History* 43 (1958): 1–13. Reprinted in Arnaldo Momigliano, *Studies in Historiography* (New York: Harper and Row, 1966).

———. "Time in Ancient Historiography." *History and Theory, Beiheft* 6 (1966): 1–23. Reprinted in Arnaldo Momigliano, *Essays in Ancient and Modern Historiography* (Middletown, CT: Wesleyan University Press, 1977).

Munn, Mark. *The School of History: Athens in the Age of Socrates.* Berkeley: University of California Press, 2000.

Murray, Oswyn. "Herodotus and Oral History." In *Achaemenid History II: The Greek Sources,* edited by Heleen Sancisi-Weerdenburg and Amélie Kuhrt, 93–115. Leiden: Nederlands Instituut voor het Nabije Oosten, 1987.

Pearson, Lionel. *Early Ionian Historians.* Oxford: Clarendon, 1939. Reprint, Westport, CT: Greenwood, 1975.

Polybius. *The Histories.* Translated by W. R. Paton. 6 vols. Loeb Classical Library. Cambridge, MA: Harvard University Press, 1922–27.

Romilly, Jacqueline de. *Histoire et raison chez Thucydide.* Paris: Société d'Édition "Les Belles Lettres," 1967.

Romm, James. *Herodotus.* New Haven, CT: Yale University Press, 1998.

Schiavone, Aldo. *The End of the Past: Ancient Rome and the Modern West.* Translated by Margery J. Schneider. Cambridge, MA: Harvard University Press, 2000.

Stahl, Hans-Peter. *Thukydides: Die Stellung des Menschen im geschichtlichen Prozess.* Munich: C. H. Beck, 1966.

Syme, Ronald. *Tacitus.* 2 vols. Oxford: Clarendon, 1958.

———. *Ten Studies in Tacitus.* Oxford: Clarendon, 1970.

Tacitus. *Complete Works of Tacitus.* Translated by Alfred John Church and William Jackson Brodribb. New York: Random House, 1942.

Thomas, Rosalind. *Herodotus in Context: Ethnography, Science and the Art of Persuasion.* Cambridge: Cambridge University Press, 2000.

———. *Literacy and Orality in Ancient Greece.* Cambridge: Cambridge University Press, 1992.

Thucydides. *The Peloponnesian War.* Translated by Richard Crawley. Revised by T. E. Wick. New York: Random House, 1982.

Trompf, G. W. *The Idea of Historical Recurrence in Western Thought: From Antiquity to the Reformation.* Berkeley: University of California Press, 1979.

Uhlig, Claus. "Auerbach's 'Hidden'(?) Theory of History." In *Literary History and the Challenge of Philology: The Legacy of Erich Auerbach,* edited by Seth Lerer, 36–49. Stanford: Stanford University Press, 1996.

Vansina, Jan. *Oral Tradition: A Study in Historical Methodology.* Translated by H. M. Wright. Chicago: Aldine, 1965.

———. *Oral Tradition as History.* Madison: University of Wisconsin Press, 1985.

Walbank, F. W. *Polybius.* Berkeley: University of California Press, 1972.

Waters, Kenneth H. *Herodotus, the Historian: His Problems, Methods, and Originality.* Norman: University of Oklahoma Press, 1985.

Wilcox, Donald J. *The Measure of Times Past: Pre-Newtonian Chronologies and the Rhetoric of Relative Time.* Chicago: University of Chicago Press, 1987.

Part Two. Christianity

Althoff, Gerd, Johannes Fried, and Patrick J. Geary, eds. *Medieval Concepts of the Past: Ritual, Memory, Historiography.* Cambridge: Cambridge University Press, 2002.

Auerbach, Erich. *Dante: Poet of the Secular World.* Translated by Ralph Manheim. Chicago: University of Chicago Press, 1961.

———. "Figura." In *Scenes from the Drama of European Literature,* 11–76. Minneapolis: University of Minnesota Press, 1984.

———. *Mimesis.* Translated by Willard R. Trask. Princeton, NJ: Princeton University Press, 1953.

Augustine of Hippo, St. "Acts or Disputation against Fortunatus, the Manichæan." Translated by Albert H. Newman. *Christian Classics Ethereal Library,* www.ccel .org/ccel/schaff/npnf104.iv.vii.ii.html.

———. *The City of God.* Translated by Marcus Dods. New York: Modern Library, 1950.

———. *The City of God against the Pagans.* Translated by George E. McCracken et al. 7 vols. Loeb Classical Library. Cambridge, MA: Harvard University Press, 1957–72.

———. *Commentary on the Lord's Sermon on the Mount.* Translated by Denis J. Kavanagh. Washington: Catholic University of America Press, 1951.

———. *Confessions.* Introduction, text, and commentary by James J. O'Donnell. 3 vols. Oxford: Oxford University Press, 1992.

———. *Confessions.* Translated by R. S. Pine-Coffin. Harmondsworth: Penguin, 1961.

———. *Confessions.* Translated by William Watts. 2 vols. 1631. Loeb Classical Library. Cambridge, MA: Harvard University Press, 1968.

———. *On Music.* Translated by Robert Catesby Taliaferro. New York: Fathers of the Church, 1947.

———. *Retractations.* Translated by Mary Inez Bogan. Washington: Catholic University Press, 1968.

———. "To Simplician—on Various Questions. Book 1." In *Augustine: Earlier Writings.* Translated by John H. S. Burlegh. Philadelphia: Westminster Press, 1953.

Barnes, Timothy D. *Constantine and Eusebius.* Cambridge, MA: Harvard University Press, 1981.

Bede. *Ecclesiastical History of the English People.* Translated by Leo Sherley-Price. Revised by R. E. Latham. London: Penguin, 1990.

———. *Opera historica.* Translated by J. E. King. 2 vols. Loeb Classical Library. Cambridge, MA: Harvard University Press, 1971.

Bloch, H. "The Pagan Revival in the West at the End of the Fourth Century." In *The Conflict between Paganism and Christianity in the Fourth Century,* edited by Arnaldo Momigliano, 193–218. Oxford: Oxford University Press, 1963.

Bourke, Vernon J. "*The City of God* and History." In *The City of God: A Collection of Critical Essays,* edited by Dorothy F. Donnelly, 291–303. New York: Peter Lang, 1995.

Brown, Peter. *Augustine of Hippo.* Berkeley: University of California Press, 1967.

———. *Authority and the Sacred: Aspects of the Christianization of the Roman World.* Cambridge: Cambridge University Press, 1995.

———. *The Cult of the Saints.* Chicago: University of Chicago Press, 1981.

———. *The Making of Late Antiquity.* Cambridge, MA: Harvard University Press, 1978.

———. "Saint Augustine and Political Society." In *The City of God: A Collection of Critical Essays,* edited by Dorothy F. Donnelly, 17–35. New York: Peter Lang, 1995.

———. *The World of Late Antiquity, AD 150–750.* New York: Norton, 1989.

Chadwick, Henry. *Augustine.* New York: Oxford University Press, 1986.

Coleman, Janet. *Ancient and Medieval Memories: Studies in the Reconstruction of the Past.* Cambridge: Cambridge University Press, 1992.

Courcelle, Pierre. *Recherches sur les Confessions de Saint-Augustin.* Paris: E. de Boccard, 1950.

Cullmann, Oscar. *Christ and Time: The Primitive Christian Conception of Time and History.* Translated by Floyd V. Filson. Rev. ed. Philadelphia: Westminster Press, 1964.

Dihle, Albrecht. *The Theory of Will in Classical Antiquity.* Berkeley: University of California Press, 1982.

Dodaro, Robert, and George Lawless, eds. *Augustine and His Critics: Essays in Honor of Gerald Bonner.* London: Routledge, 2000.

Donnelly, Dorothy F., ed. *The City of God: A Collection of Critical Essays.* New York: Peter Lang, 1995.

Eusebius. *The Ecclesiastical History.* Translated by Kirsopp Lake. 2 vols. Cambridge, MA: Harvard University Press, 1965.

Fortin, Ernest L. "Augustine's *City of God* and the Modern Historical Consciousness." In *The City of God: A Collection of Critical Essays,* edited by Dorothy F. Donnelly, 305–17. New York: Peter Lang, 1995.

Foutz, Scott David. "An Attempt to Establish an Historically Accurate Definition of Typology." *Quodlibet: Online Journal of Christian Theology and Philosophy,* www.quodlibet.net/typology.shtml.

Geary, Patrick J. *Phantoms of Remembrance: Memory and Oblivion at the End of the First Millennium.* Princeton, NJ: Princeton University Press, 1994.

Gilson, Etienne. *The Christian Philosophy of Saint Augustine.* Translated by L. E. M. Lynch. New York: Random House, 1960.

Goetz, Hans-Werner. "The Concept of Time in the Historiography of the Eleventh and Twelfth Centuries." In *Medieval Concepts of the Past,* edited by Gerd Althoff, Johannes Fried, and Patrick J. Geary, 139–66. Cambridge: Cambridge University Press, 2002.

———. *Die Geschichtstheologie des Orosius.* Darmstadt: Wissenschaftliche Buchgesellschaft, 1980.

Goffart, Walter. *The Narrators of Barbarian History (A.D. 550–800): Jordanes, Gregory of Tours, Bede, and Paul the Deacon.* Princeton, NJ: Princeton University Press, 1988.

Grant, Robert M. *Eusebius as Church Historian.* Oxford: Oxford University Press, 1980.

Gregory of Tours. *The History of the Franks.* Translated by Lewis Thorpe. Harmondsworth: Penguin, 1974.

———. *Libri historiarum X.* Edited by Bruno Krusch and Wilhelm Levison. *Monumenta Germaniae historica: Scriptorum rerum Merovingicarum.* Vol. 1, part 1. Hanover, NH: Hahniani, 1951.

Hanning, Robert W. *The Vision of History in Early Britain: From Gildas to Geoffrey of Monmouth.* New York: Columbia University Press, 1966.

Heinzelmann, Martin. *Gregory of Tours: History and Society in the Sixth Century.* Translated by Christopher Carroll. Cambridge: Cambridge University Press, 2001.

Holmes, Oliver Wendell. *Holmes-Laski Letters: The Correspondence of Mr. Justice Holmes and Harold J. Laski, 1916–1935.* Edited by Mark DeWolfe Howe. Cambridge, MA: Harvard University Press, 1953.

Horn, Christoph, ed. *Augustinus, De civitate dei.* Berlin: Akademie, 1997.

Knuuttila, Simo. "Time and Creation in Augustine." In *The Cambridge Companion to Augustine,* edited by Eleonore Stump and Norman Kretzmann, 103–15. Cambridge: Cambridge University Press, 2001.

Koselleck, Reinhart. *The Practice of Conceptual History: Timing History, Spacing Concepts.* Translated by Todd Samuel Presner and others. Stanford: Stanford University Press, 2002.

Manuel, Frank E. *Shapes of Philosophical History.* London: Allen and Unwin, 1965.

Markus, Robert. "Bede and the Tradition of Ecclesiastical Historiography." Jarrow Lecture, 1975. Jarrow: St. Paul's Rectory, 1976.

———. *Conversion and Disenchantment in Augustine's Spiritual Career.* Villanova, PA: Villanova University Press, 1989.

———. *The End of Ancient Christianity.* Cambridge: Cambridge University Press, 1990.

———. *From Augustine to Gregory the Great.* London: Variorum Reprints, 1983.

———. *Sæculum: History and Society in the Theology of St. Augustine.* Rev. ed. Cambridge: Cambridge University Press, 1988.

———. "Two Conceptions of Political Authority: Augustine, *De Civitate Dei,* XIX, 14–15, and Some Thirteenth-Century Interpretations." In *The City of God: A Collection of Critical Essays,* edited by Dorothy F. Donnelly, 93–117. New York: Peter Lang, 1995.

Marrou, Henri-Irénée. *L'ambivalence du temps de l'histoire chez Saint Augustin.* Paris: Vrin, 1950.

———. *Saint Augustin et la fin de la culture antique.* 4th ed. Paris: De Boccard, 1958.

Momigliano, Arnaldo, ed. *The Conflict between Paganism and Christianity in the Fourth Century.* Oxford: Oxford University Press, 1963.

———. "Pagan and Christian Historiography in the Fourth Century A.D." In *The Conflict between Paganism and Christianity in the Fourth Century,* edited by Arnaldo Momigliano, 79–99. Oxford: Oxford University Press, 1963.

Mommson, Theodor E. "St. Augustine and the Christian Idea of Progress." In *The City of God: A Collection of Critical Essays,* edited by Dorothy F. Donnelly, 353–72. New York: Peter Lang, 1995.

Niebuhr, Reinhold. "Augustine's Political Realism." In *The City of God: A Collection of Critical Essays,* edited by Dorothy F. Donnelly, 119–34. New York: Peter Lang, 1995.

O'Connell, Robert J. *The Origins of the Soul in St. Augustine's Later Works.* New York: Fordham University Press, 1987.

———. *St. Augustine's Confessions: The Odyssey of Soul.* 2nd ed. New York: Fordham University Press, 1989.

O'Daly, Gerard. *Augustine's "City of God": A Reader's Guide.* Oxford: Oxford University Press, 2004.

O'Meara, John. *Charter of Christendom: The Significance of the "City of God."* New York: Macmillan, 1961.

Orosius, Paulus. *The Seven Books of History against the Pagans.* Translated by Roy J. Deferrari. Washington: Catholic University Press, 1964.

Pontet, Maurice. *L'exégèse de Saint-Augustin, prédicateur.* Paris: Aubier, 1946.

Russell, Bertrand. *Human Knowledge: Its Scope and Limits.* New York: Simon and Schuster, 1948.

Sorabji, Richard. *Time, Creation, and the Continuum: Theories in Antiquity and the Early Middle Ages.* Ithaca, NY: Cornell University Press, 1983.

Spiegel, Gabrielle M. *The Past as Text: The Theory and Practice of Medieval Historiography.* Baltimore: Johns Hopkins University Press, 1997.

Stump, Eleonore, and Norman Kretzmann, eds. *The Cambridge Companion to Augustine.* Cambridge: Cambridge University Press, 2001.

Taylor, Charles. *Sources of the Self: The Making of Modern Identity.* Cambridge, MA: Harvard University Press, 1989.

Teske, Roland. "Augustine's Philosophy of Memory." In *The Cambridge Companion to Augustine,* edited by Eleonore Stump and Norman Kretzmann, 148–58. Cambridge: Cambridge University Press, 2001.

Thürlemann, Felix. *Die historische Diskurs bei Gregor von Tours: Topi und Wirklichkeit.* Bern: Herbert Lang, 1974.

Wallace-Hadrill, D. S. *Eusebius of Caesarea.* Westminster, MD: Canterbury Press, 1961.

Weintraub, Karl Joachim. *The Value of the Individual: Self and Circumstance in Autobiography.* Chicago: University of Chicago Press, 1978.

Wilcox, Donald J. *The Measure of Times Past: Pre-Newtonian Chronologies and the Rhetoric of Relative Time.* Chicago: University of Chicago Press, 1987.

Williams, Thomas. "Biblical Interpretation." In *The Cambridge Companion to Augustine,* edited by Eleonore Stump and Norman Kretzmann, 59–70. Cambridge: Cambridge University Press, 2001.

Wills, Garry. *Saint Augustine.* New York: Viking/Penguin, 1999.

Wittgenstein, Ludwig. *Philosophical Investigations.* Translated by G. E. M. Anscombe. 2nd ed. New York: Macmillan, 1953.

Part Three. Renaissance

Barkan, Leonard. *Transuming Passion: Ganymede and the Erotics of Humanism.* Stanford: Stanford University Press, 1991.

———. *Unearthing the Past: Archaeology and Aesthetics in the Making of Renaissance Culture.* New Haven, CT: Yale University Press, 1999.

Baron, Hans. *From Petrarch to Leonardo Bruni: Studies in Humanistic and Political Literature.* Chicago: University of Chicago Press, 1968.

———. *Petrarch's "Secretum": Its Making and Its Meaning.* Cambridge, MA: Medieval Academy of America, 1985.

Bishop, Morris. *Petrarch and His World.* Bloomington: Indiana University Press, 1963.

Blair, Ann. "Humanist Methods in Natural Philosophy: The Commonplace Book." *Journal of the History of Ideas* 53 (1992): 541–51.

———. "Reading Strategies for Coping with Information Overload, ca. 1550–1700." *Journal of the History of Ideas* 64 (2003): 11–28.

———. *The Theater of Nature: Jean Bodin and Renaissance Science.* Princeton, NJ: Princeton University Press, 1997.

Bodin, Jean. *Method for the Easy Comprehension of History.* Translated by Beatrice Reynolds. New York: Norton, 1969.

———. *Œuvres philosophiques de Jean Bodin.* Vol. 1. Edited by Pierre Mesnard. Paris: Presses Universitaires de France, 1951.

Bolgar, R. R. *The Classical Heritage and Its Beneficiaries.* Cambridge: Cambridge University Press, 1954.

Bouwsma, William J. *The Waning of the Renaissance: 1550–1640.* New Haven, CT: Yale University Press, 2000.

Boyle, Marjorie O'Rourke. *Petrarch's Genius: Pentimento and Prophecy.* Berkeley: University of California Press, 1991.

Brown, John L. *The Methodus ad facilem historiarum cognitionem of Jean Bodin: A Critical Study.* Washington: Catholic University of America Press, 1939.

Bruni, Leonardo. "The Study of Literature." In *Humanist Education Treatises.* Texts in Latin and English. Edited and translated by Craig W. Kallendorf, 92–125. Cambridge, MA: Harvard University Press, 2002.

Burckhardt, Jacob. *The Civilization of the Renaissance in Italy.* Translated by S. G. C. Middlemore. 2 vols. New York: Harper and Row, 1958.

Cave, Terence. *The Cornucopian Text: Problems of Writing in the French Renaissance.* Oxford: Clarendon, 1979.

Cochrane, Eric, and Julius Kirshner, eds. *University of Chicago Readings in Western Civilization.* Vol. 5, *The Renaissance.* Chicago: University of Chicago Press, 1986.

Cornilliat, François. "Exemplarities: A Response to Timothy Hampton and Karlheinz Stierle." *Journal of the History of Ideas* 59 (1998): 613–24.

Couzinet, Marie-Dominique. *Histoire et méthode à la renaissance: Une lecture de la Methodus de Jean Bodin.* Paris: Vrin, 1996.

De Vecchi, Pierluigi. *Raphael.* New York: Abbeville Press, 2002.

Durling, Robert. "The Ascent of Mt. Ventoux and the Crisis of Allegory." *Italian Quarterly* 18 (1974): 7–28.

Eden, Kathy. *Friends Hold All Things in Common: Tradition, Intellectual Property, and the "Adages" of Erasmus.* New Haven, CT: Yale University Press, 2001.

Engster, Daniel. *Divine Sovereignty: The Origins of Modern State Power.* Dekalb: Northern Illinois University Press, 2001.

Erasmus, Desiderius. *On Copia of Words and Ideas.* Translated by Donald B. King and H. David Rix. Milwaukee: Marquette University Press, 1963.

Franklin, Julian H. *Jean Bodin and the Sixteenth-Century Revolution in the Methodology of Law and History.* New York: Columbia University Press, 1963.

Freud, Sigmund. *Civilization and Its Discontents.* Translated by James Strachey. New York: Norton, 1961.

Gilmore, Myron P. "The Renaissance Conception of the Lessons of History." In *Facets of the Renaissance,* edited by William H. Werkmeister, 73–101. New York: Harper and Row, 1963.

Goyet, Francis. *Le sublime du "lieu commun": L'invention rhétorique dan l'Antiquité et à la Renaissance.* Paris: Honoré Champion, 1996.

Grafton, Anthony. *What Was History? The Art of History in Early Modern Europe.* Cambridge: Cambridge University Press, 2007.

Grafton, Anthony, and Lisa Jardine. *From Humanism to the Humanities.* Cambridge, MA: Harvard University Press, 1986.

Greene, Thomas M. *The Light in Troy: Imitation and Discovery in Renaissance Poetry.* New Haven, CT: Yale University Press, 1982.

———. *The Vulnerable Text: Essays on Renaissance Literature.* New York: Columbia University Press, 1986.

Hampton, Timothy. "Examples, Stories, and Subjects in *Don Quixote* and the *Heptameron.*" *Journal of the History of Ideas* 59 (1998): 597–611.

———. *Writing from History: The Rhetoric of Exemplarity in Renaissance Literature.* Ithaca, NY: Cornell University Press, 1990.

Hankins, James. *Plato in the Italian Renaissance.* 2 vols. Leiden: E. J. Brill, 1991.

Hotman, François. *Antitribonian.* Paris, 1603. Facsimile ed. in *Images et témoins de l'âge classique,* no. 9. Sainte-Etienne: Presses de l'Université de Sainte-Etienne, 1980.

Huppert, George. *The Idea of Perfect History: Historical Erudition and Historical Philosophy in Renaissance France.* Urbana: University of Illinois Press, 1970.

Janson, Tore. *A Natural History of Latin.* Translated by Merethe Damsgård Sørensen and Nigel Vincent. Oxford: Oxford University Press, 2004.

Jardine, Lisa. "Lorenzo Valla and the Intellectual Origins of Humanist Dialectic." *Journal of the History of Philosophy* 15 (1977): 143–63. Revised as "Lorenzo Valla: Academic Skepticism and the New Humanist Dialectic." In *The Skeptical Tradition,* edited by Myles Burnyeat, 253–86. Berkeley: University of California Press, 1983.

Jeanneret, Michel. "The Vagaries of Exemplarity: Distortion or Dismissal?" *Journal of the History of Ideas* 59 (1998): 565–79.

Kahn, Victoria. "The Figure of the Reader in Petrarch's *Secretum.*" *PMLA* 100 (1985): 154–66.

———. "*Virtù* and the Example of Agathocles in Machiavelli's *Prince.*" *Representations* 13 (1986): 63–83.

Kelley, Donald R. *Foundations of Modern Historical Scholarship: Language, Law, and History in the French Renaissance.* New York: Columbia University Press, 1970.

Koselleck, Reinhart. *Futures Past: On the Semantics of Historical Time.* Translated by Keith Tribe. Cambridge, MA: MIT Press, 1985.

Lechner, Joan Marie. *Renaissance Concepts of the Commonplaces.* New York: Pageant, 1962.

Lyons, John D. *Before Imagination: Embodied Thought from Montaigne to Rousseau.* Stanford: Stanford University Press, 2005.

———. *Exemplum: The Rhetoric of Example in Early Modern France and Italy.* Princeton, NJ: Princeton University Press, 1989.

Machiavelli, Niccolò. *Discourses on the First Ten Books of Titus Livius.* In *The Prince and the Discourses.* New York: Random House, 1950.

———. Letter No. 140. Translated by Eric Cochrane. In *University of Chicago Readings in Western Civilization.* Edited by Eric Cochrane and Julius Kirshner. Vol. 5, *The Renaissance,* 182–85. Chicago: University of Chicago Press, 1986.

Marsh, David. *The Quattrocento Dialogue: Classical Tradition and Humanist Innovation.* Cambridge, MA: Harvard University Press, 1980.

Meinecke, Friedrich. *Historism: The Rise of a New Historical Outlook.* Translated by J. E. Anderson. New York: Herder and Herder, 1972.

Montaigne, Michel de. *Essays.* In *The Complete Works of Montaigne.* Translated by Donald M. Frame. Stanford: Stanford University Press, 1958.

———. *Œuvres complètes.* Edited by Albert Thibaudet and Maurice Rat. Paris: Gallimard, 1962.

Moss, Ann. *Printed Commonplace-Books and the Structuring of Renaissance Thought.* Oxford: Oxford University Press, 1996.

Nadel, George H. "Philosophy of History before Historicism." In *Studies in the Philosophy of History,* edited by George H. Nadel, 49–73. New York: Harper and Row, 1965.

Panofsky, Erwin. *Renaissance and Renascences in Western Art.* New York: Harper and Row, 1969.

Petrarca, Francesco. "The Ascent of Mont Ventoux." Translated by Hans Nachod. In *The Renaissance Philosophy of Man,* edited by Ernst Cassirer, Paul Oskar Kristeller, and John Herman Randall Jr., 36–46. Chicago: University of Chicago Press, 1948.

———. *Familiarium rerum libri.* Edited by Vittorio Rossi and Umberto Bosco. 4 vols. Florence: G. C. Sansoni, 1933–42.

———. *Letters on Familiar Matters.* Translated by Aldo S. Bernardo. 3 vols. New York: Italica Press, 2005.

———. *Opera latine de Francesco Petrarca.* Vol. 1, *Secretum: De secreto conflictu curarum mearum.* Edited by Antonietta Bufano. Turin: Unione tipografico editrice torinese, 1975.

———. *The Secret.* Edited by Carol E. Quillen. Boston: Bedford/St. Martin's, 2003.

Pigman, G. W., III. "Versions of Imitation in the Renaissance." *Renaissance Quarterly* 33 (1980): 1–32.

Pocock, J. G. A. *The Ancient Constitution and the Feudal Law: A Study of English Historical Thought in the Seventeenth Century: A Reissue with a Retrospect.* Cambridge: Cambridge University Press, 1987.

Polybius. *The Histories.* Translated by W. R. Paton. 6 vols. Loeb Classical Library. Cambridge, MA: Harvard University Press, 1922–27.

Quillen, Carol Everhart. *Rereading the Renaissance: Petrarch, Augustine, and the Language of Humanism.* Ann Arbor: University of Michigan Press, 1998.

Redig de Campos, D. *Raphael in the Stanze.* Translated by John Guthrie. Milan: Aldo Martello, 1971.

Rigolot, François. "The Renaissance Crisis of Exemplarity." *Journal of the History of Ideas* 59 (1998): 557–63.

Saxl, Fritz. *A Heritage of Images.* Harmondsworth: Penguin, 1970.

Schiffman, Zachary Sayre, ed. *Humanism and the Renaissance.* Boston: Houghton Mifflin, 2002.

――. "Jean Bodin, Roman Law, and the Renaissance Conception of the Past." In *Cultural Visions: Essays in the History of Culture,* edited by Penny Schine Gold and Benjamin C. Sax, 271–87. Amsterdam: Rodopi, 2000.

――. *On the Threshold of Modernity: Relativism in the French Renaissance.* Baltimore: Johns Hopkins University Press, 1991.

Skinner, Quentin. *The Foundations of Modern Political Thought.* 2 vols. Cambridge: Cambridge University Press, 1978.

Spini, Giorgio. "Historiography: The Art of History in the Italian Counter Reformation." In *The Late Italian Renaissance,* edited and translated by Eric Cochrane, 91–133. New York: Harper and Row, 1970.

Stierle, Karlheinz. "L'histoire comme exemple, l'exemple comme histoire." *Poétique* 10 (1972): 176–98.

――. "Three Moments in the Crisis of Exemplarity: Boccaccio-Petrarch, Montaigne, and Cervantes." *Journal of the History of Ideas* 59 (1998): 581–95.

Struever, Nancy S. "Pasquier's *Recherches de la France:* The Exemplarity of His Medieval Sources." *History and Theory* 27 (1988): 51–59.

Trinkaus, Charles. *"In Our Image and Likeness": Humanity and Divinity in Italian Humanist Thought.* 2 vols. Chicago: University of Chicago Press, 1970.

――. *The Poet as Philosopher: Petrarch and the Formation of Renaissance Consciousness.* New Haven, CT: Yale University Press, 1979.

Vasari, Giorgio. *Lives of the Artists.* Translated by George Bull. Harmondsworth: Penguin, 1965.

Weintraub, Karl Joachim. *The Value of the Individual: Self and Circumstance in Autobiography.* Chicago: University of Chicago Press, 1978.

Weiss, Roberto. *The Renaissance Discovery of Classical Antiquity.* Oxford: Basil Blackwell, 1969.

Wilkins, Ernest Hatch. *Life of Petrarch.* Chicago: University of Chicago Press, 1961.

Witt, Ronald G. *"In the Footsteps of the Ancients": The Origins of Humanism from Lovato to Bruni.* Leiden: Brill, 2000.

Woodward, William Harrison. *Vittorino da Feltre and Other Humanist Educators.* Cambridge: Cambridge University Press, 1897. Reprint, New York: Columbia University Press, 1963.

Zarka, Yves Charles, ed. *Jean Bodin: Nature, histoire, droit et politique.* Paris: Presses Universitaires de France, 1996.

Part Four. Enlightenment

Auerbach, Erich. "Vico and Aesthetic Historism." In *Scenes from the Drama of European Literature,* 183–98. Minneapolis: University of Minnesota Press, 1984. First published in the *Journal of Aesthetics and Art Criticism* 8 (1949): 110–18.

Baron, Hans. "The *Querelle* of the Ancients and the Moderns as a Problem for Renaissance Scholarship." In *Renaissance Essays,* edited by Paul O. Kristeller and Philip P. Wiener, 95–114. New York: Harper and Row, 1968. First published in the *Journal of the History of Ideas* 20 (1959): 3–22.

Berlin, Isaiah. "Montesquieu." In *Against the Current: Essays in the History of Ideas,* edited by Henry Hardy, 130–61. New York: Viking, 1980. First published in the *Proceedings of the British Academy* 41 (1955): 267–96.

———. *Vico and Herder: Two Studies in the History of Ideas.* New York: Viking, 1976.

Blumenberg, Hans. *The Legitimacy of the Modern Age.* Translated by Robert M. Wallace. Cambridge, MA: MIT Press, 1983.

Burrow, John. *A History of Histories: Epics, Chronicles, Romances and Inquiries from Herodotus and Thucydides to the Twentieth Century.* London: Penguin, 2007.

Carrithers, David. "Montesquieu's Philosophy of History." *Journal of the History of Ideas* 47 (1986): 61–80.

Cassirer, Ernst. *The Philosophy of the Enlightenment.* Translated by Fritz C. A. Koelln and James P. Pettegrove. Princeton, NJ: Princeton University Press, 1951.

Conroy, Peter V., Jr. *Montesquieu Revisited.* New York: Twayne, 1992.

Descartes, René. *Regulae ad directionem ingenii—Rules for the Direction of the Natural Intelligence: A Bilingual Edition of the Cartesian Treatise on Method.* Edited and translated by George Heffernan. Amsterdam: Rodopi, 1998.

Durkheim, Emile. *Montesquieu and Rousseau: Forerunners of Sociology.* Translated by Ralph Manheim. Ann Arbor: University of Michigan Press, 1960.

Erasmus, H. J. *The Origins of Rome in Historiography from Petrarch to Perizonius.* Assen: Van Gorcum, 1962.

Fasolt, Constantin. *The Limits of History.* Chicago: University of Chicago Press, 2004.

Fletcher, F. T. H. *Montesquieu and English Politics.* London: Edward Arnold, 1939. Reprint, Philadelphia: Porcupine Press, 1980.

Frame, Donald M. *Montaigne: A Biography.* New York: Harcourt, Brace and World, 1965.

———. "New Light on Montaigne's Trip to Paris in 1588." *Romanic Review* 51 (1960): 161–81.

Goldmann, Lucien. *The Philosophy of the Enlightenment: The Christian Burgess and the Enlightenment.* Translated by Henry Mass. Cambridge, MA: MIT Press, 1973.

Grafton, Anthony, and Lisa Jardine. "'Studied for Action': How Gabriel Harvey Read His Livy." *Past and Present* 129 (1990): 30–78.

Hampton, Timothy. *Literature and Nation in the Sixteenth Century: Inventing Renaissance France.* Ithaca, NY: Cornell University Press, 2001.

Hobart, Michael E. "The Analytical Vision and Organization of Knowledge in the *Encyclopédie.*" *Studies in Voltaire and the Eighteenth Century* 327 (1995): 147–75.

———. *Science and Religion in the Thought of Nicholas Malebranche.* Chapel Hill: University of North Carolina Press, 1982.

Hobart, Michael E., and Zachary S. Schiffman. *Information Ages: Literacy, Numeracy, and the Computer Revolution.* Baltimore: Johns Hopkins University Press, 1998.

Hulliung, Mark. *Montesquieu and the Old Regime.* Berkeley: University of California Press, 1976.

Hume, David. *An Enquiry Concerning the Principles of Morals.* London: A. Millar, 1751.

Jacks, Philip. *The Antiquarian and the Myth of Antiquity: The Origins of Rome in Renaissance Thought*. Cambridge: Cambridge University Press, 1993.

Kaiser, Thomas. "The Evil Empire? The Debate on Turkish Despotism in Eighteenth-Century French Political Culture." *Journal of Modern History* 72 (2000): 6–34.

Levine, Joseph M. *The Battle of the Books: History and Literature in the Augustan Age*. Ithaca, NY: Cornell University Press, 1991.

———. *Between the Ancients and the Moderns: Baroque Culture in Restoration England*. New Haven, CT: Yale University Press, 1999.

———. "Giambattista Vico and the Quarrel between the Ancients and the Moderns." *Journal of the History of Ideas* 52 (1991): 55–79. Reprinted in Joseph M. Levine, *The Autonomy of History: Truth and Method from Erasmus to Gibbon*, 127–53. Chicago: University of Chicago Press, 1999.

Macfarlane, Alan. *The Riddle of the Modern World: Of Liberty, Wealth, and Equality*. New York: St. Martin's, 2000.

Malebranche, Nicholas. *De la recherche de la vérité*. Edited by Geneviève Lewis. 3 vols. Paris: J. Vrin, 1945.

———. *Treatise on Nature and Grace*. Translated by Patrick Riley. Oxford: Clarendon, 1992.

Mason, Sheila Mary. *Montesquieu's Idea of Justice*. The Hague: Martinus Nijhoff, 1975.

Mattingly, Garrett. *The Armada*. Boston: Houghton Mifflin, 1959.

Montaigne, Michel de. *The Complete Works of Montaigne*. Translated by Donald M. Frame. Stanford: Stanford University Press, 1958.

———. *Œuvres complètes*. Edited by Albert Thibaudet and Maurice Rat. Paris: Gallimard, 1962.

Montesquieu, Charles de Secondat, baron de. *Considerations on the Causes of the Greatness of the Romans and Their Decline*. Translated by David Lowenthal. Indianapolis: Hackett, 1999.

———. *Œuvres complètes*. Edited by Roger Caillois. 2 vols. Paris: Gallimard, 1949–51.

———. *Persian Letters*. Translated by C. J. Betts. Harmondsworth: Penguin, 1973.

———. *The Spirit of the Laws*. Translated by Anne M. Cohler, Basia Carolyn Miller, and Harold Samuel Stone. Cambridge: Cambridge University Press, 1989.

Pangle, Thomas L. *Montesquieu's Philosophy of Liberalism: A Commentary on "The Spirit of the Laws."* Chicago: University of Chicago Press, 1973.

Pfeiffer, Rudolf. *History of Classical Scholarship, 1300–1850*. Oxford: Clarendon, 1976.

Phillips, Mark Salber. "Reconsiderations on History and Antiquarianism: Arnaldo Momigliano and the Historiography of Eighteenth-Century Britain." *Journal of the History of Ideas* 57 (1996): 297–316.

———. "Relocating Inwardness: Historical Distance and the Transition from Enlightenment to Romantic Historiography." *Proceedings of the Modern Language Association* 118 (2003): 436–49.

———. *Society and Sentiment: Genres of Historical Writing in Britain, 1740–1820*. Princeton, NJ: Princeton University Press, 2000.

Pocock, J. G. A. *Barbarism and Religion*. 4 vols. Cambridge: Cambridge University Press, 1999–2008.

Riley, Patrick. *The General Will Before Rousseau: The Transformation of the Divine into the Civic*. Princeton, NJ: Princeton University Press, 1986.

———. "Malebranche and Natural Law." In *Early Modern Natural Law Theories: Contexts and Strategies in the Early Enlightenment*, edited by T. J. Hochstrasser and P. Schröder, 53–87. Dordrecht: Kluwer, 2003.

Sandys, John Edwin. *A History of Classical Scholarship*. 3 vols. Cambridge: Cambridge University Press, 1908.

Schaub, Diana J. *Erotic Liberalism: Women and Revolution in Montesquieu's "Persian Letters."* Lanham, MD: Rowman and Littlefield, 1995.

Schiffman, Zachary Sayre. "Montaigne and the Problem of Machiavellism." *Journal of Medieval and Renaissance Studies* 12 (1982): 237–58.

———. "Montaigne's Perception of Ancient Rome: Biography as a Form of History." In *Rome in the Renaissance: The City and the Myth*, edited by P. A. Ramsey, 345–53. Binghamton, NY: Medieval and Renaissance Texts and Studies, 1982.

———. *On the Threshold of Modernity: Relativism in the French Renaissance*. Baltimore: Johns Hopkins University Press, 1991.

———. "Renaissance Historicism Reconsidered." *History and Theory* 24 (1985): 170–82.

Shackleton, Robert. *Montesquieu: A Critical Biography*. London: Oxford University Press, 1961.

Shklar, Judith N. *Montesquieu*. Oxford: Oxford University Press, 1987.

Sorel, Albert. *Montesquieu*. Translated by Melville B. Anderson and Edward Playfair Anderson. Port Washington, NY: Kennikat Press, 1969.

Vico, Giambattista. *The New Science of Giambattista Vico*. 1744. Translated by Thomas Goddard Bergin and Max Harold Fisch. Ithaca, NY: Cornell University Press, 1984.

Waddicor, Mark H. *Montesquieu: Lettres persanes*. London: Edward Arnold, 1977.

Woolf, D. R. *The Idea of History in Early Stuart England*. Toronto: University of Toronto Press, 1990.

———. *Reading History in Early Modern England*. Cambridge: Cambridge University Press, 2000.

Epilogue

Burrow, John. *A History of Histories: Epics, Chronicles, Romances and Inquiries from Herodotus and Thucydides to the Twentieth Century*. London: Penguin, 2007.

Collingwood, R. G. *The Idea of History*. London: Oxford University Press, 1946.

Fasolt, Constantin. *The Limits of History*. Chicago: University of Chicago Press, 2004.

Franklin, Julian H. *Jean Bodin and the Revolution in the Methodology of Law and History*. New York: Columbia University Press, 1963.

Grafton, Anthony. *The Footnote: A Curious History*. Cambridge, MA: Harvard University Press, 1997.

———. *Joseph Scaliger: A Study in the History of Classical Scholarship*. 2 vols. Oxford: Clarendon, 1983, 1993.

Haskell, Francis. *History and Its Images: Art and the Interpretation of the Past*. New Haven, CT: Yale University Press, 1993.

Herder, Johann Gottfried. *Another Philosophy of History for the Education of Mankind: One among Many Contributions of the Century (1774)*. In *Another Philosophy of History and Selected Political Writings*. Translated by Ioannis D. Evrigenis and Daniel Pellerin, 3–98. Indianapolis: Hackett, 2004.

Huppert, George. *The Idea of Perfect History: Historical Erudition and Historical Philosophy in Renaissance France*. Urbana: University of Illinois Press, 1970.

Kelley, Donald R. *Faces of History*. New Haven, CT: Yale University Press, 1998.

———. *Foundations of Modern Historical Scholarship: Language, Law, and History in the French Renaissance*. New York: Columbia University Press, 1970.

Levine, Joseph M. *Dr. Woodward's Shield: History, Science, and Satire in Augustan England*. Berkeley: University of California Press, 1977.

———. *Humanism and History: Origins of Modern English Historiography*. Ithaca, NY: Cornell University Press, 1987.

Meinecke, Friedrich. *Historism: The Rise of a New Historical Outlook*. Translated by J. E. Anderson. New York: Herder and Herder, 1972.

Miller, Peter N., ed. *Momigliano and Antiquarianism: Foundations of the Modern Cultural Sciences*. Toronto: University of Toronto Press, 2007.

———. *Peiresc's Europe: Learning and Virtue in the Seventeenth Century*. New Haven, CT: Yale University Press, 2000.

Momigliano, Arnaldo. *Essays in Ancient and Modern Historiography*. Middletown, CT: Wesleyan University Press, 1977.

———. *Studies in Historiography*. New York: Harper and Row, 1966.

Phillips, Mark Salber. "Reconsiderations on History and Antiquarianism: Arnaldo Momigliano and the Historiography of Eighteenth-Century Britain." *Journal of the History of Ideas* 57 (1996): 297–316.

———. "Relocating Inwardness: Historical Distance and the Transition from Enlightenment to Romantic Historiography." *Proceedings of the Modern Language Association* 118 (2003): 436–49.

———. *Society and Sentiment: Genres of Historical Writing in Britain, 1740–1820*. Princeton, NJ: Princeton University Press, 2000.

Pocock, J. G. A. *The Ancient Constitution and the Feudal Law: A Study of English Historical Thought in the Seventeenth Century: A Reissue with a Retrospect*. Cambridge: Cambridge University Press, 1987.

———. *Barbarism and Religion*. 4 vols. Cambridge: Cambridge University Press, 1999–2008.

Reill, Peter Hanns. *The German Enlightenment and the Rise of Historicism*. Berkeley: University of California Press, 1975.

Voltaire. *Candide and Other Writings.* Edited by Haskell M. Block. New York: Modern Library, 1956.

———. *Essai sur les mœurs et l'esprit des nations et sur les principaux faites de l'histoire depuis Charlemagne jusqu'à Louis XIII.* Edited by René Pomeau. 2 vols. Paris: Garnier, 1963.

———.*Œuvres historiques.* Edited by René Pomeau. Paris: Gallimard, 1957.

Weintraub, Karl J. "Autobiography and Historical Consciousness." *Critical Inquiry* 1 (1975): 821–48.

———. *The Value of the Individual: Self and Circumstance in Autobiography.* Chicago: University of Chicago Press, 1978.

———. *Visions of Culture: Voltaire, Guizot, Burckhardt, Lambrecht, Huizinga, Ortega y Gasset.* Chicago: University of Chicago Press, 1966.

Index